ACLS History E-Book Project

Reprint Series

The ACLS History E-Book Project (www.historyebook.org) collaborates with constituent societies of the American Council of Learned Societies, publishers, librarians and historians to create an electronic collection of works of high quality in the field of history. This volume is produced from digital images created for the Project by the Scholarly Publishing Office and the Digital Library Production Service at the University of Michigan, Ann Arbor. The digital reformatting process results in an electronic version of the text that can be both accessed online and used to create new print copies. This book and hundreds of others are available online in the History E-Book Project through subscription.

Many of the works in the History E-Book Project are available in print and can be ordered either directly from their publishers or as part of this series. For information refer to the online Title Record page for each book. Inquiries regarding this series can be directed to info@hebook.org.

http://www.historyebook.org

WOMEN'S EARLIEST RECORDS

Number 166

WOMEN'S EARLIEST RECORDS

From Ancient Egypt and Western Asia

Edited by

Barbara S. Lesko

WOMEN'S EARLIEST RECORDS
From Ancient Egypt and Western Asia

Proceedings of the Conference on Women
in the Ancient Near East
Brown University, Providence
Rhode Island November 5-7, 1987

Edited by
Barbara S. Lesko

Scholars Press
Atlanta, Georgia

WOMEN'S EARLIEST RECORDS
From Ancient Egypt and Western Asia

Library of Congress Cataloging in Publication Data

Women's earliest records : from ancient Egypt and western Asia / (edited) by Barbara S. Lesko.
p. cm. -- (Brown Judaic studies : no. 166)
Proceedings of the Conference on Women in the Ancient Near East. held at Brown University in November 1987.
Bibliography: p.
ISBN 1-55540-319-0 (alk. paper)
1. Women--Middle East--History--Congresses. 2. Middle East--History--To 622--Congresses. 3. Middle East--Civilization--To 622--Congresses. 4. Women--Middle East--History--Bibliography.
I. Lesko, Barbara S. II. Conference on Women in the Ancient Near East (19877 : Brown University) III. Series.
HQ1137.M628W65 1989 89-4135
305.4'0932--dc19 CIP

Printed in the United States of America
on acid-free paper

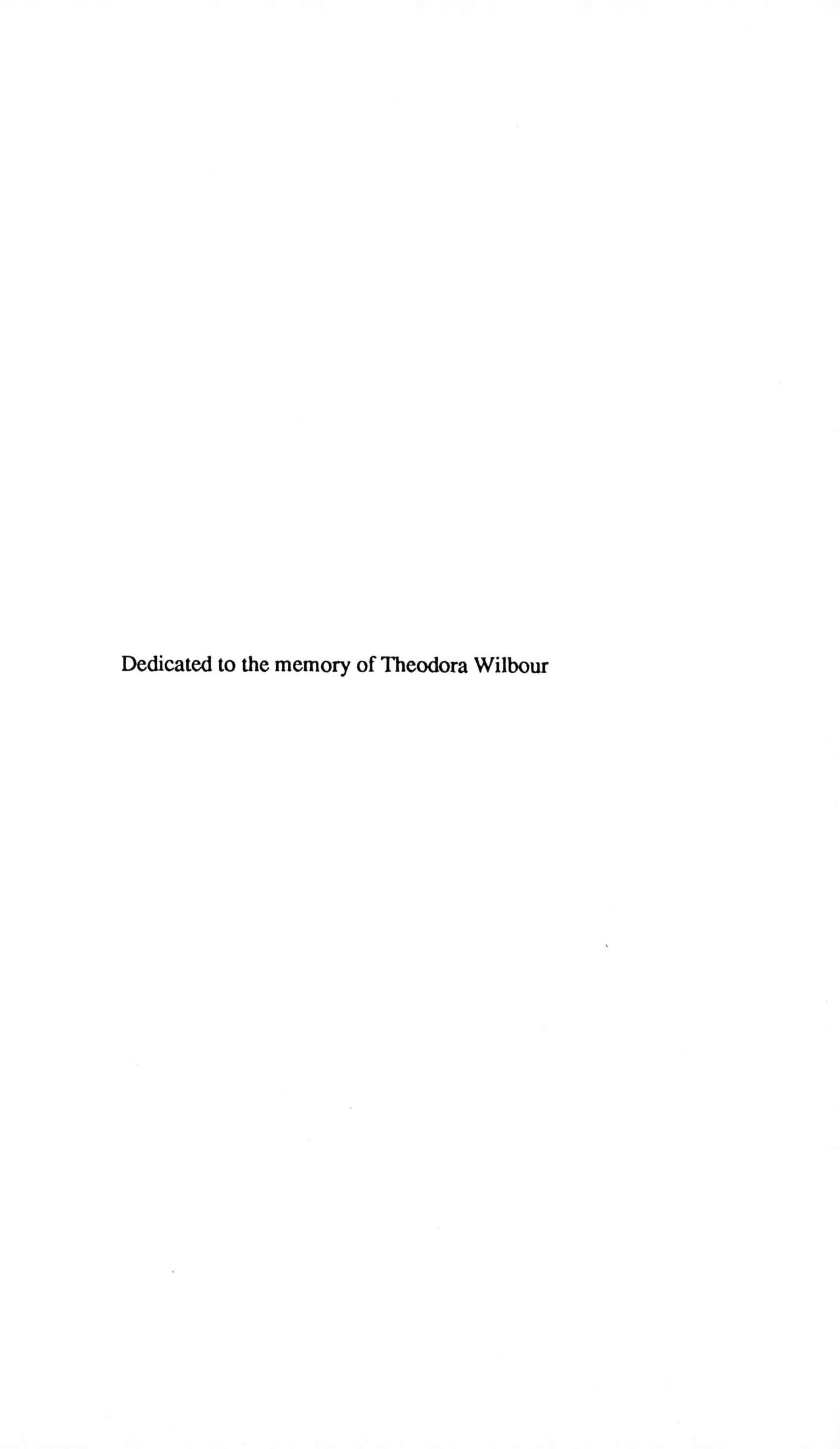

Dedicated to the memory of Theodora Wilbour

CONTENTS

Part III

Part IV

Part V

Acknowledgements

This volume evolved from the Conference on Women in the Ancient Near East held at Brown University in November of 1987 and was the intended result of that "meeting of minds." It owes much to the valued support of the National Endowment for the Humanities, whose conference grants are designed to advance scholarly research in the humanities in the United States, and also to the Mellon Foundation's Fresh Combinations Grant to Brown University, which was intended to foster innovative and productive programs in the humanities on campus. Brown's own Wetmore Lectureship Fund and the Department of Egyptology's Wilbour Fund covered almost all remaining expenses of the Conference and the Wilbour Fund continued to provide necessary assistance in the production of this publication. Without the wholehearted support of the Department's chairman, Wilbour Chair Professor Leonard H. Lesko, the project would doubtless have not progressed beyond the idea stage.

The idea itself developed out of the frustrations I experienced in researching and writing the chapter on women in the ancient Near East for the second edition of *Becoming Visible: Women in European History*, edited by Renata Bridenthal, Claudia Koonz, and Susan M. Stuard and published by Houghton Mifflin Company of Boston in 1987. I am indebted to Professor Stuard especially for her enthusiastic encouragement of the idea of a conference when I first voiced it and her continuing interest and participation in the conference. Indeed, I am very grateful to all of the active participants and especially to those who produced the various segments of this volume.

This publication has been further enhanced by the many illustrations generously provided free of charge by their sources. Special thanks for this must go to Professors Giorgio and Marilyn Buccellati of the International Institute for Mesopotamian Area Studies and to Professor Paul Zimansky of the Department of Archaeology of Boston University for their personal photos of recently unearthed material and to Dr. Gay Robins now of Emory University and to Dr. Henry G. Fischer of New York's Metropolitan Museum of Art, and Professor Carol Meyers of Duke University for providing their illustrative material. We are also pleased to acknowledge the kind cooperation of the Mss. Harper and Wilder of the Metropolitan Museum of Art and thank the Louvre Museum for permission to publish once again some of the very few images of women surviving from Near Eastern Antiquity.

I am sincerely appreciative of the help extended me by the staff of Brown's Office of Research Administration, particularly by Norman Hebert and Alice Tangredi-Hannon. Special thanks must also go to our Dean of Faculty, Professor John Quinn and to the Director of Brown's Ancient Studies Program, Professor Alan Boegehold and to the Directors of the Pembroke Center for Teaching and Research on Women, Drs. Barbara Babcock and Elizabeth Weed, for their valued moral and financial support of the conference.

Indeed, this volume owes much to the interest and helpfulness of a treasured group of Brown colleagues, and I am particularly grateful for the encouragement, advice, support and commitment of Professors Jacob Neusner and Ernest S. Frerichs of Brown's Program in Judaic Studies who have made possible the publication of the conference proceedings.

Finally, sincerest thanks is due for the helpfulness of Scholars Press editor Dr. Dennis Ford and for the editorial assistance of John Switalski, Hamish Dempster, and most especially Stephen E. Thompson, Benjamin R. Foster, Martha A. Morrison, and Leonard H. Lesko all of whose keen perceptions and special knowledge assured the final product would be worthy of all of the contributors.

Barbara S. Lesko
Deptartment of Egyptology
Brown University

Preface

Despite being a largely neglected area of research for many years, study of the roles and status of the ordinary women in the earliest societies is currently being pursued by scholars in such diverse fields as Sumerology, Assyriology, Egyptology, and by specialists in Hurrian and ancient Israelite studies. Happily, this coincides with the wider acceptability of social history as part of the historian's legitimate focus of inquiry, and the current burgeoning growth of women's and gender studies in academia.

An interdisciplinary conference was held at Brown University in November of 1987 which brought thirty scholars together across professional and international boundaries to meet and exchange information on a selected number of topics which could be examined in the light of current research on the average woman in the various ancient cultures of the Near East. The conference was organized by the Department of Egyptology, co-sponsored by the Program in Ancient Studies and the Pembroke Center for Teaching and Research on Women and funded by the National Endowment for the Humanities, together with support from the Mellon Foundation's "Fresh Combinations" grant to Brown, the Wetmore Lectureship Fund and the Wilbour Fund for Egyptology at Brown University.

This volume is the publication of that conference's proceedings, its papers, and some of the questions that they raised, together with edited parts of the discussions which followed the papers. The thirteen presenters were joined by invited discussants drawn, not only from ancient Near Eastern studies, but from the fields of classics, religious studies, anthropology, and women's history of other early periods: scholars who are involved in research and teaching on women in antiquity or in pre-industrial societies. Many of the respondents brought to the conference, not only comparative data from other cultures, but a perspective more attuned to gender studies and, in some cases, a greater familiarity with major questions and trends in the history of women and the family. The authors of the papers were chosen for their work with particular periods of history of the ancient Near East and the intense researches they are undertaking on certain bodies of evidence which throw light on the non-royal women of those times. They are not all equally well-versed in legal or social history or comparative anthropological data or gender studies. Thus the comments and questions following the papers were meant to help reach a clearer appreciation of what is known, what questions can be asked of the data, and what can yet be learned from the ancient sources. The influence of the discussions has not always been reflected in the published papers, as some remain virtually unchanged from the way they were first presented. Thus the readers are encouraged to weigh the commentaries which follow the articles and draw their own conclusions.

Several factors inspired the convening of this conference, and the most important of these were the facts that too few (and less than adequate) publications pertaining to the study of women in the Near East of antiquity are available (as opposed to a plethora of recent publications on women in classical antiquity), and that large amounts of data exist which could yield more information pertaining to women and their status, but which still await study (and even publication in many instances).

Nonspecialists often regard all ancient societies as alike, but significant differences in their socio-economic and political structures and religion and thought existed among the ancient Near Eastern societies themselves, and also differentiated them from the better known cultures of classical antiquity.

When considering the status of ancient women, some anthropologists and feminist historians are still influenced by the nineteenth century socialist Frederick Engels whose *Origins of the Family and Private Property and the State* continues to be widely read and quoted. Engels drew on classical literature for his insights into "ancient society" and theorized a connection between the establishment of private property, monogamous marriage and prostitution. He posited that with private property the egalitarian societies of prehistory and the supposed original equality between the sexes vanished, with women losing control of even the home to men who "took command" reducing women "to servitude." While patriarchy characterized most classical and perhaps all ancient societies to some degree, recent work by classical scholars, using an array of primary source materials from a broad span of periods and places, has detected varying degrees of male dominance (or female participation and prominence) and pointed to significant changes in laws, attitudes and philosophies over time, particularly with respect to the Hellenistic period and to ancient Roman women. While often assumed to be patriarchal due to the influence of the Old Testament, the societies of the ancient Near East reveal varied and suprising examples of women's status and participation in public life and the economy. Researchers of the ancient Near East must determine the true status of family and social relationships between the sexes as well as fill in details of women's varied roles in her society. They must also try to determine causes behind changes over time within each and among the several societies. Factors at work are complex, but it is important to identify root causes for changes, whether positive or negative, in the position that women held, both in theory and in practice, in a given social context.

Because the societies of the ancient world were not similar (Egypt differed quite extremely in the opinion of such classical observers and authors as Herodotus and Diodorus Siculus, even with regard to its women), it is surely mandatory for all of those who wish to study and write about ancient women to have access to primary sources or, at least, to careful translations and evaluations of them made by specialists who are able to read the ancient texts or to scrutinize a spectrum of monuments and archaeological reports.

Recent works by feminist historians on the origins of patriarchy or marriage are handicapped by a lack of understanding of the ancient languages and by preconceived ideas fostered by the theories of Engels or Levi-Strauss. Their sweeping observations and conclusions encompassing all Near Eastern cultures of antiquity have received wide acceptance even though they are not always applicable or correct. Principally, it is the lack of access to primary sources and only slight acquaintance with ancient Near Eastern cultures that is leading such writers astray, and thus it is incumbent upon the relatively few specialists who have access to primary sources to continue to pursue, study, and publish women's early records.

All types of data exist that can be brought to bear on research into women's status and roles in the ancient societies. Perhaps a million inscribed tablets, the majority of them secular texts such as letters and contracts, survive from ancient Mesopotamia and North Syria and hold a wealth of information about the daily activities and beliefs, laws and traditions of the various ancient peoples of the region. In proportion to the amount of material, the number of scholars and students engaged in translating these texts is not large, and those who currently analyze the ancient texts for information on the lives of ancient women are fewer still. A good proportion of these scholars were involved in the Brown conference.

More than twenty years ago the Assyriologist Rivkah Harris of Chicago brought out very important studies on women in the religious life of Old Babylonia and a book on the society of the great commercial city of Sippar. Only recently, however, have other scholars followed her example and begun to search out information on women in other archives. Another second millennium archive from Nuzi, the Hurrian city in north Syria is being profitably reexamined by Katarzyna Grosz of Copenhagen, and Assyriologists

Martha Roth of Chicago and Amélie Kuhrt of London are working with original sources on Neo-Babylonian women of the first millennium, while third millennium texts prove fertile fields for the Sumerologists Jean Jaques Glassner of Paris and Marc Van de Mieroop of Columbia University in New York.

While ordinary women hardly show up in the historical records left by the great civilizations of the past, minute details on their lives can be uncovered by perseverance and careful sifting of written records as well as archaeological data. In Egyptology the American researchers Henry G. Fischer, William A. Ward, and Marianne Galvin have all examined ancient Egyptian women's tomb inscriptions as well as seals, contracts and other civil documents, to discover women's titles which indicate professional and cultic responsibilities, thus elucidating women's non-domestic roles and the extent to which they participated in the economic and religious life of the nation. Two other Egyptological participants in the conference are leading experts on ancient Egyptian law--Schafik Allam of Tübingen and Bernadette Menu of Paris--and they were joined by Egyptian art historian Gay Robins, then of Cambridge, England, who analyzed the artistic repertoire (which is so extensive for Egypt) for insights it can provide into social attitudes as well as for practical information about the activities of non-royal women.

The American women scholars in religious studies who presented papers, Phyllis Bird and Carol Meyers, have been in the fore of research and revisionist writing about early Israelite or Palestinian women in the periods covered by the Hebrew Bible. Currently, the biblical record is being reexamined and a re-evaluation of traditional views as well as more recent radical feminist viewpoints is being attempted in regard to the socio-economic and cultic participation of women as revealed, not only by textual examination but through anthropological analysis of group behavior and social change as reflected both through texts and through the material remains (artifact and skeletal). Such investigations of women in ancient Israelite society are essential to correct misinterpretations both recent and long standing.

With an increasing number of women entering religious studies, it can be expected that more will turn to serious investigation of women in the formative years of the Judeo-Christian tradition. It appears that biblical scholarship has already moved from describing "what" to discovering the "why" behind institutions and attitudes in ancient Israelite society that have had prolonged impact.

The participants in the Brown conference were asked to focus upon a few main points in clarifying the image of the ancient Near Eastern woman:

Were roles for men and women stereotyped from the beginning of history? What, if any, were the ordinary woman's activities outside the home (for instance in the economy, cult, or community)? Did women ever exercise authority over others in the workforce? Did any women obtain literacy or undergo professional training of any type? Were women heirs or purchasers of real estate? What was the average woman's legal status compared to that of her male relatives? Answers to these questions would build upon data already gathered about women's legal status, marriage customs, and her status in the family.

Trends should become discernible for civilizations like pharaonic Egypt where records survive for nearly three thousand years of history. Perhaps developments in women's experiences can be linked with events or conditions (geo-political or economic)? Comparing differences in attitudes toward women among the various cultures under study will lead to investigating the root causes for those differences and a better understanding of the ancient societies themselves will result. Obviously, what is easiest to define is women's public life. Her spiritual and psychological states are almost unobtainable given the types of records which have survived. An ideal sociological/historical study of women would also include surveys of their girlhood, marriage, and old age with information on health, sexual life, and an analysis of the degree of her influence on her children. While the paper-presenters at this conference often had to deal with marriage documents, these were the contracts which reflect the economic and legal aspects of marriage, most personal data remains elusive, hinted at only in a few letters and court records which have somehow managed to survive the ravages of time and for the most part have been left unstudied. Clearly, there is much more work which yet remains to be done on the lives of ancient women, but one of the goals of the conference and this publication is to encourage further research.

Inevitably, several differing viewpoints surfaced in the papers and discussions, and many points of controversy may never be resolved. Differences in preferred transliterations of the ancient languages and variances of preferred spellings by the authors have been slightly modified by the editor for consistency's sake. The desired distinction between Akkadian and Sumerian words has been stressed by the use of italics for the former and bold print for the latter. Any resulting errors are entirely the responsibility of the editor.

To help the student gain full access to information already published on the ancient women of the Near East, a very extensive bibliography has been prepared, with the help of the conference participants. Just as all aspects of ancient women's lives have not been touched on by the papers and discussions of the conference, it will be some time (if ever) before the last word can be written on the subject. We are convinced that continued research is called for, and several of the authors of our chapters refer to problems yet unresolved and point to data still to be studied in the quest for women's earliest story.

December 14, 1988 Barbara Switalski Lesko

The Presenters of Papers in the order of their appearance:

Dr. Henry G. Fischer

The Lila Acheson Wallace Research Curator in Egyptology at the Metropolitan Museum of Art, New York.

Dr. William A. Ward

Professor of Ancient Near Eastern History and Languages at the American University of Beirut and Visiting Professor, Brown University, 1987-89.

Dr. Marc Van de Mieroop

Assistant Professor, Department of Middle East Studies, Columbia University.

Dr. Jean Jacques Glassner

An Associate at the Centre National de la Recherche Scientifique in Paris and Visiting Professor, University of Geneva.

Dr. R. Gay Robins

Fellow of Christ College, Cambridge.

Dr. Schafik Allam

Professor of Egyptology at Tübingen University in West Germany.

Dr. Rivkah Harris

Professor at the School of the Art Institute of Chicago.

Dr. Katarzyna Grosz

Research Scholar at Copenhagen's Niebuhr Institute.

Dr. Bernadette Menu

Professor of Egyptology at the Catholique Institut in Paris.

Dr. Amélie Kuhrt

Lecturer in the History of the Near East at University College London.

Dr. Martha T. Roth

Associate Professor of Assyriology, University of Chicago, Department of Near Eastern Languages and Civilizations.

Dr. Carol Meyers

Professor in the Department of Religion, Duke University.

Dr. Phyllis Bird

Professor of Old Testament at Garrett Evangelical Seminary, Evanston, Illinois.

Respondents:

Dr. Jerrold S. Cooper

Chairman, Department of Near Eastern Studies, The Johns Hopkins University.

Dr. Eugene Cruz-Uribe

Assistant Professor of Egyptology, Brown University.

Dr. Carol Delaney

Assistant Professor, Anthropology, Stanford University.

Dr. Benjamin R. Foster

Professor of Assyriology, Yale University.

Dr. Ernest S. Frerichs

Professor of Religious Studies, Brown University and Director of the Program in Judaic Studies.

Dr. Marianne Galvin

A recent Ph.D. (Brandeis) in Egyptology.

Dr. David Herlihy

Keeney Professor of History at Brown University.

Barbara S. Lesko, M.A.

Administrative Research Assistant in Egyptology, Brown University.

Dr. Leonard H. Lesko

Wilbour Professor and Chairman of Egyptology at Brown University.

Dr. Jo Ann McNamara

Professor of History at Hunter College, City University of New York.

Dr. Martha A. Morrison

Co-editor of the series *Studies on the Civilization and Culture of Nuzi and the Hurrians.*

Dr. Barbara G. Nathanson

Assistant Professor in the Department of Religion, and Director of the Jewish Studies Program at Wellesley College.

Dr. S. Georgia Nugent

Assistant Professor of Classics at Brown University.

Dr. Sarah Pomeroy

Professor of Classics, Hunter College and a member of the Faculty in Classical Studies of the City University of New York.

Dr. Elizabeth Stone

Associate Professor of Anthropology, State University of New York, Stonybrook.

Dr. Susan M. Stuard

Visiting Associate Professor of History, Haverford College.

Dr. Allan Zagarell

Associate Professor in the Department of Anthropology, Western Michigan University, Kalamazoo.

Participants from the Audience

Dr. Katalin Hegedus, Brown University

Dr. Charles Shute, Cambridge University

Stephen E. Thompson, M.A., Brown University

Dr. Raymond Westbrook, The Johns Hopkins University

Abbreviations

ABL	R.F. Harper, *Assyrian and Babylonian Letters belonging to the Kouyounjik Collection of the British Musuem*, I-XVI, London, Chicago, 1892-1914
ÄF	*Ägyptologische Forschungen*, Glückstadt, Hamburg, New York
AfO	*Archiv für Orientforschung*, Graz
AHAW	*Abhandlungen der Heidelberger Akademie der Wissenschaften, Phil.-Hist. Kl.* Heidelberg
AHDO	*Archives d' histoire du droit oriental*, Brussels
AHw	W. von Soden, *Akkadisches Handwörterbuch*, Wiesbaden, 1965-1981
ÄIB	*Ägyptische Inschriften aus den königlichen Museen zu Berlin*, 2 vols., Leipzig
AKPAPHK	*Abhandlungen, Königliche Preussiche Akademie der Wissenschaften Philosophisch-Historische Klasse*, Berlin
Allam, *Hathorkult*	Schafik Allam, *Hathorkult (bis zum Ende des Mittleren Reiches) MÄS* 4, 1963.
Allam, *HOPR*	Schafik Allam, *Heiratische Ostraka und Papyri*

	der Ramessidenzeit, Tübingen. 1973
Anchor Bible	Anchor Bible, Garden City, NY
ANET	J.B. Pritchard, ed., *Ancient Near Eastern Texts relating to the Old Testament*, 2nd ed. Princeton, 1969
AnOr	*Analecta Orientalia*, Rome
AOS	American Oriental Series
AOATS	Alter Orient und Altes Testament, Sonderreihe
ArOr	*Archiv Orientàlní*, Praha
ASAE	*Annales du Service des Antiquités de l'Égypte*, Cairo
ASAW	*Abhandlungen der Sächsischen Akademie der Wissenschaften*, Berlin
ASJ	*Acta Sumerologica Japanensis*
AWL	J. Bauer, *Altsumerische Wirtschaftstexte aus Lagasch*, Studia Pohl IX, Rome, 1972
BA	*Biblical Archaeologist*, Baltimore
Bahrein and Hemamieh	W.M.F. Petrie, E. Mackay, L. Harding, *Bahrein and Hemamieh*, London, 1929
BASOR	*Bulletin of the American Schools of Oriental Research*, Ann Arbor

BE	Babylonian Expedition of the University of Pennsylvania, Series A, Cuneiform Texts
BES	*Bulletin of the Egyptological Seminar*, New York
BIFAO	*Bulletin de l'Institut Français d'Archéologie Orientale*, Cairo
BIN	Babylonian Inscriptions in the Collection of J.B. Nies, Yale University
BLOT	Book List,The Society for Old Testament Study, London
BM	British Museum
BM Stelae	*Hieroglyphic Texts from Egyptian Stelae in the British Museum*, London
BMFA	*Bulletin of the Museum of Fine Arts*, Boston
BSFE	*Bulletin de la Société Française d'Égyptologie*, Paris
CAD	*The Assyrian Dictionary of the Oriental Institute of the University of Chicago*
CAH[3]	*The Cambridge Ancient History*, Third Edition, Cambridge
Camb.	J.N. Strassmaier, *Inschriften von Cambyses, König von Babylon (529-521 v. Chr)* (*Babylonische Texte* VIII-IX), Leipzig, 1889.

CBQ	*Catholic Biblical Quarterly*, Washington, D.C.
CdE	*Chronique d'Égypte*, Brussels
CG	*Catalogue Général des Antiquités Égyptiennes du Musée du Caire*, Cairo
CRIPEL	*Cahiers de recherches de l'Institut de papyrologie et d'Égyptologie de Lille-- Études sur l'Égypt et le Soudan anciens*, Lille
CTR.	C. Thompson, *Cuneiform Texts from Babylonian tablets in the British Museum*, London
Cyr.	J.N. Strassmaier, *Inschriften von Cyrus, König von Babylon (538-529 v. Chr.) (Babylonische Texte* VII), Leipzig, 1889-1892
Dahchour	J.J.M. de Morgan, *Fouilles à Dahchour*, Wein 1895-1903
Dar.	J.N. Strassmaier, *Inschriften von Darius*, Leipzig, 1889-1977 (*Babylonische Texte* X-XII)
DE	*Discussions in Egyptology*, Oxford
Deir el Gebrawi II	N. de G. Davies, *The Rock Tombs of Deir el-Gebrâwi* 2 vols. Archaeological Survey of Egypt, London, 1902.
DeM	Deir el Medina
DP	F.M. Allotts de la Fuye, *Documents présargoniques*, I-II, Suppl. Paris, 1908-1920

ECT	*Egyptian Coffin Texts*
Enchoria	*Enchoria*, Zeitschrift für Demotistik und Koptologie, Wiesbaden
Egyptological Studies...Parker	*Egyptological Studies in Honor of Richard A. Parker*, ed. by L.H. Lesko, Hanover, 1986.
Épron-Wild, *Tombeau de Ti* I	L. Épron, F. Daumas, G. Goyon, P. Montet,H. Wild, *Le Tombeau de Ti*, 2 vols., Cairo, 1939 and 1953
Erg. bd.	*Ergänzungs band*: supplementary volume
EVO	*Egitto e Vicino Orienti*, Rivista della sezione orientalistica della Instituto de Storia Antica Universita degli Studi di Pisa
Firth-Gunn	C.M. Firth and B. Gunn, *Excavations at Saqqara: Teti Pyramid Cemeteries*, 2 vols. Cairo, 1926.
FN	Female Name
Fs. Dunham	Festschrift for Dows Dunham= *Studies in Ancient Egypt, the Aegean, and the Sudan*, Boston, 1981
GM	*Göttinger Miszellen*, Göttingen
Hassan, *Giza*	Selim Hassan, *Excavations at Giza*, 10 vols, Oxford and Cairo, 1929-60
HSS	Harvard Semitic Series
HTR	*Harvard Theological Review*, Cambridge

HUCA	*Hebrew Union College Annual*, Cincinnati
ITT	Inventaire des tablettes de Tello
JA	*Journal Asiatique*, Paris
JAAR	*Journal of the American Academy of Religion*, Atlanta
Jacobsen, *SKL*	T. Jacobsen, *The Sumerian King List* (Oriental Institute, Assyriological Studies, 11), Chicago, 1939
JANES	*Journal of the Ancient Near Eastern Society of Columbia University*, New York
JAOS	*Journal of the American Oriental Society*, New Haven
JARCE	*Journal of the American Research Center in Egypt*, Winona Lake
JBL	*Journal of Biblical Literature*, Atlanta
JCS	*Journal of Cuneiform Studies*, Philadelphia
JEA	*Journal of Egyptian Archaeology*, London
JEN	Joint Expedition with the Iraq Museum at Nuzi
JEOL	*Jaarbericht van het Vooraziatisch-Egyptisch Genootschap (Gezelschap), "Ex Oriente Lux,"* Leiden

Jéquier, *Pepi II*	Gustave Jéquier, *Le monument Funéraire de Pepi II, Fouilles à Saqqarah*, 1936-40, Cairo
JESHO	*Journal of the Economic and Social History of the Orient*, Leiden
JNES	*Journal of Near Eastern Studies*, Chicago
JSOT	*Journal for the Study of the Old Testament*, Sheffield
JSSEA	*Journal of the Society for the Study of Egyptian Antiquities*, Toronto
Junker, *Giza*	*Wilhelm Pelizaeus' unternommenen grabungen auf dem friedhof des alten Reiches bei den Pyramiden von Giza*, ed. by Hermann Junker, Wein & Leipzig, 1929-1955.
Klio	*Klio*, Berlin
LÄ	*Lexikon der Ägyptologie*, Wiesbaden
LD	R. Lepsius, *Denkmäler aus Ägypten und Aethiopien* (13 vols.), Berlin: 1849-1913.
LNB	Neo-Babylonian Laws
Lucas, *Materials*	A. Lucas (rev. ed. J.R. Harris) *Egyptian Materials and Industries*, London, 1926/1962
MA	Middle Assyrian

M.A.R.I.	*Mari, Annales de Recherches Interdisciplinaires*, Paris
Mariette, *Mastabas*	A. Mariette, *Les Mastabas de l'Ancien Empire.* Fragment du dernier ouvrage d A. Mariette, publié d'apres le manuscrit de l'auteur par G. Maspero, Paris, 1885
MÄS	*Münchner Ägyptologische Studien*, Berlin
MCS	Manchester Cuneiform Texts
MDAIK	*Mitteilungen des Deutschen Archäologischen Instituts, Abteilungen Kairo*, Cairo
Meir	A.M. Blackman, *The Rock Tombs of Meir I-VI*, London: 1914-53
Mesopotamia	*Mesopotamia*, Copenhagen Studies in Assyriology
MET	Mond Excavations at Thebes
MFA	Museum of Fine Arts, Boston
MIFAO	*Mémoires publiés par les Membres de l'Institut Français d'Archéologie Orientale du Cairo*, Cairo
MMA	Metropolitan Museum of Art, New York
MMAF	*Mémoires publiés par les Membres de la Mission Archéologie Française au Caire*, Paris
MMJ	*Metropolitan Museum Journal*, New York

MMS	*Metropolitan Museum Studies*, New York
MVN	*Materiali per il vocabolario neosumerico*
Nbk.	J.N. Strassmaier, *Inschriften von Nabuchodonosor, König von Babylon (604-561 v. Chr.) (Babylonische Texte* V-VI), Leipzig, 1889
Nbn.	J.N. Strassmaier, *Inschriften von Nabonidus, König von Babylon (555-538 v. Chr) (Babylonische Texte* I-IV), Leipzig, 1889
NRVU	M. San Nicolo und A. Ungnad, *Neubabylonische Rechts- und Verwaltungsurkunden Band I: Rechts- und Wirtschaftsurkunden der Berliner Museen aus vorhellenistischer Zeit*, Leipzig, 1935
NS	New Series
O	Ostracon
OB	Old Babylonian
OECT	Oxford Editions of Cuneiform Texts
Oppenheim, *Beer*	L.F. Hartman and A.L. Oppenheim, *On Beer and Brewing Techniques in Ancient Mesopotamia* (*JAOS* Suppl. 10), Baltimore [1950]
Or	*Orientalia*, Nova Series, Rome
P	Papyrus

PBS	Publications of the Babylonian Section, University of Pennsylvania Museum, Philadelphia
Petrie, *RT*	Wm.M.F. Petrie, *Royal Tombs of the First Dynasty* (2 vols.), London, 1900-01.
PM	B. Porter and R. Moss, *Topographical Bibliography of Ancient Hieroglyphic Texts, Reliefs, and Paintings*, Oxford
PN	Personal Name
PSBA	*Proceedings of the Society of Biblical Archaeology*, London
Quibell-Hayter, *Teti Pyramid*	J.E. Quibell and A.G.K. Hayter, *Teti Pyramid, North Side*, Cairo: 1927
RA	*Revue d'assyriologie et de archéologie orientale*, Paris
RAI	*Rencontre Assyriologique Internationale*
RdE	*Revue d'Égyptologie*, Paris
RecTrav	*Recueil de Travaux Rélatifs à la Philologie et à l'Archéologie Égyptiennes et Assyriennes*, Paris
Reisner, *Giza*	G.A. Reisner, *A History of the Giza Necropolis*, 2 vols. (I: London, 1942) (II: Cambridge, 1955)
RHD	*Revue historique de droit français et étranger*, Paris

RIDA	*Revue Internationale des Droits de l'Antiquité, 3rd series*, Brussels
RlA	*Reallexikon der Assyriologie*, Leipzig, Berlin, New York,
RSO	*Rivista degli studi orientali*, Rome
RTC	Recueil de tablettes chaldéennes
SACT	Sumerian and Akkadian Cuneiform Texts in the Collection of the World Heritage Musuem of the University of Illinois, Urbana
SAK	*Studien zur Altägyptischen Kultur*, Hamburg
SAOC	*Studies in Ancient Oriental Civilization*, The Oriental Institute, University of Chicago
SASAE	*Suppléments aux Annales du Service des Antiquités de l'Égypte*, Cairo
SBL	Society of Biblical Literature
SCCNH	*Studies on the Civilization and Culture of Nuzi and the Hurrians in Honor of E.R. Lacheman*, edited by D. Owen and M. Morrison, Winona Lake, 1981
Semeia	*Semeia*, Atlanta

Signs	*Signs*, Journal of Women in Culture and Society, Chicago
Smith, *Sculpture*	William Stevenson Smith, *A History of Egyptian Sculpture and Painting in the Old Kingdom* Oxford, 1946, 2nd ed. 1949
SPAW	*Sitzungsberichte der Preussischen Akademie der Wissenschaften, Phil.-hist. Kl.*, Berlin
SR	D.O. Edzard, *Sumerische Rechtsurkunden des III. Jahrtausends*, Munich 1968
Studies Oppenheim	*Studies Presented to A. Leo Oppenheim*, Chicago, 1964
Studies...Wilson	*Studies in Honor of John A. Wilson* (*SAOC* 35), Chicago, 1969
SWBAS	*Social World of Biblical Antiquity Series*, Sheffield
Syria	*Syria*, Paris
TBER	*Textes Babyloniens d'Époque récente*, ed. Jean-Marie-Durand, Paris, 1981
TCL	Textes cunéiformes du Louvre
TMH 2/3	O. Krückmann, *Neubabylonische Rechts-und Verwaltungstexte*, (*TuM*), Leipzig, 1933
TuM	Texte und Materialien der Frau Professor Hilprecht Collection of Babylonian Antiquities in Eigentum der Universität Jena

TPPI	J.J. Clére and J. Vandier, *Textes de la premiére période intermédiaire et de la XIéme dynastie I* (*Bibliotheca Aegyptiaca* 10), Brussels
TT	Theban Tomb
UCP	University of California Publications in Semitic Philology, Berkeley
Urk.	K. Sethe, *Urkunden des Alten Reichs*, Leipzig, 1933-
USQR	*Union Seminary Quarterly Review*, New York
VAS	*Vorderasiatische Schriftdenkmäler*, Berlin
VS	A. Ungnad, *Vorderaisatische Schriftdenkmäler der königlichen Museen zu Berlin* 3-4, Leipzig, 1907-1917
VT	*Vetus Testamentum*, Leiden
Wb.	A. Erman and H. Grapow, *Wörterbuch der aegyptischen Sprache* (5 vols.), Berlin, 1926-1963
WO	*Die Welt des Orients*, Göttingen
Wrez., *Atlas*	W. Wrezinski, *Atlas zur altägyptischen Kulturgeschichte*, Leipzig, 1914-1935.
YOS	Yale Oriental Series, Babylonian Texts, New Haven

ZA	*Zeitschrift für Assyriologie*, Berlin
ZÄS	*Zeitschrift für Ägyptische Sprache und Altertumskunde*, Leipzig, Berlin
ZAW	*Zeitschrift für die alttestamentliche Wissenschaft*, Berlin
ZDMG	*Zeitschrift der Deutschen Morgenländischen Gesellschaft*, Leipzig, Weisbaden

List of Figures

Ancient Egypt: An Introduction

Ancient Egypt was the longest enduring of the ancient Near Eastern civilizations, spanning three thousand years of recorded history. It was an agrarian kingdom and an African culture that absorbed, throughout its history, cultural influences from Western Asia and the Mediterranean world, yet remained true to itself. For a long time (almost half its recorded history) Egypt was politically isolated, safe behind wide desert and ocean barriers, protected from major powers in distant lands, easily able to dominate its immediate, less sophisticated and poorer neighbors. It did not develop a standing army during the first fifteen hundred years of its history.

Because the Egyptians used papyrus and--even more perishable--leather scrolls to record their most important documents, few government records and no law codes have survived the enormous gulf in time which separates the Pharaonic Period from our own. More durable surfaces were utilized by the common people for letters and accounts, but, in general, fewer written records survive from the third and second millennia B.C. than from the first. Mainly royal funerary monuments and the "eternal mansions" of the gods dominate the Egyptian landscape. The rich burial places of Egypt's elite have attracted the archaeologists; the town sites, where people of all classes lived, have gone, in many cases, untouched, and most *are* untouchable now, lying as they do under intense agricultural and real estate development.

Nonetheless, there are positive things that may be said about the source material. Since the Egyptian hieroglyphs were deciphered in the early nineteenth century, steady progress has been made in translating the rich legacy of religious and historical texts (often found engraved on stone walls of existing monuments). These combine with a scattering of philosophical treatises, short stories, poems, private letters, contracts and accounts, many written in ink on durable ostraca of pottery or stone, to reveal attitudes, values, and details about how people lived. Combined with the sometimes biographical tomb inscriptions, funerary art also shows us, to some extent, how people lived and worked.

Egypt's history is divided into thirty one dynasties, and modern historians have further delineated several periods chronologically: the Archaic Period, the Old Kingdom, First Intermediate Period, Middle Kingdom, Second Intermediate Period, New Kingdom, Third Intermediate Period, and Late Period, preceding the conquest of Alexander the Great and the subsequent Ptolemaic Dynasty, which ended with the death of Cleopatra VII and the beginning of foreign (Roman) domination, which continued for several centuries.

The papers in Egyptology published here concentrate on Pharaonic Egypt, that is Egyptian society prior to the conquest of Alexander the Great in 332 B.C.

Because so little scholarship in Egyptology has concentrated on women, these papers are setting the basis for future research by sorting out the available documents and suggesting problems for future investigation. The scholars have only begun to devise appropriate questions for their ancient sources, and evaluation, for the most part, must wait until these descriptions of women's status and roles are completed.

Barbara S. Lesko

The Old Kingdom

The Old Kingdom (2686-2181 B.C.) is best known for its highly centralized government (in control of the royal family) and for the development of the pyramid as royal tomb. From the beginning of the Dynastic Period, queens either had impressive tombs of their own (as did Mer-Neith, Her-Neith, and Neith-hotep) or (later) shared their husband's pyramid (Zoser's, for instance) with their children. By the Fourth Dynasty, kings'mothers and wives received their own individual, if smaller, pyramid tombs--an architectural form reserved for them and the king and not shared even by the princes or heirs apparent. While the king, equated with the sky god Horus and also known as the son of the sun god Re, was an absolute, all powerful ruler, the kings' mothers were highly honored by their sons and were commemorated in larger than life statuary and long-lasting memorial cults. Only queens shared with kings the benefits of the royal mortuary religion by having pyramid texts engraved on the walls of their sepulchres.

Old Kingdom records of the names of the mothers of the kings, going back centuries, would suggest that matrilineal descent was significant, at least during the formative centuries of Egyptian kingship and imparted both legitimacy and divinity to the king. That some royal wives attempted to manipulate the succession, and that some of them succeeded to the throne themselves, at least briefly, is also clear. How much effect the power and prestige of the queens had upon women in the general population and their standing in the family as well as on their roles in secular and cultic life is not ascertainable. However, titles of women in responsible positions in the workforce and in religious life are comparatively numerous for the Old Kingdom and appear to become less so in subsequent periods, as will be seen from the Egyptological papers published in this volume.

With its strong central government and plentiful natural resources in a pleasant climate, rarely threatened by destructive storms, the peaceful and prosperous united kingdom of Upper and Lower Egypt was seldom disturbed (although occasionally a rebellious province or aggressive Libyan tribe might have to be dealt with). Prosperity was threatened only by an occasional extremely low Nile, whose predictable annual inundation further contributed to a secure world for the Egyptians, reflected in a religion and art comparatively free of frightening demons and vengeful gods, enjoying the benefices of a kindly and caring pantheon.

At the end of the Old Kingdom, ecological changes and the overly-long reign of an aged king conspired to darken this sunny picture. Literary and biographical texts describing the period suggest a social upheaval and, while the dire straits described for Egypt may have been exaggerated or may have pertained only to the Memphite area, where the ruling dynasty was losing control, the First Intermediate Period (Heracleopolitan Period) marks at least a century of political instability and civil war. Some old towns, shrines and services were abandoned, political power became fragmented, and civil unrest and impoverishment stalked the land.

Barbara S. Lesko

Women in the Old Kingdom and the Heracleopolitan Period

Henry G. Fischer

1. Sources

By way of preface I should point out that, while this paper deals with non-royal women, it will be impossible to avoid some comparisons with and analogies to the royal family, or not to look at the tomb chapels of kings and queens for some of my evidence for women of lesser status.

In any case tomb chapels provide the bulk of the evidence, many of them incompletely preserved, nearly all of them belonging to men, and more specifically to men of high rank and office. The sun temple of Ne-user-re[1] provides a bit of further evidence, as does the pyramid temple of Sahure.[2] Hieratic evidence is limited to a few "letters to the dead," containing some perplexing hints of domestic strife,[3] and to a small group of ostraca that accompanied the mummies of women from El Kab to Helwan.[4] There are no biographies of women that tell of their accomplishments, and the repertory of so-called autobiographical epithets is extremely limited compared to those applied to men. About the only ones that do not concern their husbands or children are: *smt-ỉb m nmḥw* "caring of heart for the orphan,"[5] *ḥzwt rmṯ* "whom people praise"[6] and *mrt nỉwt.s tmt* "whom all her town loved."[7] These

---

[1] W. von Bissing, *Das Re-Heiligtum des Königs Ne-Woser-Re*, (Leipzig, 1923-8). Vols. 1 and 2.

[2] L. Borchardt, *Das Grabdenkmal des Königs Sa3hu-re^c* (Berlin/Leipzig, 1913).

[3] A.H Gardiner and K. Sethe, *Egyptian Letters to the Dead* (London, 1928). For further examples see Reinhard Grieshammer, "Briefe an Tote," *LA* 1, cols. 864-870.

[4] Z.Y. Saad, *Royal Excavations at Saqqara and Helwan (1941-1945)* (Cairo, 1947), 105-107, pls. 42-43; Fischer, "The Butcher *Pḥ-r-nfr*," *Or.* 29(1960): 187-190. Further facsimiles will be given in my *Egyptian Studies* III, forthcoming.

[5] Z.Y. Saad, "Preliminary Report on the Excavations of the Department of Antiquities at Saqqara 1942-43," *ASAE* 43 (1943): 473 (pl. 40) and E. Drioton, "Description sommaire des chapelles funéraires de la VIe dynastie récemment découvertes...à Sakkarah," *ASAE* 43(1943): 496.

[6] Z.Y. Saad, "A Preliminary Report on the Excavations at Saqqara 1939-40," *ASAE* 40 (1941): 681.

isolated examples are all from the late Sixth Dynasty. Also, from the inscriptions of an earlier "overseer of dancing for the king" there is the more exceptional epithet *m33 nfrw n nb.s* "she who beholds the beauty of her lord."[8]

Despite these limitations it is possible to determine at least the most essential aspects of women's role in society, with the addition of some occasionally surprising details.

2. *The position of the wife and mother in tomb chapels*

Unlike queens, who have tomb chapels of their own and do not appear very conspicuously in those of their royal spouses,[9] non-royal wives normally share their husband's chapels, although there are admittedly a certain number of well-preserved chapels of men who have children, but make no mention whatever of a wife: the most familiar examples are those of Akhty-hotep, his son Ptah-hotep, Hetep-her-akhty and Khentika, all at or from Saqqara.[10] The reverse situation, where a non-royal woman makes no mention of her husband, is exceedingly rare; a single instance will be described later, in section 4. When the wife shares her husband's tomb she is clearly a secondary partner, her secondary status being apparent both in the reliefs and in the inscriptions. Even on the false door of her own offering niche she often sits on the subordinate right side of the offering table, while her husband takes the dominant left side opposite her.[11] I know of only seven cases where the woman sits on the left side opposite the man, only four of

---

[7]E. Edel, *Hieroglyphische Inschriften des Alten Reiches* (Opladen, 1981), fig. 4 and 20.

[8]Hassan, *Gîza* II, fig. 228; Fischer, "*Nbty* in Old Kingdom Titles," *JEA* 60 (1974): 99 and fig. 3.

[9]For evidence of them see Borchardt, *Sa3hu-reᶜ* 2, pl. 16 and especially pl. 48; G. Jéquier, *Le monument funéraire de Pepi II* (Cairo, 1940), Vol. 3, pl. 4 and probably Vol. 2, pls. 46, 50.

[10]Davies, *The Mastaba of Ptahhetep and Akhethetep at Saqqara* 2 (London, 1901); R.F.E. Paget, A.A. Pirie, and F. Ll. Griffith, *The Tomb of Ptah-hetep* London, 1898; P.A.A. Boeser, *Beschreibung der aegyptischen Sammlung des Niederländischen Reichsmuseums der Altertümer in Leiden: Die Denkmäler des Alten Reiches:* Atlas (The Hague, 1908), pls. 5-22; T.G.H. James and M.R. Apted, *The Mastaba of Khentika* (London, 1953).

[11]Wife and husband on both of a pair of false doors: *Bahrein and Hemamieh*, pls. 20, 22; Junker, *Gîza* 2, fig. 28 (=*LD* 2, pl. 23); 3, fig. 27; Hassan, *Gîza* 3, fig 15 (the couple are both facing right on his; opposite each other on hers); 3, fig. 91; *LD* 2, 40; T.G.H. James, *Hieroglyphic Texts from Egyptian Stelae*, etc., in the British Museum, I2 (London, 1961), pls. 6 and 7. Husband alone on his false door, with wife on hers: *ibid.*, pl. 28; W.M.F. Petrie, *Medum* (London, 1892), pls. 13, 15. Other cases where husband confronts wife on her false door: CG 1414, 1506; James, *loc. cit.*, pl. 27. Indeterminate cases: CG 1392, 1398, 1439, 1447, 1482, 1484.

them certainly involving a husband and wife.[12] While there are also many cases where each appears alone on a pair of false doors,[13] the male tomb owner almost as frequently appears alone on both false doors, even though his wife is to be seen elsewhere in his chapel.[14] If the couple are seated together on a single chair before the offering table, facing right, her legs are passed behind the seat so that she is placed behind him, while he is nearest the offerings (Fig. 1).[15] She holds on to him; he scarcely ever holds her.[16] Their relationship is always stated by identifying her as "his wife" or "his beloved wife" and while she is often "revered with her husband," the reverse is never stated, as though her opinion was of no consequence. In a rare case where a husband praises his wife he says he made her burial for her, "so great was her state of reverence in my being; she did not utter a statement that repelled my heart; she did not transgress while she was young in life."[17] In short she was submissive and virtuous.

The adjunctive status of the wife is also indicated by the frequent presence of a "redundant determinative" after her name in labels of both statues and two-dimensional representations, while such a determinative is omitted after the name of the husband. A similar situation appears on a

---

[12]Junker, *Gîza* 9, fig. 36; Hassan, *Gîza* 1, fig. 143 (her own false door, but relationship unknown); Abdel-Moneim Abu-Bakr, *Excavations at Giza 1949-50* (Cairo, 1953), fig. 95 A-B; G.T. Martin, *The Tomb of Hetepka*, (London, 1979), pl. 21; Fischer, "A Scribe of the Army of the Fifth Dynasty," *JNES* 18(1959): 271, fig. 27 (=the exhibition catalogue *Geschenk des Nil* [Basel,1978], no. 121); University Museum, Philadelphia 29-209-1 (unpublished); S. Curto, *Gli Scavi Italiani a El-Ghiza (1903)*, (Rome, 1963), pl. 2 and fig. 22 (to be discussed below, in reference to Fig. 5).

[13]E.g. Hans Kayser, *Die Mastaba des Uhemka* (Hannover, 1964), 24-25; Épron-Wild, *Tombeau de Ti* I, pl. 39 (wife); *Tombeau de Ti* 3, pls. 182, 184 (husband); Hassan, *Gîza* 3, figs. 69 and 70, 221 and 222; James E. Quibell, *Excavations at Saqqara* 3 (Cairo, 1907/08), pls 63 (husband's offering scene lost), 65. S. Hassan, *Excavations at Saqqara 1937-1938* 3 (Cairo, 1975), figs. 37b, 38b.

[14]Junker, *Gîza* 3, fig. 16, pl. I; 2, fig. 18; Hassan, *Gîza* 2, figs. 19, 22 and 25; V, figs. 67 and 70, figs. 85 and 88+91, fig. 126; 6/3, fig. 146 (the husband's false door is badly damaged; on the wife's she appears only on the inner jambs); 7, fig. 20.

[15]See Fischer, "Rechts und Links," *LÄ* 5, col. 190 and fig. 3. The example reproduced here is taken from Junker, *Giza* 6, fig. 11.

[16]For a non-royal example in statuary see MMA 48.111 *(Ancient Egypt in the Metropolitan Museum Journal, Volumes 1-11 [1968-1976]* [New York, 1977], 80); and for a royal example in relief see Borchardt, *Sa3hu-re'* 2, pl. 48. In each case the man puts one arm over the wife's shoulder, but she also puts an arm around him. In the New Kingdom a reciprocal embrace was much more commonly represented: Spiegelberg, "Notes on the Feminine Character of the New Empire," *JEA* 15(1929): 199.

[17]Edel, *loc. cit.*

number of isolated lintels and architraves where both are named. The point is that the presence of the tomb owner's body and his all-pervasive identification with the tomb chapel made the name-determinative unnecessary, while such considerations were less effective in the case of the wife.[18]

Depending on the context, children are called "his son/daughter," less commonly, when the children are isolated in the presence of the mother, "her son/daughter," but never "their son/daughter."[19] This peculiarity is only emphasized by a provincial relief where a son who stands beside both parents is called "his-her son," using both pronouns in succession.[20]

Marriage was monogamous, at least until the Heracleopolitan period, when there evidently were some exceptions,[21] and the tomb chapels depict, for the most part, only the immediate family--the tomb owner's wife and children--even though his inscriptions often proclaim: "I was one beloved of his father, praised of his mother, gracious to his siblings,"[22] or : "I was respectful to my father and gracious to my mother."[23] Siblings are much more rarely depicted, or other members of the older generation, but if the father is shown, the mother usually accompanies him.[24] And in quite a few cases the mother alone is represented, or is shown more prominently. In several instances she is

---

18*Ancient Egypt in the MMJ*, 73-91.

19Even in the context of her offering scene the wife's children are sometimes called "his": *LD* 2, 109; B. van de Walle, *La chapelle funéraire de Neferirtenef* (Brussels, 1978), pl. 6; D. Silverman, "The Priestess of Hathor *'nḫ-Ḥwt-Ḥr*," *ZÄS* 110 (1983): 81, fig. 1 and pl. 1.

20*Ancient Egypt in the MMJ*, 158f. and figs. 1-2. For this phenonmenon see also Silverman, *o.c.*, 85 (v).

21Fischer, "The Nubian Mercenaries of Gebelein," *Kush* 9 (1961): 55 n. 17, referring in particular to W.M.F. Petrie, *Athribis* (London, 1909), pl. 7.

22Cf. Edel, Untersuchungen zur Phraseologie der ägyptischen Inschriften des Alten Reiches," *MDAIK* 13(1944): §§40,41.

23*Ibid.*,§38.

24Brother: P. Duell, *The Mastaba of Mereruka*, I (Chicago, 1938), pls. 23[a], 88 (6 brothers); CG 1482 (3 brothers), CG 1449 (2 brothers), CG 1347 and 1645 (Heracleopolitan period); Hassan, Gîza 2, fig. 106; F.W. von Bissing, *Die Mastaba des Gem-ni-kai* 2 (Berlin, 1911), pl. 10. Sister: Hassan, *Gîza* 4, fig. 76. Brother, sister, father, mother: CG 1415. Father and mother: Kayser, *loc. cit.*, 37; CG 1444 (mother and perhaps father); *Meir* 4, pl. 15 (also wife's father, mother and uncle, who occupy a lesser position); Curto, *loc. cit.* (note 12 above). Also CG 5742, where the four men, all seated on chairs, at the right of the offering scene are certainly brothers (contrary to what I have surmised in "Four Provincial Administrators at the Memphite Cemeteries," *JAOS* 74 [1954]: 28). See also notes 25, 27.

represented because of her exalted status, as a queen[25] or princess,[26] but in a number of other cases she is not a member of the royal family.[27] Usually it is the tomb owner's mother that is given this attention, much less frequently his mother-in-law.[28] In one rather unusual case (Fig. 2)[29] the mother is seated opposite her son, the metalworker of the royal ornaments Wer-ka. She is, exceptionally, on a smaller scale than he, and makes the following statement concerning him: "As for any man who will do anything ill to this, there will be judgement with him because of it by the Great God." The threat is familiar, but it is usually made by the man who owned the tomb, and it suggests that she was responsible for having it built.[30] The inheritance of wealth, as well as status, undoubtedly played a part in the prominence given the mother in tomb chapels, for there is inscriptional evidence for the fact that non-royal women could own and bequeath property,[31] and in at least one case, dating to the Heracleopolitan period, a son specifically attributes his wealth to his mother's help, stressing that this help was given while he was in his father's

---

25D. Dunham and W.K. Simpson, *The Mastaba of Queen Mersyankh III* (Boston, 1974), figs. 4, 7 (the father is also shown on fig. 4); W.K. Simpson, *The Mastabas of Kawab, Khafkhufu I and II* (Boston, 1978), figs. 13 (tomb of Kawab), 26 (Khafkhufu I); Hassan, *Gîza* 4, fig. 61 (=*LD* 2, 42b; *Erg.bd.*, 37); fig. 81 (=*LD* 2, 14).

26Hassan, *Gîza* 2, fig. 32; *LD*, 20f.

27Junker, *Gîza* 3, pl. 1 (on 207 Junker notes the mother occupies the same position in the chapel of the tomb owner's father); *ibid.* 6, fig. 69; Hassan *Gîza* 1, fig 5 (but both the father and mother are shown in a statue group, pl. 30 [1] and 29); CG 1379 (named only; see Fischer, "Two Old Kingdom Inscriptions Restored," *JEA* 65[1979]: 42 f.); CG 1414 (false door of a woman who embraces her mother on left outer jamb); H.G. Fischer, *Egyptian Studies* 1 *Varia* (New York, 1976), 3ff. (false door, Bologna 1901), although the father, who is the dedicant, appears on the right outer jamb and at the bottom of the niche with the mother, the mother is far more prominent; she is shown opposite her son in the offering scene, and again opposite him on the inner jambs, as well as at the bottom of the niche with her husband); Edel, *Hieroglyphische Inschriften des Alten Reiches*, 50f. and fig. 20 (names of the owner and his wife and followed by label "his mother," which apparently applies to a woman of a different name than the wife; she is represented by a statue in the niche below the caption). Heracleopolitan period: W.M.F. Petrie, *Dendereh* (London, 1900), pl. 11B (left, second from the bottom=MMA 98.4.67); CG 1609; Fischer, "The Nubian Mercenaries of Gebelein," *Kush* 9(1961): 54 (stela of *Ini* from Gebelein, on market).

28H.G. Fischer, loc. cit., I, fig. 4, 20. See also note 36 below.

29This photograph was found in the archives of the Department of Antiquities at Saqqara in 1956. The stone is now in the Musée d'Ethnographie, Neuchâtel, Eg 323. I am indebted to the curator, M. Jacques Hainard, for permission to publish it. Cf. PM 3^2, 568.

30On the fragmentary upper part of a false door from Reisner's Giza 7766 it is more explicitly stated that the mother provided for her son's burial (Museum of Fine Arts, Boston, neg. B 6873).

31Discussed by Fischer, "The Nubian Mercenaries," *Kush* 9 (1961): 54 with reference to *Urk.* 1, 2 (10), 164 (2).

household.[32] In his own words he says: "I acquired it in the house (*ḫnw*) of my father Iti; it was my mother Ibeb who did it for me." She is depicted beside him on the funerary stela that bears this inscription. An analogous situation may explain some of the other cases, such as the son of an important governor of several provinces, who very conspicuously refers to himself as "son of Khenet," his mother, on his own false door.[33] This is particularly remarkable because filiation is not usually expressed on funerary monuments of the Old Kingdom,[34] and in other situations, such as letters, hieratic mummy tags or rock inscriptions, it is the father who is generally named.[35] In many other cases it is clear that the mother was represented because she had no other monument.[36] And such cases are, of course, greatly outnumbered by those where sons provided for their father's burial.[37] In only two cases is the role of

---

32Fischer, *ibid.*, 64, fig. 1 and pl. 10 (=Berlin [East] 24032).

33James, *Hieroglyphic Texts* 12, pl. 8 (2); cf. Fischer, "Four Provincial Administrators," *JAOS* 74 (1954): 28. This case is hardly comparable to the one in M. Alliot, *Rapport sur les fouilles de Tell Edfou*, 1933 (Cairo, 1935), 25; three sons are attributed to mothers of different names, none of these corresponding to either of the two women known to be wives of the tomb owner.

34Both parents are mentioned on a false door from Abydos, CG 1575, and a stela that may come from Dendera, Louvre E 26904, to be discussed in my *Egyptian Studies* 3.

35Rock inscriptions of Sinai: *Urk.* 1, 92(1). Wadi Hammamat: ibid., 93 (9), 95 (3); G. Goyon, *Nouvelles inscriptions rupestres du Wadi Hammamat* (Paris, 1957), nos. 20, 21, 24, 27-31, 36. El Kab: Jozef Janssen, "Mijn Verblief in El-Kab en het Verdere Nijldal (December 1949-April 1950)," *JEOL* 12 (1951-52): pls. 28-33. Aswan (inscribed pottery): E. Edel, *Die Felsengräber der Qubbet el Hawa* 2/1/2 (Wiesbaden, 1970), 70-72 (including some evidence for the mention of both parents). For a letter see Smither, "An Old Kingdom Letter Concerning the Crimes of Count Sabni," *JEA* 28(1942): 16ff., and for mummy tags see Goedicke, "Four Hieratic Ostraca of the Old Kingdom," *JEA* 54 (1968): 23ff.

36CG 1501 and *LD*, *Text* 1, 19 (two false doors, the second entirely inscribed for a woman whose son is named as the donor; on the other she again appears alone at the offering table, but the son's name is on the crossbar below, and the jambs are inscribed for him and for his wife; in both cases he is "revered" or "possessor of reverence with his mother"); Junker, *Gîza* 6, fig. 32 (the second, and largest false door is dominated by the owner's mother, who is shown opposite the owner in the offering scene; she is shown four times in all; on the right are three generations of ancestors, including herself and her husband); Hassan, *Gîza* 1, fig. 184; H.G. Fischer, *Egyptian Studies* 1, 19 (the tomb owner made false doors for his father, his wife and his mother-in-law, the last in pl. 4); CG 1306 (double offering slab for owner and mother); CG 1394 (stela of a woman dedicated by her grandson).

37Many recorded in *Urk.* 1, 9(4-7; 13-16), 15(15-17, for mother and father; cf. James, *Hieroglyphic Texts* 12, pl. 8[1]), 34 (4-6; 12-13), 40-41, 165 (8-9), 176 (6-7; 11; 13), 227 (6-7), 228 (11, grandson; 16-17, owner's name is *Wtꜣ*), 229 (7, Heracleopolitan period; 12-13; 16), 230 (6-7; 10; 13; 17), 264 (4-6; 17-18), 265 (4-5), 267 (8ff.); some further examples in Fischer, "Five

the mother graphically emphasized by showing her on a larger scale than the tomb owner, to the extent that he is evidently represented as a child; but she is a queen in both instances, and he a king's eldest son.[38] A parallel is to be seen in the statue of Pepy II sitting on the lap of his mother.[39] Even more explicit representations of the mother's role are to be found on the higher plane of goddesses who nurse kings at their breast,[40] or on the lower level of peasants who are similarly portrayed in limestone tomb models[41] and in scenes of daily life. In one case the mother and child appear at the end of a series of figures below the offering scene of a false door; the other figures are bringing offerings, straining beer and slaughtering a steer, and all bear names, including the pair in question.[42] In another case (Fig. 3),[43] the context is the making of bread, and the mother holds her child to her breast while heating moulds for the loaves. Above her an older child gives his mother a hug while she grinds grain, and she seems to reassure him by saying "Here I am, here I am my dear." All of the other examples of this motif--three in all--situate the nursing mother on a cargo boat, where she probably accompanies her husband.[44]

Despite the wife's secondary status in the tomb chapel, she seems to have enjoyed the companionship of her husband very frequently. She[45] and/or

---

Inscriptions of the Old Kingdom," *ZÄS* 105 (1978): 50, n.42 and 51, fig. 6. Also note *Urk.* 1, 32 (6-7), where the tomb was made by a daughter and son(-in-law?).

38Hassan, *Gîza* 4, fig. 61; cf. note 25 above; Reisner, "The Servants of the *Ka*," *BMFA* 32 (1934): 11, fig. 10.

39Brooklyn 39.119. For bibliography see T.G.H. James, *Corpus of Hieroglyphic Inscriptions in the Brooklyn Museum* (Brooklyn, 1974), 28.

40Smith, *Sculpture*, figs. 124, 125 and pl. 54 b; Jéquier, *Pepi II*, 2, pls. 30, 32.

41Smith, *o.c.*, pl. 27a-b and 58 (Leipzig 2446); pl. 27d and 101 (MMA 26.3.1405). Also pl. 27c, a woman in a chair, with child on lap (Cairo J 72142). The evidence from the Old to New Kingdom is discussed by Florence Meruéjol, "La Nourrice: une thème inconographique," *ASAE* 49 (1983): 311-319, but two additions should be made in her list of Middle Kingdom statuettes: MMA 22.2.35 (Hayes, *Scepter* 1, 222, fig. 138); Berlin (West) 14078 (Werner Kaiser, *Ägyptisches Museum Berlin* [1967], no. 316).

42Berlin (East) 13.466 (H.W. Müller, "Die Totendenksteine des Mittleren Reiches," *MDAIK* 4 (1933): pl. 30.

43The drawing is made from the photograph in A.M. Moussa and H. Altenmüller, *Das Grab des Nianchchnum und Chnumhotep* (Mainz, 1977), pl. 23. The translation is the one rightly preferred by Altenmüller, 68. Cf. the child who stands among women making bread in Épron-Wild, *Tombeau de Ti I*, pl. 67.

44(1) Firth-Gunn, *Teti Pyramid Cemeteries*, pl. 53; (2) CG 1536; (3) *LD* 2, pl. 104 (b). For later (New Kingdom) examples of this theme see Maruéjol, *op. cit.*

45Duell, *Mereruka*, pls. 94-95, paralleled by *Meir* V, pl. 45; relief from tomb of Nekhebu (MFA 13.4349), discussed below with Fig. 9. In W.M.F. Petrie, *Athribis* (London, 1909), pl. 1, a female

one or more daughters[46] play the harp to him (Fig. 4),[47] sometimes singing as they do. There are, in fact, so many examples of this sort that playing the harp must have been as important to the education of a young lady of the Old Kingdom as playing the spinet or piano used to be in our own recent past.

The couple repeatedly share the same offering table, in which case they are almost always isocephalic. One exception (Fig. 5),[48] probably dating to the first half of the Fifth Dynasty, not only places the woman on the dominant left side of the offering scene on her false door, but shows her on a larger scale than the man who is the principal tomb owner; both her parents are represented behind her. Elsewhere on the same wall she is on a smaller scale than the man. Their relationship is not specified, and they may be mother and son rather than (as I have assumed elsewhere) husband and wife. Otherwise the use of scale is rather variable. As in the offering scene on false doors, the wife may be isocephalic, but is more often slightly smaller than her husband, probably no more so than she was in life. In other situations she may be much smaller, depending on the context. Statue groups show all these possibilities, but the slightly smaller wife seems to predominate.

From the very beginning of the Fourth Dynasty onward, the couple often stand together as he views the manifold activities of his artisans and laborers.[49] She also accompanies him on boating trips to the marshes while he harpoons fish or brings down fowl with a throwstick. In one of the fishing

---

retainer brings a harp to the wife, undoubtedly for her own use. See also the reference to Barsanti in next note.

46Junker, *Gîza* 6, fig. 38 b (a granddaughter, lit. "daughter of his daughter" plays before the owner, behind a grandson, lit. "son of his son," who accompanies a singer); Hassan, *Excavations at Saqqara 1937-1938* 2, figs. 36-37 (a female harpist is "his beloved..." therefore probably a daughter); W.K. Simpson, *Mastabas of Qar and Idu* (Boston, 1976), fig. 38 (five female harpists, two identified as "his daughter"; they sing as they play); *LD* 2, 109 ("his daughter *Nfrt*," although the adjacent figure is erroneously a man); Hassan, *Gîza* 5, fig. 105 (=*LD Erg.bd.*, 38; two daughters); CG 1778 (=*Dachour* 2, pl. 25); *Meir* 4, pls. 9-10 (two daughters; they play and sing a hymn to Hathor); Fischer, "*Bꜣ* and the Deified Vizier *Mḥw*," *JARCE* 4 (1965): pl. 29; relief formerly in Michailides Collection (cf. PM 3^2, 761-2; the harpist is "his daughter, his beloved, *Ḫnit*"); Barsanti, "Le Mastaba de Samnofir," *ASAE* 1 (1900): 155, fig. 9 (two harpists, the tomb owner's wife and daughter). Finally it may be noted that in one case daughters identified as [hieroglyphs] sing to dancers in the presence of their parents: Junker, *Gîza* 4, fig. 9. And the first of a row of dancers is identified as "his daughter" in Simpson, *loc. cit.*

47*Meir* 4, pl. 10.

48Curto, *loc. cit.* (note 12 above); Fischer, in *Ancient Egypt in the MMJ*, 82-84 and fig. 15 (reproduced here).

49As early as the beginning of Dyn. IV (Petrie, *Medum*, pls. 9, 10, 19).

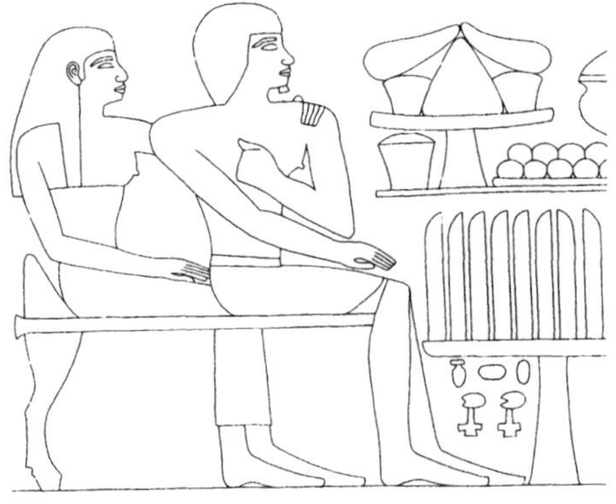

Figure 1

Example of a husband and wife sharing a chair. After Junker, *Giza* VI, fig.11.

Figure 3

Mother and child after A.M. Moussa and H.Altenmüller, *Das Grab des Nianchchnum und Chnumhotep* (Mainz, 1977), pl.23.

Figure 2

Mother seated opposite son, from Saqqara, Neuchatel Musée d'Ethnographie, Eg. 323.

Figure 4

Daughter playing a harp,
after Meir IV,pl.10.

Figure 5

Woman on Dominant side
in offering scene. H.G. Fischer,
Ancient Egypt in the MMJ, fig.15.

scenes, probably dating to the Eighth or Ninth Dynasty (Fig. 6),[50] the wife follows her husband in a second skiff, collecting lotus blossoms. In the fowling scenes she sometimes points out a likely target and may even make a comment such as "O Sire, get me this *gnw*-bird!" To which he obligingly replies: "I'll do so and get it for thee."[51] This particular example from Meir is, to my knowledge, the only conversation between husband and wife that has been preserved from the period in question. But another, of which we have only the words of the wife, is probably to be recognized in a damaged scene in the tomb of Mereruka; she says: O Meri, would that thou might give me those [goodly(?)] fowl--as thou livest for me!"[52] His response is lost.

When the tomb owner travels on one of the larger boats that plies the length of the Nile, he travels alone, as also when he travels by land, in a palanquin, but there is at least one exception in each case.[53] The exception involving travel by water, in a Fifth Dynasty tomb at Hemamia (Fig. 7),[54] is especially interesting because the husband and wife are rowed downstream in two separate boats, hers preceding his on the west wall of the tomb, while on the wall opposite she appears alone in another boat (Fig. 8).[55] Her high rank as king's daughter might explain this, but the title has been consistently erased before her name. Another likely exception, in a fragment of relief from the tomb chapel of Nekhebu at Giza (Fig. 9),[56] shows the owner seated on a barge towed by oarsmen in another boat; thus removed from the cacophony of their efforts, he listens in tranquility to a female harpist who plays, and perhaps sings, before him. She is a woman of some status, with the title *rḫt nswt* "known to the king," and is probably his wife, in conformity to the tradition mentioned earlier.[57]

The religious beliefs concerning the hereafter of the deceased applied equally to men and women. The same funerary formulas appear on the false doors where offerings were deposited. Towards the end of the Old Kingdom women, like men, could become an "akh"--a transfigured spirit--in the next

---

50N. de Garis Davies, *The Rock Tombs at Deir el-Gebrâwi* 2 (London, 1902), pl. 23.

51*Meir* 5, pl. 28.

52Duell, *Mereruka*, pl. 17; cf. Fischer, "Five Inscriptions of the Old Kingdom," *ZÄS* 105 (1978), 45-47; 106 (1980): 86f., for the interpretation.

53For the couple in a palanquin see Wresz., *Atlas* 3, pl. 8A.

54*Bahrein and Hemamieh*, pl. 21.

55*Ibid.*, pl. 24.

56The drawing shown here, by Peter Der Manuelian, makes some improvements on the tracing in the archives of the Museum of Fine Arts, Boston, although the scene (MFA 13.4349) has somewhat deteriorated in the meantime. I am indebted to him for supplying it.

57See note 45 above.

world; and in at least one case the feminine form "akhet" is used.[58] But survival in the next world ultimately entailed identification with the male god Osiris, the father of the living king, who became king of the dead. So far as men are concerned, that identification was adumbrated fairly early in the Fifth Dynasty by the representations of *ḏrt*-mourners at either end of the bier, impersonating the sisters of Osiris (of which more will be said later); by the end of that dynasty it was attested in royal tombs by the Pyramid Texts, and in private tombs by the kingly regalia that is occasionally pictured among the funerary equipment, including collars with falcon terminals and pendants with uraeus-cobras.[59] The identification of women with Osiris is first attested in the Pyramid Texts of Queen Neith and Wedjebten; here the name of the god precedes the name of the deceased, as an epithet, in spells invoking offerings.[60] The same epithet began to be applied to the funerary monuments of non-royal men and women before the end of the Heracleopolitan period, again in connection with the transmission of offerings.[61] In the next world, as in this one, a woman could only reign by becoming a king.

3. Occupations of non-royal women

There is a tendency, in the representations of wealthy households, for men to be waited on by men, women by women,[62] although, in the latter case, women did not altogether replace men in this capacity. Queen Mersyankh III, for example, has a considerable entourage of women, but her steward and

---

[58] *Ancient Egypt in the MMJ*, 173 (m).

[59] E.g. Duell, *Mereruka*, pls. 29, 30, 32, 69, 75, 76; F. W. von Bissing, *Die Mastaba des Gem-ni-kai*, with A.E.P. Weigall (Berlin, 1911), 2, pls. 36, 41.

[60] Jéquier, *Pyramides des Reines Neit et Apouit*, pls. 8-12; *La Pyramide d'Oudjebten* (Cairo, 1928), pls. 6 (25), 7 (72).

[61] Fischer, "A Stela of the Heracleopolitan period at Saqqara: the Osiris *Ỉti*," *ZÄS* 90 (1963): 36f. and pl. 6.

[62] A female retinue is particularly numerous in the case of queens: Dunham and Simpson, *loc. cit.*, figs 3a, b, 7, 8 (to which add the block shown in Simpson, *Mastabas of Kawab* etc, fig. 72); Z.Y. Saad, "A Preliminary Report on the Excavations at Saqqara 1939-1940," *ASAE* 40 (1941): pl. 79 (Nebt); Firth-Gunn, *loc. cit.*, pl. 57 (Iput); G. Jéquier, *La Pyramide d'Oudjebten* (Cairo, 1928), 16, figs. 9-12; G. Jéquier, *Pyramides des Reines Neit et Apouit* (Cairo, 1933), pl. 4. Also princesses: R. Macramallah, *Mastaba d'Idout* (Cairo, 1935), pls. 7, 11, 16, 17; Wresz., *Atlas* 3, pl. 11 (wife of Mereruka). Non-royal women: Hassan, *Gîza* 2, 207 (a maidservant on each side of false door); 4, fig. 82 (=*LD Erg.bd.* 34 a); Junker, *Gîza* 7, fig. 31; X, figs. 44-45 (man serving man, woman serving woman); Kayser, *Mastaba des Uhemka*, 37 (male retainers in upper register for husband, women in lower register for wife); CG 1558 (similar arrangement of male and female attendants); Duell, *Mereruka*, pl. 94 (maidservants behind wife, men behind husband); CG 1384; Petrie, *Athribis*, pl. 1.

Figure 6

Fishing scene showing wife in her own skiff. From N. de G. Davies, *The Rock Tombs at Deir el-Gebrawi*, II(London, 1902), pl.23.

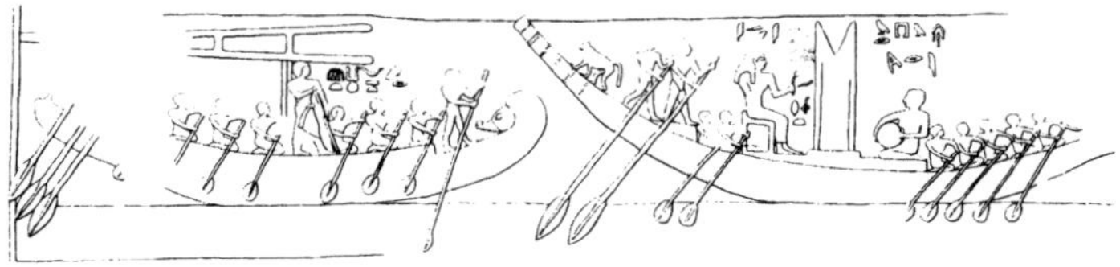

Figure 7

Wife rowed in her own boat, preceding husband's. From *Bahrein and Hemamieh*, pl.24.

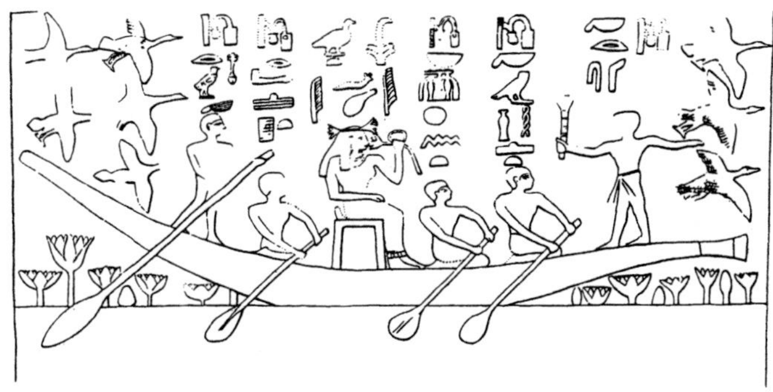

Figure 8

Wife alone in her own boat.
Bahrein and Hemamieh, pl. 24.

Figure 9

Woman playing a harp on a boat. Tomb chapel of Nekhebu at Giza. Museum of Fine Arts, Boston, 13,4349.

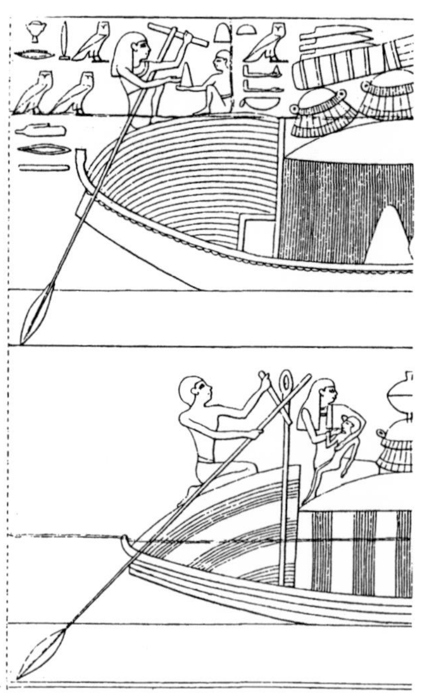

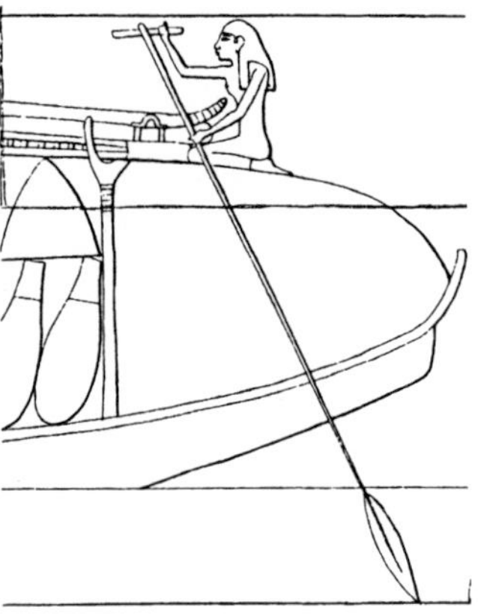

Figure 10, a & b

Woman wielding steering oar, from *LD* II, pls. 103 & 104.

scribe is a man.[63] The princess Hemet-Re, in one of Hassan's tombs at Giza, likewise has a male steward as well as a number of male scribes, and exceptionally has no female retinue at all.[64] From this class of evidence we also see that, while men prepared the master's bed, women made that of the mistress,[65] and women may even carry their mistress' palanquin.[66] Boys and girls play games separately, as seen in a familiar example from the tomb of Mereruka[67]--the only one that shows both.

Dancers also perform in separate groups of men and women, which perhaps relayed each other, and the female dancers may be supervised either by a man or woman called *sb3/sb3t* "instructor."[68] At least two female "overseers of dancers" are known and one "overseer of singers,"[69] although male overseers of singers are more numerous.[70] The professional musicians, and notably the pairs of singers and instrumentalists, one giving signals to the other, are virtually always men.[71] In the Old Kingdom men play the harp, an

---

[63] Dunham and Simpson, *op. cit.*, figs. 3 b, 7, 9, 12; similarly Junker, *Gîza* 7, fig. 31 (male overseer of priests presents papyrus).

[64] Hassan, *Gîza* 6/3, figs. 40-45.

[65] Dunham and Simpson, *op. cit.*, fig. 8; there are many examples where men make the master's bed: Junker, *Gîza* 4, fig. 10A; Hassan, *Gîza* 4, fig. 81 (=*LD* 2, 14); Hassan, *Excavations at Saqqara (1937-1938)* 2, fig. 39; Duell, *Mereruka*, pl. 92, etc.

[66] Wresz., *Atlas* 3, pl. 11.

[67] Duell, *Mereruka*, pls. 164-165; other Old Kingdom examples of children at play show boys only.

[68] Male "instructor": *Hassan, Excavations at Saqqara 1937-38* 1, fig. 7; *Gîza* 1, 67 and pl. 44 (1). Female instructor: Fischer, "Notes on Two Tomb Chapels at Gîza," *JEA* 67 (1981): 167f.

[69] Fischer, *Egyptian Studies* 1, 71.

[70] There is evidence of a lesser overseer (*sḥḏ*) of dancers (PM 3^{2}, 571); the title given by M.A. Murray, *Names and Titles of the Old Kingdom* (London, 1909), pl. 20 (cf. PM 3^{2}, 895, "overseer of the chamber of dancers") is not beyond question, since it is preceded and followed by a lacuna. For male "overseers of singers" see CG 1328, 1420, 1421, 1436, 1461 (all from Mariette, *Mastabas*, E 6-7); MFA 21.3081 (Reisner, *Giza* 1, pl. 65 b); Hassan, *Gîza* 2, fig. 226; *LD* 2, 59; A.M. Moussa and Altenmüller, *Tomb of Nefer and Ka-hay* (Cairo, 1971), pls. 42a ("overseer of singers of the Two Houses"), 26, 29-32 ("director"). Also lesser supervisors (*sḥḏ*): Mariette, *Mastabas*, 154, with the obscure addition of *tm3t* "mat(?)"; Hassan, *Gîza* 6/2, 133 (CG 57173); 7, fig. 38; Junker, *Gîza* 7, fig. 12 (discussed 36-38); Moussa and Altenmüller, *loc. cit.*, pls 29, 30, 32, 33, 36, 39; P. Posener-Kriéger, *Les archives du temple funéraire de Néferirkarê-Kakai* 2 (Cairo, 1976), 385, 605. In some cases the singers are specified as men: Reisner: *Gîza* 1, pl. 65b (determinative); Moussa and Altenmüller, *loc. cit.*, 46 (determinative red-skinned, wearing beard and sidelock).

[71] The clearest exception is to be seen in CG 1778 (*Dahchour* 2, pl. 25); here a female harpist accompanies a singer. A grandson similarly accompanies a singer in Junker, *Gîza* 6, fig. 38 b.

open-ended flute (Arabic, *nay*) and a double-tubed wind instrument with the sound of an oboe (Arabic, *zummara*). Of these three, the harp is the only one played by women, other than such things as clapsticks or the sistrum; it is only in scenes of later periods that we find them playing wind instruments such as the *nay*.[72] It has already been noted that the women who play the harp are frequently identified as the wife or daughters of the tomb owner, but they do not necessarily play alone. In some cases they evidently join in with the male musicians.[73]

Other activities sometimes bring men and women together more closely, as will be seen from a brief summary of the three types of productive work in which women were engaged.

The first, and most important type of production was weaving, which was executed entirely by women, unlike the New Kingdom, when men were likewise employed in it.[74] It is not represented as such, as it is in the tombs of the Middle and New Kingdom, but women are shown delivering cloth and receiving payment, usually in jewelry.[75] Furthermore several women are "overseer of weavers" or "the house of weavers,"[76] although a few men also hold the latter title.[77] The Old Kingdom hieroglyph for "weaver" ( ) is a seated woman who holds a long straight baton, most probably a

---

[72]For a female *nay*-player of the Middle Kingdom see Davies-Gardiner, *Antefoḳer*, pl. 23; for another of the New Kingdom see Oriental Institute, Chicago, *The Tomb of Kheruef* (Chicago, 1980), pl. 34.

[73]CG 1778 (note 71 above); Junker, *Gîza* 6, fig. 38b; Simpson, *Mastabas of Qar and Idu*, fig. 38; *LD* 2, 109.

[74]N.de Garis Davies, *Seven Private Tombs*, MET 2 (London, 1948), pl. 35 (TT 133); "The Town House in Ancient Egypt," *MMS* 1 (1929), 234 (TT 104); N. de Garis Davies, *Tomb of Nefer-hotep at Thebes*, 2 vols. (New York, 1933) 1, pl. 60 (TT 49).

[75]Men and women bringing cloth: Junker, *Gîza* 5, figs. 7-8; cloth is delivered from the house of weavers by men; a record is made by scribes, and men and women are paid for their services in jewelry; Junker compares a scene in the Louvre mastaba of Akhty-hotep, his fig. 9, where cloth is brought by men, and women alone receive jewelry. In *ibid.*, fig. 11 (=*LD Erg. bd.*, 34); Hassan, *Gîza* 4, fig. 82, the same theme is also recognized, while in fig. 10 (=*LD* 2, 103) the delivery of cloth is rewarded by food. See also *Meir* 5, pl. 15, where scribes are "registering the production of female servants (*ḥmwt*) for the requirement of the month: 84 (bolts of cloth)"; the bolts of cloth are brought by "overseers of linen"; cf. Fischer, "Notes on Davies' *Deiṛ el Gebrawi*," *JARCE* 13 (1976): 11-12.

[76]Fischer, *Egyptian Studies* 1, 71-72, to which add Moussa and Altenmüller, *Grab des Nianchchnum und Chnumhotep*, fig. 11 (three women who are "overseers of the house of weavers," while one man is an "under-supervisor (ỉmy-ḫt) of the houses of weavers."

[77]See preceding note and Junker, Gîza 5, 56; also CG 1336.

shuttle, to judge from its length. Since linen was used for cloth, one might expect women to be involved in the harvest of flax, as they were to be in later periods, and one tomb of a woman, to be discussed presently, in fact shows her supervising this activity;[78] it must be acknowledged, however, that her titles contain no reference to weavers. Women probably also made clothing, although no term for that activity has yet been identified. Oddly enough, men do the washing, as also in later periods.[79]

An equally important, if somewhat humbler, activity is the making of bread, but this, along with the closely related production of beer, is usually done in cooperation with men. In the Old Kingdom women sometimes undertake virtually all the work of making bread; they are seen pounding and grinding the grain, making dough and heating the moulds for the loaves.[80] Of these activities the one most frequently represented is grinding, and the model bakery and brewery of Meket-Re, dating to the beginning of the Middle Kingdom, reduces the woman's role to this task.[81] Only men are known to be called "baker" (*rtḥ*).[82] Occasionally a woman helps the brewers. Several tomb models show her straining the mash for this purpose.[83]

---

78 See note 122 below, and Fig. 13.

79 Contrary to *Wb.* 2 448 (9-10), the word *rḫty* "washerman" is attested before the Middle Kingdom: Hassan, *Excavations at Saqqara 1937-1938* 2, 33 and pl. 25 *bis*.; Fischer, *Dendera in the Third Millennium B.C.* (Locust Valley, N.Y., 1968), 156 and fig. 30 (Heracleopolitan period).

80 A few of the more complete scenes: Maria Mogensen, *Le mastaba égyptien de la Glyptothèque Ny Carlsberg* (Copenhagen, 1921), figs. 29, 33-35 (=CG 1534); Junker, *Gîza* 11, fig. 64; Abu-Bakr, *Excavations at Giza 1949-1950*, fig. 95 A; Épron-Wild, *Tombeau de Ti* 1, pl. 67. There are many statuettes showing the various aspects of this activity: James H. Breasted Jr., *Egyptian Servant Statues* (New York, 1948), 17ff. and pls. 15-20, 25b, 28-29a, 31, 32b; Hassan, *Gîza* 6/3, pls. 74, 75, 78, 80. Among the examples where women participate with men in the making of bread see James and Apted, *loc. cit.*, pl. 9; Dunham and Simpson, *loc. cit.*, fig. 11.

81 H.E. Winlock, *Models of Daily Life in Ancient Egypt from the Tomb of Meket-Re'* (Cambridge, Mass., 1955), 27-29 and pls. 22, 23.

82 The Belegstellen for *Wb.* 2, 459 (13) give only one Old Kingdom reference for *rtḥ* (Junker, *Gîza* 2, fig. 20), but there is also a [hieroglyphs] "director of bakers, director of cooks (Junker, "Pḥrnfr," *ZÄS* 75 [1939]: 65, who notes that the [hieroglyphs] "cook" similarly follows bakers in the aforementioned example), and a [hieroglyphs] "inspector of bakers for the king's repast" (W.M.F. Petrie, *Gizeh and Rifeh* (London, 1907), pl. 7A). It may be added that only men are shown cooking meat in Old Kingdom scenes. Although a woman of the late Old Kingdom is named [hieroglyphs] (*BM Stelae* 4, 32 [832], and ewer and basin in the Louvre), this does not show a feminine ending as would be expected of a female "cook."

83 Abu-Bakir, *loc. cit.*; W.K. Simpson, *Mastabas of the Western Cemetery I* (Boston, 1980), fig. 32; M. Saleh, *Three Old Kingdom Tombs at Thebes* (Mainz, 1977), pl. 11. Statuettes of this

The winnowing and sieving of grain is always performed by women, perhaps in teams of five, for they are called *ỉdwt* "fivers."[84] In this they are less directly associated with men, who merely pitch the straw and tidy up. There is no clear evidence that women participate actively in other aspects of harvesting. A female gleaner is shown on a fragment of relief from Saqqara, the date of which is possibly earlier than the Middle Kingdom, but that date is not certain.[85]

Of all the activities of women, their participation in the temple and funerary rituals was doubtless felt to be most important. In the temple services they hail the king as the "*mrt*-singers of Upper and Lower Egypt," who, as early as the Fourth Dynasty are under the command of a male director.[86] A great many women are priestesses of Hathor, or of Hathor and Neith, both of whom had cults in the Memphite area. The cult of Hathor was more widespread, however, with many local temples throughout the country,[87] and she is the subject of hymns sung in the household by dancers (in the tomb of Kagemni at Saqqara)[88] and by harpists (at Meir: Fig. 4).[89] At Meir the wife of Ny-ankh-Pepy is a "percussionist" of the goddess (the word is *ḫnwt*, meaning "she who beats the rhythm"),[90] and at Thebes[91] and Dendera[92]

activity: Breasted Jr., *op. cit.*, 30ff. and pl. 29, 30 (30b much restored); Hassan, *Gîza*, pl. 71. More commonly the statuettes represent a man.

84One of the most common scenes; only a few need be cited: *LD* 2, 47, 71 a, 80 a; Épron-Wild, *Tombeau de Ti* 3, pl. 155 (the most complete example); Junker, *Gîza* 6, fig. 47; 11, fig. 75; Hassan, *Gîza* 1, fig. 21; Duell, *Mereruka*, pl. 168. Male winnowers are apparently attested for the Middle Kingdom (*Meir* 1, pls. 4, 21 [4]), and more frequently for the New Kingdom (J.J. Tylor, *The Tomb of Renni* [London, 1900], pl. 14; Tylor-Griffith, *Paheri*, pl. 3; Davies, *Two Ramesside Tombs*, pl. 30; cf. L. S. Klebs, *Die Reliefs des Alten Reiches...Material zur ägyptischen Kulturgeschichte* 3 (Heidelberg, 1915), 14).

85Wresz., *Atlas* 3, pl. 55 (B) (=Quibell, *Excav. Saqq.* 1, pl. 20 [2]).

86Junker, *Gîza* 1, pl. 23; 2, fig. 34; and a lesser overseer (*sḥḏ*) of singers is a priest of the divinities themselves: Moussa and Altenmüller, *Tomb of Nefer and Ka-hay*, pls. 36, 39; for the earliest representation of the *mrt*-singer see H. Goedicke, *Re-used Blocks from the Pyramid of Amenemhet I at Lisht* (New York, 1971), 36f.

87Cf. Allam, *Hathorkult*.

88Firth-Gunn, *Teti Pyramid Cemeteries*, 113 and pl. 53 (3): "Hathor [appears] in the door of the east. 'May she be greeted,' say the gods. 'Thou art greeted,' says Re," etc.

89*Meir* 4, pl. 10: "Gold (scil. Hathor) appears in the great door. 'Thy power is exalted' says Horus."

90*Ibid.*, pls. 4, 7, 9.

91Saleh, *loc. cit.*, pl. 17.

priestesses of Hathor carry the sistrum that was particularly associated with her cult. A male *ḫnw* of Hathor is also known, however.[93] Among the less common priestesses are a *ḥmt-nṯr* priestess of Cheops[94] and a *ḥmt-nṯr* of Ptah.[95] From Akhmim we also know of a *wršt*-priestess who evidently kept watch over the god Min,[96] and a "Wife of Min"[97]--the earliest example of a divine consort, a distinction which was to assume great importance in the New Kingdom. A few women are also to be found among the men who perform the ceremonies for the king's jubilee in the Sun Temple of Neuserre at Abusir, but the nature of their duties is unclear.[98]

Women likewise play an important part in the funerary rituals, impersonating Isis and Nephthys at either end of the bier. In this capacity each of the pair is called *ḏrt*,[99] the falcon known as a kite, whose soaring flight has given its name to the aeronautic toy of our own culture. The Pyramid Texts (1280) describe the association between the falcon and the goddesses in these terms: "the screecher[100] comes, the kite comes, namely Isis and Nephthys; they have come in search of their brother Osiris, in search of their brother King Pepi." As mourners, women are also associated with the *šnḏt* "the acacia house," and in this capacity, as *šnḏtt*, they perform a funerary dance and give offerings.[101] There are other female mourners called *m3ṯrt*,[102] but it is difficult to differentiate their functions. It is also difficult to interpret the curious ritual performed by a woman in the pyramid temple of Sahure; she applies eye-paint to one of a pair of bulls in the presence of the enthroned king.[103]

Women, like men, were frequently "funerary priests," employing the feminine form *ḥmt-k3*, lit. "servant of the spirit" and there is even a female

---

92For references see Fischer, "The Cult and Nome of the Goddess Bat," *JARCE* 1 (1962): 15, n. 58 and fig. 6, where (6e) a sistrum is also shown in the hand of a dancer at Giza (Junker, *Gîza* 10, fig. 46).

93On the false door of *Ṯnmw*, Giza tomb 5233 (in the excavation records of the MFA).

94Mariette, *Mastabas*, 90.

95Fischer, *Egyptian Studies* 1, 69, n. 3.

96*Ibid*, n. 8.

97N. Kanawati, *The Rock Tombs of El-Hawawish* 3 (Sidney, 1982), fig. 26.

98Bissing, *Re-Heiligtum* 2, pls. 5, 13; 3, pls. 4 (140, 141, 142), 15 (253).

99Fischer, *Egyptian Studies* 1, 39-49.

100For the translation of this word see Faulkner, *Pyr.*, 200, n. 1.

101E.Edel, *Das Akazienhaus und seine Rolle in den Begräbnisriten des alten Ägyptens* (Berlin, 1970).

102E.Edel, "Beiträge zum ägyptischen Lexikon 5," *ZÄS* 96 (1969): 9-14.

103Borchardt, *Sa3hu-re'* 2, pl. 47.

overseer of such priests.[104] Like their male counterparts, they enjoyed material benefits in return for maintaining the provision of offerings at the tomb.[105]

Groups of women known as *ẖnr*, of whom an individual member was a *ẖnrt*, were attached to various cults, including the funerary cult.[106] Their principal activity was singing and dancing. The same designation is given to women who sing and dance for the household in the scenes shown in tomb chapels, and women only are overseers of the *ẖnr* and its activities, including the *ẖnr* of the king. Since the term *ẖnr* means "restrain" or "confine,"[107] the term in question has been translated "harem," but this meaning becomes rather problematic, as Del Nord has pointed out, when the *ẖnr* belongs to a goddess such as Hathor or Bat. A label in a tomb at Deir el Gebrawi seems to refer to male dancers as *ẖnrt*, but the use of the feminine ending at this period puts this evidence in doubt.[108] Men were eventually involved in such groups, but probably not before the end of the Heracleopolitan period, and it is unclear what their participation entailed.

A more modest role is played by women in the household service of other women, although in some cases, where the mistress is a queen or high-ranking princess, this role could convey a considerable degree of responsibility. Thus female stewards are to be found in the service of two queens, and another in the chapel of a princess within the mastaba of Mereruka. The last source also shows a female "inspector (i.e., a lesser

---

[104]Fischer, *Egyptian Studies* 1, 70.

[105]Most specifically attested by the funerary decree of *Ny-k3-Ḥr* at Tehna, *Urk.* 1, 24-27.

[106]Discussed in detail by Del Nord, "The term *ẖnr*: 'harem' or 'musical performers'?" in *Fs. Dunham*, 137-145.

[107]I find it difficult, in any case, to accept Betsy Bryan's argument ("The Etymology of *H̱NR* 'Group of Musical Performers,'" *BES* 4 [1982]: 35-39) that *ẖnr* derives from *ẖnỉ* "beat the rhythm," which is apparently 3ae inf. (cf. her n. 85). The Old Kingdom evidently makes a clear distinction between the noun *ẖnr*, referring to a group of women who are portrayed and described as dancing and singing, written [hieroglyphs] (an individual member of which is written [hieroglyphs], as in the mastaba of *Mḥw* at Saqqara) and the verb [hieroglyphs] (Pyr. 557c) on which the term "percussionist" is based (fem. [hieroglyphs], for which see n. 90 above; m. [hieroglyphs], for which see n. 93). Wm. Ward, *Index of Egyptian Administrative and Religious Titles of the Middle Kingdom* (Beirut, 1982), 132, gives abundant evidence for later percussionists. They are not, at this period, to be confused with singers and dancers, even though the activities of the latter were related to theirs.

[108]N. de Garis Davies, *The Rock Tombs of Deir el-Gebrâwi* 2, pl. 7. The confusion is compounded by the fact that the label is between a row of dancing women above it and a row of singing and dancing men below it. Although the label should apply only to the men, the term hnrt may well refer to the women.

overseer) of the treasure," an "overseer of ornaments" and an "overseer of cloth."[109] The final title occurs again in the chapel of the princess Idut. In the midst of these and other titles implying a degree of authority, the absence of female scribes is conspicuous. Several scribes are mentioned in Idut's chapel, but they are all men. Nor is it possible, as Chr. D. Noblecourt has stated,[110] that Idut herself can claim literacy on the basis of a scribal kit that is placed before her on a boat. The reliefs of this tomb were originally carved for a vizier named Ihy, whose figure has been replaced here as elsewhere, and the scribal kit belongs to him, as do the scribes. It will be recalled, however, that Queen Mersyankh III and the Princess Hemet-Re likewise have male scribes.

Among the other titles of women are "overseer of doctors" and "overseer of the chamber of wigs."[111] There is no further evidence for the first of these activities, but it is evidently to be taken quite seriously, since it occurs repeatedly on the false door of the woman who claims it. For the second title there is some related evidence: a female *ỉrỉt-šnỉ* "hairdresser" is known[112] and there is iconographic proof of her activity.[113]

4. Some exceptional cases

Now we may turn to a few details of a more-or-less surprising nature. Although women are occasionally to be found in market scenes, they are usually purchasers; in one case, however, a woman is a vendor.[114] More exceptionally, a Fifth Dynasty chapel at Saqqara shows, in two cases, a woman wielding the steering oar of a cargo ship (Fig. 10 a, b).[115] In one case (Fig. 10 b)[116] she is being offered bread by a boy who squats in front of her. To judge from the direction of the hieroglyphs, both of the statements accompanying them are spoken by the woman. They are by no means easy to interpret, but

---

109 Fischer, *Egyptian Studies* 1, 70. The "overseer of ornaments" ( ) is hardly visible in Wresz., *Atlas* 3, pl. 11; but it was seen in a projected publication of the princess' chapel by the late Alexander Badawy.

110 C. Desroches Noblecourt, *La femme au temps des Pharaons* (Paris, 1986), 190, an error already noted by H. Brunner, *Altägyptische Erziehung*, (Wiesbaden, 1957), 46, n. 151.

111 Fischer, *Egyptian Studies* 1, 71f.

112 *Ibid.*, 72, n23.

113 *Ibid.*, 47, fig. 14 and pl. 15.

114 Moussa and Altenmüller, *Grab des Nianchchnum und Chnumhotep*, fig. 10 (two women; one sells, the other buys). Other examples of women as purchasers: *LD* 2, 96; S. Hodjash and O. Berlev, *The Egyptian Reliefs and Stelae in the Pushkin Museum of Fine Arts*, Moscow (Leningrad, 1982), 38f.

115 *LD* 2, 103, 104.

116 *Ibid.*, 104.

the first statement seems to be : "Give bread (with) thy arm," and the second "(but) don't obstruct my face with it while I am putting to shore." The ship in the register below her shows the more familiar motif of a woman nursing her child.

In the chapel of Nefer and Ka-hay at Saqqara, a woman sits in a pillared canopy which is, rather curiously, the extension of an open pavilion in which cuts of meat are suspended (Fig. 11).[117] Since a small naked girl stands before her, holding her hand, she may represent the wife of the principal tomb owner rather than an instructor or supervisor of the dancers whom she is watching. That alternative is also borne out by the fact that the wife does not accompany her husband at the end of the register in question. If the wife is indeed represented here, the case is most unusual.

A false door from Busiris in the Delta,[118] probably dating to the Heracleopolitan period, emphasizes, in a very interesting way, the fact that while aged women are sometimes represented (most frequently in the feminine version of the ideogram for "being old"),[119] they are never corpulent, as men so often are. False doors of the same period and earlier contrast the tomb owner as a slender young man and in portly middle age.[120] At the bottom of the false door from Busiris the same contrast is paralleled by showing the female owner as a naked girl, her hair in a pigtail terminated by a disk,[121] and as a thin old woman with pendant breasts. At the top of the door she conforms to the ideal of young womanhood that is customary.

The tombs of non-royal women are not, in general, of great interest, with one exception--unfortunately of unknown provenance.[122] One of the two

---

117Drawn from the photograph in Moussa and Altenmüller, *The Tomb of Nefer and Ka-hay*, pl. 14.

118*Ancient Egypt in the MMJ*, 166-174 and figs. 8-9 (note particularly the latter).

119E.g. MFA 21.3081 (Reisner, *Giza* 1, pl. 65b); Épron-Wild, *Tombeau de Ti* 1, pl. 39. For other examples of emaciated old women see Fischer, "An Example of Memphite Influence in a Theban Stela of the Eleventh Dynasty," *Artibus Asiae* 22 (1959): figs. 10, 13 following 240, fig. 11, 251.

120E. g. CG 1397, 1483, 1565, 1619; see also Fischer, "A Scribe of the Army in a Saqqara Mastaba of the Early Fifth Dynasty," *JNES* 18 (1959): 246, fig. 10(e) and 244-248, where the general subject of male corpulence is discussed; and Fischer, "Varia Aegyptiaca," *JARCE* 2 (1963): frontispiece and 19, referring to an example of the Heracleopolitan period: MMA: 12.183.8.

121This style of pigtail appears throughout the representations of the princess Idut at Saqqara: Macramallah, *Mastaba d'Idout*.

122Berlin (East) 15416-21. The two scenes described here are illustrated by H. Schäfer and W. Andrae, *Die Kunst des Alten Orients* (Berlin, 1925), pl. 250. For the rest see *ÄIB* 1, 17f.

Figure 11

Woman in open pavilion, after Moussa and Altenüller, *The Tomb of Nefer and Kahay*, pl.14.

Figure 12

Woman tomb owner supervising harvesting of flax. Photograph Staatliche Museen zu Berlin, Hauptstadt der DDR, Ägyptisches Museum Inv. Nr. 1542(front side).

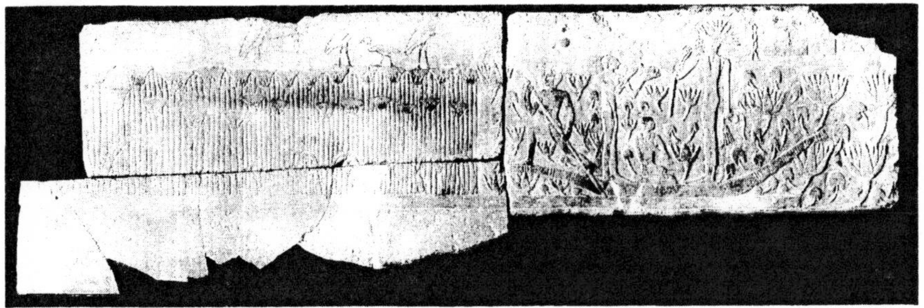

Figure 13

Woman tomb owner gathering lotus blossoms, tomb of Hetepet. Photograph Staatliche Museen zu Berlin, Hauptstadt der DDR, Ägyptisches Museum Inv. Nr. 15420.

Figure 16

False door of a Priestess of Hathor. Photograph Staatliche Museen zu Berlin, Hauptstadt der DDR, Ägyptisches Museum architrave: Inv. Nr. 15416; lintel: Inv. Nr. 15417; jamb: Inv. Nr. 15418.

Figure 14

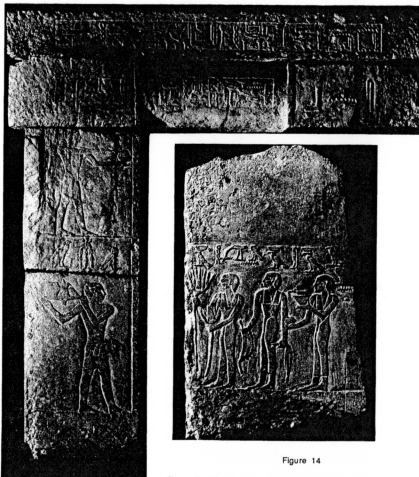

Three female retainers. Photograph Staatliche Museen zu Berlin, Hauptstadt der DDR, Ägyptisches Museum Inv. Nr. 15419.

Figure 15

Women with necklaces. Photograph Staatliche Museen zu Berlin, Hauptstadt der DDR, Ägyptisches Museum Inv. Nr. 15421(left side).

substantial pieces of relief that have been recovered (Fig. 12) shows a detail I have already mentioned: the tomb owner supervises the harvesting of flax. The other piece (Fig. 13) shows her gathering lotus blossoms in the marshes as in the scene of Deir el Gebrawi;[123] her papyrus skiff is punted by a man, but a female servant offers her a drink and another woman sits between them. A smaller piece of relief (Fig. 14) shows three female retainers bringing lotus blossoms, necklaces, a ewer and a basin, while a similar block (Fig. 15) shows other women bringing necklaces only. There is no mention of a husband on these reliefs or on the elements of a false door (Fig. 16).[124] It is true that we may not have a complete picture of the decoration of the chapel, but it seems to be devoted to feminine preoccupations to an unusual degree.

The most surprising piece of evidence concerning non-royal women in certainly the representation of a besieged town in a tomb at Deshasha (Fig. 17).[125] I have redrawn only the uppermost register, which is the one most clearly preserved; a woman stabs an Egyptian bowman at the left; a second woman leads a boy, who carries a dagger, towards a man (probably elderly) who breaks the bow of another assailant. Although the details of the lower registers are less clear, they certainly show women overpowering other invaders in one way or another. All this is quite different from an otherwise similar representation at Saqqara.[126] Perhaps the point of the Deshasha version is less to extol the bravery of the women than to deprecate the ineffective efforts of the men of the town who fight outside the walls. But there is no reason to doubt the historical veracity of the women's resistance, for there are many other examples of this kind in more recent history.[127]

In sum, if Egyptian society of the Old Kingdom was basically a man's world, reflected, for the most part in tomb chapels of which men were the primary owners, women are nonetheless seen to have participated in some of the most essential and important activities of that society; they could possess property of their own and hold positions of considerable responsibility,

---

[123]See note 50 above. These scenes might be associated with the preparation of perfume, but it should be noted that this activity is only attested for the Late Period (contrary to Lucas, *Materials*, 86); see Fischer, "The early publication of a relief in Turin," *GM* 101 (1988): 31-33.

[124]The owner is "She who is Known to the King, Priestess of Hathor, Tenant Landholder (*ḫntyt-š*), *Ḥtpt*".

[125]Redrawn from W.M.F. Petrie, *Deshasheh*, (London, 1897), pl. 4.

[126]Quibell-Hayter, *Teti Pyramid*, frontispiece.

[127]Apart from the exceptional case of Jean d'Arc, who delivered Orleans from the English in 1429, one thinks of the woman of Toulouse who killed Simon de Montfort with a stone when he beseiged that city in 1218, of Marie Fouré, who raised the siege of Péronne in 1536, and of the women of Geneva, who held off the Savoyards during the Escalade of 1602.

even though they were not scribes and therefore could not enter the governmental bureaucracy to an appreciable extent. I might add that, while the generic use of "man" is sometimes felt to be offensively exclusive in our own society, the Egyptians did not seem to have that problem. The equivalent term *rmt* "people" may be followed solely by the male determinative,[128] but that fact makes the more usual addition of the female determinative all the more significant. Thus the good opinion of women, as well as that of men, is sought in all sorts of moralistic statements such as "I never did what people dislike";[129] "I was one who did what all people praise";[130] "I was beloved of people";[131] "I never did (or said) what people contest."[132]

Figure 17

Women defenders at Deshasha, after W.M.F. Petrie, *Deshasheh* (London, l897), fiig. XXX.

[128]*Ancient Egypt in the MMJ*, 88, n. 42.

[129]Hassan, *Gîza* 3, fig. 69.

[130]*Urk.* 1, 75 (16).

[131]*Urk.* 1, 75 (13), 217 (10).

[132]*Urk.* 1, 46 (13), 193 (4).

Responses to Dr. Fischer's Paper

Herlihy: I have a special interest in the existence of women's workshops. You used the term "house of weavers," and I was wondering if you could state whether that term "house" is in any sense a technical term and whether the word "weavers" applies to married women and then whether there is any linkage between a house of weavers in the Egyptian sense and the later Greek term "women's workshops." I think that there are some references in an Egyptian context in the Hellenistic age. Did such an institution exist; is there any continuity into the Hellenistic period?

Fischer: Of course there was an establishment. It was a "house of weavers" and such a workshop is represented on the tomb walls of Beni Hasan and in a model from the tomb of Meket-Re at the beginning of the Middle Kingdom, both completely run by women. However by the New Kingdom men were very active in such establishments, and therefore after a certain date it was no longer a strictly female enterprise. And in fact that hieroglyph that I showed you of a woman with her shuttle only occurs in the Old Kingdom; it doesn't appear in later times. A different term, a rather vaguer term, is used for weavers after the Old Kingdom. I don't really see any connection with a Greek house of women. Just one more point: some connect the development of the vertical loom with men entering the profession, but I am a little skeptical about this.

Galvin: Dr. Fischer, in your presentation, you described the many and varied positions that woman held in the Old Kingdom. You said "Of the activities of women, their participation in temple and funerary rituals is most important." My own research on the Priestesses of Hathor has certainly corroborated your statement. I have investigated approximately four hundred women that were involved in the cult of Hathor during the Old Kingdom and the First Intermediate Period. These women represent a cross-section of socio-economic status, and their provenance represents a cross section of geographic locations from Momemphis in the north to Aswan in the south. During the Old

Kingdom in what I would call the middle and upper management positions of the Hathoric cult I can identify 48 Priestesses of Hathor, Mistress of the Sycamores, 10 Priestesses of Hathor, Mistress of the Sycamore in all her Places, 11 Priestesses of Hathor in all her Places. Then something really dramatic happens in the First Intermediate Period. I can find only 4 Priestesses of Hathor, Mistress of the Sycamore, 0 Priestesses of Hathor, Mistress of the Sycamore in all her Places, 0 Priestesses of Hathor in all her Places. Instead I find 19 men who claim the title of Overseer of the Priests of Hathor. They start in the Sixth Dynasty and last through to the Middle Kingdom.

So, with this lengthy introduction to my question, I'm very interested in what happens in the First Intermediate Period to cause this dramatic reversal in the authority of women. I believe it was John A. Wilson who was fond of associating the phrase "democratization of power"; with this Intermediate Period, but this doesn't appear to me to be a democratization, it appears to be the reverse for women at least. I was wondering if, from your research of the First Intermediate Period, you might elaborate on this hypothesis.

Fischer: Well, a good deal of our evidence for the so-called First Intermediate Period is from the provinces and certainly if you go to Dendera you will find that every woman who is anybody is a priestess of Hathor, again, the overseer of priests and the inspector of priests is a man. But these priestesses are very common; I think it is a question of where you look at the evidence. You have to weigh that against the evidence from the necropolis at Saqqara.

Galvin: Do you think that there was any lessening of activity within the cults during the period of turmoil that resulted in the opportunity for reformation of authority?

Fischer: Of course I must say that the dating of material from, say Saqqara, which is a main source, is extremely difficult because traditions were extremely tenacious there and there is a great deal of dispute about the dating of many of the tombs. But, as I say, in the provinces (after all in this period the provinces represented a large share of the actual power) people had a great deal of autonomy, and this is part of what we mean by democratization, that not only did these different provinces have more independence but people within the province were independent too. Within these provinces, certainly, you have plenty of priestesses.

Galvin: Priestesses, but no longer in positions of authority.

Fischer: No, and you also do find a few Priests of Hathor, as well as Priestesses of Hathor.

McNamara: One of the things that really concerned me Dr. Fischer, in listening to your speech was that you said that there are few of these tombs that are owned by women, but while you were talking I was unable to follow which ones were owned by women so that I was not clear at what point the male owner is really dominating the discourse, really making the woman, constructing the woman. I wondered particularly about the woman who was steering the boat and the doctors, women seemed to be acting more in the positions of, shall we say, autonomous activity. Are these women the owners of the tombs?

Fischer: No, not necessarily. Usually a wife would have a false door stela within the tomb of the husband. She had, so to speak, a tomb of her own within the mastaba of her husband. This is conspicuous in the tomb of Mereruka, where his wife, who was a king's daughter, had her own suite of chapel rooms, ostensibly a tomb within that of her husband's. However, this is a rather unusual situation.

Delaney: I have a comment. You were talking about the markets and you said something about most of the scenes showing women only as purchasers rather than as vendors. And I think that there is another way of looking at that, and that is compared with the contemporary Middle East. Men are mainly the purchasers and that is a prestigious kind of role for them, and in fact what women being purchasers would show is that they had freedom of movement by themselves and also control of some of the funds. I'm not sure that by saying that they were only consumers isn't reading back into it what we think of women now into times past. There is possibly another interpretation.

Fischer: You're quite right. I suppose that the reason that I did that is simply to underline the fact that they were rarely the vendor. It is the rarity of that situation that I was emphasizing.

Harris: I would like to know if the mother continues to be prominent in the tombs of the later Middle and New Kingdoms and in the literature, especially with regard to her relationship to her son. I am particularly interested in what classicists call the "ascendancy of affection" in trying to learn about the intrafamilial relationships. To find out what we can about a man who might feel much closer to his mother than to his wife. Would there be evidence for that sort of closeness which you find, for example, in China in very ancient times or in India today?

Fischer: As I indicated, one can think of a variety of motives behind the commemoration of the tomb owner's mother. In one case it was specified exactly why the man was so fond of his mother: she had helped him in a situation in which his father apparently did not. In another case the same thing seems to have happened, to judge from the way the man mentioned his mother, and in still other cases we can't guess, we simply don't know.

B. Lesko: We might add that, yes, there are New Kingdom tombs where the owner's mother is portrayed in the wall scenes along with his wife and their children. As the wife is often termed "his beloved" one is not tempted to make value judgments. There are also the queen-mothers, who are commemorated in statuary and inscriptions, perhaps the most famous being Queen Ahmose-Nefertari, from the early Eighteenth Dynasty, who, along with her son, was deified after death and whose cult was perpetuated for centuries, particularly in Western Thebes. Also the didactic text of the sage Any makes two important allusions to (1) the importance of grandmother's favorable opinion about your offspring's behavior, and (2) to the honoring of one's mother in her old age with care for her in the form of plentiful food rations, oil for her skin, and clothing for her back.

Addendum by Dr. M. Galvin

My remarks will be based on my research of Hathoric priestesses and their scope will be limited largely to the Giza-Saqqara area during the Old Kingdom.

It is perhaps most appropriate to start with a few remarks about the goddess Hathor herself. The tenacity of her faithful and the persuasiveness of her cult made her a central figure in Egyptian religion for thousands of years. She was already so well established with political authority at the inception of Egypt's Dynastic Period as to grace the Narmer palette with her likeness. Well over two thousand years later the rulers of the Saite period were still legitimizing their authority by commissioning sculpture associating the king with the protection of Hathor.[1] Even the Sed-festival, which commemorated the period renewal of kingship, required the integral participation of Hathor to make the divine recognition of pharaoh complete.[2]

Of the non-royal populace, we might interpret the expression "venerated before Hathor," which appears in many hundreds of Old Kingdom tomb inscriptions of both men and women, as an indication of a popularity so enormous that it carried itself forward for thousands of years. Hathor was identified as proprietress of love, sex, joy, music, and poetry; she was also one with drunkeness, bloodthirstiness and revenge: striding across the full range of human emotion. But, perhaps, her most appealing association was that of nurturer of humankind. Her nurturing capacity was closely linked with her cow identity as certainly the milk of the cow was recognized for its life sustaining nutrition.

In light of Hathor's remarkable longevity and enormous popularity, it is not surprising to find that hundreds of women were drawn to the priestly sorority of this female deity's cult. From the Old Kingdom and the First Intermediate Period, 226 Priestesses of Hathor have been identified, but only 10 Priests of Hathor show up in the records. Clearly, despite the fact that men and women equally filled the ranks of Hathor's faithful, women predominated in her priesthood.

During the Old Kingdom, particularly in the Giza-Saqqara area, an elaborate hierarchy of priestly positions was worked out within the Hathoric cult.[3] This was, no doubt, a necessity in order to accommodate the magnitude of cultic activity and perhaps to reward its priestly members. Within this system, we might recognize the Priestess of Hathor, Mistress of the Sycamores in all her Places as the designated authority over all Priestesses of Hathor, Mistress of the Sycamores. Finally, we might recognize the Priestess of Hathor in all her Places as designated authority in all Hathoric cult centers in Giza-

---

[1]PM III, p. 178 (and map p.174); A. Vigreau, *Le Musee du Caire* (Encyclopedie photographique de l'art, editions "Tel"), Paris, 1949, pl. 174-175; Bothmer, *Egyptian Sculpture of the Late Period*, Brooklyn, 1960, repr. 1969, pp. 64, 68, 103.

[2]Edward F. Wente, "Hathor at the Jubilee," *Studies.....Wilson*, *SAOC* 35, p.83ff.

[3]Marianne Galvin, "Priestesses of Hathor in the Old Kingdom and the Ist Intermediate Period" University Microfilm, Inc., p. 74ff.

Saqqara, Dendera, Cusae, the Re-Hathor cult, and possibly even in the interactions with the Neithic cult of the Old Kingdom.

Among these "administrative" positions, I have identified 52 Priestesses of Hathor, Mistress of the Sycamores, 10 Priestesses of Hathor, Mistress of the Sycamore in all her Places, and 11 Priestesses of Hathor in all her Places. I have identified only 2 men, both of whom served as Priest of Hathor in all her Places. It would, therefore, appear that the hierarchy of priestly titles for the Hathoric cult belonged primarily, if not exclusively, to women.

Interestingly enough, during the Old Kingdom, 19 men can be identified as holding the position of Overseer of Priests in connection with the Hathoric cult and 10 men the position of Inspector of Priests. I know of no women who held either of these positions for the Hathoric cult during the Old Kingdom or First Intermediate Period.

This sets up a curious juxtapositioning of women in authority to men in authority. Women in the Hathoric cult appear to have risen up through the ranks, starting with the position of Priestess of Hathor, progressing to the more lofty, "administrative" positions. Men, however, seem to have bypassed the upper level Hathoric titles to become Inspector or Overseer.

It should also be noted that the Hathoric priestly titles did not carry with them a hereditary status (a daughter could not inherit the position of Priestess of Hathor from a family member). On the other hand, the positions of Inspector and Overseer of the Priests, particularly within the Cusae Hathoric cult, did.[4]

I do not mean to imply an antagonistic relationship between these two administrative branches of the Hathoric cult; among the 19 overseers, 14 recorded in their tomb inscriptions a female family member who held the title of Priestess of Hathor, indicating at the very least a significant familial involvement with the Hathoric cult. However , it is quite clear that certain positions within the Hathoric cult were held by women while certain other positions were held by men.

---

[4]M. Galvin, "Hereditary Status of the Titles of the Cult of Hathor," *JEA* 70(1984): 42-49.

The Middle Kingdom

When rule of the land passed from the successors of the old royal family at Memphis (Seventh and Eighth Dynasties) to newer aspirants to power, social revolution possibly played a role. All we know for certain is that the central government of Egypt became fragmented as control of the land was shared by rival factions, one of which was the Heracleopolitan Ninth and Tenth Dynasties (c. 2150-2050 B.C.). Herakleopolis was the much later Greek name for a city in the Twentieth nome of Upper Egypt, or the Fayum province, which rose to power and wrested much of Egypt away from the Old Kingdom's successors at Memphis. This new Ninth Dynasty probably took control in the north, but the succeeding Tenth (still Herakleopolitan) Dynasty had to contend with independent southern princes at Thebes (modern Luxor) who eventually gained ascendency.

The Theban Eleventh Dynasty in turn had to deal with several surviving independent nomes or states in their own efforts to rebuild a strong central government such as had benefited the Old Kingdom. Economic, social, religious, artistic, and bureaucratic changes mark the First Intermediate Period and early Middle Kingdom, and its society was markedly different from that which had existed under the rich and mighty Old Kingdom dynasties.

However, the royal wives were still important (and may have provided links with previous royal families) and helped provide legitimacy for new aspirants to power. The Eleventh Dynasty ruler Mentuhotep had a wife named Neferu I whose "importance is attested by the frequency with which she is mentioned in her son's inscription."[1] She was the mother of King Intef. His successor, Mentuhotep II, buried his womenfolk in his temple precinct near his own tomb. These included Queen Tem, mother of Mentuhotep III and Queen Neferu III, Mentuhotep II's full sister, whose tomb was much visited in the New Kingdom and was then evidently regarded as a national shrine.

Because several hundred years are covered by the transitional period and the Middle Kingdom, and political and economic crises were almost

[1]Wm. C. Hayes, *CAH*[3] I, part 2, p.477.

constant, the status of women undoubtedly varied considerably from century to century and from region to region. More consistency could be expected once the strong centralized government and peace throughout the realm was established. How much "consistency" social practices had in such a large country in antiquity is problematic, however.

It remained for a usurper, Amenemhet, to assume the throne at the end of the Eleventh Dynasty and move his capital to the north again. He reinforced Egypt's old borders and founded the new Twelfth Dynasty, which is also known as the Middle Kingdom (2030-1786 B.C.). The crisis of Amenemhet's own assassination (an ancient text implies that women of the palace were implicated) was survived by his family, but the dream of a return to a strong kingship was not immediately realized. Indeed Egypt of the early Twelfth Dynasty, from surviving evidence, seems to have been "a feudal state more completely than ever before or after."[2] The powerful provincial families imitated royalty in the style and decoration of their tombs, in their mortuary beliefs and literature, and in the organization of their households. Indeed, even ordinary men and women now were hopeful of attaining an effective afterlife in the company of the greatest gods.

The provincial governors may have exacted tolls from river traffic passing through their provinces or commandeered taxes into their own treasuries which should have gone instead to the central government. For some reason, their independence proved intolerable to the kings, and eventually strong rulers put an end to the independence and power of the nomarchs, and the great provincial tombs came to an end in the second half of the Twelfth Dynasty.

Not very much is known about the royal women of the Middle Kingdom, until the end of the dynasty. Part of an elegant female-headed sphinx survives to tantalize us, and the pyramid of Amenemhet III erected at Dashur has proven to be the tomb of his chief queen. His daughter, Sobekneferu, succeeded his son to the throne and may have been the victor in a family feud. She is generally accepted as the second documented female pharaoh of Egypt (after Nitokerty of the Sixth Dynasty), although the possibility remains of an early dynastic female ruler and one or two others in the Old Kingdom. The fine tombs and coffins of the Middle Kingdom's leading provincial families, as well as the more modest funerary monuments of their subjects, which now proliferated, provided some of the material for the second chapter on Egyptian women.

Leonard H. Lesko

---

[2]A.H. Gardiner, *Egypt of the Pharaohs*, Oxford, 1961, 129.

Non-Royal Women and their Occupations in the Middle Kingdom

William A. Ward

At the beginning of this century, the French archaeologists Gauthier and Jequier reported the results of their excavations around the pyramid of Sesostris I at Lisht. In a shallow shaft burial just south of the pyramid, they discovered what must surely be one of the more baffling minor mysteries of Egyptian archaeology, a find for which there is still no logical explanation. The small burial pit contained ordinary and uninteresting coffins of the Graeco-Roman period indicating that the chamber was probably excavated at that time, part of a small late necropolis which grew up around the pyramid.[1]

The mystery of this burial is that the inner part of the chamber was lined with finely executed offering-tables taken from elsewhere and used to create a decorated burial chamber for what was otherwise an undistinguished tomb. There are fourteen offering-tables, thirteen of which are inscribed with the usual funerary formulae and the names and titles of several women. The date of this group of objects is clearly the Middle Kingdom so this is yet another example of the ancient Egyptian practise of raiding older monuments for finished building-stones.

Since two of these offering-tables belonged to one person, there are twelve women involved in this group. Based solely on the titles of these women--there is nothing else to go on--the excavators suggested that the offering-tables belonged to a guild of priestesses forming a religious order involved in ceremonies of the funerary cult of the dead king. The titles of nine of these women were thought to mean "Guardian of a house." One woman was considered a kind of mother superior, the remaining two as minor functionaries of the group. In short, these offering-tables represent a dozen priestesses belonging to a religious order with its own administrative staff which functioned within the funerary cult of Sesostris I.

---

[1] J.-E. Gauthier and G. Jequier, *Memoire sur les fouilles de Lisht* (*MIFAO*, Vol. 6; Cairo, 1902): 50-55. There seems to be no record of these coffins which have presumably disappeared.

With rare exceptions, these offering-tables and the ladies they represent have subsequently gone unnoticed.[2] Most of the objects were included in the Cairo Museum catalogue, but this intriguing discovery has otherwise been relegated to the obscure corners of history, the real mystery it left behind forgotten. For when we take a closer look at their titles, the definition of these women as priestesses is obviously in error. In the light of more recently available information, four of the women from Lisht were "hall-keepers,"[3] five were "housemaids,"[4] one was an "attendant" of some kind,[5] and the suggested leader of the group turns out to have been a "cleaning-lady."[6] The other titles represented are "Overseer of a storehouse"[7] and perhaps "maiden."[8] Far from being a religious order of priestesses, the women from Lisht seem rather to be from the ranks of minor household servants. Precisely where and in what capacities these women served and why women with mediocre status should have owned such well-made offering tables will probably never be known. The mystery remains a mystery.

This group of titles and the very different interpretations given to them--priestesses or household servants--illustrates one of the major difficulties in defining the status of non-royal women during the Middle Kingdom. Titles borne by women are one of the few sources of information we have on the personal situation of women as individuals in their own right, not as wives of this or that official or aristocrat. But the majority of the known female titles do not appear in any explanatory context and some simply cannot be translated with accuracy. Since the meaning and function of women's titles are often unknown, the duties and rank of an individual can rarely be determined.

One area in which some precision is possible is service to deities and temples. The numerous titles are self-explanatory and need little definition.[9] Priestesses of the two lower grades served gods and temples throughout Egypt[10] though it is of some interest that no Chief Priestesses are known. In the cult of Hathor, for example, women were very numerous but the head of

---

[2]Cf. H.G. Fischer, *Egyptian Studies* 1. *Varia* (New York, 1976): 76-77; W.A. Ward, *Essays on Feminine Titles of the Middle Kingdom and Related Subjects* (Beirut, 1986): 31-32.

[3]*iry.t-ᶜ.t*; Ward, *Feminine Titles*: 4.

[4]*wb3y.t*; *ibid.*, 6-7.

[5]*3ty.t*; *ibid.*, 8.

[6]*ḥt.t-pr*; *ibid.*, 13; a further example in J. Ferry, "Une mission en Italie," *RecTrav* III (1882), 117.

[7]*imy.t-r s.t*; Ward, *Feminine Titles*, 3-4.

[8]Fischer, *Varia*, 77.

[9]Ward, *Feminine Titles*, 20-21.

[10]*wᶜb.t* and *ḥm.t-nṯr*; ibid., 6, 10-11.

the temple personnel serving this goddess seems always to have been a man.[11] The only possible female administrative officer in the Hathor cult so far recorded for the Middle Kingdom is a Sealer at the Hathor temple in Sinai[12] (see infra.). The priesthoods thus seem to have been dominated by men, women having no place in the hierarchy except at the lowest levels.

Singers, dancers and musicians were intimately associated with temple cults so they can be included in the roster of temple personnel. However, such professionals were also attached to royal courts and the larger private households so that music and dancing had both a religious and secular function. Both men and women were prominent in these professions. It is perhaps misleading that, on the basis of the known evidence, musical directors in the Old Kingdom and First Intermediate Period were women, but in the Middle Kingdom, this position was held by men.[13] As will shortly be seen, this situation fits into an overall pattern for the Middle Kingdom.

In purely secular functions, women appear rarely in the trades and professions. We find them as hairdressers and cosmeticians, which is to be expected, but also as brewers, millers, weavers, gardeners and scribes, professions usually reserved for men. All women in these professions worked in large private households; we find none in the palaces. Nor do we hear of female overseers or other administrative officers within a profession. Those few women who did practice a trade remained in the ranks, so to speak, and were not promoted to the higher levels.

The appearance of at least four female scribes in Middle Kingdom sources raises the important issue of women's education. Two appear among household functionaries on funerary stela,[14] one is portrayed twice in the burial chamber of Aashiyet in the funerary complex of Nebhepetre Mentuhotep,[15] and the fourth was the owner of a fine rock crystal scarab.[16]

11W.A. Ward, *Index of Egyptian Administrative and Religious Titles of the Middle Kingdom* (Beirut, 1982), nos. 157a, 268-70. In the Middle Kingdom, the head of a local Hathor cult was generally the Nomarch; Sh. Allam, *Beiträge zum Hathorkult* (Berlin, 1963), 32-33.

12The *sḏ3w.ty(t) kf3-ib*, Ib-Neith; Ward, *Feminine Titles*, 18, but see infra, n.24.

13D. Nord, Review of *Der königlische Harim im alten Ägypten und seine Verwaltung*, by E. Reiser, *JNES* 34 (1975): 144, notes that the *ḫnr.wt* troupe of singers and dancers was always directed by a woman into First Intermediate Times. Other musical and dancing groups were also directed by women in the earlier periods; Fischer, *Varia*, 71. Men directed such groups in the Middle Kingdom; Ward, *Feminine Titles*, 74, nos. 22, 24.

14Turin 107 (Cat. 1534)=Ferry, *RecTrav* III (1882), 117; O. Koeford-Perersen, *Les stéles égyptiennes* (Publications de la Glypothèque ny Carlsberg, 1; Copenhagen, 1948), no. 18.

15*TPPI*, 26, 29.

Since our documentation is far from complete, it is safe to assume that if four female scribes are known, there were probably others. While little can be said about the education of women in general,[17] the existence of female scribes assumes that they must have been trained somewhere. This would not necessarily have been in the regular temple schools as such training could well have been received from tutors. The fact remains that there were some women who could read and write and were employed as female scribes, perhaps as secretaries to aristocratic women. Yet no female scribe is portrayed as such in the reliefs and paintings.

The roster of titled women at work is completed by many whose functions lay within the household. It is in this group that we must place the ladies from Lisht and it is within this range of titles that we encounter the most difficulties in defining what a particular woman did or the extent, if any, of her authority. Some twenty titles belong in this category; most are attendants of some kind or other, nursemaids and other servants with duties in private households. What these duties were is very difficult to determine. As Fischer notes: "the rank and status of such servants depended on the circumstances of their employer."[18] The common title *wb3y.t* meaning "housemaid" or "housekeeper" is a good example here.[19] Women with this title could have important duties on a large wealthy estate or rather minor ones in a smaller household.[20]

Note also the title "Sealer" (*sḏ3w.tyt*) held by two women of the Twelfth Dynasty. This was one of the most common functions performed by men whom we find at all levels from important positions in the state treasury down to the mere assistants of minor officials.[21] During the Old Kingdom and First Intermediate Period, at least eight women are known with this title, all employees of private households and mostly associated with the entourages of women of varying degrees of social status.[22] From the Middle Kingdom proper, the only sure example is the lady Tchat who was the "Sealer" and "keeper of the property of her lord" in the household of the Nomarch

---

[16]Berlin (Charlottenburg) Inv. 42/73, now published by Fischer, *Varia*, 77-78.

[17]Brunner, *Erziehung*, 45-49, who concentrates more on musical than literary education, evidence for the latter being very sparse.

[18]Fischer, *Varia*, 76.

[19]Ward, *Index*, no. 706.

[20]In P. Westcar 12,9 the *wb3y.t* of Dedi's household was apparently in charge of the food storerooms. For *wb3y.t*'s in lesser households, cf. Cairo 20561, 20649; *El Arabah*, pl. 13; *BM Stelae* II, pl. 34.

[21]Ward, *Index*, nos. 1468-1501.

[22]References in Fischer, *Varia*, 70 (6) and 79, n.60, first four references.

Khnumhotep II of Beni Hasan, a powerful provincial governor.[23] As already noted, the lady Ib-Neith was a "Trustworthy Sealer" of the Hathor temple in the Sinai, though there is some doubt about the completeness of the relevant text.[24] With the possible exception of the latter, then, female sealers normally served other women in households of varying size and wealth. Since no actual seals of these women are known, they were presumably entitled to use those of their employers to carry out the duties the title implies. As these duties were in private households, such "Sealers" probably used the personal seals of the ladies of the households in which they worked. Innumerable seals of the latter are known from Middle Kingdom times as well as the actual sealings.[25]

At this point, some general observations can be made. First of all, there is a distinct difference between the positions held by women in the Old Kingdom and those held by women in the Middle Kingdom. The list of Old Kingdom women in female administrative positions collected by Fischer[26] is replete with Overseers, Directors, Inspectors, and the like, ranks which are totally lacking in the Middle Kingdom. In the older period women held supervisory positions over other people as well as positions of moderate importance in the palace. Both aspects are missing in the Middle Kingdom. But one should be cautious about asserting the obvious conclusion that women were given more authority in the third millennium than in the second. It may well be that the general feudal atmosphere of the Middle Kingdom followed by the extensive administrative reforms of Sesostris III kept women out of the supervisory capacities they had enjoyed in an earlier age. But the evidence from both periods is sparse and it is best not to push this point too far.

Secondly, in Middle Kingdom times, authority at all levels seems to have remained a prerogative of men. We find no women in government, national or local, they have only subordinate positions in the priesthood and, according to the evidence at hand, were not appointed to positions where they held authority over other people, even in private households. With the exception of spinning and weaving, women are notably absent from the artistic

---

23W.A. Ward, "The Case of Mrs. Tchat and Her Sons at Beni Hasan," *GM* No.71 (1984): 51-59. Tchat bore three children to the Nomarch and eventually became his wife.

24Fischer, *Varia*, 79, n.69, suggests that part of the text has been omitted--"the Trustworthy Sealer (X, born to) Ib-Neith"--so that the title refers to an unnamed son rather than Ib-Neith herself. He also suggests that the gender of the figure accompanying this lable is uncertain, in his *Egyptian Titles of the Middle Kingdom, A Supplement to Wm. Ward's INDEX* (New York, 1985), 87, no. 1501.

25*nb.t-pr*: G.T. Martin, *Egyptian Administrative and Private-name Seals* (Oxford, 1971), passim; clay sealings: nos. 258, 288, 694, 1128, 1624.

26Fischer, *Varia*, 69-72.

crafts and trades. In general, then, the female work force can be found in homes and temples in subordinate positions. The inference is that they were answerable to the wife who ran a household, or a male supervisor everywhere else.

A third general observation concerns the distinction between women and men in the work force. The titles borne by women indicate that, with few exceptions, they worked inside buildings; the outside labor was left to men. In the reliefs and paintings of the Middle Kingdom, representations of women working on private estates show them in a somewhat restricted range of activities: spinning and weaving, grinding grain, making bread, and as hairdressers or attendants to the ladies of the family. Young girls are occasionally found winnowing grain. Women are also frequent in scenes of music and dancing. Female servants may be present in the traditional fishing and fowling scenes of the aristocracy, but they are passive observers rather than participants.[27] Women also appear regularly in groups of offering-bearers or rarely as passengers in sailing ships[28] but both are ceremonial rather than work functions. Only in extremely rare occurrences do we find a woman involved in work generally reserved for men.[29] Men were responsible for outside activities: agriculture, animal husbandry, fishing and fowling, slaughtering animals, washing clothes, and similar activities. The crafts and trades were likewise men's work. This same division of labor is seen in the numerous servant statues found in burials which portray women involved in the same narrow sphere of activity as in the reliefs and paintings.[30] The titles, reliefs and servant statues thus point to the same conclusion: women worked at jobs which kept them inside; the outside work was done by men.

The rather small corpus of papyri from Middle Kingdom times has little to say about the occupations of women, though the few facts that can be gleaned from these documents support the general picture gained from other sources. For example, weaving as women's work is noted several times. The correspondence of the miserly Hekanakht deals mostly with agricultural

---

[27]Cf. Klebs, *Reliefs* 2, Index, sub "Frau."

[28]Women servants in lines of offering-bearers can be found on most funerary stelae and in the larger tomb chapels. Groups of women in ships are found in the representations of the "Abydos pilgrimage," e.g., *Beni Hasan* 1, pls. 16, 29. On this, see H. Altenmüller, "Abydosfahrt," in *LÄ* 1, 42-47.

[29]E.G., a woman reaping with men: *Beni Hasan* 1, pl. 29; women gleaners following reapers: Davies-Gardiner, *Antefoker*, pl. 3; Quibell, *Excav. Saqq. (1905-06)*, pl. 20.

[30]J.H. Breasted, Jr., *Egyptian Servant Statues* (The Bollingen Series, 13; Washington, 1948), passim. A few additional activities are shown in this material such as milking a cow (p.8) and tending a kiln in a pottery workshop (p. 50).

matters, but he does note that some of the payment for the rental of fields should come from the sale of cloth woven in the household.[31] A letter from Lahun is concerned with women weavers and woven goods for a local temple which have not yet been finished.[32] And in the well-known list of household servants from a papyrus in Brooklyn, of the 29 women listed whose occupations are preserved, at least 20 worked in the weaving trade, almost all of whom were Asiatics.[33] While the people in this list, and specifically the Asiatics, are constantly refered to as "slaves" in the literature, it is more likely that this group of women weavers and similar groups of professionals came on their own to Egypt to find employment.[34]

One cannot discuss the status of non-royal women without touching on the subject of harems and concubines. It has been customary in the literature to define as a concubine almost any women with no immediately

---

31 *Hekanakht Papers*, p. 13, Letter I, Rt. 4-6. Cf. K. Baer, "An Eleventh Dynasty Farmer's Letters to his Family," *JAOS* 83 (1963): 1-9, for a detailed analysis of the economic implications of these letters.

32 F. Ll. Griffith, *Hieratic Papyri from Kahun and Gurob* (London, 1898), 75-77, pl. 32, document III.3.

33 W.C. Hayes, *A Papyrus of the Late Middle Kingdom in the Brooklyn Musuem* (Brooklyn, 1955), Chap. 4. Further discussions of the relation between this list of servants and the other texts on this papyrus are: A. Théodoridès, "Du rapport entre les parties du Pap. Brooklyn 35.1446," *RIDA* 3e ser., 7 (1960): 138-145; B. Menu, Review of *A Papyrus of the Late Middle Kingdom*, by W.C. Hayes, *CdE* No. 95 (1973): 84-87; *idem.*, "Considérations sur le droit pénal au moyen empire égyptien," *BIFAO* 81, Suppl. (1981): 57-76.

34 E.g., the Asiatics listed among musicians and dancers who performed at various festivals; Griffith, *Hieratic Papyri from Kahun and Gurob*, 60, Table 1, pl. 24. The whole question of slavery in Egypt needs re-study in spite of major essays on the subject: A. Bakir, *Slavery in Pharaonic Egypt* (*SASAE*, 13; Cairo, 1952); W. Helck, "Sklaven," *LÄ* 5, 982-87; G. Posener, "Les asiatiques en égypte sous les XIIe et XIIIe dynasties," *Syria* 34 (1957): 145-63. The general assumption is that foreigners in domestic, palace or temple service came to Egypt as prisoners of war and were impressed as slave laborers. While this may be true in some cases, the argument is a weak one when applied to Middle Kingdom times. Professional Asiatic weavers, dancers, and the like, would be more likely to come from the urban centers of Canaan rather than the tribes of the frontier area. While there was military action along the frontiers, such activity was almost non-existent in Canaan during the Middle Kingdom. Note also the study by Jac. J. Janssen, "Eine Beuteliste von Amenophis II und das Problem der Sklaverei im alten Aegypten," *JEOL* 17 (1963): 141-147, who argues on economic grounds that, in the New Kingdom, slavery on the broad scale assumed in the literature was not possible. His arguments serve as well for the Middle Kingdom. On the whole, I feel that the bulk of the Asiatics found in Middle Kingdom Egypt arrived there of their own accord, seeking employment not only in the trades and professions but in lesser positions as well.

apparent status as a family member, or one who is labelled with a title that has no obvious meaning.[35] Any woman associated with a household, the palace, or even a temple, who cannot be placed within the structure of the family or the hierarchy of servants and workers has been placed in the ranks of concubines and harem-women. It is as if all women in the texts and reliefs must be catalogued somewhere, with the status of concubine being a kind of catch-all category for any woman who cannot be placed elsewhere. This practice is no more in evidence than with the numerous burials of women associated with the funerary temple of Nebhepetre Mentuhotep at Deir el-Bahri. These women are generally considered to be the wives and concubines of that king.[36]

Such an approach was probably inevitable some years ago when individual titles could not be interpreted and when the term "harem" was generally used in a way that suggested the closed, guarded and prison-like women's quarters of the Islamic Kingdoms and the Ottoman Empire. But this is not the correct view and the terms "harem" and "concubine" have been most inappropriately used in connection with ancient Egypt. It is now evident, for example, that many words and phrases thought to identify individual women as concubines should be understood rather in terms of professional functions far removed from concubinage. Drenkhan has shown that the titles literally translated "King's Ornament" and "Sole King's Ornament" designate women who served as ladies-in-waiting to women of the royal family. They were usually married and were drawn from the higher strata of Egyptian society.[37] Nord and I have independently proved that the *ḫnr.wt* were not concubines but singers and dancers who made up professional troupes of entertainers which included both men and women.[38] Berlev's attempt to show that the title *ᶜnḫ.t*, literally "living person," is yet another term for "concubine" cannot be correct since many women with this title were married with families.[39] In

[35]H. Brunner, *Die Texte aus den Gräbern der Herakleopolitan Zeit von Siut* (*ÄF*, 5, Glückstadt, 1937), 33, nn. 46-47, refers to *šps.wt-* and *ḫnr.wt*-women as "Haremsfrauen;" *Meir* 6, 10 suggests "concubine" for *'nḫ.t nt nỉw.t*; cf. W. Schenkel, "Haremsdame," *LÄ* 2, 986-87.

[36]Hayes, *Scepter* 1, 158; *PM* 1, 2, 656, pits 3-5; H.E. Winlock, *Excavations at Deir el Bahri 1911-1931* (New York, 1942), 74; etc.

[37]R. Drenkhan, "Bermerkungen zu den Title *ḫkr.t nsw.t*," *SAK* 4 (1976): 59-67. On their married status, see Ward, *Feminine Titles*, 24-28.

[38]D. Nord, "The Term ḫnr: 'harem' or 'musical performers'?", in W.K. Simpson and W.M. Davis (eds.), *Studies in Ancient Egypt, the Aegean, and the Sudan* (Boston, 1981), 137-145; W.A. Ward, "Reflections on Some Egyptian Terms Presumed to Mean 'Harem, Harem-woman, Concubine,'" *Berytus* 31 (1983): 71-73.

[39]O.D. Berlev, "Les prétendues 'citadins' au moyen empire," *RdE* 23 (1971): 23-43; cf. Ward, *Feminine Titles*, 61-65, for a critique of Berlev's position.

other words, as scholars produce more and more detailed studies of the numerous terms previously thought to mean "concubine" or "harem-woman," it is becoming increasingly evident that such a social category did not exist.

Much the same is true for the harem as an institution where, again, it is more a lexical than an archaeological problem. It has traditionally been thought that the phrase *ỉp.t-nsw.t* means "royal harem"[40] so that wherever this phrase--or the simple *ỉp.t*--is found, one can speak of a "harem" or a "royal harem." Recent statements continue to propound this traditional view.[41] From the Old and Middle Kingdom titles including these terms, a whole hierarchy of harem officials has been created with the corollary that if the officials existed the institution itself must have existed. But *ỉp.t-nsw.t* does not mean "royal harem," therefore the officials attached to the *ỉp.t-nsw.t* do not form a hierarchy of harem administrators so that, on the basis of the lexical evidence, the harem as traditionally defined did not exist. The phrase in question can be rendered "royal counting-house" in some contexts,[42] or "(private) royal apartment" or even "royal granary" in others. The reading *ỉp.t* is itself questionable in most examples prior to the New Kingdom.[43] The lexical evidence traditionally proposed for the existence of the harem as an institution is thus capable of quite different interpretations.

On the archaeological side, two discoveries have been considered to represent the women who belonged to harems prior to the Empire--the subsidiary burials around the Abydos tombs of kings of the First Dynasty, and the numerous burials in the funerary complex of Nebhepetre Mentuhotep alluded to above. In the former case, much has been made of the fact that of ninety-seven stelae with names found in the subsidiary graves around the tomb of King Djer, seventy-six belonged to women whose burials contained rather fine objects including the remains of wigs. Female burials constitute a sizable proportion of the subsidiary graves around other royal tombs at Abydos. While it is frequently proposed that these women constituted harems,[44] there is

---

40This translation was apparently first proposed by T. Devéria, "Le papyrus judiciaire de Turin," *JA* 6e ser., 6 (1865): 343.

41E. Reiser, *Der königliche Harim im alten Ägypten und seine Verwaltung* (Vienna, 1973), 1-11; W. Schenkel, *LÄ* 2, 982-983.

42D. Lorton, Review of *Der Königliche Harim* by E.Reiser, *JARCE* 11 (1974): 98-101.

43Ward, *Feminine Titles*, Chap. 5; Nord, *JNES* 34 (1975): 144-145.

44B. Kemp, "The Egyptian 1st Dynasty Royal Cemetery," Antiquity 41 (1967): 26; G. Reisner, *The Development of the Egyptian Tomb Down to the Accession of Cheops* (Cambridge, Mass., 1936), 109-111. Reisner creates a wholly unwarrented hierarchy of rank with the supposed harems based on the relative size of the individual burials and their position with respect to the royal tombs.

nothing to support such an assumption other than the fact that a group of women were buried in the same funerary complex in the vicinity of a king. The titles preserved certainly do not support such a conclusion.[45] These women could just as well have been court ladies in the service of the queen.

We have much the same situation in the funerary complex of Nebhepetre Mentuhotep who is usually credited with eight wives and numerous concubines.[46] It can be argued, however, that he had only two queens who succeeded each other and that the six other "queens" buried behind the chapels incorporated into the construction of the main court were never queens in fact.[47] The various other women entitled "Lady-in-waiting" or "Sole Lady-in-waiting" were members of the queen's entourage and the remainder, such as the Nubian dancing-girls, can, in my opinion, in no way be construed as concubines.[48] Again, the fact that a group of women was buried

---

45The titles are discussed by Kaplony, *Inschriften*, 372-374. Kaplony asserts that it is "undisputed" that all or most of the women buried in the Abydene subsidiary graves belonged to royal harems. This includes women without titles and those with the title *zḫn(.t)-ỉ3ḫ*, borne by both men and women, which Kaplony himself argues designates a funerary priest(ess) (p. 368). Other women's titles on these stelae are rare and many are impossible to define precisely. There is one *ḥm(.t)-Ḥp*, "Priestess of the Apis;" Petrie, *RT* 2, pls. 27, 30, no. 131. The title *m33.t Ḥr rmny.t Stḫ*, "Whom Horus sees, whom Seth carries," is apparently the later queen's title *m33.t Ḥr Stḫ*, "Whom Horus and Seth see;" W. Westendorf, *Beiträge aus und zu den medizinischen Texten*," *ZÄS* 92 (1966): 141; W. Barta, *Untersuchungen zum Götterkreis der Neunheit* (*MÄS* 28; Berlin, 1973), 182-183. Kaplony, *Inschriften*, 373, suggests that the unique *wr.t-pr*, "Great one of a house," could be a harem overseer, but such an interpretation is only possible if one first assumes that the women in question did, in fact, constitute a harem. This goes as well for the remainder of the titles for which, in some cases, even the reading is doubtful, e.g., *ḥtḥ Ḥr sḳr Sm.ty* (?), and *ỉm3(.t)-Ḥr or ḥts-Ḥr*.

46To the references in n.41 supra, add: E. Riefstahl, "Two Hairdressers of the Eleventh Dynasty," *JNES* 15 (1956): 12; Nord, *JNES* 34 (1975): 143; H.E. Winlock, *The Rise and Fall of the Middle Kingdom in Thebes* (New York, 1947), 25, 27, 43; L. Kuchman, "Titles of Queenship, Part II," *JSSEA* 9 (1978): 21-25. Hayes, *Scepter* 1, 162, speaks also of a "king's Wife, Amunet," though this lady was rather a "Sole Lady-in-Waiting, Priestess of Hathor," hence neither queen nor concubine.

47Ward, *Feminine Titles*, Chap. 6. Note that one of these six was a mere child of five years and that her burial contains no titles of any kind. Kuchman, *JSSEA* 9 (1978): 123, n.5, points out from her personal inspection of the tomb of Queen Neferu that the publication of the texts by Cabet, "Documents relatifs aux fouilles de Mariette," *RecTrav* 12 (1892): 217, is in error at this point. Queen Neferu did not have the title "Great King's Wife," the supposed *wr.t* being a mistake for *s3.t-nsw*.

48As Winlock, *Excavations at Deir el-Bahri*, 74, and Hayes, *Scepter* 1, 162.

near a king does not imply a harem, but rather a group of court retainers in the queen's services and, in this case, some entertainers.

To sum up, non-royal women of the Middle Kingdom played a subsidiary role, or none at all, outside the home. While they were numerous in certain priesthoods, they are inevitably found in the lower priestly grades. This does not imply low social status since Priestesses of Hathor, the most numerous of the Middle Kingdom religious ladies, belonged to a priesthood that functioned as a protector of the kingship and Priestesses of Hathor came from the higher ranks of society. Even here, however, women did not rise to administrative or managerial posts.

Women were prominent in the performing arts both in the temples and private households, but again there is no evidence that they directed such activities. Women are totally lacking in government administration at all levels[49] and are only rarely found in the trades and crafts. In general, they pursued occupations which were not physically demanding and which were carried on inside; outside work was left to the male population. Such a generalization, however, depends on the evidence we have which does not say much about the peasant classes and nothing about village life. Still, women are notably absent in the many representations of the outdoor activities of the peasants in the fields and marshes.

We thus gain a picture of a society where authority was the privilege of men and, outside the home, women did not hold positions of administrative responsibility in any sphere of activity. We do find some female professional women in the entourages of important ladies and queens, but not important men and kings.[50] Their principal role in Middle Kingdom society was as wives and mothers and in this role they were held in particular esteem. They bore the title "Lady of the House" with pride and were honored for their contribution to the stability and maintenance of family life.

---

[49]Two examples have been proposed which go against this. Fischer, *Varia*, 78, suggests that two women held the title "Controller of Works," but the text is ambiguous and I feel the title rather belongs to their brother; Ward, *Feminine Titles*, 22. In Scharff's publication of P Boulaq 18, he has transcribed one entry as "three female members of a judicial council" (pl. 29, 1, 10). This is an error which I have perpetuated in *Index*, no. 1242, and *Feminine Titles*, 14. The actual reading of the hieratic is "three women as family members;" see my article in *GM* No. 100 (1987): 81-84.

[50]The single exception to this is the Sealer Tchat from Beni Hasan (supra, n.23) who may have served the husband rather than the wife. Otherwise, professional women seem always to have served other women.

Responses to Prof. Ward's Paper

L. Lesko: Concerning harems and concubinage, over the past twenty years we have had one carefully argued study after another attacking traditional translations. If one accepts all these arguments, he/she is forced to conclude that all ancient Egyptians were monogamous except perhaps for a few New Kingdom pharaohs for whose harem women no terminology exists! There is surely something wrong here. If indeed the *pr-ḫnr*, despite its etymological connection to "restrain" or "imprison" is not a harem but rather an "establishment of musicians," if the royal "ornaments" or "decorations" are "Ladies in Waiting" rather than concubines, then who are the women depicted in the High Gate at Medinet Habu? Who are the mothers of Thutmose II and Thutmose III? Why did the Egyptians need coregencies? If "royal wife" is sufficient, why did the kings have "great royal wives"? If no harem conspiracies occurred, what do we call it when a lesser wife conspires to get her son on the throne or kill her husband? Even if we accept polygamy for kings or separate royal apartments, even separate palaces, for women in the New Kingdom, did these concepts come strictly from foreign influences of that period? Or do the terms designating them still go undetected in our literature? Again, are the terms we do find really derived from much more innocent usages of the same words in the Old and Middle Kingdom? I really wonder!

I have many questions about the new meanings being given to old words, and about how far this will go. To cite only two Middle Kingdom examples that Prof. Ward hasn't discussed in this paper or his latest book: what of the *mt-ḥnt* in Coffin Texts 146, the spell for assembling the family of the deceased. It indicates one father, one mother, male and female children, wives (plural) and also female *mt-ḥnt* (plural), and male and female servants. Finally I wonder whether the term *sḫty* in the Execration Texts wasn't too easily put aside by Gerald Kadish in his article on eunuchs.

Ward: On the business of harems, Prof. Lesko is certainly correct, from the Eighteenth Dynasty on there were royal harems. I feel that these arose out of political marriages which Egyptian kings were then conducting with their foreign provinces and allies. There was a kind of open harem situation in the empire period. One can always duck behind this lovely phrase "we don't have enough evidence for the earlier period." Personally, I don't see harems before the New Kingdom times. I could well be wrong, with new evidence coming, but I just don't see the groups of ladies so far proposed to be members of harems as such. I think that the new meanings for old terms are by and large correct. I think that there have been really detailed studies on this vocabulary and we are dealing with married women who have families, and I don't think that we should be calling them concubines. I don't say concubines didn't exist; I'm simply saying that as a widespread social category I don't believe they did, monogamy was the rule.

Zagarell: There has been no discussion of the concept of community of work, as communities, yet there is a major discussion going on about that, for instance by feminist literary scholars like Auerbach and Smith-Rosenberg, among others. Also, one might have profited from the suggestion of certain scholars that class and profession do not automatically correspond (cf. Wright, Costello, Hachen, Sprague, for instance). Therefore to discuss professions without discussing the economic position of particular individuals within their profession or within their society, obscures more than it elucidates. For example, women may indeed be kept in subordinate positions within the house or may be involved with supposedly domestic concerns, but where are they kept within the house and what effect does the domestic economic sector have on the society as a whole? In some societies people are kept in subordinate positions and nevertheless play a critical role in shaping the nature of the society. For example, slaves and slavery in the United States had an enormous effect on the entire structure of southern society despite the subordinate position of the slaves themselves (in this vein see Adams, 1984 and Zagarell, 1986).

Also, where is the discussion about social reproduction of the family, social reproduction, not simply how women are looked at, but do women in fact train the young to adopt the social values of the society, thus reproducing the social structure of that society? Do they play that role? For a synthesizing discussion of social reproduction I recommend the work of Vogel, 1983. I'm afraid if we don't get about discussing these problems we're not going to be able to solve them.

Ward: Just very briefly, I agree with practically everything you've said. You're quite right, these questions should be discussed, but I think that when we are dealing with a society like Egypt we are literally hamstrung by the kind of evidence we have. This sort of thing should be brought up in later discussions, but in a public lecture I don't want to go into guesswork, and with all of these questions you raised I would have to get into guesswork.

Third Millennium Mesopotamia: An Introduction

A dozen years ago, the earliest history of Western Asia was comparatively simple: civilization began in Sumer in the very south of Mesopotamia where the earliest writing and first large cities emerged just before the beginning of the third millennium. Gradually, urbanism and writing spread from this Sumerian core, so that after the mid-third millennium, the focus of the light of history broadens to include more and more of the Near East. Three interrelated developments in ancient Near Eastern studies have both complicated and enriched our view of this early history. None challenges Sumer's primacy in either true writing or urbanism, but all three have revolutionized our understanding of Sumer's relationship to the rest of the Near East.

The work of D. Schmandt-Besserat has given cuneiform writing, which *was* invented in Sumer for the Sumerian language, a documentable prehistory.[1] Although her claims that clay tokens reaching back to the eighth millennium are precursors of actual cuneiform signs are not entirely convincing, she has reconstructed a sequence of tokens (representing amounts of commodities) impressed on the surface of clay balls and then sealed within them, followed by cushion-like tablets impressed with numerical signs similar in shape to the token impressions, which leads directly to the tablets on which the first cuneiform signs were written. These clay balls and impressed tablets are found in the middle to late fourth millennium not only in Sumer and neighboring Susiana, but in an arc stretching from the great bend of the Euphrates through northern Syria into Assyria and Iran.

A second recent major development in Near Eastern protohistory is the recognition that a number of these sites that have the clay balls and impressed tablets also have ceramic assemblages and architecture that show clear links to mid-fourth millennium Sumer, so much so that some scholars

[1]The most recent summary of her work is "An Ancient Token System: The Precursor to Numerals and Writing," *Archaeology* November/December 1986, 32-39. For archaic cuneiform, see H. Nissen, "The Archaic Texts from Uruk," *World Archaeology* 17 (1986): 317-334.

would call the sites Sumerian colonies. The whole concept is quite new, and was stimulated in part by recent archaeological discoveries in Syria, which prompted reexamination of earlier work at other sites.[2] Curiously, all of these Sumerianizing phenomena--clay balls and tablets, ceramics, architecture--disappear on Sumer's periphery toward the end of the fourth millennium, just as writing is invented in Sumer itself and Sumerian urbanism approaches its great climax.[3] Archaic cuneiform is *not* found in Syria or Assyria; the progression from impressed numerical tablet to cuneiform tablet is made in Sumer alone.

Thus, the invention of writing in Sumer was not an *ex nihilo* event, but the culmination of a long development of notation on clay, and the spread of "civilization" from Sumer to neighboring areas in the third millennium is actually a *resumption* of contact that had begun in the mid-fourth millennium.

A third major development has radically altered our understanding of third millennium contact between southern Mesopotamia and areas to its north and west. Syria, it was thought, was innocent of writing and sophisticated urbanism until quite late in the third millennium. The mid-third millennium Sumerianizing inscribed statues from Mari, near the present Syro-Iraqi border, were the exception. Mari, the only Syrian city included in the Sumerian King List, was considered to be the most northwesterly outpost of Sumerian culture. The discovery in 1974 and 1975 of over 10,000 cuneiform tablets of the mid-third millennium at Ebla, between Aleppo and Hama in northwestern Syria, turned the old notions upside down.[4] Writing, bureaucracy, complex patterns of state-dominated international trade were all present throughout Syria much earlier than had ever been imagined!

The discoveries at Ebla have also forced us to adjust our ideas about the relationship of the two major ethno-linguistic groups in southern Mesopotamia, the Sumerians and the Semites. Cuneiform writing was invented for the Sumerian language, and only later was adapted for writing Semitic and other languages. Sumerian is related to no other known language, and the ultimate origins of the Sumerians are a mystery, but nearly all agree

---

[2]D. Sürenhagen, "The Dry-Farming Belt: The Uruk Period and Subsequent Developments," in H. Weiss, ed., *The Origins of Cities in Dry-Farming Syria and Mesopotamia in the Third Millennium B.C.* (Guilford CT, 1986), 7-43.

[3]On early urbanism in Sumer, see R.M. Adams, *Heartland of Cities* (Chicago, 1981), Chapter I.

[4]The literature on Ebla is enormous now. A good overview of the excavations and the texts can be found in a series of articles in *Histoire et archéologie* No. 83(May 1984). A now dated bibliography is S. Beld, W. Hallo and P. Michalowski, *The Tablets of Ebla. Concordance and Bibliography* (Winona Lake IN, 1984).

that they were settled in southern Mesopotamia from at least the middle of the fourth millennium. The first appreciable number of texts found in a Semitic language there date to the dynasty of Akkade, founded by Sargon, ca. 2350 B.C. While it had come to be recognized that the rise of Sargon was preceded by a relatively long period of peaceful coexistence between Sumerian and Semitic speaking groups in southern Mesopotamia, it was thought that for most of the third millennium Semites were concentrated in what came to be called Akkade, to the north of Sumer proper, and that writing, with the exception of some votive inscriptions, remained pretty much a Sumerian preserve until the time of Sargon. It came as a real jolt to learn, in 1967, that scribes who wrote the earliest known Sumerian literary texts at Abu Salabikh, near the Sumerian religious capital, Nippur, ca. 2500 B.C., had Semitic names.[5] Semites in southern Mesopotamia, then, were old hands at cuneiform, and hence intimately involved in Sumerian cultural life, long before Sargon.

At Ebla in Syria, ca. 2500 B.C., Semites were writing in Semitic, although the connected texts that have survived use Sumerian logograms to write virtually all nouns and verbs; only pronouns, prepositions and conjunctions appear in Semitic, as do, of course, the Semitic names of those named in the texts. The Semitic used by Sargon of Akkade and his successors in southern Mesopotamia is called Old Akkadian, and is ancestral to the later Babylonian and Assyrian dialects of the language we call Akkadian. Much ink has been spilled over whether the Semitic language of Ebla is an early dialect of Akkadian or an Akkadian related language, or more closely related to later Northwest Semitic languages (Amorite, Ugaritic, Canaanite).[6] What the Ebla, Mari, and Abu Salabikh texts seem to reflect is a mid-third millennium Semitic population stretching from Ebla in northwest Syria to Sumer in the southeast, speaking and writing a variety of related dialects of what might be called Old North Semitic, one of whose descendants is probably Old Akkadian. Other dialects of this early Semitic lived on well into the second millennium at Mari,[7] and probably elsewhere in Syria, until they were replaced by Amorite as a spoken language and Babylonian as a written language.

Most importantly, the written evidence of the mid-third millennium manifests a shared scribal tradition from Ebla all the way to Abu Salabikh and

---

[5]R. Biggs, "Semitic Names in the Fara Period," *Orientalia* 36(1967): 55-66.

[6]I.J. Gelb, "Thoughts about Ibla," *Syro-Mesopotamian Studies* 1(1977): 3-30, is still valuable. See especially the contributions of Diakonoff, Von Soden and Fronzaroli in P. Fronzaroli, *Studies on the Language of Ebla*, Quaderni di Semitistica 13 (1984).

[7]See the excellent treatment by P. Michalowski, "Language, Literature and Writing at Ebla," in L. Cagni, ed., *Ebla: 1975-1985. Atti del convegno internazionale (in press)*.

Fara in Sumer. And artifacts recovered at Mari and Ebla suggest a common artistic tradition as well. What exactly was the nature of the contact between southern Mesopotamia and Syria in the early third millennium that lead to the diffusion of the cuneiform writing system and the maintenance of these shared traditions? At present, we cannot say.

We can speak more confidently about the situation within southern Mesopotamia itself. Early inscriptions[8] attest to the hegemony of the city of Kish over Akkade from about 2700-2500 B.C. and perhaps beyond, a hegemony which at times extended to Sumer as well. From at least 2500 B.C., Sumer is divided into four major city-state groupings: Uruk-Larsa-Badtibira, Ur, Umma-Zabala and Lagash-Girsu-Nina. The Uruk group eventually expanded to include Ur.

The Sumerian city states were ruled by secular princes whose economic power was based on possession of considerable royal estates as well as control of the great temple estates, which were major economic institutions. The socio-economic structure was similar to what it would be in succeeding periods as well: an elite composed of royalty and high officials, complex bureaucracy and record keeping, some blurring of distinctions between state and private enterprise, large numbers of semi-free workers and conscript labor, women used in large numbers as laborers in textile manufacturing and the milling of grain.

Frequent inter-city warfare characterized mid-third millennium Sumer. It often included cities in Akkade, and could spread even farther afield: Elam to the east and even Mari to the northwest are cited as opponents by Eanatum of Lagash. Solely due to archaeological coincidence, we have recovered the greatest historical detail regarding the centuries-long border conflict between Lagash and Umma, which around 2350 B.C. was resolved in Umma's favor when Umma merged with Uruk-Ur, and the ruler of this enlarged grouping, Lugalzagesi, defeated Lagash and exercised hegemony over Sumer.

Not long after, Lugalzagesi was defeated by Sargon of Akkade, a city near Kish that became the capital of the first documented empire in the ancient Near East. Sargon established an imperial bureaucracy for a realm that, by the time of his grandson, Naram-sin, extended over all of Babylonia and beyond

---

[8]For historical inscriptions before the time of Sargon of Akkade, see J.S. Cooper, *Sumerian and Akkadian Royal Inscriptions, I.* American Oriental Society Translation Series 1 (New Haven CT, 1986). For the history of this period, see J.S. Cooper, *Reconstructing History from Ancient Inscriptions: The Lagash-Umma Border Conflict.* Sources from the Ancient Near East 2/1 (1983).

into Assyria, Syria and western Iran. Sargonic control over the entire area was varied in both mode and degree, and rebellion was chronic, both in outlying provinces and in Sumer, which always resisted central control and tended to break apart into its component city states. Like most empires before the first millennium, that of Akkade did not last very long, not much more than a century. Southern Mesopotamia disintegrated into small, independent jurisdictions, and was often prey to invaders from the mountains to the east.

Sometime in the late twenty-second century Utukhegal of Uruk brought some stability to Sumer, and around 2100 B.C., his governor at Ur (and perhaps a close relative), Urnammu, founded a dynasty that, for a century, would rule all of Mesopotamia and territories to the east. The Third Dynasty of Ur is best known for its prodigious bureaucracy that has left us scores of thousands of government records. So much clay "paperwork" was produced that serious scholars have suggested that the empire foundered under the weight of the tablets. In reality, the empire collapsed due to pressures from both the east and west, accompanied to be sure, by internal weaknesses that are difficult to define. By about 2000 B.C., southern Mesopotamia was once again a network of vying independent city states, one of which, Isin, considered itself the successor to Ur, and continued the traditions of the empire into the second millennium.

Jerrold S. Cooper

Figure 18

Limestone statue of a woman from the Inanna temple, Nippur, Iraq, Early Dynastic IIIa. Courtesy of The Metropolitan Museum of Art, Joint Expedition to Nippur, Rogers Fund, 1962. No. 62-70.2.

Women in the Economy of Sumer

Marc Van De Mieroop

The exact chronological boundaries of Sumerian history are difficult to establish since we are not certain about when the Sumerians first arrived in Mesopotamia and when they disappeared. The use of Sumerian in writing cannot be used as a guideline as the written form of the language seems to have survived long after it died out in speech,[1] and it is impossible to determine in what language the earliest cuneiform documents are written. For convenience I will consider the third millennium B.C. as the period of "Sumerian" history, thus including Jemdet Nasr, Early Dynastic, Old Akkadian and Ur III periods. The Sumerian bureaucrats have left us with more than one hundred thousand cuneiform tablets, recording many aspects of the economic life. These unfortunately are not spread equally throughout this long period of time, but date mainly from a fifteen year period in the mid Twenty-fourth century and a hundred year period, more or less coinciding with the Twenty-first century. The documents do not originate from many different cities, but from a few which have been excavated, such as Ur and Girsu,[2] or looted, such as Puzrish-Dagan and Umma. Our evidence is thus partial, which biases any historical reconstruction. When attempting to describe the role of women in the economic life of Sumer these textual limitations naturally also apply. On the other hand, the study of their role is not necessarily more difficult, as women are represented in the same way as men. Both official inscriptions and economic documents give us much information about them.

For the first six hundred years of this period (c. 3000-2400 B.C.) we have very limited sources. Some texts from Jemdet Nasr and Archaic Ur, which are in general hard to understand, contain the word **géme** "woman (of the dependent classes)", but the contexts are unclear. From historical, royal, and building inscriptions of the Early Dynastic Period we can compile a long list of important women, almost all of them wives and daughters of rulers and

[1]See J.S. Cooper, "Sumerian and Akkadian in Sumer and Akkad," *Or.* NS 42 (1973): 239-246.

[2]The texts from Girsu were partly excavated by the French at the turn of the century, but many of them were stolen from the excavation, and the tell was probably also looted afterwards.

high officials.[3] An exceptional case is the legendary Ku-Bau, who ruled Kish for one hundred years according to later legend.[4] From legal documents of the Early Dynastic IIIa Period (c. 2550 B.C.) it is clear that women could buy houses privately.[5]

The city of Girsu has yielded some sixteen hundred tablets from the very end of the Early Dynastic Period, in the mid Twenty-fourth century. Through the accident of discovery almost all of these texts come from the archive of an institution called the **é-bau**, the household or temple of the goddess Bau. Soon after the archive was discovered, it was studied in depth by the Sumerologist Anton Deimel who, with Anna Schneider, developed the theory of the Sumerian "temple-city." He postulated that most of the land was owned by the temples in Girsu, and that these institutions dominated the entire economy. This theory has known considerable popularity, although it has been attacked by many scholars such as Gelb and Diakonoff,[6] who debate mainly the extent of the temple's role, and prove that land owned privately or by village communities also existed. It is, however, only recently that the entire concept of a large part of the economy being dominated by the temples has been refuted. The temple of the goddess Bau was not an institution existing from time immemorial in Girsu, but was actually a renaming of the **é-MÍ**, the household of the wife (of the city ruler). During the reigns of the Enentarzi and Lugalanda the **é-MÍ** was an administrative center controlled by these city rulers'[7] wives, Dimtur and Baranamtara. Originally it seems to have been only a small enterprise with some fifty persons working in it,[8] but gradually it grew. In the reign of Uru'inimgina a major change took place; in his second year as king[9] the **é-MÍ** was expanded enormously, and certain texts mention fifteen hundred men dependent on it. Also the household was renamed as **é-bau**, the temple or household of Bau. This change seems to have been related to the so-called "Reforms of Uru'inimgina" in which he claims to have given the land which was formerly owned by the **énsi**, his wife

[3]See the list in J. Asher-Greve, *Frauen in altsumerischer Zeit*, Bibliotheca Mesopotamica 18 (Malibu, 1985): 146-148.

[4]See D.O. Edzard, "Ku(g)-Baba," *RlA* 6 (1980-83): 299.

[5]Edzard, *Sumerische Rechtsurkunden des III. Jahrtausends*, (München, 1968), nos. 15, 28, 29.

[6]For a survey of the literature see K. Maekawa, "The Development of the É-MÍ in Lagash during Early Dynastic III," *Mesopotamia* 8-9 (1973-74): 81-87; B.R. Foster, "A New Look at the Sumerian Temple State," *JESHO* 24 (1981): 225-230.

[7]The Sumerian term is **énsi**.

[8]Maekawa, *Mesopotamia* 8-9 (1973-74): 101-114.

[9]Uru'inimgina ruled one year as **énsi**, then he adopted the title **lugal**, "king."

and children, to the god Ningirsu, his wife Bau, and their son Shulshagana.[10] The documents describing the activities of the household of Bau are thus not of an entirely new institution, but of an expanded and renamed household of the ruler's wife. Whether we regard this "temple of Bau" as a new institution, showing the culmination of the concept of rule by divine favor,[11] or as an administrative fiction,[12] is not important, as in both cases the "temple" administration can be regarded as still controlled by the ruler's wife.

A large part of this administration is involved with agriculture. Deimel calculated that the fields owned by it at least covered an area of c. 4,465 1/2 hectares.[13] All aspects of agriculture were controlled by the wife's household: sowing, harvesting and storage, canal maintenance, and equipment supplies. Vegetable gardens and orchards were also cultivated. The household owned cattle, pigs, sheep and goats, and some one hundred fishermen were employed by it. Certain industrial undertakings, such as work with textiles, must also have been part of the household's activities. Labor was provided by a large group of men, but more so by women and children, about whom I will say more later. All these dependents are provided with rations of barley, bread, milk, malt, and wool.[14]

A similar household seems to have existed for the ruler himself and for his children, and one may wonder about the degree of independence of his wife's administration. If indeed the reforms of Uru'inimgina were responsible for the great expansion of the **é-MÍ**,[15] one can assume that in many matters the ruler was in charge. There are some indications, however, that his wife had personal control. Under Enentarzi Dimtur was in charge of the **é-MÍ**. When her husband died she did not disappear from the administrative records, but she appeared at least in the first year of Lugalanda's reign, and she was probably still in charge of the **é-MÍ**.[16] When Lugalanda's throne was usurped

10See Cooper, *Sumerian and Akkadian Royal Inscriptions*, The American Oriental Society Translation Series; (New Haven, 1986), Vol. 1, 72 for a translation of this passage.

11Maekawa, *Mesopotamia* 8-9: 137.

12Foster, *JESHO* 24: 241.

13*Sumerische Tempelwirtschaft zur Zeit Urukaginas und seiner Vorgänger AnOr* 2 (1931): 79.

14For a description of these activities, see A. Deimel, *AnOr* 2: 71-113. He analyzed the relevant documents in a series of articles in *Or* Series Prior from 1924-1929.

15Maekawa, *Mesopotamia* 8-9: 131.

16J. Bauer, *Lagash*, 532f. Asher-Greve, *Frauen*, 149 suggests three explanations for this situation:

1. Lugalanda was not married
2. Dimtur was in charge of the organization
3. Dimtur was training Baranamtara in the administration of the **é-MÍ**.

These alternative explanations are possible, but still show that Dimtur had a continuing role.

by Uru'inimgina, it was logical that Baranamtara was replaced by Shasha, Uru'inimgina's spouse. From Baranamtara we have two texts that record the exchange of presents between her and Ninizkimti, wife of the ruler of Adab.[17] This shows that the ruler's wife could maintain diplomatic relations independently, and that probably an administrative system, similar to the one in Girsu, existed in Adab.

The **é-bau**, which was an artificial creation, disappeared after the conquest of Girsu by Lugalzagesi, and it is not attested in the following Sargonic Period. The **é-MÍ** reappears, however, although the attestations to it are rare. In the Sargonic material (dated c. 2350-2150 B.C.) we find only one attestation of this institution in Girsu,[18] and some references to it in the city of Umma.[19] This shows that in the local administration the wife of the **énsi**, now dependent on the king in Akkade, still played a role. The institution survived in Girsu under the **énsi** Gudea (c. 2150),[20] and also in the Ur III period the **é-MÍ** is attested in Nippur and Girsu.[21] It seems plausible that even after the Ur III period this institution survived. Some slave sales from Larsa under Rīm-Sîn (1822-1763 B.C.) contain a clause about the escape of the slave to "the palace, an influential person, or the **é-MÍ**."[22] The latter institution seems to be considered equal to the palace. Since references to the **é-MÍ** are very scant after the Early Dynastic Period, its function cannot be determined with certainty. From all the information one can conclude, however, that the **é-MÍ** existed throughout Sumerian history, and even later, and that several cities had such an institution. Moreover, it contained an administration separate from the palace.

Throughout the late third millennium the role of women is clear from other archives as well. From Umma in the Sargonic period we have an archive of a couple, Ur-Shara and Ama-e.[23] While the husband specialized in animal husbandry, the wife Ama-e owned large areas of land, and she is mentioned in texts recording harvests and grain expenditures. She also seems to deal with wool and metals. Also in the legal documents of the Sargonic period women

---

17M. Lambert, *RA* 47 (1953): 58-9.

18ITT I no. 1393, see A. Westenholz, "The Sargonic Period," in *Circulation of Goods in Non-Palatial Context in the Ancient Near East*, ed. A. Archi (Roma, 1984): 21 note 18.

19B.R. Foster, *Umma in the Sargonic Period* (Hamden, 1982), 96.

20RTC no. 219, MVN 6: nos. 312, 350, 397, 497 and MVN 7: nos. 256, 304, 393, 474, 494.

21See H. Waetzoldt, *Untersuchungen zur neusumerischen Textilindustrie* (Roma, 1972), 100 & note 139 for Nippur, MVN 6: no. 421 for Girsu.

22E.g. YOS 8: nos. 44, 45, 56, 57, and 72. In *AfO* 33 (1986) I translated the term **é-MÍ** as "cloister," but I believe now that the "woman's house" is intended here.

23See Foster, *Umma*, 52-78.

can act independently. They buy[24] or sell houses,[25] act as guarantor for another person,[26] and are involved in court procedures.[27]

With the rise of the Third Dynasty of Ur under Ur-Nammu and especially Shulgi, the documentation about the administration of the state becomes very abundant, and we have sources from several sites: Ur, Girsu, Umma, Nippur, and Puzrish-Dagan. More than one hundred thousand texts are preserved, many of them still unpublished. From Puzrish-Dagan texts it is clear again that the queen had an administration of her own which played an important role in the economic life of the state. In these texts the activities of one of Shulgi's queens, Shulgi-simtī, are documented.[28] She is in charge of the collection of animals and their distribution to the temples of Nippur and other cities, and to palace dependents, from Shulgi's twenty-ninth to his forty-seventh regnal years. It is interesting to note that most of the people who contribute animals are women, and that at least one of the officials who works for her, Apillatum, is also a woman. Unfortunately most Sumerian and some Akkadian names were given to both men and women,[29] so the sex of almost all the individuals in these texts cannot be determined with certainty. Among the other officials recorded, Bēlī-ṭāb, Apillia and Shulgi-ilī could be both men or women. With the death of Shulgi, Shulgi-simtī disappears from the administrative records, and her activities are taken over by a spouse of Amar-Suen, Abī-simtī, who is attested throughout the reigns of Amar-Suen and Shu-Sîn.[30] Her activities seem to be mainly related to the festival on "the day of the disappearance of the moon,"[31] and her administration seems to have been integrated into the larger structure of Puzrish-Dagan. At the accession of Ibbī-Sîn to the throne, his wife Geme-Enlila takes over the responsibilities of Abī-simtī immediately.[32] Puzrish-Dagan is not the only place where royal women

---

24Edzard, *Sumerische Rechtsurkunden*: no. 38.

25Edzard: no. 37.

26Edzard: no. 70.

27Edzard: nos. 84, 99 (1).

28For a provisional list of these texts see S.T. Kang, "The role of women at Drehem," in C. E. Keiser, *New-Sumerian Account Texts from Drehem* (BIN 3; New Haven, 1971), 3-5, which is slightly expanded in S.T. Kang, *Sumerian Economic Texts from the Drehem Archive* (SACT 1, Urbana, 1972); 264-267. Note the corrections for BIN 3 by L. Matouš, *RA* 68 (1974): 83-88, and for SACT I by T. Gomi in *Orient* 12 (1976): 11 note 6. Marc Cooper has greatly expanded the list of texts mentioning Shulgi-simtī, and will publish a study of her activities in the near future.

29See H. Limet, *L'anthroponomie sumérienne dans les documents de la 3e dynastie d'Ur* (Paris, 1968), 62.

30For a list of texts mentioning her see S.T. Kang, BIN 3, 6-7 and SACT 1, 268-270.

31**u4-ná-a** = *bubbulum*.

32P. Michalowski, *Acta Sumerologica* 4 (1982): 137.

seem to have a separate network for certain cultic activities. From Umma we have a group of texts that list the gold offerings of Ninkalla at the same occasions as those of her husband, King Shulgi, but through a separate administration.[33] She has a separate official who supervised the transaction, Ninmelam, who was the wife of the governor of Umma, and who will be treated in more detail later.

It has become clear recently that the kings of Ur must have had more than one wife, since some of them are father to some eighteen to twenty children.[34] Many discussions have appeared in the last few years discussing the names and the titles of these women, but to my knowledge, no one has discussed the purpose of these affiliations. In the table below, I listed all the names of royal spouses known to me, their titles, and a bibliography of the literature about them.

Table

Rulers	title	Bibliography
King: Ur-Nammu		
Consort: SI.A.tum	**dam**	Steinkeller 1981, 77-78; she is the mother of Shulgi, Sollberger 1967, 69. The reading Watartum proposed by Sollberger, *ibid.* has never been established with certainty, Michalowski 1982, 132.
King: Shulgi		
Consort: Shulgi-simtī	**lurkur**	Michalowski 1977, 222-4, Steinkeller 1981, 78-80, Michalowski 1982, 135.
	nin	Steinkeller 1981, 79, Kang 1971, 5 note 12.
Consort: Ea-nisha	**lukur**	Steinkeller 1979, 190, Grégoire 1979,190-1, Michalowski 1979, 176 note 16.

[33]M. Van De Mieroop, "Gold Offerings of Shulgi," *Or.* NS 55 (1986): 134-137, texts 4 and 5.

[34]I.J. Gelb, "Household and Family in Early Mesopotamia," in ***State and Temple Economy in the Ancient Near East***, Orientalia Lovaniensia Analecta, edited by E. Lipinski, 5 (Leuven, 1979), 66.

Consort: Geme-Ninlila	**lukur?**	Gomi 1976, 6, Michalowski 1977, 222-4, Michalowski 1979, 171-6, Powell 1981, 93-4, Michalowski 1982, 135.
Consort: Taddin-Eshtar	?	Michalowski 1979, 172, Michalowski 1982, 135.
Consort: Ninkalla	?	Michalowski 1979, 172, Van De Mieroop 1986, 147-8
Consort: ME-Ea[35]	?	Michalowski 1982, 135
Consort: Geme-Suen	**dam**	Michalowski 1976, 169-172. She was Shulgi's **dam** prior to his deification, Steinkeller 1981, 81.
Consort: Shu-gur-[ ]	**lukur**	Steinkeller 1981, 84 note 44.
Consort: Taram-Uram		Hallo 1972, 13-4, Hallo 1976, 31. She could also be Ur-Nammu's wife.
King: Amar-Suen		
Consort: Abi-simti	**nin**	in the reign of Amar-Suen, Steinkeller 1982, 79.
	nin-GAR	in the reign of Shu-Sîn, Steinkeller 1982, 79. She is the mother of Shu-Sîn, Falkenstein 1947, 45, Whiting 1976, 182. She cannot be equated with Shulgi-simti, Matous 1974, 84-5, Gomi 1976, 1-14, Michalowski 1977, 222-3. Jacobsen 1953, 45-7, Sollberger 1954-6, 18 note 33.
Consort: Kubatum	**lukur**	Sigrist 1986, 185.
Consort: Puzur-usha	**lukur**	Steinkeller 1981, 84 note 44.

[35] Perhaps to be read Simat-Ea?

Consort: Ú-da-ad-zé-na-ad	**lukur**	Kang 1971, 2, Steinkeller 1981, 84 note 44.
Consort: Za-ga-AN-bi(?)	**lukur**	Steinkeller 1981, 84 note 44, Michalowski 1982, 137.
Consort: [x]-natum	**lukur**	Steinkeller 1981, 84 note 44.
King: Shu-Sîn		
Consort: Kubatum	**lukur**	Steinkeller 1981, 80, Sollberger 1980-3, 265, Sigrist 1986, 185.
	nin	Steinkeller 1981, 80, Sollberger 1980-3, 265, Sigrist 1986, 185. Possibly mother of Ibbī-Sîn, Steinkeller 1981, 80; possibly mother of Geme-Enlila, wife of Ibbī-Sîn, Steinkeller 1981, 80-1, not necessarily so, Michalowski 1982, 137. Falkenstein 1947, 50, Jacobsen 1953, 46-7, Sollberger 1954-6, 18 note 33, Sollberger 1978, 99-100, Sollberger 1980-3, 265.
Consort: Tiamat-bashtī[36]	**lukur**	Falkenstein 1947, 50, Kang 1971, 2, Steinkeller 1981, 84 note 44.
Consort: Ishdum-kīn	**lukur**	Steinkeller 1981, 84 note 44.
King: Ibbī-Sîn		
Consort: Geme-Enlila	**nin**	Jacobsen 1953, 37 and note 6, Hallo 1976, 32, Steinkeller 1981, 80-1, Michalowski 1982, 136-7.[37]

[36]Perhaps to be read A-ab-ba-bashtī, see Matouš 1974, 86.

[37]The bibliographical references to the following articles:

Falkenstein 1947 = Adam Falkenstein, "Eine Hymne auf Šūsîn von Ur," *WO* 1 (1947): 43-49.

Gome 1976 = T. Gomi, "Shulgi-simti and her Libation Place (KI-A-NAG)," *Orient* 12 (1976): 1-14.

Grégoire 1979 = J.P. Grégoire, "Le sceau d'Ea-niša," *RA* 73 (1979): 190-191.

Hallo 1972 = W. W. Hallo, "Ḫabil-kīn," *RlA* 4 (1972): 13-14.

Hallo 1976 = W. W. Hallo, "Women of Sumer," *The Legacy of Sumer*, Bibliotheca Mesopotamica 4, edited by D. Schmandt-Besserat, (Malibu, 1976), 23-40.

Jacobsen 1953 = T. Jacobsen, "The Reign of Ibbī-Suen," *JCS* 7 (1953): 36-47.

Kang 1971 = S.T. Kang, "The Role of Women at Drehem," in C. E. Keiser, *Neo-Sumerian Account Texts from Drehem*, BIN 3; (New Haven, 1971), 2-7.

Matouš 1974 = L. Matouš, "Compte Rendu of Keiser, BIN 3," *RA* 68 (1974): 83-88.

Michalowski 1976 = P. Michalowski, "Royal Women of the Ur III Period, Part 1: The Wife of Šulgi," *JCS* 28 (1976): 169-172.

Michalowski 1977= P. Michalowski, "The Death of Šulgi," *Or.* NS 46 (1977): 220-225.

Michalowski 1979 = P. Michalowski, "Royal Women of the Ur III Period, Part 2: Geme-Ninlila," *JCS* 31 (1979): 171-176.

Michalowski 1982 = P. Michalowski, "Royal Women of the Ur III Period, Part 3," *Acta Sumerologica* 4 (1982): 129-142.

Powell 1981 = M.A. Powell, "Geme-Ninlila, beloved of Šulgi," *RA* 75 (1981): 93-94.

Sigrist 1986 = M. Sigrist, "Kubatum," *RA* 80 (1986): 185.

Sollberger 1954-56 = E. Sollberger, "Sur la chronologie des rois d'Ur et quelques problèmes connexes," *AfO* 17 (1954-6): 10-48.

Sollberger 1967 = E. Sollberger, "Ladies of the Ur III Empire," *RA* 61 (1967): 69-70.

Sollberger 1978 = E. Sollberger, "A Note on the Lyrical Dialogue SRT 23," *JCS* 30 (1978): 99-100.

Sollberger 1980-83 = E. Sollberger, "Kubātum," *RlA* 6 (1980-83): 265.

Steinkeller 1979 = P. Steinkeller, "Notes on Two Sumerian Votive Inscriptions," *RA* 73 (1979): 189-90.

Steinkeller 1981 = P. Steinkeller, "More on the Ur III Royal Wives," *Acta Sumerologica* 3 (1981): 77-92.

Van De Mieroop 1986 = M. Van De Mieroop, "Gold Offerings of Shulgi," *Or.* 55 (1986): 131-151.

Whiting 1976 = R.M. Whiting, "Tiš-atal of Niniveh and Babati, uncle of Šu-Sin," *JCS* 28 (1976): 178.

Wilcke 1974=C. Wilcke, "Zum Königtum in der Ur III Zeit," *Le palais et la royautè* XIXe Rencontre Assyriologique Internationale 1971, edited by P. Garelli, (Paris, 1974), 177-232.

We have evidence of one spouse for Ur-Nammu, nine for Shulgi, six for Amar-Suen, three for Shu-Sîn, and one for Ibbī-Sîn. Only one of the women found in this list was certainly married because of diplomatic reasons: Tarām-uram who was the daughter of the ruler of Mari.[38] Although the origin of the other women is hard to establish it seems to me that they may come from different cities in the Ur III state and that the king married them to establish strong bonds with their hometowns. Not only did he ingratiate himself with the local upper-class, but he probably also got a certain amount of control over an administrative system under these women. Unfortunately, the documents do not allow us at the moment to relate each of these women to a particular city. The case of Kubatum shows how certain of these women could ameliorate their status; She is first attested as a wet nurse under Amar-Suen, thus she must have born children which can only have been of the king himself. Later she becomes the chief wife of Shu-Sîn.[39]

The power of certain high-placed women in the economy of their cities may have been quite large. From several cities of the Ur III state come some indications about the role of the wife of the governor (**dam-énsi**). In Umma Ninmelam, wife of Ur-Lisi,[40] is attested in several texts from Shulgi's forty-first year through Amar-Suen's ninth. In two texts she acts as the supervisor of the gold transactions by Ninkalla, spouse of King Shulgi. She also supervises transactions involved with leather, wool and cloth, and issues grain and flour.[41] Her successor is Ninḫilia, wife of Ayakalla,[42] who is active in the economy in the first six years of the reign of Shu-Sîn. She is mainly involved with the supervision of transactions involved with wool, leather, essences and fragrant wood. Other wives of governors were active in the economic life, and many texts record them as **dam-énsi** without providing

---

38For diplomatic marriages in general see W. Röllig, "Heirat," *RlA* 4 (1972-75): 282-287. He lists several daughters of Ur III kings who were married to foreign rulers.

39M. Sigrist, "Kubatum," *RA* 80 (1986): 185.

40In *Or.* NS 55 (1986): 148 note 30 I insisted that Ninmelam was Ur-Lisi's sister based on the reading of her seal on BIN 5: no. 203, where line two seems to read *nin Ur-d[Lig-si4]*. See already N. Schneider, "Frauensiegel in Ur III," *Or.* NS 8 (1939): 60 for this difficulty. A new copy of this seal is found in M. Sigrist, *Textes économiques néo-sumériens de l'université de Syracuse* Éditions Recherche sur les Civilisations, Mémoire no. 29 (Paris, 1983), no. 206, where the reading DAM "wife," seems to be beyond doubt.

41Based on P.A. Parr, "Ninhilia: wife of Ayakalla, governor of Umma," *JCS* 26 (1974): 92, notes 24 to 26, with corrections. I omit the texts dated in Ibbī-Sîn 2 (Chiera STA 14, Oppenheim Eames Coll G34) because a copy of these texts, AnOr 7: 296, lists these women as **lukur** of Shara. Even if the Ninmelam in these texts was the same as the wife of the **énsi** several years earlier, her status must have changed.

42See Parr, *JCS* 26 (1974): 90-99.

their names. Thus we find the wife of the governor of Girsu active in the textile industry in texts dated Shulgi 10.[43] Cultic activity by the governor's wife is also clear from a plaque dedicated by Aman-ilī, wife of Ir-Nanna, governor of Girsu, for the life of King Ibbī-Sîn.[44]

Although this material is not extensive, it surely shows in my opinion that certain women apart from royal women were active in the economic life of their cities. We are not well informed about their private economic activities, but from the records of court procedures that are preserved from Girsu it is clear that they could hold considerable property. In these records[45] women are attested as owning land (nos. 99, 106, 139), orchards (no. 109), slaves (nos. 99, 173, 175, 176, 206), oxen (no. 206), and silver (no. 182). It is clear that women had the same legal rights as men, and that they could go to court to protect them.

Women are not only active in the administration in Sumer, but they also form a large part of the labor force. From Early Dynastic Girsu information about women laborers comes mainly from ration lists. They show how a large number of women were active in the textile industry. They were organized in groups of twenty, sometimes under a male but more often under a female supervisor. From the sixth year of Uru'inimgina as king we have evidence of six of these teams in the "house of the governor's wife" alone. It is very likely that the household of the ruler himself was some twenty times larger, and probably the number of women weavers there has to be increased accordingly.[46] These women are registered as experienced women or newly acquired ones. The texts also mention the number of their children, who were probably kept by the women at work, as many of them are suckling babies. When they grew up the boys were separated from their mothers and probably set to work in manual labor elsewhere.[47] The girls were probably raised to become weavers like their mothers. Groups of women at work are also attested in the art throughout the early third millennium. They are represented as textile workers, potters, and in agriculture in seals of the Uruk and Jemdet Nasr periods.[48] An inlaid frieze from Early Dynastic Mari shows in the lower

---

[43]See H. Waetzoldt, *Untersuchungen zur neusumerischen Textilindustrie* (Roma, 1972), 99 note 138.

[44]Sollberger, "Ladies of the Ur III Empire," *RA* 61 (1967): 69-70.

[45]Studied and translated by A. Falkenstein, *Die neusumerischen Gerichtsurkunden* 3 vols. (München, 1956), Vol. 2.

[46]M. Lambert, "Recherches sur la vie ouvrière," *ArOr* 29 (1961): 422-443. K. Maekawa, "Female Weavers and their Children," *Acta Sumerologica* 2 (1980): 81-125.

[47]Maekawa, *op. cit.*, 112. He thinks that many of these boys were castrated.

[48]See J. Asher-Greve, *Frauen*, 48-54 and Plate 12.

register a group of three women who are weaving and spinning.[49] Although the rest of the scene is cultic, this part may represent organized weaving activity.

Large numbers of women weavers are also attested in texts from the following Sargonic period, and this practice continues into the Ur III period. In Girsu at that time more than 6,000 female weavers are attested.[50] There was also a large number of milling women, especially after Shulgi year 48 when a new mill was built. One text from the end of that year shows that 679 women and 86 men were requisitioned at once.[51] Texts from Ur show the same intensive use of female labor. The weaving work is there sent out to women weavers in villages surrounding Ur.[52] They were supervised by overseers of whom more than 90 are attested in the texts, and probably some 60 were active simultaneously in the reign of Ibbī-Sîn. If one counts about 220 women and children for each of these 60 overseers, one obtains a number of 13,200 weavers active at the same time. Other texts allow us to estimate the number of weavers to be about 12,000.[53] Women were also active in other parts of the work force. At Umma one finds women active in outdoor work such as in agriculture, winnowing, carrying and removing grain, cutting thorns, and removing clods from furrows. They also work at the irrigation system, and tow boats. They are also active as oilpressers. Again their number seems to be very high.[54] The women were paid with rations of barley and oil, in amounts much less than those paid to men. The usual volume of barley received is between 30 and 40 liters a month, with a maximum for highly skilled women of 50 to 60 liters. Men on the other hand usually started at 60 liters a month, and they could obtain rations of up to 300 liters.[55] The problem of the status of these women has to be studied in the larger context of the status of dependent personnel in Sumer. Not all of these women can be regarded as female slaves, although that is the usual translation of the Sumerian term **géme**. The term originally seemed to refer to "women of the

---

[49]A. Parrot, *Syria* 39 (1962): 67-68 and Pl. 11, *Propyläen Kunstgeschichte* 14, fig. 93 b. I owe this reference to Zainab Bahrani.

[50]Maekawa, "Collective Labor Service in Girsu-Lagash: The Pre-Sargonic and Ur III Periods, in *Labor in the Ancient Near East*, American Oriental Series 68, ed. by M.A. Powell (New Haven, 1987), 53.

[51]Maekawa, *Acta Sumerologica* 2: 98.

[52]See T. Jacobsen, "On the Textile Industry at Ur under Ibbī-Sîn," *Studia Orientalia Ioanni Pedersen dicata* (Copenhagen, 1953), 180.

[53]H. Waetzoldt, *Textilindustrie*, 106.

[54]T. Fish, "Gemé at Umma," *MCS* 3 (1953): 47-55.

[55]See H. Waetzoldt, "Compensation of Craft Workers and Officials in the Ur III Period," in *Labor in the Ancient Near East*, 122.

mountains," i.e., captured during a campaign. This could not have been the only source for the thousands of **géme** recorded, and many of them must have been obtained locally. A great number of them seems to have been derived from the so-called **a-ru-a** institution. This term describes the practice where objects, animals, or people are donated to the temples. For the well-to-do such an act probably contained an element of piety, but for the poor this seems to have been a way to dispose of undesirables, such as widows, waifs and handicapped, who thus became protected by the temple organization. They were, however, obliged to work and the temples seem to have employed them in large industries such as weaving institutions and agriculture.[56] This practice is well attested in the Ur III period, and probably originated in the Early Dynastic Period, although no clear evidence for it is yet available.[57]

The term **géme** covers two terms used for men; the **árad** "slave" and the **guruš** "serf, helot, or the like." The **guruš** serfs form the major labor force in the Ur III period in Mesopotamia and they are derived from the impoverished classes. The **árad** are slaves captured during foreign campaigns and put to work in domestic production.[58] The term **géme** seems to include the captured prisoners of war, the outcasts of society, and the women of the impoverished classes. It is very likely that the last group formed the large majority of the **géme**.[59] The latter group probably had a family life,[60] and must have reproduced. Their offspring are accounted for in the ration lists until they were mature enough to be employed by the organizations their parents worked for. The others may have been tied entirely to the institution for which they worked, and possibly had no family life. Women form a large part of the labor force and seem to have worked together, mainly in enterprises such as the weaving workshops and mills, institutions similar to the Greek *gunoikeia*.[61] It seems likely that they kept their young children with them at work, and that they had a family-life after work.

56Gelb, "The Arua Institution," *RA* 66 (1972): 1-32.

57Maekawa, *Acta Sumerologica* 2 (1980): 113.

58See Gelb, "From Freedom to Slavery," *Gesellschaftsklassen im Alten Zweistromland*, ed. D.O. Edzard, (München, 1972), 87, chart III, and I.M. Diakonoff, "Slaves, Helots, and Serfs in Early Antiquity," *Acta Antique Academiae Scientiarium Hungericae* 22 (1974): 58-63. The two authors disagree on some points, but in general these descriptions of **guruš** and **árad** are accepted by both.

59Gelb, "Terms for Slaves in Ancient Mesopotamia," *Societies and Languages of the Ancient Near East*. Studies in Honour of I.M. Diakonoff, ed. by J.N. Postgate (Warminster, 1982), 91-93.

60See A. Uchitel, "Daily Work at Sagdana Millhouse," *Acta Sumerologica* 6 (1984): 86-87, and P. Steinkeller, "The Foresters of Umma," in *Labor in the Ancient Near East*, 100-101, for evidence that some **guruš**-serfs had a family life and were not employed full-time by the state.

61See Gelb, "Approaches to the Study of Ancient Society," *JAOS* 87 (1967): 6.

In general it is thus clear that at both levels of society women played a very active role in the economic life of Sumer. They controlled certain administrations, and they formed a major part of the work force, but our understanding of their position is hampered in many ways. One of the major problems is our inability to determine the sex of many persons active in the economic life, as the Sumerian language does not distinguish grammatically between masculine and feminine. Thus many of the persons we assume to be men may be women, and the women's role in the society may be much more extensive than we now imagine.[62] On the other hand we do not know how far these indications about women in the economy reflect the social attitudes towards them. The economic systems in which the women function may be entirely controlled by the men, and the women mentioned in administrative positions in this study, may have been very unusual. It is clear that the major economic powers lay in the hands of men, and that only a small percentage of the texts preserved reflect the women's role. On the other hand the role of the women in the work force as dependent laborers is very clear. Here their roles are not different from those of dependent male workers, except that they work in specific enterprises, such as weaving and milling institutions, and that they were provided with substantially smaller rations. The treatment they receive is the one reserved for the dependent classes. It is impossible, however, to deduce anything about their position in the domestic household from these texts.

[62]It is surely unusual in world history that there is no distinction between the names of men and women. This problem in Sumerian society requires further study.

Responses to Professor Van De Mieroop's Paper

Cooper: First of all I would like to say there is an unpublished text that is about to be published, I think of Shu-Sin, where he actually talks about a great victory, winning a great victory and capturing so many thousand women, so many thousand men. He says that he took the men, blinded them and put them to work in the orchards and he took the women and put them to work in the weaving cells. So we have a very complete picture now. Here is the one little segment that wasn't in our picture of how a lot of these women got into servitude. We assumed that this was the case, but now we have this wonderful testimony where the ruler explicitly tells us that this is where he got his work-force from. And my question to you is-- you were talking about the family lives of these thousands of women who were working, some with their suckling children, in the mills and weaving establishments-- do you imagine that they lived in small attached houses around the temple or do you imagine there were dormitories, or do you imagine that they lived in villages outside the city walls and came to work every day? How would you imagine the actual conditions of their life outside the factories?

Van De Mieroop: Well, we don't really have information about that, especially not archaeological information, but it is my opinion that these dependent laborers did have a family life and probably did own a house or were assigned a house, probably a piece of land to live on, to get part of their food from. It is clear that these women worked in almost industrial institutions so they had to come to work every morning, and they brought their babies with them. I don't think there was child daycare then.

Herlihy: On the same subject, I happen to be studying women's workshops in early medieval Western Europe where there is considerable evidence of a life-cycle arrangement in which the women who worked in the shops tend to be very young. Then at marital age frequently they are allowed to marry and disperse and their daughters then are later brought back. Now, as married women, they may accept putting-out work, but they don't come back together into the collective workshop. It was very difficult, in other words, to employ married women in the workshop because what would the husbands do? The husbands are going to be spatially restricted in terms of their own work, so this seems to have been one restraint that allowed the girls when they reached puberty to marry and actually leave the shop, at least in principle. Most references to the women working in the shops in the later period are diminutive, in other words, they would be the same for a little girl, as distinct from women, so are there any hints at all that there might be a life-cycle factor in any of the arrangements which you described?.

Van De Mieroop: Well, the texts distinguish between newly acquired women and experienced women and it is clear from the texts that the newly acquired ones had fewer children. The experienced ones do have children, the texts account for the children, so I would assume that these women were married and when they had their children they kept on working in the institutions during their marriage. The early dynastic texts do not cover a sufficient period of time to see whether these women would reach a very old age working in these institutions, but I believe they stayed there until they were too old to work. We have some evidence of older people also being supported with rations.

Harris: Did you say that it was difficult to distinguish between male and female names?

Van De Mieroop: In the Sumerian language, yes.

Harris: Now does that really mean you have females and males having the same names, do you think, or were there different readings, because that is a very important consideration I think in an attitude toward women; contrast this to Akkadian names in the Neo-Babylonian period, when you have very distinctive names, rarely do a male and female share the same name.

Van De Mieroop: The Sumerian language often does not distinguish between masculine and feminine. We only have for certain persons, female names in the Sumerian language like **géme**, Géme-Enlil, **géme** is the female servant of the god Enlil, there are many terms, many names where you cannot make that distinction.

Harris: In Old Babylonian Akkadian names women are rarely given theophoric names and women are usually given descriptive names, that's so basic, at least to me it always has been, and it says something very important also in terms of biblical women, names of women in the Bible, there is really a sharp demarcation between masculine personal names and feminine personal names; if I remember correctly.

Bird: Women have theophoric names in the biblical texts.

Harris: And it says something does it not? If women have animal names, for example, or names like "voluptuous," it says something about attitudes.

Van De Mieroop: Well, the texts only give the names and so this could be a woman or a man, we just don't know what sex, ...

Figure 19

Seated statue of a queen(?) from Mari,
First half of third millennium. Courtesy of
the National Museums of France, Louvre no. AO 18213.

Figure 20

Steatite female statue from the reign of Gudea.
Tello, circa 2100 B.C. Courtesy of the French National Museums of France, Louvre no. AO 295.

Figure 21

Plaque showing couple. From Tello, time of Ur-Ningirsu. Courtesy of the French National Museums, Louvre AO 16676.

Women, Hospitality and the Honor of the Family

Jean-Jacques Glassner

Ein Mann muss eure Herzen leiten
denn ohne ihn pflegt jedes Weib
aus einem Wirkungskreis zu schreiten
W.A. Mozart; E. Schikaneder,
Die Zauberflöte

Were Mesopotamian women of good frequentation? Since Herodotus's famous statement: "each woman in the land must, once in her life...have sexual intercourse with a stranger,"[1] their morals have been open to doubt. Without wandering off on that tangent or making moral judgements, our purpose is to understand the role and function of women in Mesopotamian family and society.

First, gazing into the mirror wherein Mesopotamian society sees itself, the poet and the mythographer will be asked to help us explain the imaginary in order to perceive the position of women from the point of view of what their creative impulse has fantasized into a social order.

Second, as the necessary complement to this image, we shall describe the position of women in the light of juridical and administrative sources; in other words, we shall draw a portrait without make-up or mirror, the nature of the sources allowing a better approximation to reality. In this instance, we will limit ourselves to evidence of the third millennium B.C.

Let us consider the Epic of Gilgamesh, the crucial moment when the two heroes, Gilgamesh and Enkidu, are to meet. The *lullû* Enkidu, the creature who used to live in the wilderness as a savage,[2] has become a human being, *awîlum*, through his initiation to sexual life, to bread and beer, and to the

[1] I 199. Equally, *Letter of Jeremias*, 42-43; Lucien, *De Dea Syria*, VI, etc.

[2] *lullû*: cf. B. Alster and H. Vanstiphout, "Lahar and Ashnan," *ASJ* 9, (1987): 14: 20ff.

wearing of clothes.[3] However, he remains an outsider to the community of Uruk and, in order to be admitted, he will have to pass through the stages that will enable him to become a full member of that community.

The tale proceeds: while he is living with shepherds, Enkidu meets a man who is going to a wedding, carrying a tray full of rich food for the feast. Enkidu is deeply shocked by what he says: during the wedding night, Gilgamesh will have sexual intercourse with the bride before her husband does:[4]

aš-ša-at ši-ma-tim i-ra-ah-hi
šu-ú pa-na-nu-um-ma
mu-tum wa-ar-ka-nu

"He takes the promised spouse, he first, the husband after,
such is the decision of the gods in their holy assembly."

Therefore Enkidu decides to fight with Gilgamesh to prevent him from approaching the bridal bed. A violent fight ensues on the very threshold of the wedding house. Gilgamesh wins, lifting his opponent off the ground and assuming the formal attitude of the winner, one knee and one foot touching the ground. At last, Gilgamesh's rage cools down and Enkidu acknowledges the right of the king of Uruk to *ius primae noctis* according to the god's will. Afterwards, the two heroes vie with one another as friends.

We have shown elsewhere how this episode is based on the elements of a social procedure, the code of hospitality.[5] To make a long story short, the integration of Enkidu into the community of Uruk is the result of his going through four successive stages:

1. A meal is served him to celebrate his arrival;

2. He is challenged and has to prove his worth; Enkidu is indignant at the *ius primae noctis*;

3. A fight follows, with normative rules, meant to gauge his worth;

---

[3]E. Cassin, Le sembable et le différent, (Paris: 1987), 36ff.

[4]Gilgamesh P IV, 32-34.

[5]J.J. Glassner, *Lois de l'hospitalité et lois de la guerre: Aspects de la questions de l'étranger en Mésopotamie ancienne*, in preparation.

4. The cycle ends with the conclusion of the matter, Enkidu acknowledges Gilgamesh's right to *ius primae noctis* and the two heroes become friends.

The interesting point for us, here, is the close link, emphasized by the epic's author, between the figure of stranger and that of woman, between the rules of hospitality and the institution of marriage. The stress placed on this by the poet is indeed quite significant. First is the episode, so many times commented upon, of Enkidu's introduction into culture through his initiation to sexual life. Then, the first manifestation of culture which Enkidu has just been introduced to is the institution of marriage, and we see him intervening violently in the ceremony.

According to some commentators, though, the ceremony thus disturbed by Enkidu is not an ordinary marriage but a hierogamy.[6] In fact, the text of the epic provides no argument in favor of such a hypothesis and it is quite obviously an ordinary marriage in which Enkidu is involved.[7]

---

[6]For bibliography see J.H. Tigay, *Literary-critical Studies in the Gilgamesh Epic*, Ph.D. dissertation, Yale University, 1971, (Ann Arbor: (microfilm) 1972), 192ff.; W. von Soden, "Gab es in Babylonien die Inauspruchnahme des ius primae noctis?" *ZA* 71 (1981): 103-106.

[7](1) In the phrase **banšur** *sak-ki-i*, "festive tray" (Gilgamesh P. IV 25) the word *sakkû* aludes to the food on the tray and not to a chapel in a temple (*AHw* cf. *sakkû(m)*, and E. Prang, "Das Archiv des Imgûa," *ZA* 66, (1976): 16; compare also *CAD S*: *sagû* A, 26-27 (however note its hesitation, 27a). (2) The place where the wedding couch is, *bît êmim* or *bît êmûtim*, that is to say the house of the girl's father, is the ordinary place for the wedding night (cf. F.R. Kraus, "Altbabylonische Heiratsprobleme," *RA* 68 (1974): 112-113. (3) In the phrase *aššat šîmâtim* which means the promised spouse, the word *šîmâtim* "the destinies," is the common term to designate the superior power who reigns over human destiny; in no way can we see there an allusion to an exceptional ceremony. (4) As to the line *a-na* ^{d}*Iš-ha-ra ma-a-a-lum na-di-i-ma* (Gilgamesh P. IV 28-29), "a bed is prepared for the goddess Ishhara," it does not alude either to the earthly image of a goddess, but it refers, in a very common way, to an ordinary wedding night. This is indeed what the myth of Atra-hasîs tells us about the union of a young couple and the institution of the wedding night (W. G. Lambert, A.R. Millard, *Atra-hasîs*, [Oxford, 1969], I, ll. 299-304):

...na-de-e e-er-ši
li-i'-ti-[lu aš-ša-]tum ù mu-sà
i-nu-ma<a-na>aš-š[u-ti] ù mu-tu-ti
i-na bi-ti [e-mi ra-bé-]e i-ta-'i-du Iš-tar
tišti u_4*-mi [li-iš-š]a-ki-in hi-du-tum*
Iš-tar [li-it-ta-a] b-bu-ú ^{d}*Iš-ha-ra*

In short, we have three characters: (1) The Mesopotamian man in the heroic form of the king of Uruk, Gilgamesh. The poet dwells on the characteristic status of the married man, *mutum*. Initiated to sexual life and to eating habits, the *lullû* Enkidu becomes a man, *awîlum*, but, moreover, dressed, he becomes *ki-ma mu-ti*, "like a husband,"[8] in other words, an accomplished *awîlum*. Later, Enkidu turns pale when he hears that the king of Uruk is to know the bride before her husband does. Finally defeated, Enkidu acknowledges the winner's right: *ul-lu e-li mu-ti re-eš-ka*, "your head has been raised above the husbands."[9] (2) The stranger in the form of the savage, Enkidu, counterpart of the king of Uruk. (3) The Mesopotamian woman, in the form of either the "prostitute," *harîmtum*, or the "spouse," *aššatum*. The former goes to meet Enkidu in the wilderness; she embodies sexual pleasure, she is the woman of the outside, offering her services *ina bâb aštammi*/**ka$_2$ es$_3$.dam.ma** "at the door of the tavern;" *ina* **sila.limmu**, "at the crossing;" *ina ribit*, "on the square."[10] The latter, whom Enkidu does not see and whom he protects, is the woman of the inside, the image of purity and procreation, attending to household duties, secluded from the outside world.

The network of relationships among the three characters is fairly easy to trace. From the experience of bestial copulation to the revelation of the civilized sex act, from consorting with the *harîmtum* to the discovery of the *aššatum* Enkidu's entrance into civilization is under woman's auspices. She allows the transition, making it possible to pass from wilderness to town, from the state of the savage to the status of a member of the human community.[11] Enkidu enjoys the prostitute but, in order to forbid Gilgamesh access to the young bride he takes his stand on the threshold[12] of the wedding house, the crossing place between outside and the inside that consecrates space by structuring it, that symbolizes the intactness of the woman, the outermost limit of human society and the boundary of woman's power. The limit of society: the nature of the relationship between Enkidu and Gilgamesh, as well as the

---

"...the bed is laid. Let the wife and her husband lie together. When, to become spouse and husband in the house of the father-in-law, Ishtar is glorified, let there be rejoicing for nine days, let them call Ishtar Ishhara!"

8Gilgamesh P III 27.

9Gilgamesh P VI, 35.

10Cf. *CAD*: *H:harîmtu*, 101; J.S. Cooper, *The Curse of Agade*, (Baltimore: 1983), 60: 240. For **es$_3$.dam**, the temple of Inanna and not a tavern cf. *CAD A$_2$: aštammu*, 473b.

11For the role of the *harîmtum*, cf. the very explicit words of the father of the hunter: Gilgamesh I, III 19ff.

12*bâbum*, "door" :Gilgamesh P VI, 12; *sippum*, "threshold:" Gilgamesh P VI, 17; for the custom of hanging figures representing two wrestlers in the doors of a house see *CAD S* : *sippu* A, 300b.

status of the outsider in the city of Uruk, depends on the result of the fight. In fact, the social order in its entirety is at stake, Enkidu being champion at that moment of the honor of all the husbands of Uruk. The boundary of the woman's power: at the crucial moment of the decision, the woman withdraws and the man remains alone.

In order to understand more clearly the nature of the relationship that is being set up between the stranger and the woman, we must try to answer another question: what is the connection between the code of hospitality and the institution of marriage? Wouldn't Enkidu's initiation, in the course of which woman's sexuality is of such paramount importance, culminate logically in the consummation of his own marriage? Because he is defeated in single combat he will become the king's friend, he will not be allowed to marry and, therefore, he will not have the status of *mutum*: "husband."

In other words, leaving aside the special case of the epic, can we suppose that hospitality is linked to the sacred character of the woman of the house? Such is supposed to be the case in the Arab world, wherein such a relationship is based, according to J. Pitt-Rivers,[13] on "the principle of the moral division of work between the sexes," a division in the name of which the man is vested with authority and the woman with purity, and which correspondingly limits the woman's activities in public matters, the woman being always liable to pollution.

In Mesopotamia, the sources give particular emphasis to the holy character of the *aššatum*-wife. We shall consider four sets of arguments:

1) Anthroponomy: *Muti-bašti*, "My husband is my honor,"[14] associates in a strikingly short formula two difficult terms rich in significance, *mutu*, "husband" but also "protector," and *baštu*, the primary meaning of which has to do with notions of vigor, modesty, dignity and honor.[15]

2) Insistence on the purity of the virgin before marriage: *ša lâ lamdat*, "who has not been known," *ša zikaram lâ idû*, "who does not know man" *ša lâ petât*, "who has not been opened," are the Akkadian

---

[13]J. Pitt-Rivers, *L'anthropologie de l'honneur*, French translation, (Paris: 1983), 158 and note 12, also 179 and 186 ff.

[14]Cf. in *CAD B: baštu*, 143b.

[15]On *baštu*: cf. A. Cavigneaux, "L'essence divine," *JCS* 30 (1978): 178, note 6.

phrases for the young virgin; in all of them virginity is seen in its negative aspect, the absence of sexual intercourse.[16]

3) The obligation to be veiled; to avoid any risk of pollution the married woman is veiled. The sources give evidence of this as early as the end of the third millennium. Sumerians and Akkadians agree on this point and it is the husband who covers the spouse's head.[17] A common metaphor underlies the concealing function of the veil: *mušîtu kallatu kuttumtum*, "night, the veiled spouse;" the explanation is to be found in an old commentary: *kallatu kuttumtu* *dGula ša mamma lâ usabbuši aššum ereb šamšî qabi*, "the veiled spouse is the goddess Gula whom nobody can look at, even from afar; the expression alludes to the sunset."[18] The veil wraps up and keeps in the woman's energy, preventing it from malevolent influences. It protects her as do the walls of the house. After all, doesn't the Akkadian *kuttumu* mean to veil a woman as well as to shut a door?[19]

4) The punishment of adultery: its punishment is severe, by the death penalty, especially if we keep in mind that death is rarely required by the judge in Mesopotamian codes.[20] The code of Hammurabi (129) which condemns the adulterous wife to be bound and thrown into the water, leaves the husband free to decide whether to kill his wife or not. Indeed the woman's purity is the husband's affair because his honor lies first in his capacity to defend his wife. The Middle-Assyrian code (13-15) which in its turn condemns the adulterous wife to death, also leaves it to the husband to decide on the fate of his unfaithful wife, whether to mutilate her instead of killing her. In either case, the lover is punished in the same way as the woman, the judge acting in the place of the husband; the wife's adultery is a breech of civil law, reflecting not only on the honor of the husband but on society as a whole. The Assyrian laws prescribe, and this is quite important, that in case of the death penalty for

---

16Cassin, *op. cit.*, 339 ff.; it is perhaps the sense of Sumerian **e_2.nu.gi_4.a**.

17A. Falkenstein, *Die neusumerischen Gerichtsurkunden*, (Munich, 1956), II, no. 23, 10. F. Abdallah, "La Femme dans le royaume d'Alep au XVIIIe siecle avant J.C." in *La Femme dans le Proche-Orient Antique: compte Rendu de la XXXIIIe Rencontre Assyriologique Internationale (Paris, 7-10 Juillet, 1986)* ed. J.M. Durand, (Paris: 1987), 14; also G. Cardascia, *Les lois assyriennes*, (Paris: 1969), §40-41.

18Refer *CAD K*: ***kuttumu***, 611b§b.

19Cf. reference in *CAD K*: ***katâmu***, 302a §5-6.

20Thus : code of Ur.Nammu §7; code of Eshnunna §28; cf. G. Ries, "Kapitaldelikte," *RIA* 5 (1980): 391-399.

adultery *aranšu laššu* "there is no fault for (the husband)," which means that in such circumstances killing does not give right to blood vengeance.

One might object that our demonstration is grounded on a single source, the Epic of Gilgamesh. The evidence, glamorous though it may be, looks rather fragile. Another document, however, a Sumerian myth, confirms this thesis and gives it more weight: the myth of the god Mardu's marriage.[21] The story is as follows: In the neighborhood of the town of Ninab a group of semi-nomads lives by hiring themselves out to the citizens for food portions in the form of loaves of bread. A single man is given one loaf, a married one is given two, and so on. Mardu, although he is a bachelor, is given two by error. This error inspires him to get married. He therefore goes to the nearest town where there is a festival, looking for a wife. There he participates in the usual wrestling matches and contests and wins. Numushda, the king of the town, wants to reward him, according to the custom, but Mardu refuses any prize other than the king's daughter, whom he wants to marry. She is prompt to accept despite her confidante's reserves. Finally the king agrees to Mardu's request.

We can read, between the lines of the narrative, the four characteristic episodes of the code of hospitality:

1) The meal in the form of a piece of bread;

2) The challenge: the error regarding the amount of bread;

3) The fight: the wrestling;

4) The settlement: Mardu is given Numushda's daughter according to his wish.

Mardu, the winner--differing from Enkidu who loses--is in the position to demand a wife. More generally, the moral of this short narrative is obvious: there is no objection to the marriage of a woman with an outsider. Moreover, because it is a myth and no ordinary tale, the narrative functions as a charter, expressing a principle essential to social organization. The relationship between the code of hospitality and the institution of marriage is clearly stated.

---

[21]S.N. Kramer, *Sumerian Mythology*, (New York: 1961), 98-101.

Let us sum up what we have said. Mesopotamian society imagines itself in masculine terms. When trying to define the features of his identity, the Mesopotamian man defines himself by opposition to the other, to the stranger whose emblematic representation is the savage, the *lullû*, be it Tiamat, the primeval goddess, or Enkidu, the primitive being.[22] Now the figure of that "other" is not the only one encountered in this quest. We find that the figure of the woman is closely associated with him. Their closeness is doubtless based on an interplay of differences: differences of communities between the stranger and the Mesopotamian man, difference of sex between the Mesopotamian man and woman. The stranger is characterized by his peripheral position, outside of socialized space, the woman, on the contrary, is nearby, within the intimacy of the house, protected by the veil.

But the image of woman is, indeed, more complex and ambiguous. She is perceived in her dual relationship to the outside and the inside, a dual relationship that is illustrated by the pair *harîmtum*-harlot and *aššatum*-wife in the epic. Hence she is the mediator without whose intervention no peaceful contact could take place between the outsider and the Mesopotamian as "every stranger is virtually an enemy."[23] The woman intervenes to facilitate the passage from one sphere to another and to allow the transformation of the outsider into a member of the community according to a specific procedure. Although she has no power over it, this procedure is the prelude to the conclusion of a legitimate union. The principle of marriage with an outsider is thus set forth. At the same time the differentiating statuses of man and woman are established.

We have but one further comment. *A priori*, it is hard to see the difference between the *harîmtum* offering her services at the door of a house or a temple, and the future *aššatum* conversing with her wooer on the threshold of her father's house (like the goddess Sud coveted by Enlil).[24] After all, one myth about the god Su'en and the goddess Ningal[25] relates that most simple union that makes a couple: "Su'en approached her to unite with her; he took her virginity without asking the permission of her father, he impregnated her without asking the permission of her mother." Yet there is a difference,

---

22On the image of the foreigner see Glassner, "La division quinaire de la terre," *Akkadica* 40 (1984): 26-27.

23H. Limet, "L'étranger dans la société sumérienne," in *Gesellschaftsklassen im Alten Zweistromland und in den angrenzenden Gebieten*, (Munich: 1972), 124; D. Lochak, *Etranger: de quel droit?*, (Paris, 1985), 14ff.

24M. Civil, "Enlil and Ninlil: The marriage of Sud," *JAOS* 103 (1983): 43-66.

25W.H. Ph. Römer, "Studies zu altbabylonsichen hymnisch-epischen Textes (2)," *JAOS* 86 (1966): 138: II 8 ff.

showing that the two terms of the couple are not equal. The difference is that, for the second term, the *aššatum*, the threshold is the limit which cannot be crossed unharmed.[26] The woman is a sacred chattel that cannot circulate indiscriminantly. Moreover, the legislator does not deem sexual intercourse, either by violence or by consent, sufficient to form a legal marriage. Hence, marriage and the wearing of the veil are forbidden to the *harîmtum*, and it is an insult to a "gentleman's daughter," *mârât awîlim* meant to be an *aššatum*, to call her an *harîmtum*.[27] We can now understand why Enkidu curses the *harîmtum* even though she had, by making a present of her sexuality, awakened him to social life.[28]

At this point in our inquiry, we would be glad to widen the range of our speculations. Unfortunately, the sources which would allow us to do so are wanting, especially as concerns criteria for the choice of brides, as the pattern for the exchange of women is totally unknown to us.[29]

Therefore we must be content to recall with W. Robertson Smith[30] that with some Arabs: "when a man had got protection within a tribe, it was natural that he should ask to have a wife," and that elsewhere they practiced sexual hospitality, the guest being invited to go to bed with the wife of the master of the household. Rather than to ridicule the wantonness of Babylonian women or Herodotus's naive credulity, can we probe further into the real meaning of such a testimony?[31]

Here I would like to put forward a hypothesis. Among the reforms of Uru'inimgina of Lagash we read :[32]

munus.u$_4$.bi$_2$.ta.ke$_4$.ne nita.min.ta i$_3$.tuku.am$_6$
munus.u$_4$.da.e.ne za.aš$_2$.da.bi i$_3$.šub

[26] On the threshold: Cassin, *op. cit*, 352 and n. 29. Compare in the biblical world: A. Lemaire, "Marriage et structure socio-économique dans l'ancien Israel," in C.H. Breteau, N. Zagnoli, et. al., ed. *Production, pouvoir et parenté*, (Paris, 1981), 139.

[27] See *CAD H*: *harîmtu*, 101a-b.

[28] Gilgamesh VII, iii 5 ff.

[29] On exogamy see P. Attinger, "Enki et Ninhursag," *ZA* 74 (1984): 4.

[30] Cited by J. Pitt-Rivers, *op. cit.*, 193.

[31] On woman as intermediary between the man and the stranger, cf. the episode of the violation and murder of the concubine of the Levite: Judges XIX 25; similarly, cf. A. Nikitine, *Le voyage au-delà des trois mers*, French translation: (Paris, 1982), 45, where this Russian traveller from the fifteenth century explains why, in Pegu, women have sexual intercourse with their husbands by day and with foreigners by night.

[32] For bibliography see J.S. Cooper, *Presargonic Inscriptions I* (New Haven, 1986), 77.

the usual translation of which is: "Women in the past used to have two husbands. Women today have given up such an abomination."

Whatever their disagreements, scholars generally see in this passage evidence of a former state of polyandry.[33] Could the Sumerian society have passed from polyandry to polygyny? For, if marriage is generally monogamous, polygyny is also present in the form of concubinage or of the second wife.[34] Closer consideration, though raises doubt.[35] We therefore propose to translate this difficult passage as follows: "the women of old, each had two men. The women of today have banned this crime."

We may then venture a hypothesis which is but a conjecture. Could the epic of Gilgamesh be the echo of an ancient and obsolete custom to which Uru'inimgina would have put an end, the *ius primae noctis*? There is no philological argument to support this hypothesis. We can only point out that sexual intercourse with a woman is not free from danger for men and that the first time especially is not without danger. To deflower a virgin a man needs to have as much holy aura at least as the virgin herself or the group to which she belongs. Such is the function of Gilgamesh, raised by the gods above other husbands. The question here is whether or not Gilgamesh keeps to himself the privilege usually imparted to a **nimgir.si**/*susapinu*, a friend of the betrothed.[36] And we must finally not forget that the woman is the one who gives birth to children. Now the child she bears (as incantations sustaining the

---

33Ibid. 77, note 8; for a complete bibliography see B. Hruška, "Die Innere Struktur der Reformtexte Urukaginas von Lagaš," *Archiv Orientalni* 41 (1973), 121-122.

34Cf. for example, I.J. Gelb, "Household and Family in Early Mesopotamia," in E. Lipinski, ed. *State and Temple Economy in the Ancient Near East* Orientalia Lovaniensia Analecta 5/1, (1979), 61-62.

351) The context does not refer to marriage; the preceding paragraph is about a woman who, when addressing a man, is loud of speech (compare Sumerian proverbs Coll. III, 174, 186; equally, Lambert, *Babylonian Wisdom Literature* (Oxford, 1969), 236:III 3-4; 5-8). Moreover the subject of divorce is touched upon, in the same source previous to this passage (III, 20-21). 2) The phrase **nita...tuku** is not known to refer to a marriage: we should expect **dam...tuku** in which **dam** means either man or woman (*SR* 85 where **dam** signifies husband). In the case of divorce, the same source uses the terms **lu2** and **dam** to refer to the bridegroom and the bride. In the place of **lu2** and **dam** the present passage has **munus** and **nita** meaning female and male. The Mesopotamian jurists have made us familiar with these terms **nita**/*zikaru* meaning man and **munus**/*sinništu* meaning woman outside marriage. Finally, the use of the verb **tuku** is not reserved for the context of marriage: it is often found for instance in relation to debt.

36S. Greengus, "Old Babylonian Marriage Ceremonies and Rites," *JCS* 20 (1966): 68-69.

woman in labor show)[37] is moving about in his mother's womb like Atra-hasîs in the ark when he goes through the flood or Sargon in his basket when he is left to float on the river. And this child follows on his way to the canebrake or to the forest like Lugal.banda in the mountain or Sargon in the dark woods.[38] In short, the woman, with her body, is the access to the other world.

So far we have listened only to the voice of poets and mythographers. There is yet another approach to the Mesopotamian woman. Though less glamorous, administrative and legal documents can allow investigation further into the realm of actual experience. For credibility's sake, we have chosen to keep to a particular time, the third millennium B.C. and to specify archival contexts, mainly the pre-Sargonic archives of Lagash.

Women play a role at every level of society. At Girsu, the prince's wife runs the **é.munus**, a large agricultural and commercial establishment and workshop. At Kish, if we are to believe the Royal Sumerian Kinglist, Ku.bawa, a former tavern-keeper, reigned for a time on the throne, the first recorded woman ruler in history. At the other end of the social scale, women are servants. They are designated by the generic term of **geme$_2$**, generally translated "slave." In fact, this refers to a relationship of authority, to the dependant status of one group or one individual on another. The women called **geme$_2$** are given the most varied tasks and enjoy the most varied status:[39] **sag.dub.me**, regularly registered employees with full fractions; **gu$_2$.ba.me**, their auxiliaries; **geme$_2$.u$_4$.bi.ta**, those with long service; **geme$_2$.be$_2$.gal.me**, those who receive extra rations; **sag.sam$_x$.me**, chattel slaves. Between those two extremes, women are present everywhere; priestesses, overseers in workshops or heads of teams, etc.

As far as we can see, those who held the various administrative and religious functions were recruited from three major groups in Lagashite society: the **lu$_2$.SU.a.me**, the **lu$_2$.IGI.NIGIN$_2$.ne**, and the **usar.re$_2$.ne**. All members of the three groups occupied similar functions and offices, enjoyed the same advantages and privileges, had at their disposal fields for subsistence and rations, and received a special share of wool, textiles, or food on certain

---

37For example, J.J. van Dijk, "Incantations accompagnant la naissance de l'homme," *Or.* 44 (1975): 52-79.

38On *namaru/namâru*, cf. the commentary cited by M. Civil, "Medical Commentaries from Nippur," *JNES* 33 (1974): 332: 38.

39K. Maekawa, "Female Weavers and their children in Lagash--pre-Sargonic and Ur III," *ASJ* 2 (1980): 81-125.

festival days.[40] All these groups consisted of both men and women with apparently no distinction between them beyond that of sex.[41] In short we may consider that in Mesopotamian society of the third millennium women behaved in the same way and on equal terms with men, whatever their social status, assuming the same tasks and the same duties and enjoying the same privileges as men. We shall refrain from too hasty a conclusion.

Beginning with the basics and making an exception for servants in the workshops who are given smaller rations than their male counterparts, we observe that women are mainly identified by their qualities as **dam**, "wife," **ama**, "mother," **nin**, "sister," or **dumu (.munus)**, "daughter." In other words, they appear as belonging to someone else, subordinate to their father, husband and children respectively. This is clearly seen in the way they are referred to by the scribes, who usually omit to mention the woman's proper name preferring to call her **dam** PN, "wife of so-and-so," even the wife of En.iggal,

---

40Even if it is not always easy to tell one from the other, the three terms relate to three distinct groups. Briefly, **lu2.SU.a.me** or **lu2.SU.a.ensi2.ka.ke4.ne** "of the prince," is the name for a group which is linked to the prince through family ties or some other undefined connection. We can identify in this group members of the royal family; moreover, lexical sources give the equivalence SU=*Nisû*, "people, members of the family," (on **SU**=*nišû* see A. Shaffer, "Gilgamesh, the cedar forest and Mesopotamian History," *JAOS* 103 (1983): 310; **su.sa.mu.ta**=*ina nišiya*, "of my family," D.W. Myhram, *Babylonian Hymns and Prayers*, University of Pennsylvania, The University Museum Publications of the Babylonian Section, I, (Philadelphia, 1911), 135:17. For another explanation see J. Bauer, *AWL*, 343-344. In the group of **usar.re.ne**, the sources make a distinction between **usar.e2.munus**, "u. from the queen's household," and **usar.nam.dumu**, "u. from the children's household." M.A. Powell showed some time ago that the word refers to the circle of friends and companions (Powell, "Graphic criteria for the dating in the Old Babylonina Period," *Or.* 42 (1973): 401. As to the **lu2.IGI.NIGIN2.ne**, the phrase refers to a fairly numerous group that is subdivided into **gal**, "big," and **tur**, "small." Two identical administrative documents prove that **lu2.IGI.NIGIN2.ne** can be replaced by **ab.ba**, "father," "elder," "notable" (cf. *AWL* 129 and 130; **Šeš.tur, lu2.IGI.NIGIN2** in *AWL* 130, IV, 5, is **ab.ba.e2.gal**, "notable of the palace," in *DP* 184, I,2. We therefore suggest seeing in **lu2.IGI.NIGIN2** an allusion to a group of people of distinction.

41Among the lu2.SU.**a.me**, we find a Nar, wife of a **sanga.GAR**, Geme2.šu.ga.lam.ma, a **nu.gig** priestess, or He2.dba.wa, the prince's sister (*AWL* 124, I, 1ff.; on the possible reading **Gan** of the sign **He2.(gan** for **geme2**, "servant") see A. Westenholz, *Early Cuneiform Texts in Jena* (Copenhagen, 1975), passim; but D.O. Edzard, *Or.* 55(1986).) Among the **usar.re2.ne** we reckon E2.ul.le, usar of the children's house, wife of a certain Ki.tuš.lu2, he himself getting perhaps the **usar** of the house of the queen who bears the same name, also Pu2.ta the wife of a dignitary, as her name "Out of the Well" shows (*DP* 129, I, 8-11, 1; etc.) is a foundling. Finally, among the **lu2.IGI.NIGIN2.ne** we should mention a group of women, the **HAR.TU.munus.me**, who are employed in domestic service. (*AWL* 68 III, 9-IV 2; etc.)

the administrator of the queen's household, who is mentioned numerous times, is only known as **dam En.ig.gal nu.banda**, "wife of En.iggal the administrator." Her proper name, Hal.hal, is rarely mentioned.[42]

If, therefore, the woman holds the rank of her male relative (and the case of Puta the foundling proves it), this does not mean that she lives in his shadow and this is precisely one of the characteristic features of the time. Three examples will suffice to show that women have a share in public life with a high degree of autonomy:

> 1. The custom was that on some solemn occasions, the notables and dignitaries would bring presents to the sovereign, yet husbands and wives brought their gifts separately. In the same lists we find registered, for instance, first the gift brought by the **sanga** "the administrator," of the Temple of Nanshe, and then his wife's gift.[43] Elsewhere, En.iggal, already mentioned, makes a gift of ten **sa$_2$.du$_{11}$** of strong beer to the prince while his wife brings five.[44]
>
> 2. A woman, **dam.Šubur nu.banda**, "wife of Šubur the administrator," deals directly with the hierarchy of the **e$_2$.munus** without her husband's intervention, although he is doubtless still alive; she has sheaves of reeds delivered, and receives the use of a parcel of land.[45]
>
> 3. A married woman can give a surety for someone or buy real estate without her husband's intervention.[46]

Other sources such as the archaic *kudurru* for instance, which record the transfer of land or movable goods, provide us with complementary evidence, enabling us to define more precisely women's position in her family context.

According to the **LUM.ma.TUR** inscription,[47] in the name of a Lagashite prince, four groups of persons sell parcels of land to this prince. Among the sellers, the text makes a distinction between the **lugal.gana$_2$.me**, "masters of the land," the owners and the alienators of the land, on the one

---

[42]*AWL* 175, 3-5; 176 V, 7-9.

[43]*AWL* 175 II, 3-4; III, 1-2.

[44]*AWL* 176 I, 4-6; V, 6-9.

[45]*AWL* III, 9-IV, 1; *DP* 352 I, 2-3.

[46]*SR* 25; 35; 69; 70.

[47]*SR* 117.

hand, and on the other the **TUR.gana$_2$.me**, literally "small ones of the land," people associated in some way with the sale. We shall examine only the fourth transaction, although interpretation is sometimes made difficult by breaks in the tablet. Among the parties called **lugal** we find the name of E.bara.šudu, Amar.TU's wife. The other names (there must have been two or three) are lost in a break in the tablet. Then the text goes on and we see E.bara.šudu, along with Ama.barage.si, another **lugal** probably, receiving a gift. Then comes the list of the **TUR.gana$_2$.me**, that is: six sons of Amar.TU among whom are Inimani.zi, two sons of Ur.Dumuzi, possibly another **lugal**, and finally Nin-urunishe.hili, the wife of Inimani.zi, Amar.TU's daughter-in-law with her four children.

The conclusion is obvious that Amar.TU is dead and his widow is now at the head of his household with the status of **lugal**. Among the **TUR.gana$_2$.me** the presence of the wife of one of Amar.TU's sons at the side and on an equal footing with her husband is somewhat remarkable: the wife is fully associated in the transaction.

A second example, this time from Girsu, concerns the sale of a house by three brothers who receive an equal share of the sale price.[48] Three other persons are associated in this sale and each receive the same gift: E.ule, the wife of one of the brothers, along with apparently her two children. Thus one brother, married with children, is living under the same roof with his two brothers. When selling the house, his wife is associated in the sale on an equal footing with her children.

One last example comes from Adab. There we see a certain E.sudaga selling a piece of land of his own.[49] His wife, his children and a son-in-law, **mi$_2$.us$_2$.sa$_2$**, are partners in the sale.

Hence we can draw several conclusions: 1. In household affairs, the woman is usually and regularly associated with her male relations. With its groups of **lugal.gana.$_2$.me** and **TUR.gana$_2$.me** Sumerian society seems to be relatively egalitarian. However, the wife is on the same rank as her husband only if he is simply associated with the sale. If, on the other hand, he is one of the sellers, she is then only on the same level with her children. 2. The presence of a son-in-law or a daughter-in-law among the members of the family associated in a sale is a problem. Related as she is to three genealogical branches, that of the father or brother, that of the husband, and finally that of the son, is the woman, at the intersection of genealogical lines, the means for

[48]*SR* 33.

[49]*SR* 119.

the transmission of property? The easiest way to identify an individual is to relate him to the members of his family, and first of all, to his father. Yet, someone may happen to be related to his father-in-law and we find the phrase PN **mi$_2$.us$_2$.sa$_2$.ensi$_2$.ka**, "So and so son-in-law of the prince"[50] or PN, a dignitary, **mi$_2$.us$_2$.sa$_2$** PN "So and so, a dignitary, son-in-law of So and so."[51] Must we understand that in these two examples the son-in-law owes his social rank to his marriage, or more simply that he has opted for an uxorilocal residence? As matters stand, we can not give that question a well founded answer. 3. A widow has the power to be head of the family. A document from Girsu,[52] listing twelve families in the service of the goddess Bawa shows that four of them have a widow **nu.ma.su** at their head; one of them has a woman called **ama**, "mother," who could well be a grandmother, and seven have men, **ab.ba** "father." The total reads as follows:

šu.nigin$_2$ 7 ab.ba
6 ir$_{11}$ lu$_2$
11 ša$_3$.du$_{10}$ nita
9 ama TUR
17 ša$_3$.du$_{10}$ munus
5 geme$_2$ lu$_2$

55 lu$_2$.tur.mah.ba

Total: seven fathers, six servants, eleven sons, nine mothers, seventeen daughters, five maids; (all in all) fifty-five **lu$_2$.tur.mah.ba**.

The widow is head of the family but in the total she is classified among the "mothers," that is to say married women whose husbands are still alive. Moreover, the term **ama** is followed by the sign **TUR**, "small," which obviously echoes the final phrase **lu$_2$.tur.mah.ba**, containing the same word TUR. It is an ambiguous phrase. It is found at the end of numerous accounting documents that summarize distribution of rations (the families mentioned in our text, belonging to the goddess Bawa, are in fact among those who receive rations), and can be read in two ways: "man, small and big" or

---

50H. de Genouillac, *Tablettes sumériennes archaiques*, (Paris, 1909), 2 III, 1-2.

51*DP* 125 I, 7--II, 2 and parallel documents.

52M. Vasil'evich Nikolskij, *Dokumenty Khozyaystvennoy Otcetnosti Drevneysey epokhi Khaldei iz Sobraniya... (Documents of Economic Ability of the Most Ancient Period of Chaldea from the collection of N.P. Likhachev)*, (St. Petersburg: 1908), 19 (in Russian).

"men with small and big rations."[53] In any case, the widows' heads of families, belong to the **TUR** category. Between the widow, head of family, and the man, also head of a family, but not included in this **TUR** category, there seems to be a notable difference.

Now, if we compare the Sumerian sources we have just examined with the contemporary Akkadian documents, a significant difference is found. The obelisk of Man-ištusu relates the acquisition by this king of important pieces of land from eight groups of sellers.[54] Among those, women are totally absent. Thus, out of the three sons of a certain Enna-ilum, only two are present at the sale, the third is absent, but his children are associated in the transaction. We may rightly suppose that the third has died. Here, in contrast to what happens in Sumerian-speaking areas, the widow is not mentioned.[55]

We would like to raise one last question. In the middle of the third millennium, Mesopotamian society is undergoing profound changes. There are two modes of owning property, one collective, the other individual. In the first case, groups of land holders exploit in common large patrimonies of which they are the holders. In the second, the owners of the land are individuals. The important change of this period is the gradual disappearence of the large patrimonies in favor of individual property. The existence of such patrimonies is known to us only through the sale documents that attest their division.[56] If we turn to the Isle of Tory, the farthest Gaelic region of the Northwest of Ireland,[57] we are struck by the similarity between certain practices of that country and those of Mesopotamia: for instance the family group or *clann*, a Gaelic word meaning "child, offspring, descendant." One never says of someone else "the *clann* he belongs to" but So-and-so, *clann* of So-and-so." Curiously enough, *clann* proves to be the equivalent of **DUMU.DUMU** on the Man-ištusu obelisk, having exactly the same meaning and the same use. Indeed, *clann* is a cognatic descent group whereas **DUMU.DUMU**, in Akkadian contexts, refers to a group of agnates, but we

53Cf. the bibliography in Dominique Charpin, "Un nouveau compte de rations presargonique," *RA* 71 (1977): 105 *sub* 15, 1.

54V. Scheil, *Textes élamites-sémitiques*, premiere serie, Mémoires de la Délégation en Perse, 2, Paris: 1900, 1-55.

55Cf. the geneological table in Glassner, "De Sumer à Babylone: familles pour gérer, familles pour régner," in A. Burguière, Ch. Klapich-Zuber, et al., editors, *Histoire de la famille*, (Paris, 1986), 1, 108.

56J. Glassner, "Aspects du don, de l'échange et formes d'appropriation du sol dans la Mésopotamie du IIIe millénaire, avant la fondation de l'Empire d'Ur," *Journal Asiatique* 273 (1985): 39-59.

57R. Fox, *The Tory Islanders*, (Cambridge, 1978).

have no document that could give us the exact meaning of the word **dumu.dumu** in Sumerian sources.[58] Besides, just as the Mesopotamian group of land holders, the *clann* works as a system of usufruct. Granted these similarities (there are others) we come to another possible similarity pertinent to the question we raised. There is in Tory a mode of union in which the husband and wife live separately, each for instance living in the house in which they were born. Today, according to R. Fox,[59] of fifty-five couples, ten live this way. The woman lives with her family and works for it; her husband lives in his; he is a privileged guest in his wife's house, and it is a duty for him to help the male relatives of her family. Did ancient Mesopotamia have similar or comparable customs?

At the present state of knowledge, it is impossible to answer positively. Yet there are, here and there, in the Mesopotamian landscape of the third and second millennia, obvious traces of similar institutions.

In the realm of the gods, the temple of Dumuzi at Bad.tibira is called **a2.na2.da** "contiguous bed," of the holy Inanna.[60] The temple of Ningirsu at Girsu is the "contiguous bed," **a2.na2.da** or **e2.na** of the goddess Bawa.[61] As to the temple of Ningal at Ur, it is the "contiguous bed," **a2.na2.da** of the god Su'en.[62] Elsewhere it is the chapel of Enki which is the "bedroom," **ki.na2.a** of the goddess Nammu.[63] In short, gods and goddesses, husbands and wives, live in separate dwellings, and visit each other. In the state of Lagash there are a certain number of temples called **e2.dam**, apparently "house of the husband/wife," but its name is in fact the shortened form of a much longer phrase, **e2.dam.e.gar.ra**, the "temple placed at the husband's/wife's place," a phrase very near to similar phrases such as **e2.dNanše.šeš.e.gar.ra**, "the temple of Nanshe placed at the brother's house," or **dNin.gir2.su.nin.ne2.gar.ra**, "Ningirsu of the temple placed at the sister's house."[64]

58R.R. Jestin, *Tablettes sumériennes du Šuruppak*, (Paris, 1937), 245: R 2-3; 539 **dumu.dumu** 7 **im.ru** = "539 **dumu.dumu**, 7 families."

59Fox, *op. cit.*, 157ff.

60A. Sjöberg, E. Bergmann, *The Collection of the Sumerian Temple Hymns*: Texts from Cuneiform Sources III, (Locust Valley, N.Y., 1969), TH 17:211.

61Gudea, Cylinder B IX, 8ff.

62Reference in Charpin, *Le clergé d'Ur au siècle d'Hammurabi*, (Genève-Paris, 1986), 196-197.

63R.C. Thompson, *Cuneiform Texts...in the British Museum*, XVI, (London, 1903), 46: 191 ff.

64Reference in A. Falkenstein, "Girsu," *RlA* 3 (1968), 387-388.

In the realm of kings, the queen of Mari in the eighteenth century B.C. seems to have had a separate dwelling place, distinct from that of the king, at least for a certain time in the year.[65]

Have we not, in Lagash, in the institutions of the **e$_2$.munus** and the **e$_2$.gal**, another piece of evidence attesting to such separate residences? We may wonder. The **e$_2$.munus** is the estate of the queen which she governs in her own interest and on which she lives, surrounded by a court of relatives, friends and servants.[66] As to the prince, he lives in his palaces, the **e$_2$.gal** or the **e$_2$.ensi$_2$**; in fact he probably has several palaces, since at least two **e$_2$.gal** are known to us.[67] We know that he often travels, staying in various places[68] and in particular in the **e$_2$.munus**. Indeed, several documents mention his presence in the following terms: **ensi$_2$ e$_2$.munus.še$_3$ e.gin$_2$.na.a**, "when the prince went to the **e$_2$.munus**;[69] "**ensi$_2$ e$_2$.munus mu.ti.la.a**, "when the prince dwelt in the **e$_2$.munus**."[70] On the other hand, the queen frequently goes to the **e$_2$.gal**, where, it seems, she has reserved quarters: **e$_2$.gal.la ki.munus.še$_3$**, "in the **e$_2$.gal** to the palace of the queen."[71]

Hereafter it will be essential for us to reconsider the relations between the **e$_2$.munus** and the **e$_2$.gal** using a new approach, as there is obviously a division of labor between the prince and the queen. We thus need to make a new perusal of the administrative sources as well as Uru'inimgina's reforms.

We come to the conclusion that the image of the veiled woman, confined inviolate in her house, does not fit Sumerian society of the third millennium. From the anonymous woman of administrative sources to the widow in charge of her family, not to mention the complex interplay of relationships between husband and wife, the different status of man and woman may be defined.

In Sumerian-speaking countries (such is not the case, apparently, in Akkadian-speaking regions) the woman is not confined in the family house.

---

[65] Study to appear by Jean-Marie Durand, announced by B. Lafont, *Nouvelles Assyriologiques Brèves et Utilitaires* 2, (1987), 24; Abdallah, *op. cit.*, 14; Charpin, *op. cit.*, 306.

[66] Maekawa, "The Development of the *é.mí* in Lagash during Early Dynastic III," *Mesopotamia* 8-9 (1973-74), 77-144; B. Foster, "A New Look at the Sumerian Temple State," *JESHO* 24 (1981), 225-241.

[67] J. Bauer, *AWL* 32.

[68] For example: *AWL* 169 I, 6--II, 2.

[69] *DP* 218 I, 3ff.

[70] *AWL* 176 X, 1-2.

[71] *DP* 319 IV, 1-2, etc.

She is active in association with her male relatives or sometimes alone, and her role seems to extend even to the cohesion of the social groups that compose the city-state, as is suggested by the following examples:

1. Officers and dignitaries of the **e$_2$.munus** from time to time make a gift of pure malt and pure milk to notables of other institutional estates or the capital. Now, out of the 42 recipients, only eight are men; all the rest are women. We must note in passing that when En.iggal presents a notable with his gift, his wife receives the *equivalent* gift at the hands of another person.[72]

2. At the death of the former queen Bara.namtara, Sasa, the reigning queen, organizes grand funeral ceremonies[73] with 177 female mourners, 92 male lamenters, as well as 48 "wives of notables," **dam.ab.ba**; in short a group of women representing the whole community accompanies, under the queen's supervision, the deceased queen to her last resting place.

3. The royal spouses and princesses have access to the ancestor cult. Several administrative texts list those to whom sacrifices[74] are offered, or whose statues are donned in stately attire.[75] We can read the names of Nin.hilisu, wife of En.mete.na; Ašume'eren, wife of En.ana.tum, LU$_2$.šessig.TUR, wife of En.entar.zi; Bara.namtara, wife of Lugal.anda; Geme.Bawa, daughter of En.entar.zi; Mi.saga, daughter of Lugal.anda; and finally Gišri, mother of a prince or He/Gan.Bawa, sister of a prince.

Obviously, there are still numerous gaps, and we could gather only scraps of information which are not enough to come to a precise definition of women's status. We know nothing, for instance, of the principles that governed the choice of a spouse. In the royal family of Umma, in pre-Sargonic times, we find the case of a marriage between two parallel cousins, Gišša.ki.du uniting with his cousin Bara.irnun.[76] This marriage may strengthen the claim of a cadet branch of the royal family to the throne at the expense of a senior branch. But royal families, in order to remain in power, may sometime adopt uses alien to common custom, and Umma's example cannot be considered as reflective of the norm. Moreover, Bara.irnun is called **e$_2$.gi$_4$.a** of her husband's father, a Sumerian term for which translation is difficult. The meaning of its Akkadian counterpart, *kallatum*, is quite

---

[72]For example, de Genouillac, *op. cit.*, 5 I, 1-6; III, 2-4.

[73]*Ibid.* 9; *AWL* 66.

[74]*AWL* 165.

[75]*AWL* 167; 168; etc.

[76]See the reference in A. Sjöberg, "Zu einigen Verwandschaftsbezeichnungen in Sumerischen," *Heidelberger Studien zum Alten Orient*, (Wiesbaden, 1967), 209-210.

controversial too, as it has two very diverging connotations in Babylon and in Nuzi.

Responses to Dr. Glassner's Paper

Roth: There is a legal document, which you discuss in your paper, the reforms of Uru'inimgina that dictates certain social and economic reforms of this period, one of which has been always understood to say "formerly, women had two husbands; now they only take one," and what you are now saying is that the Sumerian has not been understood properly and it has nothing to do with marrying two husbands, it says...

Glassner: The expression in Sumerian is **Dam tuku**: "The man takes a woman for wife." And we have these Sumerian texts, where instead we have the term **nita**, which signifies sexual, not necessarily marital, activity. In all practical tablets, marriage is written about using **dam tuku**, never with **nita**. So, to give a translation for those who do not understand Sumerian, I would translate "formerly, women had two men" not "married two men."

Roth: Correct. **Nita** appears most of all in adultery passages, to indicate sexual relations outside of marriage, so in fact what we now have is, if you're right, and I really think you are, what we have from a legal and a more functional document as well as from a literary text is evidence for what I have always thought was just nonsense.

Cooper: Well, I would disagree completely with my colleagues here. The text in question is a very important text and it is seized upon many times by people who are writing about early Mesopotamia. It is a text from 2350 B.C. by the last independent ruler of the city-state of Lagash before Lugal-zagesi conquers all of Sumer and then is in turn conquered by Sargon of Akkade, so we're talking about a period just at the end of this so-called pre-Sargonic time before the first Akkadian empire. And this Uru'inimgina, who was an usurper, introduces a series of what we call euphemistically, reforms; he changes a lot of things in the social order and in the economic order, especially, and masks them as reforms, and talks about what happened in the bad old days and what's going to happen now in the good new days. A lot of things in his text have to do with who gets to use certain kinds of land, and it is masked as if it's a conflict between the clergy and the secular ruler, whereas in fact as Marc told us under the guise of defending the Gods' right to their domain against that of the secular ruler he's really expanding his own realm, that is the realm and the economic power of the secular ruler, so we are already warned that we can't take this text in a terribly literal way. Then he goes on to say at a certain point that in the old days "women of old days used to" and then the word that means either "have" or "marry" two men, and, as Jean Jacques says, they don't use the normal word for spouse, which is "spouse," it says "men." That doesn't really bother me. Then it says "today this abomination has been done away with." The important thing to the interpretation to me is that in the context he goes on and talks about what is done now-a-days to punish disrespectful wives, that's something like they get their teeth bashed out with a brick, it's a very obscure passage. The brick is then displayed on the city wall, so, I have always understood this passage as trying to show how, in the old days before he came into power, even the women were running around and being immoral and disrespectful to their husbands and Uru'inimgina brought this rather threatening force, this kind of female sexuality and aggression, that always is very frightening to any established order, he has brought this under control. I've always understood this as being pure hyperbole and have always objected strongly to people who have seized on this passage to say "Aha! Echoes of polyandry." And then they go from polyandry, and I'm not sure how, to matriarchy, and draw a picture of an earlier Sumerian society that was run by women who had several husbands each, but then gradually women were repressed by the rise of the male power authorities, the rulers of the city, and so resulting already by this early time in women in a subordinate, suppressed role; but supposedly we still have echoes of the golden age of female dominance in the form of this matriarchal, polyandrous society, which to me is just ridiculous.

Harris: Is it promiscuity, then?

Cooper: What he's saying is that the two men refers to the ruler and the husband, that in the Gilgamesh story it is said that Gilgamesh slept with the bride and then was followed by the husband, and what Jean Jacques is saying is that perhaps in the Uru'inimgina reforms it says "in former days women had two men, but this abomination has been abolished," it doesn't mean that they had more than one husband, but it means that they had to have sexual relations first with this other guy before they had them with their own husbands, and that Uru-'inimgina is abolishing this terrible institution.

Harris: Why would the woman be punished?

Cooper and Glassner: She isn't punished.

Cooper: No, no, no, that's a second reform. You see what I was saying, the point is that you also have this other business about disrespectful wives, I would prefer to interpret the woman's behavior of having two men as reflecting back on the woman, where Jean Jacques interprets it as reflecting unfavorably on the earlier rulers who used to force them into doing this.

Zagarell: I've heard this kind of suggestion about the first night and everything. Given the size of the city, how many women would Gilgamesh have to sleep with? It can't mean exactly what it is being said that it means, because I can't imagine anyone really playing that kind of role; it must mean something symbolic.

Glassner: First of all, I don't know the size of the city, and I can't directly for myself give you an answer because I never witnessed such a custom. But if you go to Mexico and if you look at archives you can see that *ius primae noctis* was still being used at the beginning of the 20th century.

McNamara: The *ius primae noctis* as far as we can make out, was never a sexual act, it was either one of two things. It may have been a tax, it may have been money that people paid, with some overlay, this wasn't what happened. The other thing, which is more likely, is that people paid money to have the right to sleep with their wives on the first night of their marriage, being forgiven for the three nights that they're supposed to pray in chastity before they consummate the marriage.

Cooper: So you mean it has only existed as a sexual thing in the minds of Assyriologists?

McNamara: Or in the minds of modern novelists, or something of that sort. In fact, as far as anybody can tell, the Christian Middle Ages did not have that practice.

Roth: Would you just elaborate a little bit more on the connection you made at the beginning of your paper between Enkidu civilized by woman and then Enkidu going to civilization to save women.

Glassner: I think that it is clear that the text itself of the progression of Enkidu is complete, at the beginning he is a *lullû*, in the second step, he is an *awîlum* when he knew a woman and when he had eaten food and his mind became intelligent. He was then dressed and behaved like a *lullû*. So the progression of Enkidu is clear, and he, after his behavior shows that he takes charge and tries to stop Gilgamesh.

Cooper: Well, the alternative, of course, is that the reason he is angry is because Gilgamesh had been promised to him as a special friend, he was really jealous of Gilgamesh's involvement with women. He wasn't so much protecting the women as venting his fury at Gilgamesh for preferring the women to him.

Glassner: Sure, we can have many interpretations of the epic and you can add and note some interpretations but I think the question is relevant that in the Sumerian texts always Enkidu speaks to *lullû* and to Gilgamesh as "my king, my **lugal**, my master" and Enkidu is *arab*, and as you said, *arab* is servant of Gilgamesh. The connection between the two is not as easy as we can imagine.

Discussions at the end of Day One

Stuard: I really have a question about division of labor, economic relations, and I would like to go back to this morning's speakers in particular. It would appear to me that in terms of work assigned in a gender fashion that there are certain fields which reveal more gender divisions than others, particularly the linen making, beer and such. We have exactly those same divisions in the early medieval period. My question has to do with another aspect of economic relations, and that is, it would appear also, that women and men may own the same kind of wealth, that there is no particular devolution to women and no particular devolution to men, either in inheritance or in marriage prestations. Because we also have that; it is an unusual parallel. You wouldn't find that, for example in Sub-Saharan Africa, or in India, but you do find it in medieval Europe, and you seem to be indicating to me that you find it in ancient Egypt, and I would like to hear more on that.

Allam: What we have been seeing with the papers presented by three Egyptologists: the reliefs, depicting women, sometimes women working in the fields, and participating in other kinds of activities. To my knowledge, tomb representations don't reflect exactly or completely the complete variety of activities even done by men, so because we have here women in tombs, the tomb representation had a different purpose of grouping representations and had a specific attitude toward these things. So, on the whole, these representations don't reflect the whole range of activities. The artist wanted in most cases to represent religious forces, religious aspects, of the main figure in the tomb, which was really the man, in the first instance. So if we notice that the artist in some cases drew women doing some activities I would say here we have caught a few glimpses into the actual picture of women, but I would add that the text and the information given by the text shows that we have other categories of activities carried out by men and women not shown in the representations. So, we shouldn't assess these representations at face value because we must differentiate these representations from contexts, they are not to be understood as simple representations of actual daily life. We have also the information given by the texts to rely on. I can't imagine myself that the woman in ancient Egypt was kept at home. What would she be doing at home? So I would expect her working in agriculture, sometimes, of course not to the same degree as man. As far as, we said weaving, we said agriculture, women were also at home dealing with children, etc., etc. As regards the wealth of women, I will be treating this question more. We shall be seeing that women inherited from their parents. The dowry women were sometimes also given by relatives she could pass this wealth on to her descendants, both female and male, so in this way women got involved also in having wealth.

Khurt: I think there is just a very slight confusion which is that Susan Stuard was asking that while the division of labor may exist in Egypt, it was very widespread and not to be disputed, certainly women and men carried out all sorts of jobs. Do women in Egypt inherit the same kind of possessions, wealth, goods, slaves lands, and so on, that men inherit? Or do women inherit cash and house property, for example while men would inherit land? That I think is the question she is trying to ask, and that I believe you have the answer to.

Allam: Yes, well. We see through extension from the Old Kingdom, the earliest period of Egyptian history, from which we have information based on texts we see that the king in most cases gave land to men. We don't see that the king ever gave land to a woman. But in one case, and I will be dealing with this case tomorrow, in one case we see that a woman has conveyed her estate which contains about 2000 arouras, and that is a good deal of land, she conveyed this land to her descendants. So we can ask from where this woman got this land? We can't detect that for the moment. But we have the evidence that she holds land and that she could dispose of this land as she wished, you see. The queen too is given estates by the king. I would say we should concentrate on the common people. I will deal with this question also tomorrow.

Shute: I have worked with my wife Gay Robins to some extent on Egyptian mathematics and one of the things that struck me in doing that work was the subtlety of the Egyptian grasp of mathematics. One way to know what the ancient Egyptians were like was to see what was thought about them by their near-contemporaries, the Greeks, who regarded them as a very subtle people. The Egyptians had a very strong appreciation of verbal puns. What I wanted to ask any of the speakers was whether the Egyptians may have had an equal appreciation for visual puns? For instance, when a woman is shown standing behind a man would they see this in reality as two persons standing side by side and at the same time symbolizing the proper subservience of women, or if you like when they portray a dog underneath a master's chair would they at the same time see it as a dog under a chair and a dog beside a chair. Of course we don't know this, we can't ask them but we can try to intuit, I suppose, to some extent. It seems to me perhaps in trying to evaluate the scenes in painted tombs Barbara Lesko has said before that they are very unreliable as an indication of what went on in ordinary life, perhaps one should see them on different levels as related to ordinary life, as carrying all sorts of messages, symbolic messages which we may or may not have a key to, but which we can possibly reach out to by trying to understand more about this people. Of course no two people are going to have the same ideas, hence a great deal of heat is generated between Egyptologists who discuss these very important matters. Did these people see visual puns?

Galvin: I have a partial answer for your question. I agree with you that the Egyptians loved to play with words, but I can't answer for visual puns. My response is that what we do not see is a woman standing behind a man, or as you also suggested, an animal under a chair; what we see is the Egyptian's curious perspective, so they in fact did love puns, but I would say that the joke is on us because we aren't able to understand their perspective.

Stuard: If I understood Prof. Glassner correctly and if I understood the Egyptologists correctly, it seems to me that a whole other area of discourse can be opened up that nobody has yet attacked, and that is the question of death and the afterlife, which is obviously a very important world to these people. I have been listening to the discussions about the tomb art and that many of these tombs belonged to men and that what we see, when we see this art, is a man's paradise. How the perfect is going to be, and in a perfect afterlife, whatever women may do in this life, they're not going to be doing it in the afterlife at least; whereas I thought I heard that Sumerian women are equal, in fact. Did I hear that? That they are buried in large, expensive tombs, with great numbers of mourners and they are even equal among the ancestors. I may have misunderstood but I thought that, in any case, let me just conclude by asking for some kind of discussion about the place of women in the afterlife.

Glassner: Yes, I spoke about the place of women after death, but it's not completely clear how it compares to men's. Perhaps it would be easier to explain with some women belonging to the upper classes, especially royal, but do we differentiate those in a certain social sphere in which some people who enter that sphere during their life are sure after death they will enter the ancestors' cult and benefit from it. Some women belong to that sphere. I don't know if there are texts enough to tell you if they got more or less sacrifices, this would be the kind of quantifiable answer. So I don't say that they are all equal after death. I can't state it for sure.

Fischer: Since the question has been raised concerning women in the afterlife I thought I might read something I cut out of my paper. I said "Up to now I have talked about the life of non-royal women, and it may be well to add a word about the prospects for the life to come. It is obvious from what has already been said that the here-after of women was provided for by offerings, at least if they had sufficient means. By the end of the Old Kingdom, they, like their husbands, were said to become a "glorified spirit" (the word is *3ḫ*). They either used the masculine form *3ḫ* or sometimes *3ḫ.t*, feminine; but their survival in the next world ultimately entailed a rather bizarre identification with the God Osiris, who of course was male. He was the dead king. This was, however, no more bizarre that the assumption of male attire by queens such as Hatshepsut, who had to wear a ceremonial beard. The identification with Osiris is found in the Pyramid Texts of two queens of Pepi II at the end of the Sixth dynasty, and Osiris becomes an epithet at some point in the following period. So then, ultimately this kind of democratization of the assumption of the role of Osiris by the King, this right was assumed by everyone, including women."

B. Lesko: I would like to add something to that if I may. In the Pyramid Texts and in the Coffin Texts there is an important role given to the goddess Nut in the mortuary religion; and I have been looking at coffins of women from later periods and I find, comparing with coffins of men, that the figure on the bottom of the coffin or on the bottom of the coffin lid in a man's coffin is often Osiris, in a woman's coffin it is often the goddess Nut, so I think that this is something that really has to be studied, perhaps in a doctoral dissertation, and I think that our graduate student in Egyptology, Stephen Thompson could probably fill us in with more on this association, he has been working on the Nut Texts.

Thompson: For my MA thesis I have been working on the use of the pyramid texts in Middle Kingdom coffins from Saqqara and on the lids of several of these coffins are collected a series of Nut spells from the west walls of the sarcophagus chambers in the pyramids. The purpose of these spells seems to be to allow the deceased to become a star on the body of Nut. It has been argued that one of the earliest strata, one of the earliest goals of the deceased was to become a star, and Nut represented the sky. And in my coffins, some of which belong to women, they seem to have just as much of an opportunity to become a star on the body of Nut as the men do; the only difference in the texts is the use of the feminine endings instead of masculine endings. The scribes were fairly consistent in the use of the correct endings, particularly in coffin Sq3C. But from what I have looked at it does appear that women had the same opportunity to enter this type of afterlife as a star as men do. They didn't make a distinction between the two.

Fischer: This assumption of the role of Osiris initially seemed to have been not so much assuming the identity of Osiris but to use this assumption of the role of Osiris as a means of obtaining offerings, so this had a very specific purpose.

Thompson: Also I should mention that within these texts the woman is referred to as Osiris.

B. Lesko: It is also interesting that Dr. Ward mentioned in his paper the very finely executed offering tables of women who held very low or menial rank. That was certainly interesting, I hope he can add more to that.

Ward: This is in my *Feminine Titles* book. The woman was a kind of a scullery maid, working in a kitchen at Beni Hasan. There are several Middle Kingdom texts in which the owner of a stela specifically states: "I have put pictures and names of my relatives and all my servants and all my followers here on this stela or in the tomb precisely so they can get to paradise with me." I think that women believe that this was a male paradise; it wasn't a male paradise at all. In fact, as I see it, all the pictures of the peasants and offering bearers are in the tomb so that they will be magically transported into paradise along with their owner. And this is why you always find that in the man and the wife representations you always have the wife looking like she is sitting behind him, or standing behind him; there is a very simple reason for this, the Egyptians wanted to show as much of the human person as they could which is why you get all of these strange positions in tomb art, they wanted to show in two dimensions a three dimensional figure. You can't show the whole wife if she is standing beside her husband. So you see her standing behind him so that you can see the whole lady, so that she gets into heaven as a whole person. I can very well see a peasant coming down to the cemetery on his day off with his family and showing them: "look, there is daddy up there on the wall, because I'm there with my name on it we all get into heaven too, we don't need any fancy tomb." So I think sometimes we overlook the very simple explanations for this sort of thing.

McNamara: Actually, when I asked that question I wasn't overlooking that, I was thinking about that, that if we eliminate women doing all these different kinds of work from tombs, which we think that perhaps they did do in real life, then in the next world women who did all that sort of work are not going to appear, they're not going to get on that wall. Daddy's on the wall, but mommy's not.

The Egyptian New Kingdom

The New Kingdom or empire period of Egyptian history (1567-1085 B.C.) was a direct outgrowth from the humiliation of Asiatic, i.e., Hyksos, penetration and to some extent domination of Egypt. The expulsion of these foreign overlords by a new Theban family of nomarchs produced a number of social as well as political changes. Egypt was no longer content to try to enjoy the relative security of life within protected borders. Numerous and frequent military expeditions were now sent abroad, mainly to Syria/Palestine; towns were captured; alliances were formed; and hostages were taken, some to be Egyptianized and some to be enslaved. The capital was again established at Memphis in the north, but the spoils of these imperialistic forays were, in large part, sent south to embellish the seat of the ruling family's patron god, Amun-Re of Karnak, who was now regarded as the head of the pantheon.

The roles of the famous and greatly revered women of the founding years of the Eighteenth Dynasty, i.e., Tetisheri, Ahhotep, and Ahmose-Nefertari, were certainly emulated and indeed surpassed by the likes of the later Eighteenth Dynasty royal female personalities. Indeed, that dynasty has been termed "formidably feminine," and it did enjoy the twenty year reign of the most significant of female pharaohs--Hatshepsut--and saw the chief royal wives gain more publicly acknowledged stature in both religious and public life than perhaps ever before. Queen Tiy, consort of Amenhotep III, and their daughter-in-law Nefertiti are the most obvious examples.

This and the following dynasty became a truly international age with royal diplomatic marriages, international peace treaties, and a general balance of power among the major states in the Near East of the fourteenth and thirteenth centuries B.C. Egypt benefited from the importation of foreign goods and from a greater cosmopolitanism, but the imposition of a new religion of the Aten at the expense of the powerful old cult of Amun-Re, brought with it a severe reaction: a conservative polytheism promoted particularly by the Nineteenth Dynasty, a reaction that also seems to have had its effect on the status of, or attitudes towards, women. Whether the status and the roles which society offered women changed often during the empire must be the subject of more investigation before anything certain can be deduced.

Surely the great social, economic, and religious changes which mark the Egypt of the New Kingdom had to effect the female half of the population directly, but where one stood in society as well as where one lived would have also effected women's experiences. While documentation of all types is comparatively rich for this period, it is scattered rather thinly over the four centuries of its duration.

Much of the data we do have for the social, economic, and legal positions of women of this period have come from excavations begun more than fifty years ago at the ancient village site of Deir el Medineh in the Theban necropolis area. This village contained the houses and tombs of the community of civil servants and craftsmen who worked in the nearby royal tombs. The workmen's own family tombs provide portraits, genealogical data and scenes of their activities and of everyday life in the village and environs. The remains of their houses yield some paintings, objects, and ostraca documents as well. The plan of the village reveals the changing layout and efforts to accommodate an increasing population while still maintaining familial ties, as many of the positions--from scribes to draughtsmen and artists--eventually became hereditary. Numerous papyri, including a single bibliophile's collection of over forty documents, preserves some of the formal writing that was current at the time, including stories, poetry, letters, and wills, while ostraca in the form of potsherds and also limestone flakes, preserved artists' trial pieces as well as the more useful and valuable data of day to day accounts. The individuals who occupied the village for over three centuries, their work routines, their accomplishments, their economy, their beliefs, and even their disputes are all coming to light.

The royal residence and administrative centers in the north were far removed from the Theban necropolis, however. The Ramesside pharaohs of the Nineteenth Dynasty in the thirteenth century B.C., particularly Ramses II (or "Ramses the Great") lived in royal splendor much like other oriental potentates did, with a large harem including foreign princesses who had been given to seal national alliances, in palaces probably built, to some extent, with the slave labor we read about in the Book of Exodus, though we can still argue that slaves in Egypt did not fit the strict definition of slavery. Early in the reign of Ramses II there had been an inconclusive war with the powerful Hittites of Anatolia that resulted in a rather long truce between the superpowers, but in the reign of his successor Pharaoh Merneptah, Egypt had to contend with a new menace, the Sea Peoples. Egypt's New Kingdom essentially came to an end with Ramses III of the Twentieth Dynasty, who had to contend with Libyan invasions, corruption in the bureaucracy, and strikes by his own work force, including the men and women of Deir el Medineh. He eventually succumbed to a harem conspiracy in about 1060 B.C.

Even though the more important political center seems to have been almost always in the north during Egypt's New Kingdom period, the rulers never forgot their roots and returned to be buried at Thebes, as we have noted. Here too, in the limestone hillsides, the tombs of many of their courtiers and government officials, were hewn, particularly those who had responsibilities for the Upper Egyptian administration or the city and temples of Thebes. Their tomb walls are decorated with brilliant paintings reflecting, to some extent, their owners' private and professional lives. The next two papers, dealing with the New Kingdom, utilize the artistic and then the written evidence surviving from this period to elucidate the status and activities of the ordinary women of that time.

Leonard H. Lesko

Figure 22

Tomb owner libating accompanied by his wife,
Theban tomb 52, after N. de G. Davies,
The Tomb of Nakht at Thebes, (New York, 1917).

Some Images of Women in New Kingdom Art and Literature

Gay Robins

Evidence for the nature of Egyptian society comes from a number of sources: archaeological, textual and representational. In this paper I want to examine some of the representational and literary evidence concerning non-royal women in New Kingdom society with a view to discovering how they were perceived in these contexts.

In assessing the available material, it is essential to understand why it was created and for whom. Most of what we regard as Egyptian art was made for a specific purpose to serve the gods or the dead. This is the case with temples, and with royal and private tombs, stelae and sculpture. The decoration of less monumental items like pots, bowls, cosmetic objects, furniture and boxes may have been of lesser import and, I suspect, often primarily designed to satisfy the Egyptians' appreciation of beauty, although the motifs employed usually had a symbolism appropriate to the context.

The clientele for whom this art was produced were the elite class formed by the male scribal bureaucracy of Egypt, from whose ranks were selected the state officials, and their families. As the only fully literate group they were also responsible for writing the literature of ancient Egypt. Below them in the social hierarchy were the various kinds of artists, craftsmen and other professionals, and at the bottom, supporting the whole of Egyptian society, were the peasants. The king, of course, acted as the capstone of this pyramidal social structure.

Egypt has left a vast artistic legacy, even though much has been destroyed. The surviving corpus of literature is much smaller. Most of the representational material on which I shall draw for this paper is to be found in private tombs. In temples the major decoration is concerned with ritual and with the relationship between the king and deities, but occasionally sub-scenes give information about temple personnel. Material from royal tombs is not relevant to a study of non-royal women. The private tombs, on the other hand, relate not only to their elite owners, but also to the many other classes of Egyptian society who are depicted in the scenes of daily life found in them. The literary texts to which I shall refer are the "Instruction of Any," probably written in the Eighteenth Dynasty, the narrative texts "The Two Brothers" and "Truth and Falsehood," both probably Nineteenth Dynasty in date, and the love poetry of the late Eighteenth, Nineteenth, and Twentieth Dynasties.[1]

It is important to realize that in the public domain Egyptian society was dominated by men: the king was traditionally a man; the scribal bureaucracy was staffed by men; artists and artisans were male. Although exceptionally a woman might gain entry here, it was not the norm, and for instance, the female pharaoh Hatshepsut adopted male iconography when she assumed the kingship. Thus, when it comes to evaluating the representational evidence, we must remember that most of it was commissioned by male members of the scribal elite and executed by male artists. The images of women that we receive from this material are therefore likely to be the images that such men in Egyptian society had of women. This suggests that they will be one-sided, showing us a male ideal rather than the realities of life. For instance, as we shall see, women often appear simply as appurtenances to men and their affairs, while essentially female matters which do not involve men remain unrepresented. Nevertheless, since so much of our evidence from ancient Egypt is in the form of art, we cannot afford to ignore it in trying to understand Egyptian society and the place of women in it. We must therefore explore the material that is offered us and in recognizing its bias avoid being led astray by it. My aim here is to present the various images of women that the male official class convey on their monuments and in their writings.

I shall begin by looking at the women associated with the elite male owners of private tombs, since women in general in the New Kingdom did not themselves own tombs. In such tombs the decoration revolves around the owner, in order to secure for him existence in the afterlife and to commemorate his life on earth. Members of his family, however, are often depicted alongside him, and his mother and wife are usually given a prominent

---

[1]Translations of "The Instruction of Any," "The Two Brothers," "Truth and Falsehood" and some of the love poems are to be found in *Ancient Egyptian Literature*, Vol. 2, trans. M. Lichtheim (Berkeley, 1976). The two narrative tales and the love poems are also translated in *The Literature of Ancient Egypt*, ed. W. K. Simpson (New Haven, 1972). M. V. Fox, *The Song of Songs and Ancient Egyptian Love Songs* (Madison, Wisconsin, 1985) gives texts, translations and commentaries for the love poems. The latter are also translated and discussed in J. B. White, *A Study of the Language of Love in the Song of Songs and Ancient Egyptian Poetry* (Missoula, Montana, 1978).

position. Scenes divide into those which are connected with funerary ritual, and those representing aspects of this world. In the first, the owner of the tomb is frequently accompanied by his wife or mother, and other members of the family, especially sons and daughters, may also be present. However, when shown as a couple, either standing (fig. 22) or seated (fig. 23), the man in two-dimensional art is placed on the flat drawing surface in front of the woman, thus occupying the more prestigious position of the two. In offering scenes, it is normally the man who carries out the ritual, while quite often the woman is simply present without performing any specific action (fig. 22).

The owner and his wife share the ritual pilgrimage to Abydos, but scenes which show the funerary procession to the tomb refer only to the death and burial of the owner himself, while his wife appears in these scenes as a distraught mourner. Although the tomb also served as the burial place of the owner's wife, the husband mourning the wife is not a standard scene, despite the fact that due to death in childbirth, many wives must have preceded their husbands to the tomb.

In the second class of scenes, those representing life in this world, the subject matter usually relates to aspects of the tomb owner's office and to the management of his estates, and here he is most often shown alone. There is, however, a common scene type portraying the owner spearing fish and fowling in the marshes, in which his family usually accompanies him (fig. 24), and I shall have more to say of such scenes later.

Unlike the tomb owner, his wife and mother seldom appear alone engaged in their own occupations. An exception is found in TT 93, where the owner's mother, a royal nurse, is shown holding the king on her lap.[2] Another royal nurse, in TT 85, is shown suckling a prince.[3] The inclusion of these scenes ultimately reflects on the tomb owner, since he is linked through the royal nurse to the king. Even so, such scenes are rare; a number of other women who are known to have borne the title 'king's nurse', and who must have been involved in the upbringing of royal children, are not shown carrying out their duties.

Many of the high-ranking women in these tombs who accompany the owner are shown carrying a loop sistrum (fig. 22). Some bear the title 'Chantress' of a deity. This refers to their participation as music makers in temple ritual, but this part of their life is not usually depicted in the tombs. An exception is found in TT 75 in a scene which shows the tomb owner being

---

[2]N. de G. Davies, *The Tomb of Ken-Amun at Thebes* (New York, 1930), 2, pl. 9A.

[3]L. Manniche, *City of the Dead. Thebes in Egypt* (London, 1987), fig. 26.

installed as Second Priest of Amun.[4] He is depicted approaching the temple and being met by a procession of women carrying sistra. The leading figures are members of his family and bear the title "Chantress of Amun". Once again, however, the scene commemorates the office of the tomb owner and the women are there by virtue of their participation in his ceremony. By contrast, women are sometimes shown in subsidiary temple scenes taking part in religious ritual: women may appear alongside male priests (fig. 25), and female musicians and dancers perform in temple ceremonies (fig. 26).[5] Further, on private stelae[6] and votive cloths,[7] women may be shown directly before a deity, often Hathor, without the male intermediary found in the tombs. This may indicate that they had a more active part in private cult than the tomb scenes reveal, suggesting that such a role was regarded as irrelevant to the female image presented in the male world of the tomb owner.

On the whole, in the majority of tomb scenes women of the official classes have a fairly passive role and it is difficult to see from them how in reality they would have spent their time. One may speculate that, as in many other societies and in Egypt today, the female sphere of action lay not outside, as did the man's, but inside the house in domestic occupations. This is suggested by the contrast in the skin color given to the two sexes (fig. 23). Men are generally shown as a dark brownish red, which could be supposed to indicate a tan acquired from prolonged exposure to the sun. Women are much paler, usually a light yellowish brown, possibly as a sign that their lives were mostly spent sheltered from the sun inside the house. Although the artistic convention almost certainly represented an ideal situation rather than reality, it does suggest that it was considered desirable for women to have pale skins and men dark, and this no doubt related to what were perceived as the different types of activity appropriate to the two sexes.

Although Egyptian artists followed fairly strict conventions, they were also careful observers. For instance they were at pains to distinguish the bodily proportions found in men and women. The level of the small of the back is usually shown higher in a woman, and the buttocks are wider-

---

[4]N. de G. Davies, *The Tombs of Two Officials of Thutmosis the Fourth* (London, 1923), pl. 14.

[5]E.g. P. Lacau and H. Chevrier, *Une chapelle d'Hatshepsout à Karnak* (Cairo, 1977), figs. 18, 25-27, pls. 9, 18, 19.

[6]E.g. S. Bosticco, *Le stele egiziane del nuovo regno* (Rome, 1965), nos. 48, 63; J. Černý, *Egyptian Stelae in the Bankes Collection* (Oxford, 1958), nos. 6-7; S. Hodjash and O. Berlev, *The Egyptian Reliefs and Stelae in the Pushkin Museum of Fine Art, Moscow* (Leningrad, 1982), nos. 100-101; M. Tosi and A Roccati, *Stele e altre epigrafi di Deir el Medina* (Turin, 1972), nos. 50035, 50050, 50060.

[7]E.g. T.G.H. James, *Egyptian Painting* (London, 1985), fig. 82.

Figure 23

Tomb owner and his mother before a table of offerings, Theban tomb 45(Djhuty), author's photograph.

Figure 24

Tomb owner fishing and fowling in the marshes accompanied by his family. Theban tomb 52(Nakht), after Davies.

Figure 25

Male and female temple personnel on a block from Hatshepsut's *chapelle rouge* at Karnak, author's photograph.

Figure 26

Woman shaking sistra and female dancers on a block from Hatshepsut's *chapelle rouge* at Karnak, author's photograph.

spreading and more pronounced. The widths across the shoulders and small of the back are narrower, and the female form is also usually less muscled with more slender limbs than the male (fig. 22). All these differences relate to features found in nature. In a man and a woman of the same height, the woman's back is generally shorter and her legs longer because she has smaller vertebrae and therefore a shorter spinal column. This brings the top of the buttocks and so the small of the back to a higher level.

The contrast in art between the two sexes tells us something of their different images in Egyptian society. The man is the physically stronger figure, whom we see engaged in various outdoor sports like hunting, spearing fish, fowling and chariot driving. The woman is more slender and more elegant, never more than a passive observer of these activities, probably more at home indoors than outside. Nevertheless, there are no scenes in which the owner's wife or mother is shown engaged in domestic activities. In life, she may have supervised the running of the house, as her husband supervised the estate, but this does not form part of the repertory of tomb scenes. She may also have been much involved in the domestic cult, but this again is not recorded in tombs. Once again such matters seem to have been irrelevant to the male tomb owner, as the focal point of the tomb's decoration.

Overt sexual activity on the part of men and women is not shown in the tombs, nor on the whole are the peculiarly female preserves of pregnancy, childbirth and suckling, although all of these can be found elsewhere, for instance, on ostraca and probably in the decoration of private houses. In tomb decoration, however, there occur various symbols that may refer to fertility, the renewal of life, and rebirth, such as the lotus and the tilapia fish as found in the typical tomb scene where the male tomb owner is portrayed in a skiff in the marshes hunting birds but also spearing a pair of tilapia fish. He is accompanied by his wife and children (who may possibly be present to suggest fertility). Likewise the duck, which even adorns the prow of the skiff, has been taken to have erotic significance. In banquet scenes guests hold and wear lotuses and women are often shown playing with round fruit (fig. 27). Furthermore, although the guests do not appear to eat, the servants are shown pouring drinks for them (fig. 28). The Egyptian word *sti* "to pour" was similar in sound to the word meaning "to impregnate" and the pun is unlikely to have been overlooked by the Egyptians. In addition, the guests are often entertained by naked or partially clad female musicians and dancers who also enhance the erotic content of the scene. In other words, the typical tomb scenes involving the owner's own activities and those of his social peers may not be simply straightforward depictions of family outings and social life with friends, but may be replete with references to fertility, rebirth and renewal for the tomb owner.

In tombs, then, sexual activity, while not depicted openly, was perhaps subtly alluded to by a set of symbols. Nevertheless, the art of the New Kingdom and of the Eighteenth Dynasty in particular, does have a more frankly sensuous character than other periods. The image of a nearly naked adolescent girl, which surely must have sexual connotations, is common among maid servants (fig. 27) in tomb scenes. Outside the tomb, this image is sometimes used to decorate pots, bowls, and cosmetic items. Motifs associated with fertility and rebirth, such as the lotus and tilapia, and duck are also found on these objects. Also popular as a motif are lithe hunting dogs and gazelles, which probably connoted gracefulness, a quality the Egyptians valued in both men and women. There is always a delicacy and charm about the image of the girl; it is subtly suggestive and full of promise, but never coarse. By contrast, men and women are shown coupling quite explicitly in graffiti and sketches on ostraca, and also in the famous Turin Erotic Papyrus, which depicts the adventures of a man with a prostitute.[8]

In literature, the love poems of the New Kingdom center on the relationship between young lovers and are highly erotic. They contain both explicit references to sex and also, since the Egyptians delighted in puns and double entendre, oblique allusions,[9] many of which we miss today. Sexual intercourse is touched on quite openly, as for instance, when the girl in one poem says 'I found my brother in his bedroom, and my heart was exceedingly joyful',[10] and in another '...it began when I lay with you.'[11] However, the act itself is never described. The poets delight in the sensuous side of love, the smell of sweet scents, the blossom of flowers, the touch of fine linen and the beauty of the girl who is '...like Sothis rising at the beginning of a good year: shining, precious, white of skin, lovely of eyes when gazing...Long of neck, white of breast, her hair true lapis lazuli. Her arms surpass gold, her fingers are like lotuses'.[12] The reader can only be reminded of the less formal side of New Kingdom art: the delicate touch used in ornamental motifs, but not the crudity of the graffiti and the Turin Papyrus.

Problems arise, however, when we try to work out how far the poems reflect actuality, that is, the social mores of the time. The couples seem to be

---

[8]L. Manniche, "Some aspects of ancient Egyptian sexual life," *Acta Orientalia*, 38 (1977), 11-23; J. Omlin, *Der Papyrus 55001 und seine satirische-erotischen Zeichnungen und Inschriften* (Turin, 1973).

[9]B. S. Lesko, "True art in ancient Egypt," in *Egyptological Studies in Honour of Richard A. Parker*, ed. L.H. Lesko (Hanover, New Hampshire, 1986), 93.

[10]Fox, *op. cit.*, 23, no. 14.

[11]*Ibid.*, 26, no. 17.

[12]*Ibid.*, 52, no. 31.

Figure 27

Part of a banquet scene with woman holding lotuses and mandrake fruits, Theban tomb 52 (Nakht), after Davies.

Figure 28

Servant pouring a drink for a guest at a banquet, Theban tomb 100, after N. de G. Davies, *Paintings from the Tomb of Rekhmi-Re at Thebes,* (New York, 1935).

Figure 29

Agricultural scene showing men cutting grain with a woman gathering ears into a basket, and women pulling flax from the ground, Theban tomb 52 (Nakht), after Davies.

unmarried, and although future marriage is occasionally envisaged, it is not a prime concern of these poems. Did society turn a blind eye to sexual intercourse before marriage, or was this sort of behavior acceptable in poetry but not in reality for one's sisters and daughters? Love was clearly a pleasant concept to be enjoyed as entertainment, but did it play a part in the making of marriages or did this depend more on economic and social factors? Egypt would not be the only society to express concepts in literature which would not have been acceptable in everyday life.

On the whole, the written sources, penned by the official elite, give little information about the other classes in society, and much of our knowledge in this area comes from the scenes of everyday life in private tombs. These are, however, generalized and idealized, and with regard to the division of labor between men and women and the areas in which each might work, they no doubt recorded what was considered proper. It is problematic, of course, how far this corresponded with reality.

Scenes in tombs belonging to officials whose jobs included supervising the running of various royal and temple workshops show that the craftsmen are men; women are rarely, if ever, included in any capacity, making it clear that the ideal workshop was a distinctly male preserve. Other tomb scenes deal with activities on estates belonging to or administered by the tomb owner and show the different occupations of the peasants who provided the labor force. A common group of scenes shows the agricultural year: ploughing, sowing, hoeing, reaping, winnowing, threshing, counting, transporting and storing corn, and pulling and carrying flax. The majority of workers involved are men. During the grain harvest, women are often shown following the male reapers gathering fallen ears of grain into baskets, and sometimes women bring refreshment to the workers in the fields, but they are not depicted wielding a sickle for themselves. By contrast, they often take part in harvesting flax, which is not cut; instead the stems are pulled out of the ground (fig. 29).[13]

There are many other activities on the estate which are also shown as being almost exclusively carried out by men: for instance, netting fish in the canals and marshes, catching birds in clap nets, gathering papyrus, rope-making, building papyrus skiffs, and wine-making. I have so far found only one example which depicts a woman helping two men to pick the grapes.[14] Herds of cattle and other livestock, which were kept for meat, are shown in the care of male herdsmen. A frequent sub-scene in tombs shows the butchering

---

[13]E.g. J. J. Tylor and F. Ll. Griffith, *The Tomb of Paheri at El Kab* (London, 1894), pl. 3.

[14]*Ibid.*, pl. 4.

of these animals with knives; only men are involved. A number of tombs show the preparation of meat, fish and fowl, which after jointing or gutting with a knife were usually hung up to dry. The workers depicted are men, and women are not shown as having a part in this aspect of food preparation (fig. 30).

Scenes of cooking meat are rare in the New Kingdom, but in those few the cooks are men.[15] Such scenes were more common in Old and Middle Kingdom tombs and, as in our material, it was always men who were involved. The other major kitchen activities were baking and brewing, usually depicted side by side because beer was brewed from fermented loaves. Again, scenes showing these were common in the Old and Middle Kingdoms, and they sometimes still occur in the Eighteenth Dynasty. In the earlier periods these activities employed both men and women, and the two sexes are also found working side by side on our material.[16]

Guests in banquet scenes are usually entertained by musicians and dancers. The players depicted may be of either sex, and although the groups are more often of one sex only, they may be mixed (fig. 31). Both male and female servants wait on the guests. In the early part of the Eighteenth Dynasty, men may wait on women and women on men (fig. 32). Later, female servants tend only to wait on women (fig. 27) and males on men, suggesting a possible change in attitude in the area of acceptable male and female contact.

One activity in tomb decoration where women are very prominent, as in Egypt today, is in mourning the dead.[17] Groups of mourners are depicted in the procession taking the body to the tomb, and while male mourners do occur, women are far more frequent.

Clearly then, in the art at least, the roles of men and women of the non-official classes were often conceptualized differently. Women were not shown with a role in royal and temple workshops, nor did they play a major part in agricultural work, although here they seem to have accepted roles both in gathering the ears of grain into baskets as they were cut by the men and in participating with the men in the flax harvest. Women are not shown wielding sickles; flax is harvested, not by cutting it, but by pulling it from the ground. Other jobs involving the use of sharp blades also appear in the tomb scenes as the prerogative of men, so it is men who are shown butchering animals and also preparing meat, fowl and fish. In addition, the few scenes we have of

[15] E.g. J. Vandier, *Manuel d'archéologie égyptienne* (Paris, 1964), 4, pl. 8, fig. 103.

[16] T. Säve-Söderbergh, *Four Eighteenth Dynasty Tombs* (Oxford, 1957), pl. 22.

[17] M. Werbrouck, *Les pleureuses dans l'Égypte ancienne* (Brussels, 1938).

Figure 30

Men preparing fish and fowl for food, tomb of Paheri at el-Kab, author's photograph.

Figure 31

Group of male and female musicians from shrine 11 at Gebel es-Silsila, author's photograph.

Figure 32

Banquet with women waiting on men, tomb of Reneni at el-Kab, author's photograph.

cooking, as opposed to baking, show men performing the activity, and this is so also in Old and Middle Kingdom tombs. By contrast, both men and women are shown engaged in brewing and baking, as was true too in earlier times. Further, musicians and household servants waiting on guests at banquets may be male or female. Thus according to the representational evidence, men may work on the land, in workshops or in the house, while women have a smaller part to play on the land, are absent from workshops, but have a role in domestic duties. Despite a rare scene in TT 162 which shows a woman in charge of a market stall,[18] it is plain that in art, created by men for mainly male patrons, the sphere of activity for women was perceived as being much narrower than for men. It is necessary to stress, however, that these so-called scenes of everyday life on the whole represent activities on the large estates owned by high officials or managed by them on behalf of the king or the temples. In general they ignore, for instance, the small landholder struggling for a bare subsistence, commercial and industrial enterprise outside state and temple workshops, and domestic life in small village houses as opposed to the great houses of the elite. In other words, what we are shown has been carefully selected, and activities of daily life which do not relate directly to the image of the tomb owner as high official and land holder do not form part of the repertory of private tomb scenes.

I would like to conclude by returning to the image which the representational evidence gives of women of the official class. We have seen that both the tomb owner's wife and his mother are usually given a prominent position in the scenes connected with funerary ritual. They are shown seated by the owner's side to receive offerings or standing with him while he himself offers. Other members of the family, especially offspring, both male and female, often appear in these scenes and may actively join in the rites by offering to the tomb owner. The evidence shows that participation in these scenes of funerary ritual was not limited by sex. But in many of the other scenes where the owner is involved with activities relating to his office or the running of his estate, he more often appears alone, unaccompanied by the women of his family. I suggested that this was because the main sphere of male activities was held to lie out of doors and that of female activities indoors. Nevertheless, the prominence of these women in tomb decoration suggests that they occupied an honored and important position within the family.

This is of a piece with what we know of the legal and economic position of women from official documents. Like men, they could own and inherit property and dispose of it as they would, they could adopt heirs,

[18]N. Davies, *Scenes from Some Theban Tombs* (Oxford, 1963), pl. 15.

transact business deals and go to court as principals or witnesses all in their own right on a par with men, without any question of having to have a male guardian.[19]

It is also an attitude reflected in some of the literature. The honor in which a man should hold his mother is made clear in the Eighteenth Dynasty "Instruction of Any." "Double the food your mother gave you, support her as she supported you; she had a heavy load in you, but she did not abandon you. When you were born after your months, she was yet yoked to you, her breast in your mouth for three years. As you grew and your excrement disgusted, she was not disgusted, saying 'What shall I do!' When she sent you to school, and you were taught to write, she kept watching over you daily, with bread and beer in her house. When as a youth you take a wife, and you are settled in your house, pay attention to your offspring, bring him up as did your mother. Do not give her cause to blame you, lest she raise her hands to god, and he hears her cries."[20]

According to the author, the role of the wife is to have children, "Take a wife while you're young, that she may make a son for you."[21] The text also implies that she is in charge of running the house. "Do not control your wife in her house, when you know she is efficient; don't say to her: 'Where is it? Get it!' When she has put it in the right place. Let your eye observe in silence, that you may recognize her skill; it is a joy when your hand is with her, there are many who don't know this." This passage continues by advising the man not to quarrel with his wife, "If a man desists from strife at home, he will not encounter its beginning. Every man who founds a household should hold back the hasty heart." It ends with a final piece of advice concerning women, "Do not go after a woman, let her not steal your heart."[22]

This warning points toward a rather darker side of the male attitude to women found in the literature. The Instruction also advises, "Beware of a woman who is a stranger, one not known in her town; don't stare at her when she goes by, do not know her carnally. A deep water whose course is unknown, such is a woman away from her husband. 'I am pretty,' she tells you daily, when she has no witnesses; she is ready to ensnare you, a great deadly crime when it is heard."[23] It is plain that men feared the wiles of

---

19S. Allam, *Some pages from everyday life in ancient Egypt* (Giza, Egypt, 1985), 9-54.

20Lichtheim, *op. cit.*, 141.

21*Ibid.*, 136.

22*Ibid.*, 143.

23*Ibid.*, 137.

predatory women, a side of the relationship between the sexes that is not apparent in the art.

This negative image is also very prominent in the two narrative tales, "The Two Brothers" and "Truth and Falsehood". The first begins with the attempt of Anubis' wife to seduce her husband's younger brother Bata. Then Bata's young wife betrays her husband time after time until she is outmaneuvered and finally gets her just deserts. In the second, the woman who rescued Truth after he had been blinded was censured by her son for the way in which she had callously treated Truth; she had made him her door-keeper rather than treating him honorably, once she had sated her lust for him.

The presence of this darker image of women in literature but not in art is easily explained. The wisdom texts give practical counsel for the male individual's conduct in society which includes the advice to treat honorable women honorably but to beware the wiles of others. It has been suggested by L. H. Lesko that the narrative stories may have had a propaganda purpose on behalf of the Nineteenth Dynasty against the powerful royal women of the Eighteenth Dynasty.[24] In formal tomb art, however, the purpose is to record the ideal. There was no place here for unfaithful, unsatisfactory women. Only the image of the devoted wife and mother attendant on their menfolk is suitable.

To sum up, the various images of women presented by the art of the New Kingdom are incomplete and to some extent distorted because they represent the viewpoints and ideals of the men who commissioned the monuments. Artists were not asked to show women, either of the official class or from other social strata, carrying out their daily routine within the household, although evidence from the "Instructions of Any" and indeed the ubiquitous female title *nbt pr* "mistress of the house" indicate that the woman's place was within the home. The small number of women compared to men who appear in the scenes of "everyday life" set out of doors surely reflects an idealized view of life on the great estates of ancient Egypt. Village life and the daily round of the peasant women, who made up the majority of the female population, are ignored, but it is quite probable that in poorer families women helped the men in the fields and did other outdoor work. On this point, for instance, one can contrast the impression given by the tomb art that trapping birds is a male occupation with one of the poems from Papyrus

---

[24] L. H. Lesko, "Three Late Egyptian Stories Reconsidered," in *Egyptological Studies... Parker*, 98-103.

Harris 500 where it is clearly a girl who traps birds.[25] It is, therefore, important to understand why and for whom particular types of material were created before drawing on them as evidence. Little from ancient Egypt can be taken at face value, and the dominance of men in the creation of monuments and the writing of texts means that artistic and literary evidence concerning women needs extreme care in its interpretation.

---

[25]Pap. Harris 500, Group B: No. 10. Fox, *op. cit.*, p. 19. I would like to thank B. S. Lesko for this reference and for her original idea to hold a conference on "Women in the Ancient Near East."

Responses to Dr. Robins' Paper

B. Lesko: I am becoming increasingly skeptical about the usefulness of the Eighteenth Dynasty tomb paintings as a source reflecting actual life conditions. Any corpus that says women never cooked, any corpus that gives more importance to furniture manufacturing than to the second largest industry in Egypt, the linen-weaving industry, (which I certainly do not believe was only a cottage industry)--I would say that we have to look very skeptically at the source material of the Eighteenth Dynasty tomb-paintings and I think Dr. Robins suggests this when she stresses their religious and magical intention.

Galvin: Dr. Robins, you used the expression two dimensional art to qualify one of your first slides that showed a man apparently followed by a female. The slide that immediately followed showed a male and a female seated on a bench, the female's legs were on our side, the front side of the bench. This slide was very similar to one that Dr. Fischer showed us. In that instance the woman's legs were on the far side of the bench. Now in fact if these couples are seated on a bench it is absolutely necessary that they were beside one another; it is only the artist's rendition that makes it seem as if one is in front of the other. I think your comment on two dimensional art is the key here; that it is the peculiarities of Egyptian perspective in two dimensional art that makes us see the one behind the other. Now I am wondering if this in fact is true, if when we see two individuals standing, presumably male in front, female in back, what we actually are seeing is the Egyptians' peculiar perspective, and should it not in fact be interpreted as individuals side by side? This is reinforced in a slide at the end of your presentation where you showed women participating in a harvest scene; you suggested that the woman was standing behind the male. Again, I would suggest perhaps what we are meant to see is a woman either beside the other male reaper or perhaps they are standing randomly about in the field. It is only the peculiarity of two-dimensional art that makes us perceive them as in a row or in a register.

Robins: Yes, with the standing and seated couples you're quite right, that they are to be seen side by side, and we know this from statuary, and also from statuary we know that the man normally stands or sits to the right of the woman, which is the more prestigious side. And this is translated in two dimensions by putting the man in the more prestigious position of the front, in front of the woman.

Galvin: More prestigious in the New Kingdom. Certainly in the slide that Dr. Fischer showed us it was clear by the position of the woman's legs that she is seated beside her husband. Therefore prestige is not determined by placement of one individual in front of the other.

Robins: If you are now talking about the overlapping to show that when you have a right-facing group you wish to show that the woman is on the man's left by overlapping the man's buttocks. For some reason this is very seldom done by the New Kingdom, there are examples in tombs but it is rare, but statuary on the whole continues to place the man on the right and the woman on the left.

Galvin: I have found in a cursory search over one dozen New Kingdom examples where the woman is shown seated with her knees overlapping her husband.

B. Lesko: Further, we should remember that the wall scenes were not the only representations of women in the tomb. Life-sized and often over-life-sized statues, sometimes free standing and sometimes hewn into the rock walls of the tomb, depict the owner and his wife in equal stature seated side by side.

Fischer: There is one point worth making and that is that in the New Kingdom sculptures the man and woman frequently cross their arms behind one another. To have such interaction and embrace in the Old Kingdom is extremely rare, so there are some changes.

Galvin: Are these standing representations in the New Kingdom?

Fischer: These are usually seated figures with the arms interlaced behind.

Robins: I've been thinking recently that costume, as shown in the art, actually has a lot to tell us. Male costume is far freer, suiting the image of the man striding out on his official duties, whereas the sheath dress is so restrictive, it suggests that the wearer would have little freedom of action to do much. This could well be specifically an artistic image as surviving clothes and those given in laundry lists often seem to be different from those represented in the art (e.g. the common use of long sleeves as published by Hall). Indeed, a woman could hardly move in the body-hugging sheath dress depicted by artists unless it was elasticized! She certainly couldn't kneel with one leg raised as so often is shown in the art. This way of depicting female dress seems to me to be a device by which the artist can show the shape of the body, including the erotic zones of stomach, buttock and thigh with its hint of the pubic area. One breast, due to artistic conventions, is also prominent and usually half-uncovered if not completely naked, whereas, in reality, the straps or bodice of the dress would cover the breasts. With the change in costume dating from the mid-Eighteenth Dynasty onwards, whereby female dress becomes looser and more elaborate, it is interesting that the full outline of the female body is still shown under the dress. While not expecting them to wear petticoats, the transparency of the garment is surely exaggerated and seems to be shown to a greater degree on women than men.

Fischer: So we have lots of clues and there are a few cases where we can specify the interpretation. I'd like to comment in relation to New Kingdom art that there are a couple of developments that are interesting in relation to earlier periods and that is in weaving men are now involved much more than before. They were not involved at all in the Old Kingdom, it was strictly a woman's job, so there is an assumption that it was a house of women who did the weaving. Now in the New Kingdom that situation has changed, also winnowing, women still do winnowing, but now, certainly as early as the beginning of the New Kingdom men also do winnowing along with the women. It is really curious. As for flax, the harvesting of flax, I would relate that, as I suggested in my talk, it was an interest of women because flax was the material raised for linen and used by women. In terms of the physical activity involved in harvesting flax, actually pulling up flax is a tougher job than cutting grain. It is an extremely arduous job.

E. Stone: My question is addressed to anyone who wants to answer it. Dr. Robins talked about the tomb paintings as really representing the "ideal" state of the world. If that is the case then can we really use tomb paintings to show males as exclusively acting in agriculture as representing reality? To a large extent at least in many cases I think that people will say "well, men should work in the fields," but when harvest time comes in the modern Middle East, everybody is working in the fields, the women alongside the men. The other aspect that I would perhaps suggest would be that a well-run estate would be one in which the men would be able to take care of everything whereas one that is not so well-run, therefore less ideal, wouldn't.

Robins: That's right. What happens to a peasant who happpens to own a small plot of land and is trying to make a living for himself and his family. If he couldn't pay the taxes, he got beaten up by the authorities. Reality could be very nasty. And obviously when you get back to that level I suspect that there was much less difference between men and women. You call on whatever labor you have, you do whatever needs to be done. The scenes show men doing washing, doing laundry, but again is this a professional laundry service? I mean today women go down to the river.

Fischer: Right. Doing the laundry in antiquity is rather arduous because you have to beat the laundry. Of course it's done today by women. Women do go to the river and beat clothing where they don't necessarily have detergents. But it is a very vigorous job, and you wonder, how much work the male launderers gave the women weavers. It must have been prodigious, because they obviously wore the clothing tremendously by beating it. Another thing that interests me was your comment on color. The fact is that children are also depicted, even the very young, just as women are, and so are old men. When men become portly then presumably they are scribes working indoors and they too then are yellow just as women are.

Stone: Just in terms of following what I was asking, what I was suggesting was that even on the big estates, it is only in an ideal situation that you can insure that only men are doing this. In fact, in the big estates you might have had the women being dragged out to the harvest just by necessity.

Nugent: As far as the skin color being gender related of course that's true in Minoan wall paintings, you get precisely the same kind of picture where the men are more or less the shade they are in the Egyptian materials and women are absolutely chalk-white, and the interpretation is the same sort of interpretation, the ideal would be that the woman is interiorized. My question is I am a great skeptic, at least in classical texts, of reading artistic, whether literary arts or visual arts, as social evidence and I was especially curious about your suggestion that perhaps some of the wall paintings might involve discrete, and I would say more or less allegorical, erotic allusions. I thought that was intriguing but it also strikes me that if that were the case in this particular area that might well lead over to being the case much more broadly, i.e., that what is being represented might often be--I don't know enough about Egyptian material-- but it seems to me to open the possibility that it might often have something rather more allegorical in the ideological sense than the picture represents.

Robins: That's quite true. But there are a lot of people, I think who would object to the interpretation of the marsh scene and the banqueting scene. So even though you can go so far, you start seeing things and you have no evidence of whether you are correct or not.

Zagarell: Let me suggest some other areas where an exchange with, or a working knowledge of the results of work by scholars in other disciplines would strengthen the papers just presented. The position of women as represented in male elite tomb art might be interpreted differently if one gave some consideration to the concept of discourse, as represented in the works of Foucault or gave some consideration to the Frankfurt school (for example, Bottomore). In the last paper attention was given only to one of what are really several interconnected levels of "reality," the conscious or unconscious ideological statements represented in the paintings. The context of the representation is at least as important as the representation itself. For example, if we were to look at the world through the eyes of the relatively recent Near Eastern elite males, women would have been represented in one way, that is, confined to the house. But they are often working in the fields. While high status women were supposedly to be protected, kept in the home, rural and non-elite women had a very different experience. I'm not sure we are getting the total picture, since in reality almost all the views we get are those of the male elite, looking at women. Women are not representing themselves to us. Therefore, we must recognize that these are constructions of women's lives rather than descriptions of the actual conditions of those lives.

Women as Owners of Immovables in Pharaonic Egypt

Schafik Allam

In order to assess the legal position of women we have no other choice than to resort to the documentation available describing the practice of law, such as private records and official documents. It remains to derive law-in-action from the documents themselves. In so doing we shall encounter facts bearing on the daily affairs of the people. In the present paper we shall deliberately disregard the position of women of the monarch's family.[1]

As for our sources in general, we have documents dating back as far as the Old Kingdom (2640-2155 B.C.). It is true that the information we can draw from them is quite meager. But they provide us with valuable inklings that women were indeed holders of rights in immovables at a very early stage in our history. During the course of time, however, our sources become more and more instructive. Consequently, further light is shed then upon the picture of women. Yet, I shall deal only with texts in hieroglyphic or hieratic writing, leaving out the rich documentation in demotic for separate consideration.[2]

We begin with the sources from the Old Kingdom. One of them, dating from the Fifth Dynasty (around 2465-2325), contains stipulations of a man from Giza, Tjenti by name, for the maintenance of his household.[3] According to the concept of the time, members of a well-off household should be provided for, not only on earth, but also beyond death (*prt-ḫrw*-service), as a deceased person needed to be looked after by bringing offerings to his tomb

[1] The Adoption Stela allows us a glimpse of the real estate of Princess Nitocris, daughter of King Psammetichus I (664-610 B.C.): R. Caminos, "The Nitocris Adoption Stela," *JEA* 50 (1964): 100. As for the so-called harem of a king, see E. Reiser, *Der königliche Harim im alten Ägypten und seine Verwaltung* (Wien, 1972), 48ff.

[2] S. Allam, "Women as Holders of Rights (during the Egyptian Late Period)," in *JESHO*, forthcoming.

[3] *Urkunden* 1, 163f.; H. Goedicke, *Die privaten Rechtsinschriften aus dem Alten Reich* (Wien, 1970), 122f.; I. Harari, "La fondation Cultuelle de N.k.wi.Ankh à Tehneh," *ASAE* 54 (1957): 335f.

and performing other religious rites. In this respect Tjenti mentions two equal plots (1 *st3t*: aroura=2756.5 m2) of land formerly belonging to his mother. One aroura is now given to his wife, whilst four servants (*ḥm-k3*)[4] are assigned to her and named as usufructuaries. Likewise, the other aroura goes to his brother.[5] In return, both his wife and his brother have to maintain the *prt-ḫrw*-service and, consequently, care for him and his mother. It is to be noticed that Tjenti stresses in this connection a favor bestowed upon him by the king.

The second text informs us that King Menkaure (Mycerinus: around 2490-2471) of the Fourth Dynasty created an endowment consisting of two plots (arouras) of land to help maintain the cult of the goddess Hathor at Tehne in Middle Egypt.[6] Many years later, King Userkaf (around 2465-2458), who began the Fifth Dynasty, reaffirmed the endowment, with the two plots being then in the hands of the local chief priest, one Niankhka. This man now disposes of the land for the benefit of his wife and sons as well as other persons, on the condition that they all should continue upon his death the required services in the temple. In addition to that, they all should care for the dead of the family of one Khenuka, who presumably was their ancestor.[7] It is remarkable that the woman mentioned obtained as much usufruct as any male beneficiary; in fact she had to carry out her obligations during one month a year, as every son had to do.

Besides, a biographical inscription from Saqqara, dating back to the end of the Third Dynasty (around 2570 B.C.) gives us amongst other things details about the possessions of a certain dignitary called Metjen.[8] Although

---

[4]Our documentation, texts as well as representations, reveals positively that such persons were engaged in a given household to perform special services for their master during his lifetime. After their master's death, they had to pursue their functions in the same household; in addition, they had to carry out religious and funeral rites for the deceased. See my investigation: "Le *ḥm-k3*, était-il exclusivement prêtre funéraire?" *RdE* 36 (1985): 1ff.

[5]For the pure and simple interpretation of *sn-ḏt* as "own" brother (literally: brother of the body, i.e., of the body of the person in question), see J. Perepelkin, *Privateigentum in der Vorstellung der Ägypter des Alten Reiches*, trans. R. Müller-Wollermann, (Tübingen, 1986), 35ff.

[6]*Urkunden* 1, 24ff.; Goedicke, *Rechtsinschriften*, 131ff.; T. Mrsich, *Untersuchungen zur Hausurkunde des Alten Reiches--Ein Beitrag zum altägyptischen Stiftungsrecht*, (Berlin, 1968), 70ff.

[7]The mortuary services for Niankhka are thus alluded to, as he himself was one of the Khenuka's family.

[8]*Urkunden* 1, 2, 9ff.; Goedicke, *Rechtsinschriften*, 17; K. Gödecken, *Eine Betrachtung der Inschriften des Meten im Rahmen der sozialen und rechtlichen Stellung von Privatleuten im ägyptischen Alten Reich* (Wiesbaden, 1976), 11; cf. I. Harari and B. Menu, "La notion de propriété privée dans l'Ancien Empire Egyptien," *CRIPEL* 2 (1974): 131.

scholars are strongly divided on the interpretation of some passages of the text, we can rightly take for granted that Metjen's mother had once possessed fifty arouras of land. Accordingly she could convey them to her children. That happened by means of an instrument specified as "house-document" (*i͗mi͗t-pr*).[9] The conveyance was thereupon declared to some offices. This information is of major significance, as it reveals beyond all doubt a woman with rights in immovables at the dawn of Egyptian civilization, before the era of the great pyramids.

Unlike the preceding texts which were recorded in private tombs, one papyrus written in hieratic came down to us with the bulk from the Middle Kingdom excavated at Illahun. It was found in perfect condition, vertically folded and sealed with the impression of a scarab of scroll pattern. Its text embraces two distinct sections relating to ownership.[10] According to the first, which was written down in regnal year forty-four (evidently of Amenemhet III: 1844-1797 B.C.) a Superintendent of Works, one Ankhren, gave by means of a house-document (*i͗mi͗t-pr*) all his "property (*i͗ḫt*=things) in country and in town" to his brother. Some years later this brother made in turn a house-document conveying all the property (*i͗ḫt*) in question to his wife. Since the term *i͗ḫt* connotes a general sense for property,[11] one might hesitate about whether the property mentioned included immovables as well. Yet, the brother goes on in his deed and says explicitly, "as to the dwellings (*ᶜw.t*) that Ankhren...built for me, my wife shall be therein, without allowing her to be put (forth) thence on the ground by any person."

Another interesting inscription has come to light in Edfu on a small crude stela, which possibly dates to the Seventeenth Dynasty (roughly 1650-1551). It belongs to an ordinary soldier who had spent six years on military service in Nubia.[12] In a passage of the inscription he says, "I acquired land of

[9]This is a type of document to which one used to resort when possessions of importance were to be conveyed; cf. E. Seidl, *Einführung in die ägyptische Rechtsgeschichte bis zum Ende des Neuen Reiches*, 3rd edition (Glückstadt, 1957), 22, 47 and 58.

[10]P. Kahun 1,1: F. Ll. Griffith, *Hieratic Papyri from Kahun and Gurob--Principally of the Middle Kingdom* (London, 1897-98), 31ff., pl. 12; A. Théodoridès, "La vente à credit du Pap.Kahoun I,2 et ses conséquences," *RIDA* 8 (1961): 43ff.

[11]For some examples of this term dating from the Ramesside period see Théodoridès, "Le testament dans l'Egypte ancienne," *RIDA* 17 (1970): 199, n. 320. Allam, *HOPR* (Tübingen, 1973), 339.

[12]Cairo Stele, Journal d'entrée 52456: B. Gunn, "A Middle Kingdom Stela from Edfu," *ASAE* 29 (1929): 5ff. For a recent study of the pertinent portion of the text see P. Vernus, "Allusion au partage des acquêts dans une autobiographie de la deuxième période intermédiaire," *DE* 6 (1986), 79ff. W. A. Ward, "Some Aspects of Private Land Ownership and Inheritance in Ancient Egypt

two (square) cubits, one (cubit) is for (my wife) Hormini as her property (*iḫt*=things), the other (cubit) in her (possession) is mine; I (also) acquired one cubit of land to be given to (my) children." This relevant inscription discloses people of apparently lower social status, they are dealing here with exceedingly small plots of ground, the cubit (*mḥ*) as a land measure being around 27.50 square meters. It is remarkable, furthermore, that the woman got from her husband as much land as the children.

We embark now on the rich documentation which encompasses particularly the Ramesside Period (1306-1070 B.C.), supplementing it with a few records from the beginning of the first millennium. It is mostly written in hieratic script, thus closely related to everyday life. The first document is a papyrus emanating from the ancient town Spermeru in Middle Egypt. Its exceptionally important record unfolds that in Egypt the legal fiction of adoption could be carried to extremes.[13] In the year 1099 B.C., a stable-master, having no children, adopted his wife before witnesses so that his entire property might pass to her, despite the fact that he had a sister as well; subsequently the property involved could be disposed of henceforth in accordance with the desires of his wife. Seventeen years later the stable-master, still childless, purchased a slave girl who gave birth to one son and two daughters of her own. Years passed, and the wife, now widowed, felt old age creeping upon her. Not having children, she resolved in her turn to make a will. She emancipated the slave girl's children, one of whom is married by that time to her brother. Furthermore, she adopted her brother and the slave children as well, and stated that all four adopted persons would share as her heirs any of her "property (*iḫt*=things) in the world" including "fields in the country" (*3ḥt m sḫt*).

We direct our attention to two other records, both written on ostraca and thus relating to still lower strata of Egyptian society. The first, which represents a letter, indicates that a woman offered her partner a plot of ground (*3ḥt*) located in Hermonthis (Armant) as payment for a female donkey.[14] The other ostracon records a session of the local law-court in the community of workmen at Deir-el-Medineh in Thebes.[15] In the course of the session it is reported that a woman who wanted to bury her deceased husband wished to obtain a coffin from a man in exchange for a dwelling (*ʿt*) which had belonged

ca.2500-1000 B.C.," in *Land Tenure and Social Transformation in the Middle East*, edited by Tarif Khalidi (Beirut, 1984), 70ff.

13P. Ashmolean Museum 1945.96: A. H. Gardiner, "Adoption Extraordinary," *JEA* 26 (1940): 23ff.; Théodoridès, "Le Papyrus des Adoptions," *RIDA* 12 (1965): 79ff; Allam, *HOPR*, 258 ff.

14O. Gardiner 165: Allam, *HOPR*, 184.

15O. Deir-el-Medineh 225: Allam, *HOPR*, 106.

to her husband. It emerges from such cases that women, desiring to extinguish claims of their partners, would dispose of their own rights in immovables.

The state of affairs demonstrated above is corroborated also by a fragment from a papyrus which originally served as a journal for the community of workmen at Deir-el-Medineh.[16] Its subject matter is a division of the immovables (*swt*)[17] of a man who had presumably passed away. Side by side there were two sons of his and two women, a mother with her daughter, upon whom all the succession to the immovables devolved. We are told first that one woman was apportioned a dwelling (*ᶜt*) next to the temple of Queen Ahmose-Nefertari, while her daughter was assigned the pyramid of a tomb (*mr ntỉ m t3 ᶜḥᶜ.t*). As to the two sons one got likewise a pyramid (*mr*), while the other was given amongst other things a building (*št3yt*)[18] next to a tomb. After the apportionment every beneficiary had to take an oath assuring that she or he would not contest in the future the rights devolved upon the others.

Another papyrus from the community of workmen informs us of a similar case.[19] There is a man who himself undertakes the division of his immovables (*swt*=places) among five sons and one daughter, whilst his immovables are described by their measures. Accordingly some buildings and grounds as well as a pyramid go to his sons; as far as his daughter is concerned, she has to share a certain dwelling (*ᶜt*) with one of her brothers.[20]

---

[16]P. Turin 2070 verso, col. 2: M. Muszynski, "P. Turin Cat. 2070/154," *Oriens Antiquus* 16 (1977): 183ff.; Allam, *HOPR*, 327f.

[17]This specific term, which literally means "places" is attested in many texts. It can be used in singular or plural form; for some examples see J. J. Janssen and P.W. Pestman, "Burial and Inheritance in the Community of the Necropolis Workmen at Thebes," *JESHO* 11 (1968): 158; Théodoridès, "Le 'testament' de Naunakhte," *RIDA* 13 (1966): 42, n. 46; Allam, *HOPR*, 340.

[18]For a discussion of this word, see Janssen and Pestman, "Burial and Inheritance," 162; M. Megally, *Recherches sur l'économie, l'administration et la comptabilité égyptiennes à la XVIIIe dynastie d'après le papyrus E. 3226 du Louvre* (Le Caire, 1977), 39ff. For a "tomb or part of a tomb," cf. O. UC London 31922: V. Raisman, "UC 31922", *Wepwawet-Papers in Egyptology* 1 (1985): 1.

[19]P. Cairo 58092 (P. Boulaq 10) verso: Janssen and Pestman, "Burial and Inheritance" 137ff.; Allam, *HOPR*, 290ff.

[20]The term indicating both shares is *dnỉt* (for some examples see Théodoridès, *RIDA* 17 (1970), 191, n. 291; Allam, *HOPR*, 340) which would be frequently used in demotic texts. Note furthermore that rights in immovables could be nominally divided into shares as early as the Ramesside period without a real division of the immovables in question. Such shares (*pro parte indivisa*) are quite familiar in demotic documents.

Upon the division all the beneficiaries have to promise not to contest in the future one another's rights.[21]

On the recto of the same papyrus we have a different text bearing on a dispute over the inheritance of a lady who was buried by one son without the assistance of her other children. This son claims subsequently the whole inheritance for himself. In order to substantiate his claim, he puts forward a legal rule set up by the king as well as a precedent, that previously occurred in the community. Owing to this precedent, the immovables (*st*=place, here in singular form) of a woman went to a man who cared for her after her death. This particular precedent is advanced again in another dispute regarding the succession of another lady.[22] Upon her death this lady was looked after by a workman to whom went then her share (*pš*) in a store-room (*wḏ3t*). Now her daughter claims this share to be her own. From the foregoing we can reasonably deduce that women's rights in immovables could be passed on to other persons, male or female, by way of inheritance.

The evidence forthcoming thus far can be reinforced by some facts mentioned in the great Wilbour Papyrus from the reign of Ramesses V (around 1145 B.C.). This vast document (over ten meters in length) with its immense bulk of information in different directions represents a unique record of holdings of land. It is a cadastral survey made by the Egyptian administration with the measurement and assessment of fields in Middle Egypt. One of its main interests lies in the proof it brings of the coexistence of temples, crown and small-holders, of their closely interwoven obligations, and of the control exercised over all of them by one supreme assessing and fiscal authority that must in theory have received its mandate from the crown. For our purposes it suffices to say that besides land-owning institutions (such as temples) there is a large number of small-holders of land (such as stable-masters, soldiers, priests, herdsmen, scribes, and farmers). Their position either was, or else

---

21In the last two papyri the beneficiaries had to renounce mutually any claim to one another's share. This was essential in many transfers of property; see my remarks "Bermerkungen zur Abstandsschrift," *Enchoria* 13 (1985): 1ff. Nevertheless, we are told of a similar situation through O. Louvre E 2425 (O. Anastasi): Allam, *HOPR*, 202ff. where three buildings (two *wḏ3* and one *št3t*) were divided into shares (*pš*) among two men and four women, whilst each building was given to two of them; presumably we are concerned here with the division of their parent's property. Although the text does not specify that they promised to respect one another's rights, we are inclined to suppose that they actually did so.

22O. Petrie 16: Janssen and Pestman, "Burial and Inheritance," 153ff.; Théodoridès, "A propos de la loi dans l'Égypte pharaonique," *RIDA* 14 (1967): 111ff. and "Les ouvriers-magistrats en Égypte à l'époque ramesside (XIXe-XXe dyn.)," *RIDA* 16 (1969): 141ff.; Allam, *HOPR*, 232ff. Yet, in the aforesaid precedent the word *ḫrt* is alternatively used instead of *st*.

resembled, that of private owners, since various scraps of evidence point to the fact that their holdings were, or at all events might be, hereditary. There are among them no less than one hundred and thirty-one female holders mentioned; like the men their holdings vary mostly between three and five arouras.[23] Like men farming land on behalf of someone else, two ladies are reported in our survey to be tilling plots for two scribes. Other entries name either a man or a woman holding a plot, together with his or her brethren (*ḥnᶜ snw=f/s*). This suggests an estate divided among several children after the parent's death. In a few cases a woman holding land is declared to be dead, with her plot being in the hands of her children (*m-ḏrt msw=s*); similar cases are common, of course, with men. We have then presumptive evidence of the continuance of the property in the same family for at least three generations. All this points then to the fact that a woman's field could be inherited, as men's plots were.[24]

The female capacity to own immovables prevailed also among Egyptians resident far away in the south. This is displayed by a stela found at Amarah (between the second and third cataracts of the Nile); it dates in all probability to the end of the Ramesside Period.[25] In the main the text deals with a lady who was a singer of the god Khnum. Presumably after her father had departed, she has conveyed to her by her mother all the acquisitions (*sẖprw*) of her father, which devolved first upon her mother; in return she has to support her mother in her old age. Moreover, her brother assigns her all possessions of their deceased father, consisting of "fields in the country (*3ḥt m sẖt*), male and female slaves as well as trees." She will obtain these things, as her brother puts it, "for the son of her son and the heir of her heir."

As we are passing in review miscellaneous texts, one more ostracon from the community of workmen at Deir-el-Medineh deserves to be mentioned in our context. In a lapidary style we are told there that a lady held in her possession various kinds of buildings at one and the same time: a store-room

---

23A. H. Gardiner, *The Wilbour Papyrus* (Oxford, 1948) 2, 75ff.; cf. B. Menu, *Le régime juridique des terres et du personnel attaché à la terre dans le papyrus Wilbour* (Lille, 1970), 112 and 124ff.

24Such individuals are placed on exactly the same footing as the land-owning institutions where complete ownership seems obvious. Yet, the question arises as to the relation of these small holders to the land-owning institution mentioned in the heading of their lists; Gardiner, *Wilbour Papyrus*, 105; cf. W. Helck, *Materialien zur Wirtschaftsgeschichte des Neuen Reiches* (Wiesbaden, 1961-69), 2, 237. Our holders might have been then tenants for life with their holdings being nevertheless inheritable but not divisible (cf. *ager vectigalis* in Rome).

25Helck, *Materialien*, 2, 239; Théodoridès, "La stèle juridique d'Amarah," *RIDA* 11 (1964): 45ff.; for a photograph of the stela see H.W. Fairman, "Preliminary Report on the Excavations at Sesebi (Sudla) and Amarah West," *JEA* 24 (1938), pl. 11,3.

(*wḏ3*) of Osiris, another store-room (*wḏ3*) at the temple of Ptah, a dwelling (*ʿt*) at the temple of Amun-Re, again a store-room next to the tomb of a certain man, a small [shrine (*ḥb*)] next to---as well as a pyramid (*mr*) upon the tomb of another man.[26]

Our next task is to investigate the question whether women's titles to immovables were also recognized by common law. We set out to glean information from a papyrus written in the Ramesside period with a *procès-verbal* of a trial before a law-court at Thebes. There, a soldier accused a lady, Erenofre, of having wrongfully used property belonging to another lady, Bekmut, in order to purchase for herself two slaves from two different merchants.[27] During the hearing the judges asked the soldier amongst other things to produce before them witnesses to a tomb (*ʿḥʿ.t*) which he said was in the possession of the *citoyenne* Bekmut and the *citoyenne* Erenofre gave it to one merchant, who then gave to her a man-slave in exchange for it. This context implies clearly that women could likewise acquire tombs and alienate them, as they well pleased.

The next document is again an ostracon from the community of workmen at Deir-el-Medineh. Its contents are absolutely authentic in so far as they recur in two separate records.[28] Its subject matter is legal proceedings which took place in the twelfth century B.C. about the ownership of a burial place. The man who claims the place brings forward that it had been assigned by the local authorities to one of his ancestors, Hay by name, at the time of king Haremhab over one hundred and fifty years ago. Since Hay had no son, the title to the place devolved then upon his daughter, one Hener. Consequently, the title of this lady should go afterwards to one of her descendants. This is just what is now claimed by the man before the law-court.

Dealings with regard to the property of a lady called Naunakhte, who was twice married, are recorded in several papyri. We are in this instance concerned with her last will in the form of an oral deposition which she made in 1144 B.C. before the local court at Deir-el-Medineh; it was subsequently

26O. DeM 586: Allam, *HOPR*, 139f.

27P. Cairo 65739: Gardiner, "A Lawsuit Arising from the Purchase of Two Slaves," *JEA* 21 (1935): 140ff.

28O. British Museum 5624: A. M. Blackman, "Oracles in Ancient Egypt," *JEA* 12 (1926): 176f.; Allam, *HOPR*, 43ff. The two other documents are O. Florence 2621 and P. Berlin 10496: Allam, *HOPR*, 148 and 277.

written down by a professional scribe.[29] There, Naunakhte disinherits some of her children, whom she bore to her second husband, from her own property, amongst other things, from a store-room (*wḏ3*) which apparently had earlier devolved on her from her father. Naunakhte further stresses that these children are also to be excluded from the division of any property of her first husband, including immovables (*swt*=places). Since her first husband is totally absent from the documents we possess from the time, we may safely assume that he was already dead and that Naunakhte has consequently obtained some rights over his property.[30]

Besides, many a record in our documentation explicitly states an order of the court concerning a given litigation about the titles of a woman to immovables. In the community of workmen at Deir-el-Medineh we have already met with a lady who was cared for upon her death by one of her sons without the help of his brothers and sisters. Therefore this son initiates a claim to her property against his brothers and sisters. In so doing he advances a legal ordinance set up by the king as well as a precedent that happened before in the community. There was a man who likewise undertook the burial of his mother. Thereupon he was assigned her immovables (*st*=place, here in singular form) by the law-court. Incidentally, this court was presided over not only by the local dignitaries but also by a god, namely the deceased, deified King Amenhotep I.[31]

Another law-suit is known to us through an ostracon found in Deir-el-Medineh. Here we are informed of a lady who, while bringing an action against three workmen, sought to be assigned the immovables (*swt*=places) of her husband.[32] Thereupon the judges pronounced on deliberation the decision, "the lady is in the right." We are told furthermore that she was indeed given the immovables in dispute. It is true that we are ignorant of all the details which gave rise to the litigation; nor can we determine the exact title of the woman in this case. Yet, it is sufficient for our purposes to state that the woman was given the immovables by law.

---

[29] P. Ashmolean Museum 1945.97: Jaroslav Černý, "The Will of Naunakhte and the Related Documents," *JEA* 31 (1945): 29ff.; Erwin Seidl, "Vom Erbrecht der alten Ägypter," *ZDMG* 107 (1957): 274ff.; Théodoridès, *RIDA* 13 (1966): 31ff.; Allam, *HOPR*, 268ff.

[30] Cerny, "The Will of Naunakhte," 44 and 49.

[31] P. Cairo 58092 recto: *vide supra*, n. 19. Cf. Théodoridès, *RIDA* 14 (1967): 114ff. and *RIDA* 16 (1969): 144ff.

[32] O. DeM 235: Helck, Materialien, 3, 344; Théodoridès, *RIDA* 16 (1969): 172ff.; Allam, *HOPR*, 109.

Two other documents have come down to us at other places. The first is preserved on the walls of a tomb at Saqqara. It introduces one Mose who lived in the Ramesside period.[33] Mose gives us a vivid account of a whole series of law-suits that dragged on for around half a century concerning private land-holdings of a considerable size. The story began when King Ahmose I (sixteenth century B.C.) conferred a tract of land upon a forefather of Mose, a ship's captain, as reward for his services. After the death of this captain his estate passed on as a whole to numerous heirs who continued to have indivisible shares (*communio pro indiviso*). In the time of King Haremhab, however, a litigation arose among the surviving heirs, of whom a lady called Urnero was apparently the eldest. Therefore the high law-court was called upon, with the consequence that Urnero was appointed as "trustee/administrator)" (*rwḏw*) for her brothers and sisters; this probably means that Urnero was henceforth responsible for the cultivation of the estate which she managed on behalf of herself and her brothers and sisters. Yet, a sister, being discontented, appealed to the court for a revision, and the estate was then parcelled out among the brothers and sisters. But in the course of time and on account of further litigation one Hui, son of Urnero, regained actual possession of the estate and cultivated it year after year. On his death the management of the estate devolved upon his widow, Nubnofret by name. But she had a bitter experience, as her rights were totally contested later by a man, one Khay, who alleged that Hui and his wife had forcibly seized his land, which he claimed by virtue of a title-deed testified to by witnesses. Thus was Nubnofret despoiled of her rights. After some years, however, her son Mose, who then came of age, launched an appeal to the notables of the village where the estate was situated; his appeal does not seem to have been successful. The present context proves beyond doubt that agricultural land could be held indeed in the hands of women and that law-courts fully recognized women's titles to land tenures.

The second relevant inscription is on a limestone stela that has an unusual provenance, as it comes from the distant oasis of Dakhlah. An interesting aspect of the stela is that its most fascinating contents disclose a trial bearing on the ownership of a plot of land adjacent to a flowing well.[34] The plaintiff there, a priest of the god Seth, claims the ownership of the land

---

33A. Gardiner, *The Inscription of Mes--A Contribution to the Study of Egyptian Judicial Procedure* (Leipzig, 1905); G. Gaballa, *The Memphite Tomb-Chapel of Mose* (Warminster, 1977), 22ff.; S. Allam, "Some Remarks on the Trial of Mose," in *JEA*, forthcoming.

34A. Gardiner, "The Dakhleh Stela," *JEA* 19 (1933): 19ff.; for dating the stela to the reign of Shoshenq III see now Helen Jacquet-Gordon, "Deux graffiti de l'époque libyenne sur le toit du temple de Khonsou à Karnak," *Hommages à S. Sauneron, Bibliothèque d'Etude*, LXXXI (Le Caire, 1979), vol. 1, 180ff.

alleging that the well had belonged to his mother, who had lived under Libyan pharaohs at the beginning of the first millennium B.C. His claim is based in the first instance upon the fact that a new sheet of inundation water has appeared in the neighborhood and that the area covered by it is fed by his mother's well and by no other. Apparently the ownership of the land is closely connected with the ownership of the well, so that the possessor of a well is deemed to have good title to all the land irrigated by it. In the end the court decides that the plaintiff's claim is just, and that the inundated ground did in fact belong to his mother, for the well is found inscribed in his mother's name upon authoritative official records.[35] Incidentally, the judgement was pronounced by the god of the oasis, Seth. Needless to say, it was the governor of the oasis who really determined the issue; nevertheless the verdict was devoutly accepted by the people as coming from the god. It is significant that the god affirmed also that the wells in the whole area were private waters (*mw nmḥw*) and not crown property (*mw Pr-ᶜ3*); they could belong therefore only to private individuals. Furthermore, the god ordered the wells in question be confirmed unto the plaintiff, "they being confirmed to son of his son, and heir of his heir, to his wife and to his children."

Viewing these disparate pieces of evidence, spread as they are over a period of some fifteen centuries, we may conclude that Egyptian society recognized women's rights in immovables to as great a degree as men's. The cases dealt with so far show quite clearly that women from different strata could avail themselves of such rights. And it emerges from the great Wilbour Papyrus that in given situations women were even liable to taxation/rent with regard to their land-holdings. For defining the limits of women's titles to immovables we can take some hints from the records available. There seems to be a wide range of personal rights: usufruct, diverse kinds of possession or ownership, and in some cases complete property is almost certain.[36]

---

[35]Nine wooden tablets from the oasis of Khargeh contain in Greek a systematic survey of eighty-six hydreumata (water-sources/pools) available near Hibis (Hibiton Polis) the capital of the oasis. In the text, written circa 246/49 A.D., the surveyor gave each source a number and a name; some of the names are half-Egyptian toponyms; the text indicates also the current owners or the first diggers of the well in question. The technical terms used in this Greek text provide striking parallels to the vocabulary of our Dakhlah Stela. For these Greek tablets, now in the Ashmolean Museum, see P. J. Parsons, "The Wells of Hibis," *JEA* 57 (1971): 165ff; cf. G. Wagner, *Les oasis d'Egypte (à l'époque grecque, romaine et byzantine d'après les documents grecs)* (Le Caire, 1987), 279 ff.

[36]This presumptive evidence can be drawn from three texts dealt with above: O. BM 5624, the Inscription of Mose, and the Dakhlah Stela. Through the ostracon we learn of the ownership of a tomb which lasted within the same family for some one hundred and fifty-two years. The inscription tells us of a succession to fields over two and a half centuries. The stela attests to the

Women could further transfer their titles to immovables and dispose of them by several means (sale, adoption and other inheritance conventions). The question which arises now is to know where women used to derive such rights from. In most cases we have seen them enriched by way of inheritance practices or by some undertakings on the part of their immediate families (through dowry, wills and the like). Were women otherwise entitled to acquire by purchase immovables on their own behalf? In this respect our present material is too scanty as regards women of lower social status, so that we have to turn towards some inscriptions in the Karnak temple relative to the property of some prominent ladies of the Twenty-first Dynasty (1070-945 B.C.). There we are told that two women (mother and daughter) did obtain fields and houses by purchase.[37]

This fairly positive picture, however, cannot induce the legal realist to imagine that every woman in pharaonic Egypt could enjoy such rights. In fact a glance at the data as reflected in the aforementioned Wilbour Papyrus would

---

ownership of a flowing well during one and a half centuries at least (from the reign of Psusennes I or II until Shoshenq III). For a further discussion of the problem of private land property, see W. Helck, *Materialien* 2, 237ff.; B. Menu, "Le Régime juridique des terres en Égypte pharaonique," *RHD* 49 (1971): 555ff.; Ward, "Some Aspects of Private Land Ownership," 63-77.

37We are concerned with two lengthy inscriptions which are admittedly very defective. Yet, a careful reading of the surviving passages will leave no doubt that their sole subject was the personal property of two prominent ladies, one of whom was Maatkare, daughter of King Psusennes II (960-945 B.C.). The other, Henttawy, must have been one of the most important personalities of the period, perhaps the wife of a High Priest of Amun or the sister (and wife ?) of King Smendes II, cf. K. Kitchen, *The Third Intermediate Period in Egypt*, (Warminster, 1986), 57. Although both inscriptions bear close resemblance in most respects, it would be wise to take into consideration only the inscription of lady Henttawy, since it is less mutilated. It describes recourse to the great Theban triad in order to obtain divine approval of her proprietary rights. Here we get to know that the property of this lady comprised amongst other things "fields which Henttawy obtained by purchase (*ỉn r snwt*)..." as well as "houses which (her mother) Isimkheb bought from their (the houses) master(s) for Henttawy." On this occasion the god Amun-Re said, "I will confirm the houses...in the hand of Henttawy my servant, in the hand of <her son>, the son of her son, the heir of her heir, and the child<ren> of her children eternally." A. Gardiner, "The Gods of Thebes as Guarantors of Personal Property," *JEA* 48 (1962): 57ff. That Henttawy obtained at least fields by purchase is clear from the use of the unambiguous expression *ỉn r swnt*; for the same expression occurring in another sale of fields (three arouras) see P. Berlin 9784, recto ll. 16-17: A. Gardiner, "Four Papyri of the 18th Dynasty from Kahun," *ZÄS* 43 (1906): 28ff. Difficulty may arise for the translator with regard to the common verbs *ỉn* and *dỉ* (without any explanatory adjunct), both of which can occasionally discard their ordinary meanings of "bring" and "give" in order to take on the more specialized senses of "buy" and "sell." Cf. Gardiner, "The Gods of Thebes as Guarantors of Personal Property," 65f.

suffice to give us a more realistic idea. From the land-holders, great and small, recorded in this cadestral survey appear about twelve percent as coming from women; even if, as is highly probable, I have counted wrongly, the percentage given will provide a roughly accurate picture of the female holders of land in the agricultural districts covered by the survey of our papyrus.[38] No wonder, ancient society generally had a patriarchal structure and was largely dominated by men.[39]

---

[38]For the sake of comparison with Greece we may point to the fact that in Athens and Delos, for example, only male citizens could own land; D. Schaps, *Economic Rights of Women in Ancient Greece* (Edinburgh, 1979), 4ff.

[39]See S. Allam, "Zur Stellung der Frau im Altägypten (Zum Katalog einer Ausstellung in Hildesheim), *DE* 5 (1986): 7-15.

Responses to Prof. Allam's Paper

Cruz-Uribe: Prof. Pestman has written: "It is known that women in Ancient Egypt enjoyed legal rights that were for all practical purposes equal to men." Thus women were able to own property, dispose of property as they wished; they could also enter into contracts that would be acceptable in court. This seems more or less what Prof. Allam says in his paper. After surveying a number of documents, he concludes that indeed women could own, inherit, dispose of, and generally have equal rights to property as men do. Prof. Allam points out a major factor which I wish to comment upon. He notes that the number of documents concerning women's property rights is limited in number. Although they go back to the earliest historical periods of Egypt, they comprise only a small percentage of the total number of documents dealing with property. He also notes that women comprise only 8% of the land-holders in the cadaster-survey of the Wilbour Papyrus. A question begs to be asked. Can this number be significant in regard to how we are able to approach the legal position of women in ancient Egypt? I think it may be. In my own dealings with Egyptian legal texts I have begun to form a hypothesis such that it is certain that women possessed legal rights, putting them on a legal equality with men. However, depending on how one interprets individual documents it is also possible that simple legal rights meant little in relation to the power that women held in the social sector. Yes, women had legal rights. But did they have the power to exercise these rights completely and unreservedly? Were there societal strictures that may have held back the advancement of women? Again I would tend to argue yes. For example, many of the documents dealing with transfers of legal property involving women may be viewed as exceptions to the rule rather that the norm. Taking the case of *i͗myt-pr*'s of property of the priests of El-Kab of the late Middle Kingdom: in each document very exceptional dealings are referred to in order to transfer property of the office of count of El Kab. It is because of the exceptional nature, i.e., passing on to a nephew in one case, and to a wife in another, that these texts were written. If the eldest son had inherited, it is likely that no document would have been written. Take the case of the will of Naunakhte. There Naunakhte is disinheriting some of her children because they had failed to care for her. If there had been a normal situation where each child was to inherit the same amount no document need have been written. Now, Prof. Allam, would you agree or disagree that while the legal role of women in Ancient Egypt was near to equal with men that the evidence which survives suggests that women may not have been able to exercise those rights?

Allam: Well, we have in our documentation texts dealing with the affairs of women, and in order to assess the position of women, if I try to work out her legal position, I don't pretend that in doing so I would grasp the whole position of women in the society. What is coming now would only be a portion of the evidence, so we have also what we call literary texts, texts dealing with literature, religion, education, etc., and we have to try to work out the position of women from such texts too. That is what Dr. Robins was trying to show us. We have to gather different pieces of evidence so that, putting them together, we might be able to have a general idea of the position of women in the society. My presentation was dealing with such legal texts, but I don't pretend that this legal position, or this piece of evidence, is enough to size up the position of women in the society. Then, using our legal texts, which are very scanty or very rare, they might appear to be only exceptional situations. I would say that it is a matter of interpretation. If you have thirty percent of the material coming from Egypt dealing with women, would you consider that thirty percent of the material is exceptional? I would say that you would be going too far. So, I would put the question in a different way. I would say that the society we are dealing with was in ancient times and ancient society was dominated by men, but we see in these different pieces of evidence discussed today that women played a certain role. So, I'm trying to define the limits of the role of these women and I don't pretend that every woman in a society had such rights, or could have access to such rights, I am trying to define the limits of the extent of her legal position as in our own society. In our society not every woman can avail herself of every right of a man, but we can't say that women are not on equal footing with men. So, I would say that on the whole ancient Egyptian society, as we see from the evidence written and drawn, was in fact dominated by men, but women were also acknowledged; the capacities of women were acknowledged; and in order to assess the legal position of Egyptian women I would rather compare her capacity with the capacity of her contemporaries, for instance, in Mesopotamia, or for comparison, take the later Greek civilization, I would rather also compare the capacity of Roman women with these Egyptian women. So, although all these civilizations came later, they don't show us the same capacity that Egyptian women had some 1000 years before.

Roth: I would like to ask a question of Katarzyna Grosz, because her paper later this afternoon, is, I think, arguing that women in Nuzi do control and own immovables, but only in certain circumstances. Now my question is how many individual texts from Nuzi, which can show us a part of family relations, might resemble some of these under discussion here?

Grosz: Yes, I think that you are absolutely right, many of the things that you have said today about women and immovables could very well apply to Mesopotamia. The difference is perhaps that, as far as I know, you don't find that many women as holders of crown-land, of royal land, of royal plots and this probably has nothing to do with women but with the structure of crown-property. I really feel that the important thing to state is establishing that women did have these rights to immovables, and that they passed their land on to their children, and I don't think that it's so extremely important that women did not very often do so, the important thing is that they did have this right. It is clear that we have a patrilineal society with a patrilineal devolution of property and so on. So it's obvious that the property devolves mainly through men, but the important fact is that, for instance, when a man dies, his widow gets his property; it's not his brother's, but his widow's. This shows that women's right to own property was completely self-evident. Women were perhaps a bit suppressed at times because of the patrilineal system, but certainly, in the absence of male heirs, a woman inherits her father's property, or a widow inherits, and this I think in Mesopotamia and Egypt are similar.

Fischer: I'd like to add that, in the Old Kingdom, a number of women had the title of *ḫnty-š*. *Ḫnty-š* is of course a title that is ill defined, usually it's taken to mean somebody who controlled property, or even found to be connected with an estate of a pyramid. And this is further evidence for some control of property by women in the Old Kingdom. And then, of course, we mentioned the prominence of women, and the specific evidence that in some cases this was because the mother could help the son. In the First Intermediate period a man, instead of saying "I didn't get my property entirely from my mother," said: "the property of my mother and father." And there is also, further evidence from the Middle Kingdom, where a woman is specifically entitled to bequeath her property to any heir she wished.

Figure 33

Old Babylonian plaque with female image, From Terqa, Syria. Courtesy of the International Institute for Mesopotamian Area Studies. TQ5-54.

Figure 34

Hurrian female figurine from Tell Hamida. Courtesy Paul Zimansky, Boston University.

Western Asia in the Second Millennium

The second millennium in ancient Mesopotamia may be divided into two main phases. The first of these may be called the "Amorite" or "Old Babylonian" Period; the second the era of "national states" or the "Kassite Period." "Old Babylonian" is a linguistic term; "Amorite" is an ethnic term referring to Semites believed to have their ultimate origins in North Syria or the Jezirah. Many of these "westerners" (as the Sumerians called them) began to appear in Mesopotamia towards the end of the third millennium and in greater numbers at the beginning of the second millennium B.C. They were loosely organized into various tribes or confederacies. Some of them were pastoral nomads; others may have come from the villages, towns, and cities of their land of origin.

Despite the efforts of native Mesopotamian rulers to keep them out or under control, the Amorites gradually infiltrated the Mesopotamian heartland and its urban centers. Through force of numbers and arms, wealth, guile, and ambition, they took control of the main Mesopotamian cities and established new cities of their own. They founded numerous dynasties that vied one with the other in arms and diplomacy for control of the cities, their agricultural hinterlands, and certain strategic watercourses on which the Mesopotamian cities depended.

Although some Mesopotamian urbanites ridiculed the Amorites as outlandish barbarians, recent explorations in Syria have shown that, in addition to their nomadic pastoral background, the Amorites could boast a long tradition of high urban culture in their homeland. Whereas the Amorites of Mesopotamia became well imbued with traditional Sumero-Akkadian culture, they brought with them their own language, beliefs, social, familial, and commercial practices. The amalgamation of these with the cultural patterns of Mesopotamia resulted in a new, vigorous civilization that is in many respects well documented and known.

Mesopotamia and North Syria became a patchwork of Amorite states. Some of the most celebrated rulers of this time include Naram-Sin of Eshnunna, Shamshi-Adad of Shubat-Enlil, Rim-Sin of Larsa, and Hammurabi of Babylon, all of whom ruled at different times substantial domains in Mesopotamia and beyond. This is the age of the famous palace at Mari, the enormous archives of which have shed so much light on the period.

Most germane to the purpose of this congress are certain social developments of this period. For example, in the first few centuries of the second millennium we seem to see the building-up of large family patrimonies through land purchases, livestock management, and money-lending. We see foreclosure on debtors and their property, the property to become an asset of the creditor, and the debtor a debt slave. Numerous letters and documents dealing with family affairs have come down to us, many of them written about or concerning the activities of women.

From the Assyrian trading colony of Kanesh (Kultepe, near present-day Kayseri in Turkey) have come extensive archives of Assyrian merchant families and their associates. Scores of letters, especially from the wives of prominent merchants, shed light on the personal and commercial concerns of these women, on whose industry their husband's firms to some extent depended.

From another city, Sippar, in Babylonia, thousands of documents have turned up that are the records of a cloistered group of women of high social standing who lived in a sort of compound near the temple of the sun god, Shamash. We are fortunate to have the leading expert on this material, Rivkah Harris, to share her researches on these people.

The second half of the second millennium begins after what we call a "dark age," a time for which we have practically no documentation. "Dark" of course refers to our knowledge of it rather than the period itself, which may well have been prosperous for all we know. Once sources become again available, we see important social and political changes throughout the Near East, some of which must be attributed to changes in population.

In the realm of politics emerges what we may call "national states," large entities ruled by a warrior elite living off a sometimes depressed countryside. We see scattered across the Near East "palace economies," large scale establishments that alternately make war on one another and exchange gifts of precious materials, valuable livestock, and the like, together with a lively if often querulous correspondence. These palace economies depended on the villages and towns under their control for produce, livestock, corvee labor, and military contingents.

New people seem to be in charge: the Hittites in Asia Minor, Hurrians in parts of North Syria and North Mesopotamia (including, for a while, Assyria), and Kassites in Babylonia. Towards the end of the second millennium Assyria emerges as a formidable military power at the expense of both the Hurrians and the Kassites. In the twelfth century the Kassite dynasty disappears, soon to be replaced by a proudly native Babylonian dynasty, the best known ruler of which is Nebuchadnezzar I.

In the steppe country not far from the present Iraqi oil center at Kirkuk lay the Hurrian statelet Arrapha, including the town called Nuzi, a dependent of Arrapha in the late sixteenth and early fifteenth centuries. Who were these Hurrians, and where did they come from? We wish we knew more, and current archaeological research promises to increase our knowledge substantially. They were not Semites, for example, but spoke a language that is still imperfectly understood. They settled in great numbers in northern Syria and Iraq towards the end of the third millennium, and may have been responsible for the sudden emergence of a high urban civilization in that region. Their land of origin is unknown; one tends to look north and east into Anatolia for this. The Hurrians amalgamated with other peoples, such as the Hittites and the indigenous peoples of Syria and Mesopotamia, to produce distinctive local cultures of the Late Bronze Age.

At Nuzi we find a local palace economy which has been reconstructed in wonderful detail; indeed, this admittedly marginal locality still holds pride of place in our knowledge of this whole region at the time. The late E.A. Speiser, one of the pioneers of Nuzi studies, was wont to twit his Egyptological colleagues by claiming that more legal material has turned up in two or three square meters of Nuzi than in the whole of ancient Egypt. Whether or not his claim is true or meaningful, nowadays we take a more balanced view of the importance of Nuzi than did Speiser did. We see at Nuzi the strength of family ties, both as genealogical reality and legal fiction. More on this from two of our contributors.

Nuzi is of course not the whole story: important records from Assyria during the second half of the second millennium illumine for us the business affairs of several prominent families, of which certain members labored, with heartlessness and acumen, to increase their patrimonies at the expense of their neighbors and less fortunate relatives. The outgoing second millennium seems to have been marked by violence and social upheaval throughout much of Western Asia. We lack the detailed documentation such as we had for Kanesh, Nuzi, or the various Amorite urban centers.

Benjamin Foster

Independent Women in Ancient Mesopotamia?

Rivkah Harris

In ancient Mesopotamia the center of woman's activities was in the domestic sphere just as the locus of men's activities was community or society wide. Mesopotamian women's traditional roles are best summed up in a verse from the late Babylonian hymn to the goddess of healing, Gula, who declares: "I am a daughter, I am a daughter-in-law, I am a spouse, I am a housekeeper."[1] And there is no reason to think that any would have wanted it otherwise.

The study of women's lives in ancient Mesopotamia is in its infancy. But the 1986 *Rencontre Assyriologique Internationale* on women[2] and this conference are watersheds in furthering this area of study for which I am particularly grateful. I began my work on the *nadītu* women of the city of Sippar some three decades ago; far too early to learn and benefit from the methodologies and insights of feminist scholarship. Assyriologists are, I think, still at the juncture of finding the right questions to put to the available sources rather than offering definitive answers to those questions. Unfortunately, we are always at the mercy of fragmentary, accidental materials, visual and written, which with few exceptions are male-authored, male-produced, and male oriented. All too often these "scatter-grams" skew the data and can easily mislead us into drawing fallacious conclusions about the quality and content of women's lives down the centuries. My guess is that there was far more continuity and uniformity than the extant documentation suggests and that although Mesopotamian history was characterized by periodic political upheavals, the lives of ordinary people may have changed less drastically than one might think.

Now to my topic. Were there women in Mesopotamia who had control over their persons and their activities? Were there women who were

---

[1] W.G. Lambert, "The Gula Hymn of Bulluṭsa-rabi," *Or.* 36 (1967): 121:65.

[2] See now the publication of many of the papers presented at this meeting: *La Femme dans le Proche-Orient Antique* ed., J.-M. Durand, *Éditions Recherche sur les Civilisations*, (Paris, 1987).

free of male financial support, who could survive economically without male control, whether of father, husband, brother, or son? Were there women whose influence and power did not depend on their relationship to men? Did economic independence imply the opportunity to develop personal and psychological independence? Let me be clear. I am not asking whether there were "liberated" women in Mesopotamia who could "do their thing." Such a phenomenon is a twentieth century reality and goal and not really applicable to the ancient world.

I will try to respond to these questions by first suggesting avenues which might be fruitfully explored in following through on these questions and then focus on the unique institution of the cloister of Sippar, the *gagû*, and its residents: the *nadītu* women.

Throughout Mesopotamian history women of means are attested as having the right to conduct legal transactions on their own and to witness legal transactions. Women engaged in trade and in lending and borrowing. They might give gifts, dedicate objects to the gods, and acquire property. What is difficult to assess is how freely they could do all this. To what extent must male consent be assumed for their actions when no male appears alongside them? Were wives ever able to act without spousal assent?

Attention must be paid to special categories of women, beginning with queens or women married to rulers. In Mesopotamia, only one woman became king--Ku-Bau, a barmaid, who lived in Early Dynastic times. The Sumerian King List notes that she "consolidated the foundation of Kish, became 'king' and reigned a hundred years."[3] Not surprisingly, her reign was viewed as an ominous anomaly which did not augur well for Mesopotamia.[4]

Far better known are the extensive responsibilities of the queens of Mari and Karana, Shiptu and Iltani, who lived in the Hammurabi era.[5] These remarkable women managed and supervised, not only their own complex households, but also the industries of the palace workshops. More unusual are their diplomatic functions. B.F. Batto[6] puts it well when he writes that in her activities Shiptu "cuts across the boundaries of various offices, the queen enjoyed a certain amount of independence and personal initiative in her own

[3]Jacobsen *SKL*: 104.

[4]For references to Ku-Bau see W.W. Hallo, "Women of Sumer," *The Legacy of Sumer* ed., D. Schmandt-Besserat *Bibliotheca Mesopotamica*, 4 (Malibu: 1979), 28.

[5]For a description of their activities see S. Dalley, *Mari and Karana: Two Old Babylonian Cities* (London, 1984), 97-111.

[6]In his *Studies on Women at Mari* (Baltimore: 1974), 17.

right. But more commonly she seems *to have been used by the king* (my italics) as a kind of personal representative who carried out his wishes in extraordinary circumstances." So though queens might be expected to be assertive and resourceful, the concentration of power resided in the conjugal unit. It is the king who delegated to the queen; she remained an agent of her husband. Not only the wives of rulers, but the daughters of rulers as well were instruments of political policy, the intermediaries for cementing alliances between greater and lesser power bases.[7] S. Pomeroy in her *Women in Hellenistic Egypt from Alexander to Cleopatra*[8] provides valuable insights into queenship that might be fruitfully utilized in studying Mesopotamian queenship. The correspondence of queens such as Shiptu and Iltani should be evaluated more carefully in terms of this very issue of independence. So too do the sources on the earlier and later queens require closer examination.[9]

Another group of women that merits special scrutiny are widows. Undoubtedly widowhood in Mesopotamia, as elsewhere and at all times, went hand in hand with poverty.[10] The vulnerability of the *almattu*, the widow, is frequently attested in Mesopotamian sources. Nevertheless, widowhood too might have a liberating effect as evidenced by Middle Assyrian texts. C. Saporetti comments that the position of "the *almattu* widow in Assyria...seems a desirable situation in many respects." There is confirmation from this period that the widow, in certain cases, is a "woman [who] seems free to act on her own and to handle her own affairs."[11] Widowhood could thrust a woman into control of her family and might grant her the possibility of exercising personal power and making independent decisions for herself and her children. All too often one must guess whether a woman who acts alone is a widow.[12]

7For example see Hallo, "Women of Sumer," 31 as well as P. Artzi, "The Influence of Political Marriages on the Internal Relations of the Amarna Age," *La Femme dans le Proche-Orient Antique*, 23-26 and B. Lafont, "Les Filles de Zimri-Lim, ou la Politique matrimoniale du Roi de Mari," *ibid.*, 113-123.

8(New York, 1984), 3-30.

9For queens in general see *RlA* 6, 159-162 under Königtum. Of interest is J. Reade, "Was Sennacherib a Feminist?" *La Femme dans le Proche-Orient Antique*, 139-145. See also *ibid.*, the articles by P. Artzi and Z. Ben-Barak.

10*CAD* A/1, 364 notes the ambiguity of the position of the *almattu* who "on the one hand, is in need of legal protection, and, on the other hand, *may freely dispose of herself* (my emphasis)." Thus the vulnerability of the widow existed alongside the potential for real independence. It is noteworthy that there is no masculine equivalent in Akkadian for *almattu*.

11*The Status of Women in the Middle Assyrian Period, Monographs on the Ancient Near East*, 2 (Malibu, 1979), 19.

12See e.g. B.F. Batto, "Land Tenure and Women at Mari," *JESHO* 23/3 (1980): 239ff., who discusses women who were recipients of royal land allotments who he suggests "were legally

Prosopographical information and the intuition of the specialist can be of enormous help here. If possible, the situation of divorced women should be studied.

As for the autonomy, especially economic, of married women, the spotlight should be on women such as the wives of the Old Assyrian merchants (c. 1900-1800 B.C.).[13] There seems to have been a pattern at this time of wives (and other female kin) being involved in large scale transactions, known especially from their letters. These women represented their husbands in various commercial and legal transactions. The question is whether they in any way acted independently or were working solely for the profit of their husband's firm. Did they earn monies which they could spend as they wished? What decision making, if any, was theirs alone?

Worthy of more investigation is the world of women's work[14]--the issue of gender and the division of labor. The textile industry might be fruitfully explored, not only for upper and middle-class women, but for women of the lower strata of society. Were there ever independent female artisans? If so, in what areas? Were women barred from certain occupations where one might expect to find them? What supervisory positions were held by women? A thoroughgoing study of work options available to women, their access to paid employment, how much they were paid in comparison to men, would tell us much about women's potential for independence. Of interest, for example, is the position of the *sābītu*,[15] the woman responsible for brewing and selling beer, who was involved in credit transactions just like the *tamkaru* merchant. She disappears from the scene at the end of the Old Babylonian Period.

Thus far the women considered lived in the traditional mode. Let us turn now to women who lived outside the usual norms and categories, women who were customarily not nurturers, who were not mothers, mothers-in-law,

---

independent (*sui generis*), unmarried, and free of paternal authority." Many of these were probably widows.

13See the discussion by K.R. Veenhof on some of these women in *Aspects of Old Assyrian Trade and its Terminology* (Leiden, 1972), 109-123.

14The observation by P. Sanday, *Female Power and Male Dominance* (London/New York, 1981), 114 is particularly relevant: "Females achieve economic and political power or authority when environmental or historical circumstances grant them economic autonomy and make men dependent on female activities." It is doubtful that the last ever pertained to Mesopotamian women.

15On her role see Oppenheim, *Beer* 12.

wives or daughters-in-law.[16] First a look at prostitutes (*harimtu*), as "a socially identifiable group of women [who] earned their living primarily or exclusively from the commerce of their bodies."[17] The legal status of prostitutes was regulated by Mesopotamian law codes, at least theoretically.[18] Then, as throughout history, girls became prostitutes as a result of poverty, war, and male violence. They came from the ranks of the poor, captives of war, and foreigners. No in-depth study to my knowledge has been made of prostitution in Mesopotamia.[19] There was presumably the "streetwalker" and the high-priced "courtesan." The blessing and curse of the prostitute in the Gilgamesh Epic by the despairing Enkidu informs us about both.[20] At times the temple and one of its officials might have jurisdiction over a group of prostitutes as was the case in Sippar. I might add that I do not consider them to have been *cultic* prostitutes.[21] Some may have had relatives who served as pimps. Presumably those who were self-employed and free agents might accumulate enough in fees to be free of any ties to a man.

Throughout Mesopotamian history elite women, and not-so-elite women, married women and also unmarried women functioned as priestesses. The most famous of these is the *entu* priestess of the moon god Nanna of Ur, Enheduanna, the daughter of Sargon, founder of the Akkad Dynasty (2334-2279 B.C.). She is fortuitously known both from her literary compositions and from visual sources. Sumerologists consider her to be the author of a sizeable

---

16I.M. Diakonoff, "Women in Old Babylonia not under Patriarchal Authority," *JESHO* 29/3, (1986) 225-238 also singles out priestesses and prostitutes as the two groups of women who might achieve independence. In his view whether a girl became a priestess or a prostitute depended "on whether her father could afford to give her a sufficient dowry (229)." Diakonoff (226) thinks that women outside of these two groups were unable to act on their own.

17This is L. Otis' definition in her *Prostitution in Medieval Society* (Chicago, 1985), 2.

18For references see *CAD* H 101.

19The article by G. Lerner, "The Origin of Prostitution in Ancient Mesopotamia," *Signs: Journal of Women in Culture and Society* 11/2 (1986): 236-254 is in my opinion highly problematic. For example she draws major conclusions from the curse of the prostitute by Enkidu in the Gilgamesh epic without sifting the historical data from literary motifs. Diakonoff, "Women in Old Babylonia...," 232ff. makes some telling remarks about Mesopotamian prostitutes.

20See *ANET* 86 VII iii.

21See my *Ancient Sippar: A Demographic Study of an Old Babylonian City 1894-1595 B.C.* (Istambul, 1975), 332. Some of these prositiutes are clearly foreigners requiring regulation and protection. An official of the Shamash temple, the main temple of Sippar, was the logical person to be in charge of this. Note this was so even though there was apparently an Ishtar temple in Sippar (*ibid.*, 185f.). Following up on the activities of the sons of prostitutes, identifiable by the use of the matronymic rather than the patronymic, would be informative.

group of temple hymns. W.W. Hallo[22] has described her "as a kind of systematic theologian, well versed in the subtleties of a--perhaps already traditional--set of Sumerian beliefs and capable of adapting them to a new point of view." If as he says "her poetic efforts must have served as a model for much subsequent hymnography," then this remarkably creative women would be the only Mesopotamian woman to date of whom we can say developed a personal and psychological independence made more possible, presumably, by her celibate life within the confines of the *giparu* where the *entu* priestess lived. And yet if not she, her office at least, was the instrument utilized by her father to integrate the older Sumerian cultural traditions with those of the conquering Akkadians.[23] Therefore this princess, like princesses earlier and later, was a means of achieving the male quest for power.

The types and functions of the various priestesses, their chronological and geographical distribution have been exhaustively studied by J. Renger.[24] Distressingly little is known about most of them. Information is incredibly sparse about their interior lives. L. Oppenheim[25] has commented in his *Ancient Mesopotamia* on the reticence of the cuneiform sources which serves to veil rather than reveal the thoughts of these ancients. This in contrast to biblical and classical materials. Even the *nadītu* women about whom hundreds of legal, economic, and epistolary texts are available, remain frustratingly elusive, their personalities and thoughts beyond our reach.

The Old Babylonian Period (1894-1595 B.C.) is characterized by a plethora of "priestesses" whose functions and duties in the cult are little known: *entu, ugbatu, nadītu, kulmašītu, qadištu, ištaritu, sekretu.* In describing most of these women, the *Chicago Assyrian Dictionary* states that they were "women of special status." All are dedicated to one god or another in northern and southern Mesopotamia: some may marry; others must not. Some may have children; others may not. Some are cloistered; others are not. For the rest of this paper, I will concentrate on the *gagû*, the cloister, and the *nadītus*, devotees of the god Shamash of the city of Sippar, some 65 miles

---

22*The Exaltation of Inanna* (New Haven, 1968), 4.

23This is Hallo's view. See also I. J. Winter, "Women in Public...," *La Femme dans le Proche-Orient Antique*, 200f. who notes that "the careful inscription identifying the person of Enheduanna on the reverse of [her] disk" highlights the role "she serves through her office to solidify the traditional base of the whole Akkadian regime."

24"Untersuchungen zum Priestertum in der altbabylonische Zeit," *ZA* 24(1967): 110-188.

25(Chicago, 1964): 177.

northeast of the capital Babylon, whom I have studied and written about at length.[26]

Theirs was a unique institution, a strange blend of characteristics, probably based on an earlier prototype but transformed radically, it would seem, to meet the new challenges of this period. Before focussing on our topic of independence and autonomy, I will briefly describe the institution of *nadītu* women of Shamash who lived in the *gagû*. The term *nadītu* derives from the root, *nadû* meaning "to leave fallow" (the comparison of women to fields is common in ancient Near Eastern texts). The *nadītu* was then a "fallow woman"; she was prohibited from sexual relations throughout her life. This was a basic prohibition for all *nadītu* women dedicated to different gods as well and therefore possibly living under different regulations. (For example, the *nadītu* of Marduk of Babylon might marry, but she too was forbidden to bear children and so had to provide or permit her husband a secondary wife for that purpose.)[27] The *gagû* of Sippar was apparently the most prestigious of all the cloisters of Mesopotamia because women went there from Dilbat even though the Kish cloister was closer. More importantly, princesses of the royal house of Babylon and Mari were installed in Sippar.

In the midst of Sippar, surrounded by a wall was the cloister where some one to two hundred *nadītu* and cloister officials lived in private dwellings--some owned, others leased by their residents. The girl would be brought here by her father or guardian at an age when girls ordinarily married, in her mid-teens. Here she would live away from the "outside" or *kidu* as the *nadītu* referred to the world outside, until her death when she would be buried in the *gagû* cemetery alongside her sister *nadītus*. Though there were times when the *nadītu* of Shamash might have the freedom to leave for short family visits or have her relatives visit her, she lived until death in the cloister, viewed by later lexicographers as a gloomy prison.

But the life of the *nadītu* was by no means a passive one. In crucial and striking ways the *gagû* and *nadītu* women bear no resemblance to the

---

[26]The details can be found in my articles on the *nadītu* of Sippar: "The *nadītu* Laws of the Code of Hammurapi in Praxis," *Or.* 30/2 (1961): 163-169; "Biographical Notes on the *nadītu* Women of Sippar," *JCS* 16/1 (1962): 1-12; "The Organization and Administration of the Cloister in Ancient Babylonia," *JESHO* 6/2 (1963): 121-157; "The *nadītu* Woman," *Studies Oppenheim*, 106-135; "Notes on the Babylonian Cloister and Hearth: A Review Article," *Or.* 38/1 (1969): 133-145; "Hierodulen," *RlA* 4/5 (1975): 391-393; *Ancient Sippar*, 305-312.

[27]For a discussion of this kind of sororal marriage see "The Case of the Three Marriage Contracts," *JNES* 33/4 (1974): 363-369. The sororate would have provided the two women with a united front in dealing with their husband.

medieval nunnery and its nuns. Each *nadītu*, as I have noted, lived in her own private house within the cloister compound. She had her own slaves or slavegirls to take care of the household tasks. A life of poverty was no ideal. On the contrary, many, if not most of them, were born into the wealthiest and most respectable families. Among them were princesses, even a sister of King Hammurabi, the daughters of temple, military, and cloister officials, members of the top echelon of the bureaucracy. Some were daughters of city administrators, of wealthy scribes, judges, physicians, and diviners. When these girls were brought to the cloister they did not come empty-handed. Most received as their dowry fields, plots of land, slaves, jewelry, and prized household furniture and utensils. The Code of Hammurabi even stipulated that if the *nadītu* was not given a dowry before her father's death she was (quite exceptionally) to receive a full share of the inheritance equal to that of her brothers!

In my view herein lies one of the major reasons for the establishment of the cloister at this particular point in Mesopotamian history. Celibacy was not unknown before the Old Babylonian Period. There was the earlier institution of the *entu* priestess,[28] who was a princess selected for life to participate in the annual sacred marriage, the *hieros gamos*, and remain unmarried and live in the *giparu* residence. But the Old Babylonian Period was the only time when a *community of women* lived as celibates and virgins. What is remarkable is what I.J. Gelb[29] referred to as "the uniquely 'capitalistic' development of the *nadītum* institution at Sippar...[which] seems beyond anything that can be connected with the aims and activities of cloisters and monasteries of all times." The hundreds of *nadītu* texts are mainly business documents: contracts of sale, lease and hire. With few exceptions it is a *nadītu* who buys houses and fields, leases out fields, houses, and plots of land, and hires out her slaves as farm hands to Sipparian farmers or as menials in their households. What emerges then is the amazing picture of a community of female celibates acting throughout the Old Babylonian Period as a significant economic power in their community.

E. Stone,[30] who has studied the *nadītu* of the god Ninurta of Nippur, found much the same situation. However, she calls attention to significant differences in the textual finds: a major portion of the Sippar texts are *nadītu* texts, in Nippur only 10% are *nadītu* texts. The Nippur texts may therefore give a more realistic glimpse into the relative importance of the *nadītus* there and their interrelationship with other Nippurians. The Sippar material may

---

[28]On the *entu* see Renger, "Untersuchungen," 114-134.

[29]"The Arua Institution," *RA* 66 (1972): 4.

[30]"The Social Role of the *naditu* Women in Old Babylonian Nippur," *JESHO* 27 (1982): 50-70.

thus inadvertently present a somewhat exaggerated perspective of the *nadītu*'s importance. Stone accounts for the institution this way: "Perhaps then, as now, the daughters of tribal leaders, constrained by endogamy and rank, often had difficulty finding a suitable spouse. Entrance into the *nadītu* institution could have provided a viable alternative. The god could supplement the protective role already played by her brothers, while the economic arrangement would free her from want and allow her to establish an independent household."[31]

In my work, done much earlier, I described the economic and legal stimulus for the institution of the *gagû* and its *nadītu* in the following way: When a girl married, she took her dowry *away* from her family; the dowry of a *nadītu*, though it belonged to her during her lifetime, *returned to* her brothers or their heirs at her death. In short, the *gagû* provided a respectable alternative to marriage which deescalated the dispersion of the patrimonial estate. Bolstering this assumption is the fact that successive generations of women in certain families became *nadītus*. I could trace this phenomenon at times for three to four generations and the relationship was always patrilinear.

In the Old Babylonian Period, for the first time in Mesopotamian history, much wealth is in the hands of private individuals. The position of the temple has changed considerably from earlier times: "the identity of temple and state has entirely vanished; the temple is now only one of the many institutions in the city and state. Beside it stands the palace and private properties and enterprises of the free middle class; the temple and its priesthood now become closely involved with private interests and private rights."[32] As Stone remarks: "around 1800 B.C. [in Nippur, and I would add that this was probably true in other cities as well] *nadītus* were the only members of society who had ties with more than one social institution. On the one hand they were members of their natal lineages, while on the other hand they belonged to the *nadītu* institution. The records of their economic transactions reflect their dual role, as they exchanged property with both kinsmen and with other *nadītus*."[33]

The religious underpinnings of the *gagû* are more elusive than we might wish for. Significant, however, are their names--the most popular among them and distinctive of the *nadītu*--express their special relationship to the god Shamash and his consort Aya: Amat-Shamash, "Servant girl of Shamash," Erishti-Aya, "Request from Aya," Erishti-Shamash "Request from

---

31*Ibid.*, 65.

32Jean Bottéro et al, *The Near East: The Early Civilizations* (New York, 1965), 215f.

33"The Social Role of the *nadītu* in Old Babylonian Nippur," 66.

Shamash." These names may have been given to them at birth, their future destiny already decided. (But other names are names of ordinary women.) Their correspondence is characterized by pious salutations and phrases.

Two administrative accounts[34] are key texts in informing us to some extent about the installation of a *nadītu*. One deals with the expenses incurred by the cloister on the "entrance" of a girl into the cloister, which took place at the beginning of a three-day festival. The terminology of the text is similar to that of marriage expenditures. The girl's guardian, father or brother, receives a betrothal gift from the cloister administration. The girl may have been clothed in bridal dress, which may have been the distinctive dress of a *nadītu*. The second day of the festival called "the day of the dead" was the highlight of the festival for all *nadītus*. On this solemn day, once a year, the living *nadītus* remembered the dead *nadītus* by performing for their "spirits" the rituals usually performed by the progeny of the deceased. The neophyte may have been brought to the cemetery on that day to witness her guarantee of eternal care in the afterlife, after the gods had called her to join them in banquet, to use a characteristic *nadītu* idiom. During this festival the young girl may have been brought into the awesome presence of the images of the gods Shamash and Aya, a privilege few were granted.

From the second account we learn that the "thread of Shamash" was placed on the arm of the entrant, an act which must have symbolized her new and intimate relationship to the god.

Now to the issue of the autonomy of the *nadītu*. The data are perplexing and contradictory. There is on the one hand evidence for the vulnerability of the *nadītu* who might be subjected to male violence. J. Renger[35] has suggested that it is for this very reason that she was sequestered. There is evidence that the cloister administration served the important function of maintaining the records of their transactions, as well as of their numerous litigations in which many were involved with their brothers, uncles, and even cousins who failed to supply them with the food, oil, and clothing allotments to which they were entitled. And on the other hand there is the evidence of their autonomy, of their living in private dwellings, which they owned or rented, tended by their slaves. Most importantly, these women had to care for themselves when they grew old and perhaps feeble, for this was not a function of the cloister administration. Dozens of adoption texts remain which tell of *nadītus* adopting slaves, male and female, or younger *nadītu*, many of whom were their relatives, to care for them when they grew old. A slave would be

---

[34] They are discussed at length in "The *naditu* Woman," 110-116.

[35] "Untersuchungen," 156.

manumitted after the adoptive mother died; the adopted *nadītu* would receive a bequest of property which at times was contested by the male relatives of the adoptive *nadītu*.

There is, on the other hand, evidence that at her death the *nadītu*'s property reverted to her male relatives. At the same time there is clear evidence that the *nadītu* might receive "ring money" from her father which was her very own to utilize in investments and the income of which she could dispose of as she wished. She had the power to disinherit a male heir who did not supply her with the necessary allotments already mentioned. At the same time there are the many pleading letters of the *nadītus*, usually to their brothers, beseeching them for food because they are destitute. Here, however, we may be dealing with stereotyped Mesopotamian female rhetoric, (an area which has yet to be studied). There is strong evidence that some *nadītus* concentrated their investments in certain transactions such as lending money or leasing out field slaves. Although most of these were conducted via male business agents, I believe that at least some of the *nadītus* were directly involved in business decisions.

In the earlier part of the Old Babylonian Period *nadītus* themselves might hold cloister administrative positions and have had some measure perhaps of self-governance. Later only males fill these offices. There were scribes among the *nadītu* who must have had a lengthy education; some were daughters of scribes. A few, one can assume, though based on slight evidence, may like Enheduanna have been scribe-poets or even scribe-scholars.[36]

The community of *nadītus* represented an alternative kinship structure, especially in the area of funerary obligations. It was a sisterhood that served in many ways as a substitute for natal kin who may well have died and forgotten about their sequestered aging relatives. And yet a basic reason for the establishment of the cloister was to ensure the integrity of the paternal estate. Perhaps a factor in these contradictory features is the anomalous nature of the *nadītu* herself. She was a virgin and yet a mother who can adopt a child whom she may marry off. And this "fallow" woman was also a "male" for she received a share of the paternal estate "like a son (*zittam kīma aplim išten*)."[37] Some had the right to dispose of their own property just like the male head of a

---

[36]The question of women's literacy in Mesopotamia is discussed in my forthcoming essay "The Female 'Sage' in Ancient Near Eastern Literature," to be published in *The Sage in Ancient Israel*, eds., J.G. Gamie and L.G. Perdue.

[37]CH 180.

household. Many initiated litigations just like a man. "As money lenders they are...the female counterpart of the Old Babylonian 'merchant' (*tamkarum*)."[38]

One way of understanding the anomalies and contradictions of the life of the *nadītu* is in terms of the interstitiality of the sacred status of the *nadītu* which relates to her intermediary role. The letters of the unhappy princess Erishti-Aya,[39] daughter of Shiptu and, less probably, of Zimri-Lim of Mari, especially highlight this. She refers to herself as "the praying emblem (*šurinnum kāribum*) who prays constantly for her father's life." She (and all *nadītus*) mediated between the god to whom she is dedicated and her community. As M. Beard[40] observed in her study of the vestal virgins: "mediation is ambiguity in action."

In later times when the *gagû* and *nadītu* have long disappeared, an institution such as theirs was unimaginable. They were then considered to be prostitutes and witches, marginal women who were threats to the social order of the community.

Perhaps the Sumerian and Akkadian myths which describe the taming of the powerful goddess Inanna-Ishtar, whom I elsewhere discuss as a paradox and a coincidence of opposites,[41] incorporate the fears of Mesopotamian males toward the autonomous female. There was no understanding of, and no tolerance for, women who lived outside of the traditional norms.

---

[38] J. Bottéro et al, *The Near East*, 217.

[39] These have been treated by Batto, *Studies on Women at Mari*. See especially 96f.

[40] "The Sexual Status of Vestal Virgins," *Journal of Roman Studies* 70 (1980): 24. This article stimulated me to look afresh at the *nadītu* of Shamash.

[41] In a paper presented at the AOS meeting held in Los Angeles in March 1987. A revised and expanded version will appear in the near future.

Responses to Prof. Harris's Paper

Stone: First of all, I liked your suggestion that we are constantly talking about discontinuity in the practices of Mesopotamia. As an archaeologist I can't help but note that all of the buildings we have uncovered from the Ur III period are public buildings and so we also find a great mass of public archives, yet all the buildings of the Old Babylonian period are private buildings, virtually. It is possible that there was a change between those societies, but it probably wasn't the radical change we see, but reflects simply where we have dug. But other than that I think you mentioned my discussion of the different samples from Nippur and Sippar. I think that one of the real differences is that the Nippur texts don't come from the cult-place of the *nadītus*, they come from the houses of their relatives; so you see the other side of the transactions, and I think that maybe looking at the Nippur material can help understand the Sippar data. One of the things that seems to be clear at Nippur is that you have restrictions on the degree to which property can be alienated between families. Female property especially is only found being sold between very close kinsmen, and this may have restricted the families in terms of their freedom to increase the size of their holdings. Putting these women into this institution for some reason that changed things. The women themselves could buy property from their brothers and sell it to other naditus who could then sell it back to their brothers, in a way skipping across these barriers.

A little later on, as you mentioned concerning ownership of temple offices: the men started doing that on their own, and from that point on the *nadītu* institution takes a nose-dive. In that situation we see especially in regard to the Sippar material that there were similar restrictions in terms of whom you could sell land to. I think that there is another aspect of the Nippur data: there seems enough information to make it pretty clear that a *nadītu* is being run by her brothers. I don't think she was making this complicated transaction all on her own, but there are known court-cases that suggest her brothers are keeping pretty close tabs on what she is doing: in fact, dictating what she is doing. And there is another thing that suggests that in terms of independent action the unmarried women really couldn't act very well: I don't think they could leave their houses. At Nippur, unlike Sippar, there are very few texts which deal with slaves. Those that do almost exclusively deal with female slaves, and they are associated with *nadītus* and other unprotected women like unmarried heiresses. At the point that an heiress's father dies, all kinds of exchanges take place involving a female slave. That suggests to me that the mistress had to have somebody who could go out shopping for her. It suggests that at that point such elite women may well have been closeted in the household and closeted in actual fact. So I think that what we need to look for in terms of the Sippar material is probably to look at it for the sort of changes in administrative positions which the data could hold, but look at it also in a long term diachronic perspective at Nippur. I should add that we are getting tablets coming from the Sippar excavation, in which we do find that a *nadītu* will take over the property debt once belonging to her father. It may be, in fact, that the *nadītus* were able to act autonomously.

Foster: Are you suggesting in fact that this was an ingenious device to expand the family patrimony by having such women handling family investments?

Stone: Yes. Also I think there was at Nippur more than one tactic that different families had of concentrating wealth; *nadītus* run in families and often it is a case of where one had to have a maternal aunt who was a *nadītu*, and she passed on her property, and by this continuity of a particular piece of property in the hands of women, it never gets dispersed. The other type of practice that some other families had was giving cash to several of their sons and dividing the property only among certain sons. But with the very wealthy families from which the *nadītu* come, I think it's not so much trying to make the family fortune larger, but trying to counteract the devastating effects of partial inheritance. In fact your early comment that the first half of the second millennium was a period of the increase in size of families at least at Nippur is correct, they did increase over time. I think they were trying to keep some kind of power-base together instead of dispersing it every generation among three or four sons.

Foster: For the benefit of those of you who may be irritated by this institution, you may get some satisfaction in knowing that most of these *nadītu* women outlived their brothers and outlived the other members of their generation.

Harris: Their longevity is a very important issue here and that by the way is evidence that they were celibate, or at least didn't have normal sexual relations. That's very important.

Nugent: I am struck particularly by this bizarre institution of the *nadītu* whereby there is what seems to me to be a modern analogue in surrogate motherhood, more or less. The *nadītu* provided that her husband had a child by another woman?

Harris: Yes, at least the *nadītu* of Marduk, which is really an odd thing, when you think of it. I have always been troubled by these ladies and that they are living with a man but yet not having sexual relations. However, the *nadītu* of the god Marduk of Babylon came from very wealthy families and married men (some of them married men of Sippar) who were also wealthy. So they then helped cement alliances between wealthy families.

Nugent: The other thing is that, it sounds like the *nadītu* are perhaps not so much mediating in a marginal position but specifically co-opted as males, they relinquished their female sexuality, and it sounds like what that enables them to do is become sort of a fictional or surrogate male in the inheritance system.

Harris: At the same time they don't give up their femininity: they're always whining and moaning, but really more so, and I really think its part of an act, of how women are supposed to sound. Yes, you're right, it is anomalous, they're virgins and yet they are male, they are vulnerable yet they are independent, and I think those are contradictory aspects of a woman in the world at any time. In fact with the goddess Ishtar we also find this, she is both male and female, highly paradoxical at the same time.

Roth: They're not called sons, they're not called males. The passage that Rivka quoted is that they inherit like a single heir, not like a son, but as a single heir.

Harris: But their activities are masculine type activities,....

Grosz: I'm not quite sure I agree with your theory that putting women into the cloister was devised to keep their patrimony intact, because , first of all, we have several pieces of evidence that women adopted other women and they did keep their property. Another is that they can get married, and what happens to their dowry property then? I think what happens is, if a *nadītu* dies childless, (that is without having adopted someone first) her property reverts to her male kin. This is exactly what is happening, again, to her brothers. Exactly the same thing would have happened if one of the brothers died childless: his brothers would take over his estate. Yet another thing, they could not negotiate their own marriage. They always had to have it arranged by someone. So what I have been asking myself is whether it is not the more efficient way to control a woman's inheritance share, by keeping her in the family and not arranging her marriage? Because if you introduce her into a new group you have to give her the inheritance, and in some respects this gets out of control; this is one problem. Another problem was, as you mentioned, that upon entering the cloister a *nadītu* entered a life where she didn't have much to do with the outside world. However, I think we have so much evidence, practically everything we have on *nadītu* (such as estate texts which are still unpublished in many cases), testifies to the fact that the *nadītu* are extremely involved in the life of their community.

Harris: Yes this is very important, I never raised this point, which is incredible because I think we gain more insight into what was going on: who were they writing to, who was writing to the *nadītu*? What I did do with that was to say that many of them employed business agents, while they were whining and crying to their brothers about what they weren't getting, they were also involved in making transactions. The fact of the matter is that I think that within the 300 some odd years represented by this material, there may have been changes in their freedom, that they were more free at some times that at other times. It is very difficult to put one's finger on that; but I think that obviously there were some women among them who were good business people, entrepreneurs, one might say, and really involved in the job.

Grosz: My last question is: do you have any comments on who were the men who married the *nadītu*? Do we know anything about the men?

Harris: Remember, when you say *nadītu* you have to specify which *nadītu*. *nadītu* of Shamash did not marry. *Nadītu* of Ninurta did not marry. For the *nadītu* of Marduk, recent texts that Charpin published show there were *nadītu* of Marduk who lived in a cloister in Babylon, but there were also *nadītu* of Marduk who did travel to Nippur and did marry, at least the ones we know about. Apparently there was great flexibility in their life styles, so I would say that the *nadītu* of Marduk married, based on my files. These were again the upper echelon, the families that they married into likewise: it was rich people marrying rich people.

Stone: This is really a comment about the issue of *nadītus* adopting other women who very often became *nadītus*. The real question is who were those other women, are they in fact their nieces? Not until you can chart genealogy will you get that type of information.

Harris: Let me respond that most of the young women they adopted were relatives, nieces or cousins, or the daughters of neighbors, by the way, which...

Stone: Neighbors very often were also relatives.

Harris: The whole thing is very complex, very interesting, and a lot of work can still be done....

McNamara: First of all I'd like to say that it's not really so different from Medieval nunneries as you seem to think, because, although lots of medieval nuns did pursue an ideal of poverty, the fact is medieval legislation is constantly concerned with the reality, which was that they did not always do this. The noble women "went into convents," living in their own houses, sometimes they had servants, they had pets, they had fancy clothes, although constantly cloistering (like every 5 or 6 years they would have to be cloistered). Yet every time a bishop goes around to visit them what does he discover? They are wandering, they are visiting, they are going out, they are having parties in the convent, they are entertaining in their rooms. A large portion of medieval monastic life of women was very similar to this. I don't know how to ask this question, because probably you don't know the answer, but it's something to think about: we have been looking at very objective evidence, that is what business the women do, but at the heart of this there is the ambiguity of the single woman. Who may have chosen this life for her? We don't know. Well you say, the parents had control over them; medieval parents had control over their daughters also, and yet we know hundreds of daughters who fought not to marry, who forced their parents to let them go into convents, to let them live a life in a nunnery.

Harris: That we don't really know. And I think a very important point here is one that I made in some of the reviews I've written of feminist writing: I think that there is a totally different world view here from the Christian view. Celibacy is no ideal here. Sexuality is good. In ancient Mesopotamia they had no ambiguous attitudes towards sexuality. Celibacy is not a more sacred state than marriage.

B. Lesko: But you're forgetting something, and that's the danger of childbirth death. Maybe they were afraid to have children, perhaps having known many women who had died quite young because of their pregnancies. I would think that fear of childbirth in such societies was a real incentive to going into cloistered life.

McNamara: Many medieval nuns had babies; they weren't supposed to but they often did. What I'm trying to argue, and I know how hard it is, and yet I feel we can't let this go by without making a strong push to at least remember that what we must struggle to do is to get in behind the sources, get in behind these institutions and try to understand what is moving the women who are there. What are they doing? What are they choosing? How are they relating to each other? I know this will be difficult.

Herlihy: I don't mean to prolong this, but I was interested in what you seem to be describing, which is frequently called a strategy of heirship. In the Middle Ages particularly the medieval nobility similarly had a strategy of heirship but it operated much differently. The way it operated was primarily to restrict male inheritance. Now, if you really want to concentrate patrimony what you do is prevent some of your sons, younger sons, whatever, from marrying. Now why is it that your Babylonian strategy apparently concentrates on women (which is not the most efficient way of achieving that goal)? I would like to ask if there is any male equivalent to this procedure, and if not, why not?

Harris: None that I know of.

Herlihy: Then why are women selected as a means of controlling...

Harris: You see this type of institution was nonexistent in the Old Akkadian period, so what caused it to develop? One can only surmise. I still think the women are used as instruments and that is a very important thing wherever, whenever, however.

Herlihy: Could I ask one question then, on the assumption that the sex ratio is balanced, and you do have a significant number of unmarried women.

There must be unmarried men somewhere in society and the problem would be where are they?.

Harris: One of the things that I did when I was collecting material long ago was to try to collect sizable family statistics. Many of these women, by the way, came from families where there were many brothers. In fact two sisters would enter the cloister and sometimes it would be the case that the older sister would become a *nadītu* of Shamash and the younger sister would join another group. But again, truly, I don't know. Were there many unmarried men? Even when war is so much a factor of life?

Herlihy: One solution would be female infanticide. Is there any evidence of that? In other words if the sex ratio is not in balance then why not? Because it is obviously not natural.

Delaney: One of the things that I wanted to note are some of the problems that we are running into, some of these contradictions and anomalies have to do, not so much with the material, but the perspective with which we are dealing with it. In other words, we keep reading back into the material ideas that we have currently. One of those is certainly the issue of independence and autonomy, as if this would be a mark of a kind of freedom of women or status of women, which is the way we might view it now, but we have no idea whether that was at all meant that way for either men or women. Surely the whole notion of individual independence and autonomy is a very western, modern notion, and to read that back into antiquity and look there for evidence for that sort of thing seems to me distorting what is there, and we can't find out exactly what was going on. Another problem related to that is that we keep talking about celibacy. The fact is that these women were not having babies, but that does not imply that they were necessarily celibate. The two cannot be equated, and I think it is wrong for us to say that they were celibate when in fact they could have been very much sexually active but simply that they were prohibited from having babies, and that seems to be confirmed by the fact that they would allow another woman to have children for their husbands.

Harris: The first issue raised is so crucial. I stated at the beginning that you have to ask questions and maybe we can get some answers. And you're right about the whole issue of autonomy and independence, do we even have a word in Akkadian for independence or autonomy?

That's fallacious. The only thing is how else do we operate with our methodology? We have to be careful that we are not improvising.

Galvin: This is to take that point one step further. The language that was being used indicates to me that the point of view was that the male was the standard. We discussed that the female who was not sexually active was male-like, we also said that activities of the women were male-like activities, or masculine activities, so you repeatedly set up the man as the standard and compare the woman to what she did not have and what she was aspiring to. I feel, as an Egyptologist, like pulling Mesopotamian women out of some kind of quicksand; I can't figure out what she is. It's too much from a male point of view.

Westbrook: I'd like to make three small points about practices that have been discussed. First of all on the question of whether a *nadītu* could go out of the house. There is a clause in the Code of Hammurabi which places severe penalties on a *nadītu* who is caught drinking in a tavern. If she could go into a tavern to drink and presumably be punished for it, presumably she was allowed to go walking around the streets of her town. The second point, on inheritance: somebody asked about the division of estates; well in male inheritances it was a severe problem resulting in extremely small holdings, even rooms in houses split between brothers, and there are clauses in the laws which enjoined the elder brother not to swindle the younger brothers who are forced to sell off at a discount because their holdings were not viable. So I agree that just the economic aspect, saying that was the purpose of keeping *nadītu*s, doesn't seem to be adequate, because this didn't deal with the main economic problem which came on the male side. That brings me to the third point, which I am a bit surprised hasn't been raised; that is the religious aspect. Should we forget that these women were women of religion? Our view is skewed by the texts we have, which happen to be economic texts, economic legal texts. Religion was central, and women of religion presumably played some important role, but we just don't happen to know what was going on.

Harris: You're so right, and I was always aware of that. By the way, in terms of the Code of Hammurabi, one has to be very careful in using the Code of Hammurabi for expressing reality. First of all, it's very vague what kind of *nadītu*. I wrote something way back in the '60's in *Orientalia* on the *nadītu*-laws of the Code of Hammurabi, and the legal texts as they were on the *nadītu* and Hammurabi. Hammurabi simply reinforces some of the things then in effect. I think that one has to use Hammurabi very carefully.

Westbrook: As far as Hammurabi is concerned I think he is a very true mirror of the law.

Allam: I would like to point out that we have in our Egyptian evidence something which could be similar to the situation under discussion. We have a category of ladies, who were devoted to the chief god in Thebes, Amun, and we have now the impression that these women were kept celibate all their lives, and they came usually from rich families. They were, or their parents were of a very high stratum in Egyptian society. We know that at the height of this institution, which is of a religious nature, the holder of the office, the Divine Adoratrice, was celibate and she remained as such, and she was of a very high position in Egyptian society. Very often she was the daughter of the King, and these women used to induct new members into this order by adoption, and these obtained considerable property, as Professor Menu has explained. We have many documents pertaining to this especially what is known in Egyptology as the Adoption Stela from which we see the office-holder having already adopted the princess, or daughter of the king. Because of a change of rulers, she was obliged by the new king to adopt his daughter and to pass over her property to her.

Some Aspects of the Position of Women in Nuzi

Katarzyna Grosz

1. Introduction

The ancient city of Nuzi was located in the northern part of Mesopotamia close to the modern city of Kirkuk. It flourished in the period 1450-1350 B.C.[1], a period which is scantily documented in the rest of Mesopotamia. In this period Nuzi was a part of the kingdom of Arrapha which in its turn belonged to the Hurrian state of Mitanni. The population of Nuzi was mainly Hurrian and so was the spoken language, but documents were written in a corrupt form of Babylonian. Assyriologists have always considered this city as atypical and certain social and legal practices attested in the sources are traditionally considered alien to the rest of Semitic Mesopotamia. Whether or not this is correct is, in my opinion, still a matter of belief rather than knowledge.

2. Sources

Some five thousand cuneiform tablets were found at Nuzi--a major part of them during archaeological excavations. Tablets concerning women consist of legal, administrative and economic documents, both of private and official character. The latter are lists of palace personnel and various rations issued to them. They have not yet been adequately studied. Although many women were mentioned in these documents, the structure of evidence requires an approach different from that applicable to private documents.

There are numerous private documents originating from various family archives, but unfortunately, in the 1920's when the tablets were found, it was customary to publish cuneiform documents according to their legal genre rather than archival context and many family archives were thus

[1]G. Wilhelm, "Grundzüge der Geschichte und Kultur der Hurriter," *Gründzuge*, 45 (Darmstadt:1982), 61.

dispersed. Scholars wishing to study the family structure and other social phenomena related to the family are therefore often forced to re-assemble the archive(s) as the first stage of their investigations.

The private family archives of Nuzi have been found in two places: the main tell of Nuzi and a small mound outside of the city where mansions of the rich and influential members of the society were situated. Thus, all tablets come from an urban area but they nevertheless concern people who derived their livelihood mainly from land. There is a great degree of variation in their wealth and status. The documents cover some five generations of these families' history. A majority of tablets deal with various forms of transfer of land and although women do sporadically appear in them, it is marriage documents, divorces, transfers of dowry and bridewealth, and wills that constitute our most important sources. They provide insight into such spheres of women's lives as: the position of daughters in their fathers' household, marriage and divorce, position of widows and heiresses, spheres of women's economic activities, etc. The documents are very formulaic in structure, consisting of standard clauses, arranged in set patterns which the scribes, no doubt, learned by heart. The Nuzi documents throw light on a very limited range of (legal) aspects of life while the entire universe of thoughts, beliefs and ideologies, remains completely outside of our reach.

In this paper I would like to offer some remarks on a range of topics relating to various aspects of women's position in Nuzi society. I have dealt with these topics in some detail on other occasions and will therefore only present my conclusions here, without getting into a detailed analysis of sources. My comments will concentrate on the following issues:

a) The function of marriage payments, bridewealth and dowry.

b) The role of women in the patrilineal system of kinship and inheritance of Nuzi as expressed in the position of daughters appointed as sons and wives appointed as guardians.

The private documents of Nuzi have been investigated in the first half of this century by a number of eminent scholars of law. The result was a series of studies of great scientific interest and merit.[2] The research was based on

---

[2]It is impossible to mention a representative selection of them here. A bibliography of Nuzi studies up to 1969 is available in M. Dietrich, O. Loretz and W. Mayer, *Nuzi Bibliographie*, *AOATS* 11 (Kevelaer, 1972).

the theory of legal evolutionism and differences observed in legal institutions were perceived as developmental stages of a single structure which was gradually evolving into institutions such as we know them in our own society. Legal or social practices which could not be explained as developmental stages of this particular structure were sometimes more or less dismissed as legal tricks serving to camouflage various transactions which for some reasons were reprehensible. This way of perceiving the evidence in some cases led to studies of ancient social practices in terms which, although appropriate to our own society, were nevertheless alien to the cultures investigated. In my own research I have found methods developed by social anthropology very useful for a study of social relationships. This concerns for instance the study of marriage payments.

3. Bridewealth[3]

Nuzi marriages are as a rule accompanied by two payments--bridewealth and dowry. The bridewealth, since it is a transaction between the bride-giving and the bride-receiving family is often mentioned in the marriage contract itself. The amount of bridewealth is stated, as well as the terms of payment often involving instalments over a period of time. Generally, all marriage contracts in Nuzi include statements concerning bridewealth. There is also a number of documents recording transfer of movables such as livestock, silver, etc. which are called "money of FN." The amounts mentioned in these cases correspond nicely with what seems to have been accepted as instalments on bridewealth and therefore, even though no word "bridewealth" is mentioned in these texts, I assume that transfers of "money, or silver of FN" concern payments of bridewealth.

It sometimes occurs that the bridewealth or a portion of it is given to the bride, obviously to constitute her dowry.[4] Historians of ancient law interpreted this custom as one of the developmental stages of the marriage institution, when the price for the woman was slowly being transformed into

[3]Cf. my "Dowry and Brideprice in Nuzi," SCCNH 1, 161-182, subsequently cited as Grosz, 1981. In this article I investigated these two marriage prestations, comparing their usage in Nuzi with the theories of J. Goody and S. J. Tambiah. Cf. Goody and Tambiah, "Bridewealth and Dowry," *Cambridge Papers in Social Anthropology*, 7 (Cambridge: 1973), subsequently quoted as Goody and Tambiah, 1973. I used the term "brideprice" instead of "bridewealth" because the former was the accepted form in Assyriology. I have since then abandoned "brideprice" in favor of "bridewealth"--cf. "Bridewealth and Dowry in Nuzi," *Images of Women in Antiquity*, A. Cameron and A. Kuhrt eds. (London, 1983), 193-206.

[4]Cf. Grosz 1981; 171. The phraseology is *X ina qanni FN rakāsu*, "to bind X in FN's hem."

her dowry. According to them,[5] the institution of marriage underwent several stages of development. In the beginning women were more or less bought like chattels, the bridewealth being the purchase price paid for the woman in question. The next stage of development occurred when the bridewealth, or a portion of it, was turned over to the bride as her dowry. The last stage was marriage with dowry.[6]

I have tried to find a different explanation for both the bridewealth itself and its transfer to the bride. Several parallels to this practice in different societies exist all over the globe where it typically occurs in relatively poor families. This payment is called "indirect dowry" by social anthropologists.[7] In India and China, for instance, the transfer of bridewealth to the bride conceals the fact that bridewealth is being given at all--in both these societies there are different forms of marriage, associated with different social classes and bridewealth is practiced by the lowest ones. Marriage with bridewealth and indirect dowry ranks somewhere in the middle of the scale.[8]

The social stratification of marriage payments in Nuzi must for the time being remain within the realm of conjecture. There are only very few marriage contracts concerning women from high levels of the society and in them bridewealth is not mentioned. So far, Nuzi seems thus to conform with the above pattern. However, in international royal marriages between the kings of the ancient Near East in the Amarna age bridewealth and dowry occur together. This is a significant indication that attributing different marriage payments to different strata of the society may be an oversimplification in the case of the ancient Near East.

---

[5]Cf. for example P. Koschaker, *Rechtsvergleichende Studien zur Gesetzgeburg Hammurapis*, (Leipzig, 1917), esp. Chapter II "Eherecht," 111 ff.; same author, *Neue Keilschriftrechtliche Rechtsurkunden aus der El-Amarna-Zeit*, *ASAW* 39 (Leipzig, 1928); Koschaker, Fratriarchat, Hausgemeinschaft und Mutterrecht in Keilschriftrechten, *ZA* 41, 1933; A. Van Praag, "Droit Matrimonial Assyro-Babylonien," *Allard Pierson Stichting*, *Archaeologische-Historische Bijdragen*, XII, (Amsterdam, 1945).

[6]Now, since the dowry is an expression of female inheritance rights (I shall return to this point later on) the implicit conclusion must be that female inheritance rights were a developmental stage of a system in which women originally did not have inheritance rights at all.

[7]Cf. Tambiah in Goody and Tambiah 1973, 71-72.

[8]It is important to remember, however, that there are societies which practice one form of marriage payment to the exclusion of the other. Goody's theory associates dowry with monogamy, bridewealth primarily with polygyny. Dowry systems are believed to be an Asiatic form, while bridewealth is characteristic of Africa. No opinion is expressed on societies where both dowry and bridewealth are practiced. Cf Goody and Tambiah, 1973.

An important part of the socio-anthropological theory of bridewealth concerns its strongly ritual aspect. Even though the amount of bridewealth depends on the bride's qualifications, such as her looks, diligence and skills, and social position, and even though establishing the actual sum can be accompanied by ferocious haggling, the transfer of bridewealth is not considered as purchase. The transaction, even though it undoubtedly has economic aspects, is not perceived in the same terms as purchase of commodities or livestock and a suggestion that a woman is being transferred as chattel is considered offensive in societies where bridewealth is being practiced. In some societies the bridewealth can only be paid in certain goods which circulate in the society, handed over as bridewealth from family to family. This circulation of bridewealth items demonstrates more clearly that the transfer has extremely strong ritual aspects which simply cannot be overlooked for the advantage of the economic ones.

I believe that the bridewealth in Nuzi (and in the rest of Mesopotamia as well, for that matter) should be perceived along the same lines. I do not wish to deny the economic aspects of bridewealth transfers. But I think it is more important to place them within the realm of ritual rather than sale/purchase. The phraseology of the bridewealth contracts, from which the sale/purchase terminology is conspicuously absent, substantiates my claim.[9]

4. Dowry

While the bridewealth is a transaction between two families, dowry, on the other hand, is in essence a transaction between the bride and her father, since it concerns her patrimonial inheritance share.[10] While sons have to wait for their share of patrimony until the death of their father, daughters are paid off at the moment of their marriage. Therefore, even though dowry and bridewealth occur together at the moment of marriage (and even though the groom's family can influence the size of dowry) the two transactions are completely different in nature. Bridewealth does not and cannot exist without marriage or transfer of marrying rights, but dowry does since it is simply an expression of female inheritance rights in a specific situation--that of marriage. Transfer of a portion of the patrimonial estate to a daughter is in both cases essentially the same whether it occurs at the moment of her marriage or at the death of her father.

---

[9]I have recently argued that several other transactions involving women in Nuzi should also be studied from the viewpoint of their social and ritual, rather than economic, character. Cf. K. Grosz, "On Some Aspects of the Adoption of Women at Nuzi," *SCCNH*, II (Winona Lake, 1987), 131-152. Subsequently quoted as Grosz 1987.

[10]Cf Goody and Tambiah 1973, 17 & 61-64.

There are only a few records of transfer of dowry in Nuzi and they all concern immovable property.[11] This is not surprising since all transfer of land required a written document, while that of movables was only seldom recorded in writing.[12] However, no matter how rare transfers of land to daughters as dowry (or, for that matter as inheritance share in wills)[13] are, the fact remains that daughters could and did receive land.

There is reason to believe that a standard dowry consisted of movables rather than land.[14] When Nuzi girls were given land as their dowry they presented their father with a payment which I have called a "counter-dowry payment"[15] consisting of movables such as livestock, silver and textiles, i.e., items which a daughter could probably acquire through her own work or be given as gifts at various occasions. Why did the daughter transfer these objects to her father when she was given land? My assumption is that these movables made up a standard dowry, which a girl collected throughout her life in her parents' household. When she then received the dowry in immovables she may have given up her claim to the movables. Interestingly, household utensils and furniture were not given as counter-dowry payments, even though there is some evidence that such items were given to daughters at their marriage.[16] It is therefore possible that we have to distinguish further between dowry and trousseau, that is between the inheritance portion and items given specifically to enable the daughter to set up her own household.

---

[11]Cf. Grosz 1981, 170.

[12]However, transfer of bridewealth, even though involving movables, was recorded in writing because it was seldom transferred in one portion--the payment was as a rule made by instalments; see Grosz 1981, 176-177. The contractual situation stretched thus over several years and therefore needed a written record.

[13]For daughter's inheritance share as reflected in wills cf. Grosz 1981, 168.

[14]When daughters are given land, their brothers' inheritance is automatically diminished. While brothers' patrimony will in the future provide livelihood for themselves and their families, the daughters' share is (therefore?) as a rule much smaller than a son's and whenever it is possible, it is given in movables rather than land. Cf., for instance, E. Le Roy-Laduria, "Family structures and inheritance customs in sixteenth-century France," *Family and Inheritance: Rural Society in Western Europe 1200-1800*, J. Goody, J. Thirsk, E.P. Thompson eds., (Cambridge, 1976), 37-70. Other contributions to the same volume also provide much insight into this subject.

[15]Cf. Grosz 1981, 173.

[16]See for instance the document published in cuneiform by G. Contenau, *Contrats et lettres d'Assyrie et de Babylonie*, No. 1 *TCL* IX (Paris, 1926) and in transliteration and translation by C. Gordon, *Nuzi Tablets Relating to Women*, *An. Or.* 12, 178-179. It is a list of household utensils given by a man to a woman (she is not called his daughter or sister). The purpose of the transfer is not stated. Another, clearer indication is from the will HSS XIX 10 in which the testator describes some furniture, oil, wine, and copper as "utensils from her (i.e., the wife's) father's house."

The evidence is so scarce, however, that conclusions on this subject are not possible.

5. Women, land and lineage--daughters appointed as sons

Women's inheritance rights to land have very far reaching consequences for the entire society. Let us consider some possible implications. If the daughter marries a man from a neighboring village, arrangements must be made as to tilling her dowry land, perhaps leasing it to the woman's brothers, etc. The link between the two families is therefore strengthened by additional ties of mutual expectations and obligations concerning the administration and cultivation of the dowry land. Women's right to own land has therefore consequences on the social level as well as on the purely material one. Unfortunately, the reconstruction of the family archives from Nuzi is not yet sufficiently detailed to permit tracing such relationships.

Let us consider further the implication of women's right to inherit immovable property. In a hypothetical family where a man has two sons, his property, immovable as well as movable, will be divided between them after his death.[17] Even though each son will own less of the paternal land than his father did, the entire property will remain within the same lineage. Let us now consider a family in which a man has a son and a daughter and he choses to give land to both of them. The daughter's land will be lost to the family because her children who would eventually receive it would not belong to her patrilineage but to that of her husband's. It is most probably this consideration which makes the fathers reluctant to equip their daughters with immovable property.

What happens in situations when no sons, but only daughters are born in a family? There are two problems inherent in these situations: a) the question of transmission of property within the family, and b) the continuation of the patrilineage. When a Nuzi family had no male descendants, daughters could fulfill the role which was habitually reserved for sons. I have treated this subject recently and attempted to demonstrate that the society of Nuzi and that of the Syrian city of Emar found similar ways of dealing with the problem of patrilineal family in which only daughters are born.[18]

---

[17]Cf. my forthcoming *The Archive of the Wullu Family*, Carsten Niebuhr Institute Publications, V (Copenhagen, 1988) (subsequently cited as Grosz 1988), chapter on "Ownership of Land" for a discussion of various models of divisions of property at Nuzi.

[18]Grosz, "Daughters Adopted as Sons at Nuzi and Emar," *La Femme Dans Le Proche-Orient Antique*, XXXIIIe Rencontre Assyriologique Internationale (Paris, 1987), 81-86.

There are two wills from Nuzi and two from Emar dealing with this situation. The phraseology is slightly different in Nuzi and Emar: in the former the daughters are given the rank of sons or, we could perhaps say, heirs; in the latter they are established as "man and woman." Through this procedure the daughters obtain a status which makes it possible for them to inherit their parents' entire property.[19] More important still, in three of the four wills (both wills from Emar and one will from Nuzi) the daughters are given their fathers' gods and made responsible for carrying on the cult of the family spirits.[20]

Now, the fact that in the absence of men women could inherit the family gods and officiate in the family cult is of great importance. There is no doubt in my mind that the cult of the family gods and dead ancestors, even though not often referred to in legal, administrative, or economic evidence,[21] played an important role in the social life of the family and was one of the sources from which its members derived their identity. Perhaps even more so because last names, or family names were not used--the name as such did not identify a person as a member of a given family. The fact that women could not only participate in, but sometimes also could carry on the family's cult is therefore of tremendous importance. In this context it is immaterial that they could do so only in special circumstances.

Let us now consider the question of lineage. A woman's children belonged normally to her husband's lineage--therefore, if she had no brothers her line ended with her. Two different solutions were found to this problem. If the daughter was married, her father would adopt his son-in-law and in this way bind his daughter's children to his own lineage. Adopted sons-in-law were prohibited from alienating any part of the family estate, from disinheriting their children, or selling them into slavery under the penalty of forfeiting their inheritance. Their authority remained thus limited even after the death of the father-in-law. Whether the son-in-law ever became a full member of the new family or functioned simply as a producer of heirs, is therefore open to discussion. In my eyes his position is equal to that of a wife

---

[19]I have established that the testators in three of the four wills had brothers, the situation in the last will is unknown. I believe that, were the daughters not given the status of heirs, the testator's brothers would have probably taken over his property and equipped their nieces with standard dowries of movables.

[20]Or so I assume. The phrasing is "she will respect/obey my gods and spirits." The same vague verb "to respect/obey" (*palāhu*) is used with reference to men in other contexts. No specific acts of worship are ever mentioned.

[21]Cf. forthcoming Grosz 1988, chapter "The cult."

in her husband's household and definitely not comparable to that of a naturally born son.

The other way of attaching a daughter's children to her own lineage was, I believe, through giving her the full status of son and the right to inherit the family gods and take care of the family spirits. The phraseology of the wills in question seems to indicate that the daughters mentioned in these documents were not yet married.

I have noticed that in some documents from Nuzi men appear who use matronymics rather than patronymics. Their status seems to have been exactly the same as that of any other man--they appear as witnesses or parties to transactions. It seems therefore improbable that they could be illegitimate children of the women in question.

> Cf., however, R. Harris' contribution to this volume where she states that men using matronymics were sons of prostitutes. The word *harimtu* "prostitute" appears also in Nuzi and the Chicago Assyrian Dictionary quotes three occurrences. JEN text 666 is a lawsuit between two men, Hutija, son of Kuššija and Mušteja, son of the woman Zilija. Hutija declared that his (deceased) brother, Tarmija, made a public declaration that the woman Zilija was not his wife, but his *harimtu*. He was able to produce witnesses in front of whom this declaration has been made. The witnesses and Mušteja are then asked to submit to a divine ordeal,[22] but since Mušteja refused to do so, Hutija won the case. It seems that the object of the lawsuit was establishing Mušteja's legitimacy--he obviously postulated that his mother was Tarmija's wife. Although the document is not perfectly preserved, there seems to be no reference to Tarmija's property which is not at issue here. Of course, had Mušteja succeeded in establishing his legitimacy, he would also have a valid claim to his father's estate. The other document, JEN text 671, is a declaration made by several men who state that a daughter of a certain man under no circumstances is to be brought up as a prostitute.[23]
>
> The third document, JEN text 397, concerns a stolen young animal whose carcass was found in a certain house. The woman living in

---

[22]This ceremony was called "to lift the gods"--the party who refused to do so lost the ordeal. For an investigation of divine ordeals and river ordeals in Nuzi, cf. T. Frymer-Kinsky, "Suprarational Legal Procedures in Elam and Nuzi," *SCCNH* 1, 115-131.

[23]This declaration does not concern JEN 666 as was postulated by H. Lewy in *OR*. NS 10 (1941), 218.

> this house attempts to shift the blame on others and claims innocence and finally declares "my daughter is a prostitute, she brought the animal into my houses." The implication seems to be "since she is a prostitute you can expect anything of her, even accepting stolen animals." An examination of occurrences of the abstract noun harimutu "prostitution" also clearly indicates that this profession was not held in high esteem in Nuzi.
> To return to the main argument: JEN text 666 proves that a man bearing a matronymic could indeed be a son of a prostitute. However, is it a coincidence that in this single certain case the son of the prostitute is engaged in legal proceedings trying to establish that his mother *was not a prostitute*? His attempts ending in failure, he disappears from our sources. It is dangerous to draw conclusions from a single piece of evidence, but I think it is possible to tentatively conclude that sons of prostitutes in Nuzi did not enjoy a high rank, first of all, because prostitution as such was not esteemed and secondly, because born out of wedlock, they did not have a natural place in a patrilineal society. I do not believe that prostitutes' children with their low status would be asked to act as witnesses in economic and legal transactions. Given the dominant importance of witnesses in legal proceedings, only persons enjoying respect of their community were likely to be chosen for this role.

I believe it is legitimate (no pun intended) to consider the possibility that other men in Nuzi who used matronymics instead of patronymics were sons of women appointed as sons. These men did not attempt to prove their legitimacy, to exchange their matronymic for a patronymic. They appeared in the same roles as other men, who used patronymics; they acted as parties in transactions and as witnesses. There were also women who used matronymics, even though they were married and the name of their father was also known from other contexts.[24]

In my study of daughters appointed as sons I have quote an Indian practice which seems to present a striking parallel to the Nuzian and Emariote custom of adopting daughters as sons:

> The *putrika-putra* "the daughter treated as son" or to give another construction, "the son of an appointed daughter," is a justly famous

---

[24]For instance, the lady Tulpunnaja whose archive (found in a temple) demonstrates clearly that she was a wealthy and important person. She used a matronymic even though the name of her father is known and even though she was married. Apart from the fact that her archive was found in the temple, there is no evidence that either she or her mother were priestesses.

concept in traditional Hindu law, which highlights the fact that in the absence of male issue the daughter becomes the link in the chain of continuity. In the case of appointed daughter the classical formulation was that she was appointed in order that she might raise a son for her sonless father. The daughter so appointed resided uxorically with her father's family, and her son was considered the son of her father (and not her husband's). Thus an heir was produced to continue the line. The logic of the operation was something like this according to some commentators. The appointed daughter herself was considered equivalent to a son, and therefore her son was equivalent to a grandson. As the merits of a son and grandson are equal (e.g. in offerings made to ancestors) the latter ranked as a son.[25]

6. *Women as guardians*

Let us now briefly investigate the status of wives appointed as guardians. There exists a group of wills in Nuzi in which testators appointed their wives as guardians over their children and property.[26] The guardian's status persisted until her death and entailed an almost total control over the property and members of the household.

It is extremely important and cannot be stressed enough that only women were appointed guardians.[27] This is true even in cases when a reconstruction of the archival context of the wills leaves no doubt that the testator had brothers. They did not automatically become guardians over his children and property. It is of course possible that the situations recorded in documents were entirely unusual (which is why they were recorded in the first place) and that in more "orthodox" situations guardians were chosen from among men and not women. On the other hand, one is tempted to suggest that guardians were appointed exactly *in order to avoid* any interference from the husband's male kin. A man's wife was a safer bet than his brothers when it came to taking care of the children's interests.

There were two limitations to the guardian's authority: a) she was not allowed to alienate any part of the property to a stranger (in case she wished to remarry she was to leave all her possessions behind her), and b) she was not allowed to disinherit the children or sell them into slavery. These two

---

[25]Tambiah in Goody and Tambiah 1973, 79.

[26]Cf. J.S. Paradise, *Nuzi Inheritance Practices*, unpublished Ph.D. Dissertation, University of Pennsylvania, 1972, 285-297. Cited here as Paradise, 1972.

[27]Cf. Paradise, 1972, 285: "In most cases the guardian is the testator's wife. However, in the attested cases of equal division she is either the mother or daughter of the testator."

limitations have always been interpreted as a clear indication of the women's generally inferior status.

However, a study of the documents in which sons-in-law are adopted by their fathers-in-law demonstrates that exactly the same limitations were imposed on husbands of heiresses.[28] They too were not allowed to transfer anything to strangers, to sell or disinherit their children under the penalty of forfeiting their inheritance rights. In short: all efforts were made to ensure that property and descendants remain in the father-in-law's lineage. Exactly the same was the case with women appointed as guardians. The husband whose patrimonial property formed the core of the family estate made sure that in case of his wife's second marriage the estate would not be transferred outside of his family.

It is true that limitations were imposed on women more often than on men, simply because women in patrilineal societies are the ones who cross the family borders. When they marry they do not become members of their husband's lineage--only their children do. Thus, women could be termed a "foreign element" in their husbands' families--an element recruited in order to perpetuate the lineage, but simultaneously potentially dangerous to it in the event of the husband's death.[29] Dangerous exactly in the same way in which an adopted son-in-law was to his wife's patrilineage.[30] And therefore the same measures were undertaken to neutralize his potentially dangerous activities. In this context it is perhaps more useful to conceptualize the effort to keep children and property inside the lineage as a characteristic of the patrilineal system rather than one of the manifestations of women's inferior position.

This should not lead us to the conclusion that women's rights were anywhere equal to men's. There is of course no doubt whatsoever that

[28]Cf. Grosz, 1987, 84.

[29]Probably especially in cases when the link between the wife/guardian and her native family (brothers) was strong. The situation was most dangerous in the case of the guardian's re-marriage, since a perfect stranger could then make decisions about the first husband's property and children. This situation is well illustrated in the document HSS XIV 8, where a man claims that his mother's second husband, upon receiving the family gods, sold his wife and her daughter into slavery. Cf. E. Cassin, "Une Querelle de Familie," *SCCNH* 1, 41-46 and K. Deller, "Die Hausgötter der Familie Šukrija S. Huja," *SCCNH* 1, 59-63.

[30]This is well illustrated by a group of documents in which a man is adopted by his father-in-law but upon his death transfers his entire property to his own brother, in violation of the terms of his adoption. Cf. Grosz, 1987, 84 and note 16.

women's position was different from men's--this is simply inherent in the patrilineal system of any ancient society.

Women were born under the authority of their father, later on they passed under that of their husband. But let us not forget that in the beginning they were not worse off than their brothers. All childrens' rights were limited as long as their father was alive--he arranged his sons' as well as his daughters' marriages, he also had the ultimate right to his family members' private property, whether they were his sons or daughters.[31] The position of sons and daughters changed radically at the moment of the father's death because, while sons, or at least adult sons, obtained full authority over themselves, the same was not the case with daughters. They needed someone to take care of their interests and their brothers were natural candidates for this. Documents from Nuzi make it clear, however, that brothers' authority over their sisters was not the same as fathers'. This can be seen from the fact that when brothers arranged their sisters' marriages the latters' explicit consent was necessary. Brothers probably also administered their unmarried sisters' property although the extent of their authority in this respect is unknown. It depended probably on the character of the property--it is conceivable that in case of immovables which required tilling or such the brothers' authority was complete if they provided the labour required for the task. It is also possible that enterprising and energetic women could attain much independence in this respect.

The one domain in which women simply could not act for their own behalf was that of marriage negotiations. A number of the so-called sistership contracts in which women appoint persons (they are called "brothers") who will arrange their marriage for them clearly indicates that go-betweens were necessary in this case.[32] Marriage negotiations were as a rule the only task expected of these appointed brothers. It is worth stressing that these so-called brothers were not appointed by anybody but the women themselves. It seems therefore that at least in the case of adult women (or perhaps only widows) there were no kinsmen apart from the father and brothers who *automatically* had any authority over them. Nor was there any official authority who would appoint their guardians.

---

[31]This can be clearly seen from the fact that this property is often mentioned in wills. The clause in question reads either that there will be no "private accumulations" or that these will be respected. Cf. Paradise, 1972, 253-258.

[32]Cf. B. Eichler, "Another Look at Nuzi Sistership Contracts," *Ancient Near Eastern Studies in Memory of J.J. Finkelstein*, edited by M. de Jong Ellis, (Hamden, Connecticut, 1977); and Grosz, 1987, 150-152.

There is clear evidence that mothers rranged their sons' and daughters' marriages.[33] I am sure that these were mothers who were invested with the status of guardian. Thus, while women could not negotiate their own marriage they could do so, at least in special cases, on behalf of others. It may have been a question of propriety or decorum which forbade a woman to enter into negotiations concerning her own marriage. A female guardian negotiating marriage for her children was obviously entirely admissible.

In conclusion I would like to underline that to my knowledge, there is no single economic or legal genre of document in which women do not appear as active participants. It is true that they are rare, but they write wills, adopt, and disinherit, receive their family gods, inherit their fathers' entire property and pass on their name to their sons. The fact that these cases are few and perhaps exceptional is counterbalanced by the fact that women could and did engage themselves in all spheres of life. This could be perceived as a sign of weakening of the strictly patrilineal system of Nuzi. I believe that such a conclusion would be erroneous. Even though women could act independently in some cases there is no doubt that their special position in these cases *ensured* further existence of their patrilineage and of its property. Instead of breaking down the patrilineal system of descent and inheritance they acted as a security measure for its smooth working even in extreme situations in which the patriliny was threatened. Therefore, I do not believe that we should perceive female guardians or daughters appointed as sons as champions on the path of equality between men and women. The mental framework of the Nuzi society could not house such a concept. Women could and did achieve important positions as integral parts of this system and not in opposition to it.

Therefore, I think, it would be more appropriate to describe Nuzi as a strictly patrilineal society which, in order to preserve itself, invested women with special properties which ultimately served to preserve the patriliny of kinship and inheritance.

---

[33]Cf. forthcoming Grosz, 1988, Part Six: Peripheral Archives, *dossier* Šekar-tilla, son of Wanti-muša.

Responses to Prof. Grosz's paper

Morrison: First of all I would like to review the central point of the paper. Women can be viewed as transmitters and as preservers of the family estate, especially real property, in cases where there are no sons or other men in the family to do so. Nuzi had certain social and legal vehicles designed to legitimize this role, among them the adoption of daughters and various guardianship arrangements. I agree with this completely. At Nuzi there was great concern for the integrity of the family property. Real estate, i.e., fields, houses and orchards, was, after all, both a limited resource and one of the primary bases of wealth in that fundamentally agricultural economy. The quantity, quality and location (including contiguity of the various parcels the family owned) of real estate determined the family's ability to produce, not only its means of subsistence, but also its ability to enter the markets of the community. Many archives document the efforts of family members to keep family property intact. These include straightforward steps such as a man's drawing up his will in such a way that his real estate is not over-divided or adopting as his heir a nephew or other family member who owned or would own part of the family estate so as to reconsolidate family holdings. Among more well-to-do families, there are instances in which family property that had passed to strangers was re-acquired by successful members of the family. There are other cases in which a wealthy branch of a family contracts with other, less prosperous branches either to purchase or lease family property. In such a society, then, where family attachment to land was so strong, it is not surprising that women, when they were the surviving representatives of the family line, would function as Dr. Grosz has described. I would like now to take this opportunity to offer some additional observations concerning "women at Nuzi."

The Nuzi corpus is one of the richest sources of information that we have for the social and economic dynamics of a second millennium Western Asian community. Tracing six generations of this community, the Nuzi texts originate in both private and palace archives. They document activities of the rich and poor, free and slave, and urban and rural residents. Publication of this extensive corpus is still in progress so all of the data have not been available for analysis. Therefore, my remarks must be understood as descriptive and tentative. Nonetheless, I believe that we will hear echoes of presentations throughout the symposium and, I hope have glimpses of the role that women played in Nuzi society.

A note of caution concerning the Nuzi texts is in order, however. Tablets were kept by their owners because they continued to have meaning. Contracts that were still in force, texts that proved ownership of property (contracts, law suits, wills, marriage documents, and a host of others, including the texts Dr. Grosz discussed) and administrative texts from active households are found in the corpus. Texts from early generations that were no longer useful, such as contracts that had expired, old administrative materials and the like, we believe were cleared from the archives periodically. Therefore, our information is skewed to the later period. Furthermore, because the number of wills and marriage documents that we have represents only a small fraction of the number of families for whom inheritance and marriage were concerns, it is believed that the texts that were written describe anomalous situations. With these caveats, we can examine the materials that pertain to women.

First of all, one very important source of information that Dr. Grosz mentioned was the ration lists from the palace and the household of Prince Šilwa-Tešup. These texts have been studied at some length, and we can draw some conclusions about the composition and operation of the households of the great estates. Among the workers on the great estates, both private and public, there were many women. Most of these were weavers in the large-scale textile industry that produced one of the important trade goods of the community. Among the weavers there were both male and female supervisors. One can document the rise of these supervisors through the ranks from their youth to maturity when they were entrusted with substantial responsibilities. In another industry, women are found receiving grain and malt for brewing. As might be expected, women are also nurses. We have at least one gate keeper (*maṣṣartu*) and even one woman who appears among the herdsmen, though only in a single reference. For their labor, the women received grain rations, oil rations, and garments. The male and female workers are identified by the city, town, or village in which they lived, so they appear to have been dispersed throughout the holdings of the great estates.

We can also reconstruct the family and household of the prince, albeit a royal fellow. He had one chief wife and seven to nine women in one household and two to four in another who are designated *esrīti*, usually translated as "concubines." The chief wife and some of these concubines had children. The chief wife standardly received significantly larger rations of all types than the concubines. Further, the children of the chief wife were the principle heirs and were given special privileges within the household. The children of the concubines also received special attention in the ration texts, though not to the degree of the chief wife's children, and the sons are brought up and trained much as the sons of the chief wife. They do share, though not equally, with the sons of the chief wife in the status of the Prince. The concubines who bore children received special treatment as a result of their motherhood: additional rations, servants, clothing, etc. Among the wives, therefore, was a hierarchy based on child-bearing.

A similar pattern is clear among private citizens. A primary wife's position in the household was just that--primary--and her children were chief heirs. A secondary wife, when an individual could support one, held lower rank, and her children shared according to their rank. In situations where the primary wife had no children, the secondary wife's children would inherit. As for inheritance practices, a number of wills were drawn up so as to entrust the husband's estate to his wife and grant her "fathership" of the family or to make special provisions for his wife's care after his death.

Marriage contracts are, of course, an important source of information concerning women. The issues of child-bearing and inheritance were so significant that there are marriage contracts stipulating that the financial arrangements surrounding the marriage were not to be concluded until the wife had conceived. Families involved in such transactions chose not to exchange property until there was a clear line of inheritance. Other marriage documents point to a similar interest in the division of property. On the highest level of the society, a princess' marriage document stipulates that her sons will be the primary heirs of the groom's property. (Another text itemizes the property she receives as her dowry.) In the city, a middle-class man remakes his will to give all of his property to a single son, apparently to reach an agreement with the bride's father.

In this case the bride seems to have been an only child who was herself a property owner. Through this arrangement, two family estates were joined to be inherited by the couple's children. Aside from these, a number of texts include property as part of the marriage agreement.

Through such marriage contracts, in which real estate is involved, the bride and groom's children ultimately have more property at their disposal than they would otherwise. In the cases where the bride's father transfers property, the bride's children, though officially "belonging" to the groom's family, end up with real estate transmitted through their mother. Thus, marriage agreements, like the daughtership and guardianship arrangements, were among the legal vehicles whereby women served to transmit family property.

Outside of the households, contracts testify to the economic activities of the women of Nuzi. They buy and sell real estate and slaves, contract for the herding of their livestock, and engage in exactly the same kinds of economic activities that men do. In the legal sphere, they can become guardians, go to court for legal remedy for their fiscal and social problems, and testify as witnesses and plaintiffs in court. They adopt men in real adoption texts and they bequeath their property, apparently as they choose. This holds true not only for well-to-do women but also for slave women. We have one text, for instance, in which one of the servants in Šilwa-Tešup's household leaves what amounts to her pots and pans to her son and puts them into the care of the major-domo of the house for her son.

Therefore, women at all levels of Nuzi society functioned in the economic and legal life of the community exactly as men did. Indeed, some to the most famous figures in the Nuzi archives are women. The lady Tulpun-naya was among the first known of these women. She was adopted frequently as a "son" in order to acquire real estate by the device that Dr. Grosz mentioned, the real estate adoption. She also acquired a considerable number of personnel who were received into her household as servants, and she receives a number of young women as "daughters" in order to arrange their marriages. An interesting counterpoint to this powerful woman was one of her slave girls for whom Tulpun-naya arranged a marriage. She objected to Tulpun-naya's choice, went to court, and won. Another private citizen, Winnirke, mother of Teḫip-tilla son of Puḫi-šenni, acquired extensive real estate holdings through land adoption agreements. On the royal side, Ammin-naya, wife of the king, received a substantial land grant from the king (as did one concubine) and she had her own households in Nuzi and elsewhere.

This leads me to an observation that speaks directly to the issue of the role of women in the transfer of land. In my experience, in every single significant archive at Nuzi, there is at least one woman who played a major role in the formation or dissolution of the family's estate. In the Teḫip-tilla archives, Winnirke, Teḫip-tilla's mother, a member of the second generation of the family, acquires substantial tracts of real estate. Teḫip-tilla and his descendants use this property and expand on it to amass enormous estates. She certainly appears to have acted on her own in acquiring the land and she passed it on to her son. The prince Šilwa-Tešup ran his mother's estates for a while and then seems to have owned them. In the less illustrious families-- the middle class of the city-- we find numerous instances of female family members playing important roles in the movement of property. In one case a widow contracts jointly with her son to lease or sell the family real estate, to her brother-in-law, incidentally. Her family's situation becomes increasingly desperate to the point that she and her daughter are sold off into a foreign land. (It is, of course, noteworthy that she could, on the one hand, be intimately involved in the transfer of real estate and, on the other, be sold off herself.) Another widow gives her daughter and the property her husband left her to a son on the condition that he care for her. Also from these urban archives come a number of cases of young women who are the final heirs to the family property. The circumstances of each are different. In the case that I mentioned previously, the woman is married to the son of the next-door neighbor. Because her family was more prominent, the groom's father had to change his will and leave all his property to the groom. Two large estates were thereby merged. Another young woman is left both property and debts. She contracted with a more prosperous older man to turn over her property on the condition that he pay the debts. This same older man not only transfers real estate as his daughter's *mulugu* but also takes in another woman as his charge. Throughout the urban archives, there are isolated texts involving the transfer of real estate as part of marriage or daughtership contracts. Further, other women were property owners who leave contracts, wills and legal texts. We see that, in this middle-class group, arrangements concerning women occupied some considerable attention and in nearly every case, that attention involved real estate.

While women's legal and property rights may have been the same as men's, the fact is that the greater percentage of the Nuzi contracts involve men contracting with men. This returns us to the issue of women and property. Most of the contracts involve the transfer of property or the rights to property of one kind or another and most of the court cases refer to disputes over real estate, slaves, silver, livestock and the like. Men who do not own property or are not engaged in its transfer, therefore, do not appear in the texts. The women who do appear clearly are property owners engaged in the management or disposition of their property. The relatively small percentage of texts involving women suggests that women's access to property was limited.

Aside from inheritance, an individual at Nuzi acquired real estate by purchase or lease and other property by purchase or any of a number of other arrangements. These transactions required a significant amount of excess wealth and the means to care for the property whether it be real estate, personnel, livestock, or anything else that had to be maintained. Women's access to the wealth necessary for property acquisition varied. Among the rich, wives and daughters seem to have received allowances which they could use as they pleased. Some women controlled property because they inherited it from their fathers or husbands. Some were custodians of their husbands' estates. Women who had such wealth could expand their holdings, dispose of their real estate to meet their immediate needs, or simply be the chief administrators of family estates.

The underlying factor in all of these situations is that the women receive their wealth or property in one way or another from a man. Only when the man ceases to exert his control either by choice or by death does the woman have the means to enter the economic life of the community. Furthermore, I believe that it is safe to say that the women who acquire property are all affiliated with an established family. They are identified as "wife of so-and-so" or "daughter of so-and-so." A number of the women who enter guardianship contracts through which they release their property to someone else have been left or would be left when their parents die with no surviving family. While these latter women had all of the legal and economic rights to own and maintain their property, they needed the protection that a guardian afforded and needed to "belong" to an existing household. At least one will suggests that it was possible for a woman to inherit property from her father, remain single, and retain both the property and her independence. Further evidence for such a situation, however, is not forthcoming from the Nuzi corpus.

To fully explore the relationship between women and property at Nuzi, we must also examine the complex matters of affiliation, inheritance practices, and family structures. The expression of this relationship that we find in the Nuzi texts appears to be a function of the more deeply embedded familial role of both men and women. Dr. Grosz's paper addresses one very interesting aspect of this question.

Grosz: Yes I would just like to comment on the last point of women adopting young women who will take care of them in their old age. I think it is important to realize that we also have men doing the same. On the question of people who have no relatives, I think the texts are both structurally and functionally very different from the ones in which women appoint guardians to negotiate their marriages.

Morrison: I agree. I would also like to point out that it is not just women who need to find a guardian. We have a number of instances of men, specifically men coming from outside the community with no particular association with a household or family, entering servitude or some kind of affiliation agreement with varying terms of labor. So the need for guardianship and affiliation is not limited to women.

Stone: One thing that I want to ask both of you is in terms of the documents about marriage, do you have about the same number as you do of inheritances or just a very small number of documents of marriages (which would suggest that the marriages that you see are perhaps the exceptional ones). The reason that I'm asking this question is that it really comes down to the question of endogamy. I think that was what was going on, and that's why we don't get very many marriage contracts. If this was an endogamus society then the reason you never turn to your father's brother, who might be the normal person, to whom to say "alright, you take care of this," is because he is also a potential father-in-law and would have incredible conflicts of interest under those circumstances. You don't want to put your daughter in a complete position of dependency on someone who might turn out to be her father-in-law. That is the reason that I am asking the question.

Grosz: I think it requires a reconstruction of genealogies which we unfortunately don't have yet. Well, now I really wanted to try to find some evidence for cross-cousin marriages taking place. Unfortunately it didn't work out.

Stone: But what percentage exists for the documents between inheritance and marriage? This is something people only do about once a lifetime: die and pass on their possessions, for men, or if they're women they get married. So if the percentages are equal then you can assume that what you are seeing in terms of marriage documents is most of the marriages that take place. Certainly, in the Old Babylonian period what you see is virtually no marriage documents, which presumably would relate to the fact that whatever was going on is not really critical, the ones that we do see are those in which you have a crisis and in which you have marriages that clearly are alliances. So that my question to you is do the Nuzi archives give you any information that might throw light on this? Would you have a lot of marriage documents?

Grosz: Oh, no. We have less than 10 and while I think it is so, I can't say whether there is anything special about these marriages. In the Code of Hammurabi it says that a marriage without a written document is not valid, which is of course simply Hammurabi's way of saying things which do not apply in this society. I think the writing of a marriage contract (and now I might be sticking my neck out) could have something to do with the marriage ritual and the ritual use of writing, which sort of made the occasion even more important. This is just one theory. I have no way of saying anything special about the families that conclude these marriages; and again marriage contracts are not usual, they are not more usual than any other....

Stone: What about dowry texts?

Grosz: I think I have something like six cases of dowry texts.

Morrison: A number of the texts that deal with women or with marriages survive because the deed to the property that was being transmitted from one family to another was built into the text. So, we have a third generation individual's text relating to marriage or whatever in which the transfer of real estate is included and those tablets are preserved to the end of the Nuzi corpus. In some instances we can actually trace where the real estate is, the hands through which it has passed and why it would be included in a particular archive.

Westbrook: Could I just take a moment to clarify a point which you made. What did you say about the Old Babylonian Period?

Morrison: I think that at Nippur you have something like six marriage documents, four of which are adoptions of second marriages and two would seem to be adoptions of heirs, a very complicated situation....

Westbrook: That's true of Nippur, but in the Old Babylonian period as a whole you have over 100 marriage documents.

Morrison: But compared to inheritances those numbers are very small. Even if there are over 100....

Westbrook: That's because most of the inheritances come from the cloister at Sippar, I think that is the reason. There are numerous marriage documents. We shouldn't get the impression that they are quite rare, they're not business documents, they're obviously not like check-stubs....

Grosz: I think that transfer of immovables are very rarely recorded in marriage contracts. But I think that marriage contracts as a rule don't include anything on immovable property and I think daughters normally were bought off, or paid off, whatever the expression is, in movables. This was one of the devices to keep the property as undivided as possible. I mean it's known in certain societies in Europe of the Sixteenth or Seventeenth centuries, that some of the sons may be bought out, or some of the sons buy out their brothers. This is something that I think you will find went on at Nuzi too. That brothers buy out their brothers in order to keep the paternal land intact.

Egypt in the First Millennium

Egypt of the final thousand years before our era was a changed world. Her greatest days were in the past, and her competing power centers during the Third Intermediate Period faced economic hardships and generally had lowered expectations and less impressive accomplishments. At Thebes the High Priests of Amun were the effective political rulers in the south, where now written and artistic records are much less plentiful. Tombs were, for the most part, no longer built, but burials were made instead in earlier sepulchres. The pharaohs of the Twenty-first Dynasty resided in the north--based at Tanis--but the area of the Delta has not received as much archaeological attention and has not preserved its antiquities as well, due to the high water table of the region.

The two political camps were tied together by marriage, if not by blood, and were not hostile rivals. Princesses were sent from the royal family at Tanis to become the wives of the High Priests in Thebes. The old sacerdotal post once the prerogative of the royal women in the Eighteenth Dynasty--the "God's Wife of Amun"--was now revived and bestowed upon a daughter of such unions.

Later in the Twenty-first Dynasty, marriage alliances also were arranged between the Tanite kings, the Great Chiefs of the Ma (Libyans) at Bubastis, and the High Priests of Ptah at Memphis. More obviously political was the marriage of the daughter of the last king of the dynasty to King Solomon of Jerusalem, to whom she brought the Palestinian town of Gezer as her dowry.

The political situation in Egypt during the Twenty-second Dynasty worsened and was fraught with hostilities for years between the North and South, verging on civil war, which disorganized and weakened the country. However, the celibate office of the God's Wife, perpetuated by adoptions, continued. Although the Nubian invasion of the Twenty-fifth dynasty restored order, it was apparently at the cost of many lives and the new unity and peace finally gained was not to be enjoyed for long before Egypt again fell victim to repeated attacks from abroad. This time the enemy was mighty Assyria, which first attacked the periphery and later launched two invasions of Egypt: the first under Esarhaddon, sacking Memphis, and the second under Assurbanipal, penetrating up river to Thebes, which was devastated and stripped of its treasure. The Assyrians had to withdraw soon thereafter, but left lackeys among the natives in both north and south to do their bidding.

Their loyal dynasty at Sais in the Delta eventually grew strong and more independent and was able to encourage a remarkable nationalistic and artistic revival of ancient Egyptian culture and to become the new masters of Egypt as the Twenty-sixth Dynasty. Psametichus I continued the practice of exerting influence in the south through the women of the royal family, by sending his eldest daughter Nitocris to be adopted as the succeeding God's Wife at Thebes, where she reigned for over 60 years. Her office brought with it great rewards (as was traditional) in the form of real-estate--more than 2000 acres in both Upper Egypt and the Delta--as well as large quantities of food rations to pay the vast personnel under her command. In time the First Prophet (or High Priest) of Amun's position was abandoned with its responsibilities apparently having been taken over by the God's Wife, who is now more popularly known as the "Divine Adoratrice."

Defeated by the Persian's invasion in 525 B.C., the Saite kings were followed by three Egyptian dynasties which made attempts to throw off the Persian yoke, and the Thirtieth Dynasty actually had some success before the second Persian domination, which was followed by the conquest of Alexander, who was certainly welcomed by many Egyptians in the late 4th century.

Considerable documentation exists for the average person from this late period, but from the seventh century on it is primarily written in the difficult demotic script, and is much less known than the abundant Greek material that survives from the relatively few Greek mercantile centers flourishing in Egypt at that time.

Leonard H. Lesko

Women and Business Life in the First Millennium B.C.

Bernadette Menu

From the advent of the priest kings to the intervention of Rome, Egypt experienced restless but very fertile times that can be divided into four periods:

1) The Tanite-Theban diarchy followed by the government of dynasties called Libyan (Twenty-first to Twenty-third Dynasties).

2) The Nubian Restoration and the Saite "Renaissance" (Twenty-fourth to Twenty-sixth Dynasties).

3) The Persian domination and the last national dynasties (Twenty-seventh-Thirty-first Dynasties).

4) The Macedonian conquest in 332 B.C. and the subsequent Hellenistic hegemony under the Ptolemaic Dynasty.

As far as law, social relations, and the economy are concerned, the first millennium in Egypt saw the development of a very elaborate system that expresses itself in texts of remarkable legal precision but one must ask what facts these documents actually cover and what do they reveal about the part played by women in business life.

For the four periods previously defined, the instrumentary sources can be divided as follows:

1) The stelae and reliefs of the Twenty-first-Twenty-third Dynasties including oracular decrees, donation and foundation stelae, as well as a boundary stele showing the constitution of an agricultural estate. In addition to these texts engraved in stone, there are the decrees of the High Priest Pinudjem and his wife Nesikhons that we have in several versions (on papyrus and on wood) as well as the contracts of Papyrus Berlin 3048 published by

Möller. Most of these documents concern women. Listed in chronological order the principal ones are the decrees for Henttawy and Istemkheb,[1] for Nesikhons[2] and for Princess Maatkare;[3] the decree of Shoshenq I, founder of the Twenty-second Dynasty, instituting the daily supply of an ox to be offered the god Arsaphes,[4] the donation stele of the fourth year of Pharaoh Shoshenq I;[5] the Dakhleh Stele of the fifth year of that same king;[6] the Apanage Stele of the tenth year of his son Osorkon I;[7] the Louvre Stele E 8099 of the same reign;[8] the Berlin Papyrus 3048 of the thirteenth and fourteenth years of one of the Takelot of the Twenty-second Dynasty;[9] and lastly the Cairo Stele JE 36159 of the twenty-fifth year of Takelot II and the Cairo Stelae JE 45948 and 11/9/21/14 of the tenth year of King Pwf-tjua-awy-Bast.[10]

The great cadastral papyri of that period, which are enumerated in Malinine's contribution to *Hommage Champollion*,[11] are still unfortunately largely unpublished. They would undoubtedly provide a considerable extra amount of information on the part played by women as landowners or as persons liable for taxes.

---

[1]G. Maspéro, *Les momies royales de Deir el-Bahari*, *MMAF* 1 (Cairo, 1894): 704-706; A. H. Gardiner, "The Gods of Thebes as Guarantors of personal property," *JEA* 48 (1962): 57-69.

[2]B. Gunn, "The Decree of Amonrasonthêr for Neskhons," *JEA* 41 (1955): 83-95, with an "Appendix," by I.E.S. Edwards, 96-105.

[3]Maspéro, *Les momies royales*, 693-697; Gardiner *op. cit.*, 64-69.

[4]P. Vernus, "Décret de Chéchanq I réglant la fourniture du Boeuf de l'offrande d'Arsaphès à Héracléopolis," *Tanis: l'or des Pharaons* (Paris, 1987): 107-108.

[5]D. Meeks, "Les donations aux temples dans l'Egypte du 1er millénaire avant J.-C.," *State and Temple Economy in the Ancient Near East* (Leuven, 1979), 665. E. Graefe, "Ein neue Schenkungstele aus der 22. Dynastie," *Armant*, 12 (1974): 3-9 & plate.

[6]A. H. Gardiner, "The Dakhleh Stela," *JEA* 19 (1933): 19-30 & pl. V-VII.

[7]Hieroglyphic transcription by G. Legrain, *ZÄS* 35 (1897): 12-16 and commentary by Adolf Erman, *ibid.* 19-24; J. Pirenne and B. Van de Walle, "Orient Ancien: 1. Egypte," *Archives d'Histoire du Droit Oriental* 1 (Bruxelles, 1937): 41-63; J. H. Breasted, *Ancient Records of Egypt*, 4 (Chicago, 1906), 405; H. Sottas, *La préservation de la propriété funéraire dans l'ancienne Égypte* (Paris, 1913), 161-165; B. Menu, "La stèle dite de l'Apanage," *Mélanges Pierre Lévêque* (Besançon, 1989).

[8]Meeks, "Les donations aux temples," 666.

[9]G. Möller, "Zwei ägyptischen Eheverträge aus vorsaitischer Zeit," *AKPAPHK* 3, (1918); Möller, "Ein ägyptischer Schuldschein der Zweiundzwanzigster Dynastie," *SPAW*, 15, (1921): 298-304.

[10]Meeks, "Les donations aux temples," 667 and 672.

[11]M. Malinine, "L'hiératique anormal," *Textes et langages de l'Égypte pharaonique: Hommage à Jean-François Champollion* 1, (Cairo, 1973), 32.

The Twenty-fourth Dynasty left us only two donation stelae dated to Tefnakht's reign in the late eighth century B.C.[12]

2) For the second period considered (Twenty-fifth Dynasty and first part of the reign of Psametichus I), besides the donation stelae and the great stele of the adoption of Nitocris[13], the eldest daughter of Psametichus, as God's Wife of Amon, which follow the former tradition, and the great Saite Oracle[14] which corresponds to previous legal practices, documents of a new kind appear, i.e., contracts written on papyrus already prefigured in the deeds of Pap. Berlin 3048. They clearly differ in their formulation from the late Neo-Egyptian documents. Those contracts were written in abnormal hieratic or in archaic demotic.

An important evolution in the conception of law appeared in the formulary of sales contracts--of which I have lately proposed an analysis and interpretation.[15] It was possible to place the chronological interruption introducing the third period between the eighth (maybe the fourth) year and the twenty-first year of Psametichus (circa 660-640 B.C.)

3) Contracts of the Saite and Persian period written in Demotic: the work of Hughes, Malinine, Parker, Reich, as well as more recent publications[16] will be used as the basis for defining the sources belonging to the second and third period thus delimited.

4) The fourth and final period provided a great many legal deeds written in Ptolemaic demotic. Because of the large number of documents whose investigation would lead us too far, I have limited my survey by stopping at Alexander's conquest of Egypt in 332 B.C.

---

[12]Meeks, "Les donations aux temples," 672.

[13]R. A. Caminos, "The Nitocris Adoption Stela," *JEA*, 50, (1964): 71-101 & pl. VIII-X.

[14]R. A. Parker, *A Saite Oracle Papyrus from Thebes* (Providence, 1962).

[15]B. Menu, "Les actes de vente en Egypte ancienne, particulièrement sous les rois kouchites et saïtes," *JEA* 74 (1988).

[16]The main ones are: N. J. Reich, *Papyri juristischen Inhalts in hieratischer und demotischer Schrift aus dem British Museum* (Vienna, 1914); M. Malinine and J. Pirenne, "Documents juridiques égyptiens: Deuxieme série," *AHDO* 5 (Bruxelles, 1950); G. R. Hughes, *Saite Demotic Land Leases* (Chicago, 1952); Malinine, *Choix de textes juridiques en hiératique 'anormal' et en démotique*, (Paris, 1953) & Plates (Cairo, 1983); Parker, *Saite Oracle*; E. D. Cruz-Uribe, *Saite and Persian Demotic Cattle Documents* (Chico, California, 1985). See also F. Ll. Griffith, *Catalogue of the Demotic Papyri in the John Rylands Library* (3 vol., Manchester, 1909); E. Seidl, *Aegyptische Rechtsgeschichte der Saiten- und Perserzeit* (Glückstadt, 1968).

As marriage contracts and divorce settlements have been widely studied and as matrimonial and successoral laws are well-known, thanks to the work of Lüddeckens, Pestman, Janssen, Allam, Théodoridès,[17] I will only take into account the documents giving us information about the right of ownership, contractual relationships, and incidentally judicial dispositions.

Before starting the analysis of sources, together with a commentary on the role of women in the pharaonic society of the first millennium, a few remarks about the functions fulfilled by the women mentioned in the documents are in order.

Most of those who appear as parties in the writ or are merely quoted, for example in enumerations of plots of land, bear titles in relation to divine worship or funeral rites. At the top of the hierarchy was, of course, the God's Wife, the Divine Adoratrice of Amun, whose domain was composed of fields, lands and buildings, and whose household consisted of a roster of officials at whose head stood the First Majordomo.[18] The Divine Adoratrice enjoyed services and incomes; land revenues, taxes (cf. for instance the Valençay Letter).[19] Then the records show numerous Superiors of the Recluses of Amun (and one for Arsaphes) and Chantresses of Amun, and finally, on the lowest level Choachyte women. The only title which is not linked with sacerdotal or funerary activity is "King's nurse," born by a lady Sesy whose fields were contiguous to the land which is the object of the conveyance related in Papyrus Berlin 10117.[20] Papyrus Louvre E 3168[21] presents a woman weaver selling to a Choachyte a certain amount of thread for a sum of 2 1/4 *kite* of silver, but no particular title defines the vendor who is only referred to as "woman" (*s-ḥm.t*), the usual manner of referring to contracting

[17]F. Ll. Griffith, "The earliest Egyptian Marriage Contracts," *PSBA* 21 (1909): 212-220; E. Lüddeckens, *Aegyptische Eheverträge* (Wiesbaden, 1960); P.W. Pestman, *Marriage and Matrimonial Property in Ancient Egypt* (Leiden, 1961); R. Tanner, "Untersuchungen zur ehe- und erbrechtlichen Stellung der Frau im pharaonischen Aegypten," *Klio* 49, (1967): 5-37; S. Allam, "Ehe." *Lexikon der Aegyptologie* (Wiesbaden, 1975), col. 1162-1181; Allam, "Quelques aspects du mariage dans l'Égypte ancienne," *JEA* 67, (1981): 116-135; A. Théodoridès, "Le droit matrimonial dans l'Égypte pharaonique," *RIDA* 23, (1976): 15-55; P.W. Pestman, "The Law of Succession in Ancient Egypt," *Essays on Oriental Laws of Succession* (Leiden, 1969), 58-77; J. J. Janssen and P.W. Pestman, "Burial and Inheritance in the Community of the Necropolis Workmen at Thebes," *JESHO* 9, (1968): 137-70.

[18]E. Graefe, *Untersuchungen zur Verwaltung und Geschichte der Institution der Gottesgemahlin des Amun vom Beginn des Neuen Reiches bis zur Spätzeit*, 2 vol. (Wiesbaden, 1981).

[19]Gardiner, "A Protest against Unjustified Tax-demands," *RdE* 6, (1951): 115-133.

[20]Malinine and Pirenne, *AHDO* 5, 26.

[21]Malinine, *AHDO* 5, 54-55.

women in the notarial deeds of the Twenty-fifth and following Dynasties; whereas the Apanage Stele mentions two "citizens" or "city-dwellers" or more simply "inhabitants" (*ᶜnḫ-nt-niwt*) as well as a "woman settler" (*mnḥ*).[22] In the same way, *ᶜnḫ-nt-niwt* refers to the woman vendor of shares of a field in the Memorandum number two of Papyrus Brooklyn 16.205,[23] dating from the beginning of the reign of Pemay, successor of Shoshenq III. The title *ᶜnḫ-nt-niwt* is also usually born by the women who entered into contracts during the New Kingdom.[24]

Part 1: Documents of the Twenty-first-Twenty-third Dynasties

These texts can be partly related to the preceding New Kingdom period by the practice applied and the terminology and legal formulae used. On the other hand, they constitute an important stage of transition paving the way for the notarial deeds of the subsequent period.

Oracular texts confirm the theocratisation of power. Amun is appealed to through the agency of his clergy (by the ruling families as well as the less powerful priestly circles), for important political issues, which is in keeping with the tradition of the New Kingdom seen as early as the Eighteenth Dynasty, as well as for private matters.

The oracular decree in favor of Henttawy and her daughter Istemkheb[25] consists of the solemn and public guarantee (displayed on the northern side of the tenth pylon at Karnak) given by Amun and the Theban triad confirming that they own the properties acquired by Queen Henttawy and a part of her mother's inheritance which was transmitted to her by her brother, the High Priest Smendes. The decree for Henttawy indicates the matrilinear filiation several times, about the beneficiaries of the disposition as well as about the possible protesters. A quite similar disposition was taken for Princess Maatkare[26] and placed on the northern side of the seventh pylon of Karnak. The divine guarantee involves the properties Maatkare had bought from private owners and those she had come into possession of as a child.

22Gardiner, *JEA* 19, (1933): 27.

23Parker, *Saite Oracle*, 50 & pl. XVII.

24For example: Gardiner, "A Lawsuit arising from the Purchase of Two Slaves," *JEA* 21, (1935): 140-146; Gardiner, "Four Papyri of the XVIIIth Dynasty from Kahun," *ZÄS* 43, (1906): 27-47.

25See note 1 above.

26See note 3 above.

In addition to those two reliefs, there are the documents discovered in the "cachet" of Deir el-Bahri near to the mummy of Nesikhons, wife of the High Priest Pinudjem II: two papyri and three wooden tablets relate Amun's decision concerning the divine destiny of the deceased: "Amun clearly asserts that she owes her felicity to her good behavior with her husband. The decision is strongly justified and must accurately reproduce the wording of the sentence pronounced by Pharaoh and his judges. Once again we can notice that the customs in the next world are the exact reproduction of what was going on in this world."[27]

Women's property deserves divine guarantee because women transmit hereditarily the legitimacy of rights. This is how Amun expresses himself again in the Apanage Stele: "I confirm them (i.e., a rural estate and its outbuildings) in favor of the Prophet of Amun-Re, King of the Gods, the chief of the district, Khaemwase, deceased, his son brought into the world for him by the royal son's daughter Tadenitenbast, for ever."[28]

Princesses and priestesses of the Twenty-first to Twenty-third Dynasties play an essential part in the maintenance and legitimate transmission of the rights and powers. They have the right to acquire properties by inheritance or in return for payment and this they can do very early in their lives, if we follow the interpretation suggested by Gardiner for Princess Maatkare's decree.[29] They can also make use of their incomes thanks to a royal decision confirmed by Amun's oracle; thus the Superior of the Recluses of Arsaphes, daughter of the Chief of the (Libyan) Ma, must supply three oxen a year as her contribution to the daily offering of an ox to the god Arsaphes. The Donation Stelae support the same principles, which are also true for citizens of a lower rank or common birth. In the Dakhleh Stele the Prophet of Seth claims the private use of a well: "for (it is) a private well (*nmḥy*), he says, "and it belongs (*ny-sw*) to my mother Tewhenut, whose mother was Hententere."[30] This outstanding statement shows the matrilinear hereditary transmission of ownership such as we understand it for ancient Egypt, i.e., a prerogative of authority together with full right of use. In the Apanage Stele, several women seem to be in possession of holdings: one of them cultivates

[27]Maspéro, *Les momies royales*, 614.

[28]"Stèle de l'Apanage," (see note 7), lines 23-24.

[29]Gardiner, *JEA* 48: 66: "...with any things of any sorts which the people of the land sold to her (or?) which she obtained as a child of their property." The translation given by Maspéro, *Les momies royales*, 696, is "les biens de toute sorte que lui ont donné les gens du pays, pour qu'elle prît [sa part] de leurs pauvres richesses."

[30]Gardiner, *JEA* 19, (1933): 22.

her fields with her brother,[31] the other one with her three sons.[32] In the list of tenant-farmers, the wife of a shield-bearer and a woman settler (*mnḥ*) can also be found. The two last ones are undoubtedly widows still exploiting (with or for their children) the plot given to their husbands as payment for their military services. This is akin to the conclusions I had drawn about the analysis of Papyrus Wilbour.[33] In memorandum number 2 of Papyrus Brooklyn 16.205 already quoted, a woman is found alienating her shares of a field through the agency of a relative, trustee or member of the household.[34] Finally, in a donation stele we find the unique and interesting case of a priestess managing (*m-ḏr*) fields offered to a member of the clergy of the goddess Hathor through the instrumentality of the "Royal Son of Ramses."[35]

In short, women of the Twenty-first to Twenty-third Dynasties seem to have enjoyed an important legal capacity, although they are mainly entitled to land rights (land property in ruling families, simple holding among small farmers or peasant soldiers). Their main role seems to be the maintenance and transmission of those rights to legitimate heirs; the inheritance of a patrimony seems to take place even from mother to daughter. They may, however, alienate their real property, more or less freely and even perhaps under the control of their relatives (see note 34 above). On the other hand, we can wonder if they could actually *manage* their estates or their holdings. According to a certain number of clues we may doubt it. Even the case of Louvre Stele E8099 seems to be quite exceptional.

Part 2. Documents of the Twenty-fifth to Thirty-first Dynasties

The documentation is very unevenly distributed between a few stelae and a number of papyri.

The Adoption Stele of Nitocris is in keeping with the decrees for Henttawy and for Maatkare as it defined the properties and incomes of the Divine Adoratrice acquired by adoptive filiation and transmitted by the solemn act "*ỉmyt-pr*." It differs from them by its resolutely more worldly and contractual aspect and by the absence of divine oracle. We enter a period of

---

[31]"Stèle de l'Apanage," line 15.

[32]"Stèle de l'Apanage," line 18.

[33]Menu, *Le régime juridique des terres et du personnel attaché à la terre dans le Papyrus Wilbour* (Lille, 1970): 124-126 and *passim*.

[34]Parker, *A Saite Oracle*, 50: "They disputed again today about payment for the sections (*dnyt*) of field of citizeness Ipip which Peneferher son of Harsiesi, her male kinsman (*šnw*), sold to Ikeni."

[35]Louvre Stele E8099=Meeks, "Les donations aux temples," 631.

juridical renewal, of the assertion of the individual against a power that is recovering. Under such circumstances, women's rights can but improve.

As a starting point for our investigation, we will deal mainly with private contracts written in abnormal hieratic and later in demotic.

If we do not take into account the donation stelae which constitute a very specific genre well represented in the Twenty-second to Twenty-sixth dynasties, documents engraved in stone do not seem necessarily to refer to a former state of contractual relationships. They may simply prove that contracting parties are economically better off and can afford to reproduce in stone the essentials of a contract previously written on papyrus. If the Cairo Stele published by Legrain[36] and dating from the eighth year of Tanutamun still uses terminology belonging to the preceding period, the Louvre Stele C 101[37] of the eighth year of Psametichus I shows for the first time the important legal change which I have already alluded to and which consists in a conscious conceptualization of the legal link.[38] The Louvre Stele comes from Memphis; the documental renewal took place from the north to the south, through the language and the writing used (demotic) as well as through the formulae adopted which reveal a real juridical reflection.

In the Cairo Stele from Thebes we are confronted with a sale of property drawn up according to the ancient pattern: date; *on this day*; definition of the juridical act (*smn*); designation of the contracting parties (the representative of the Divine Adoratrice and a Recluse Singer of Amun); description of what is sold (ten arouras of private fields; high lands in Amun's domain in such and such a district); specification of the price received; signature of the scribe and the witness; boundaries of the field sold which seems to be surrounded by canals; finally the beginning of an imprecatory formula.

In spite of the marked juridical change that took place in the eighth year or possibly the fourth year of Psametichus I, I will examine together Nubian, Saite and Persian documents in order to present my exposé in two main chronological parts:

---

[36]Georges Legrain, "Deux stèles inèdites," *ASAE* 7, (1906): 226-227; Pirenne and Van de Walle, *AHDO*, 1: 63-64.

[37]Malinine and Pirenne, *AHDO* 5: 40-41; Malinine, "Vente de tombes a l'époque saïte," *RdE* 27, (1975): 168-174; Sergio Pernigotti, *EVO* 2, (1979): 37.

[38]See note 15 above.

Papyrus Berlin 3048 contains two marriage contracts and a loan contract concluded between a certain Petekhons and the Prophet of Amun and Steward of the Royal Treasury Ankhefenkhons. It previews, by its form and spirit, contracts of the Nubian period. The pattern: date; *on this day,* "so and so came to so and so (or spoke to him or to her) in these terms;" with a quotation of the dialogue between the parties and the list of witnesses, is replaced by the simple declaration of the debtor to the creditor (or of the vendor to the vendee) in this way: date, "*so- and- so says to so- and- so*;" statement of the debtor's or of the vendor's obligation and signature of a greater number of witnesses who more or less repeat the terms of the agreement.

The juridical deeds being much more numerous than those of the preceding period, I will not list them all but will analyze them in groups after making a few general remarks about their features:

1) The double filiation of contractants is mentioned, yet the father comes before the mother; no longer are found purely feminine expressions of filiation as in the decree for Henttawy or in the Dakhleh Stele;

2) In the clauses of guarantee against the action for recovery of property by heirs or against the risks of eviction, the constant preeminence of the masculine over the feminine item can be noticed; father, mother, brother, sister, son, daughter, master, mistress, but we can also notice that women as well as men can still bring an action. (Papyrus Rylands 1 includes the two genders: "neither children nor brethren.")[39]

3) The total absence of women as notaries and witnesses to the act can be stressed. The only women appearing as guarantors are wives and daughters in renunciation clauses (for example in British Museum Papyrus 10117;[40] Papyrus Lille 26.[41]

In the following categories of contracts that have been preserved--loans, renting of fields, selling of land, houses or offices, prebends, and tombs, domestic animals, thread, and lastly transfers of services--women make up, on the whole, about ten percent of the parties in the act.[42] However, the distribution of women is very irregular according to the nature of the contract. The close examination of the contracts of loans, partnerships or land-leases

[39]F. Ll. Griffith, *Rylands Papyri*, 3, 46.

[40]See note 20 above.

[41]H. Sottas, *Papyrus démotiques de Lille* (Paris, 1921): 53; *AHDO* 5, 33.

[42]About 30% during the Ptolemaic Period.

shows that no woman operated that kind of transaction at this time. Even if we don't want to draw a definite conclusion by using "*a silentio*" arguments, this observation seems to confirm the remark made about the preceding period, i.e., that women seldom performed administrative work in everyday life. However, they can be found in disposition deeds and in higher proportion in the land sales and transfers of shares and services than in the sales of domestic animals.

Let us take up these various categories and start with the specific case of Papyrus Louvre E 3168 registering the sale of thread. The woman (*s-ḥm.t*) Benatenherimen sells an indeterminate amount of thread to a Choachyte who, not only pays her for the raw material, but also for the weaving; this document confirms the permanent role of women in textile manufacturing. It stresses the autonomy of a craftswoman who can freely sell the product of her toil.

Few women apparently dealt with domestic animals, notably cows. The reason for that must be found in the fact that most of these deals are made for or by the herdsmen themselves or persons responsible for cattle or peasants, among whom women are definitely a small minority. As my colleagues at this conference have stressed, women worked inside; spinning and weaving were suitable for them but not the looking after of herds, which was regarded rather as a man's job. The case of Papyrus Michigan 3525A,[43] in which a farmer of Edfu temple buys a fat cow, with a woman (*s-ḥm.t*) whose name is lost but who may be his wife, can be accounted for as an exception to the principle of the sharing of tasks, and more probably by the implementation of matrimonial law ruling property acquired in common.

Besides, the presence of women--in important agreements leading to the selling of fields within a family or in the transfer of a wife's or mother's shares--is obviously due to the implementation of matrimonial or successoral law (cf. Papyrus Turin 2118 and 2120 below).

Papyrus Turin 2118 to 2121[44] register the successive transactions concerning a tenure of (ten plus one)[45] arouras of land in Amun's domain. These archives are made up of five documents dated from the thirteenth to the

[43]Cruz-Uribe, *Demotic Cattle Documents*, 17-19.

[44]Pernigotti, "Un nuovo testo giuridico in ieratico 'anormale.'" *BIFAO* 75, (1975): 73-95 & pl. XI-XII.

[45]Pernigotti, *BIFAO* 75, (1975): 78.

forty-seventh year of Psametichus I of the Twenty-sixth Dynasty, numbered 2118, 2118A, 2119, 2120 and 2121.[46]

In Papyrus Turin 2118, the woman (*s-ḥm.t*) Ese(n)kheb who holds her fields in joint possession with her brother sells them, with him, to a singer (*šmᶜ*) of Amun's domain. Note that she is mentioned before her brother (she may have been older) and that another woman, the vendor's aunt, also owns a share to the west of the field on sale, as a large estate had been divided up in the previous generation among several heirs.

Papyrus Turin 2118A is a renunciation, by a member of this family, of the rights he could claim. Papyrus Turin 2120 contains a second sale contract according to which the Prophet of Amun and Prince of Thebes, Peteese, buys the same ten arouras from the Singer of Amun who had acquired them previously. Finally Papyrus Turin 2121 contains a foundation act whose author is Peteese's widow who acts together with her children to donate the ten arouras in question to Osiris, the Lord of Abydos, in order to have the funerary cult of her husband instituted there in the care of the Choachyte Ienharow.

Thus, through these very interesting archives, one sees how a funerary property is constituted, passing from the domain of Amun to that of Osiris after being exploited by the temple's tenant farmers, and how women have an essential role in this legal fiction in which the same plot of ten arouras changed hands four times in seventeen years, with every time the payment of transfer duties to the suzerain temple. Papyrus Louvre 10935,[47] of the fifteenth year of Amasis, preserves a contract according to which a certain Psammetek-menkh grants the Choachyte Nesmin in charge of her funerary service a piece of land of ten arouras constituted by him as a foundation for his mother, Tsenhor. The plot, situated in the domain of Amun in Coptos, was subjected to several transactions, the first of which was made by a Neskhons whose wife, a Recluse Singer of Amun called Nitocris, had brought it as her dowry.

In British Museum Papyrus 10117 and Lille Papyrus 26, the wives of the owners--whether wife or divorcee--intervene in the transaction to assert their consent explicitly, thenceforth giving up their own rights. Thus, women

---

[46]Turin Papyrus 2118 (=246): Malinine and Pirenne, *AHDO* 5: 12-19; Malinine, *Choix de Textes juridiques*, 56-71; Turin Papyrus 2118A was published for the first time by Pernigotti (note 44 above); Turin Papyrus 2119 (=244): Griffith, *Rylands Papyri*, 3, 18, no. 8; Malinine, *Choix*, 83-84; Turin Papyrus 2120 (=267): *AHDO* 5: 19-25; Turin Papyrus 2121 (=248): Malinine, *Choix*, 117-124.

[47]Malinine, *Choix*, 125-131.

of the Nubian and Saite Dynasties retained their essential role, which is to maintain the rights they are entitled to and pass them on to their children, whether girls or boys. They can also transfer them in return for payment, for instance when a joint ownership is shared, and they can do it quite freely: something which did not appear clearly in the preceding period.

The Choachyte families of western Thebes enjoyed intense economic activity, and several women can be found selling their shares of incomes of a hereditary function they could also fulfill. There are several indubitable cases where women bear the title *w3ḥ-mw*, Choachyte, for example in Papyrus Louvre E 3228 c: "The 'man of the north' whose services I acquired, whom I later sold, and whom Lady Hetepese, my sister, the Choachyte of Lady Meriesamun gave up."[48] Papyrus Louvre E 9294 is a "sale contract of an inheritance consisting of various incomes allotted to the function of Choachyte which Lady Tamenkhawase inherited from her mother and which she now sells to the Choachyte Pherbes."[49] The vendor tells the buyer that she is satisfied with the money she received for the shares that are hers in the countryside, in the temple, and in the town, for the shares of the properties that are dependent on the function of Choachyte--"Osiris' rations" (offerings), the tomb, the house, the vacant plot, the servant, the sycamore (wood), the field, etc.--which she inherited from Lady Ruru, her mother, the daughter of the Choachyte Khausenmut.

This leads us to mention briefly the contracts of transfer of services[50] which are made in Theban sacerdotal circles, mainly in Choachyte families:

Not only is there a case, which is hardly surprising at first, of the voluntary engagement of a woman as servant,[51] as well as the transfer of a servant with her son,[52] but we often come across women carrying out transfers of servants and getting for that a transfer duty. Out of the thirteen deeds of conveyance for services that are known for the Nubian and Saite period, to

---

48Malinine, "Une jugement rendu à Thèbes sous la XXVe dynastie," *RdE* 6, (1951): 157-178, particularly 159; Menu, "Cessions de services et engagements pour dette sous les rois kouchites et saïtes," *RdE* 36, (1985): 78-79.

49Malinine, *Choix*, 113; Louvre Papyrus E 9294 (not 9204): *Choix*, 113-116. See also Cruz-Uribe, *Enchoria* 9 (1979): 33-34.

50Menu, *RdE* 36, (1985): 73-87. See also Menu, "Les rapports de dépendance en Egypte à l'époque saïte et perse," *RHD* 55 (1977): 391-401; Cruz-Uribe, "Slavery in Egypt during the Saite and Persian Periods," *RIDA* 29, (1982): 47-71.

51Coupe Louvre E 706: Menu, *RdE* 36, (1985): 81-83, with the former bibliography, 82.

52F. de Cenival, "Une vente d'esclaves de l'époque d'Artaxerxès III (Inv. Sorbonne Nos. 1276 and 1277), *RdE* 24, (1972): 31-39 & pl. III-IV.

which must be added the double contract of the Persian period, two involve servants, but above all five were negotiated by women for servants often defined as "northern people." We may wonder if the taking on of servants in Theban Choachyte circles fell half within women's responsibility.

To conclude, the examination of the contracts that contain transfer, disposition or alienation deeds, shows that during the Nubian and Saite period, women, as far as the law is concerned, acted in total freedom, in their own name and without any male intermediary, whether a tutor or a curator. The evolution that one can be inclined to point out, between the Twenty-first-Twenty-third dynasties and the following period, concerns the development of the exercise of women's rights on two levels:

1)"Middle class" women have access to legal life;

2) With smaller dowries than their elders of the upper sacerdotal class, they are not protected, as these latter were, by measures such as the intervention of a male warrant supported by divine guarantee or the matriarchal transmission of real properties. Women of the Nubian and Saite periods seem to assume their legal capacity much more fully than their predecessors. This feature will but become more marked later on, during the Ptolemaic period.

During the whole period considered here (from 1080 to 330 B.C.), the sharing out of tasks and thence of juridical operations between the sexes somehow followed a natural line: women were housekeepers; they maintained their children's rights, having at the same time the possibility of practicing an economic activity, whereas men were more involved in business life, acting as witnesses or notaries, concluding contracts of partnership, loans, sales of moveable properties and land leases which were not yet, or were very seldom, made by women. It seems that women had a full *capacity* of rights, but that in daily life they often left to their husbands the *exercise* of those rights.

Responses to Prof. Menu's Paper

Pomeroy: Since you did not go into the Ptolemaic period at all, I would like to say briefly that the evidence from the Greek documents confirms that Egyptian women continued to be able to own immovables, and this distinguishes them from Greek women, who did not own property such as land. The type of land that women with Egyptian names owned is different from that which men owned, however. That is to say, they tended to have vineyards and orchards rather than grain-producing lands, and I think this is because they don't own cattle like oxen. They didn't have to plow the land they owned. We do find that they kept smaller animals such as sheep and goats. Now in agricultural societies, men often tend to influence the land reforms, and I wonder to what extent the marriages between brothers and sisters that we have evidence for in Greek literature--that is the Greeks described brother/sister marriage among the Egyptian commoners--I wonder if this was the result of the fact that Egyptian women owned immovables. They could thus end up owning a share of a house, a share with brothers and sisters, or they owned strips of land which really shouldn't be divided.

Allam: This kind of marriage was frequent only in the Roman period in Egypt, but very rare earlier. In the Pharaonic period it does not involve siblings of the same parents, they are of different mothers or of different fathers.

L. Lesko: I would just like to point out that we have a little evidence for Greeks getting this misconception based on their visiting ancient tombs, such as that of Sennefer at Thebes. His wife is called "his sister" just as the lady love in the love songs is called "sister" as a term of endearment. This is very common in Egyptian tomb inscriptions.

Cruz-Uribe: In my own work I have been noticing that there probably is more brother/sister marriage in Egypt showing up in the Demotic documents. Not necessarily full brothers and full sisters, but half-brothers/half-sisters. In other words, one man may have two wives during his life and the children from each side of the marriage may be forced to get married; that we don't know for certain. However, there does seem to be some connection here with them marrying to keep property in the family. Prof. George Hughes mentioned this to me a number of years ago, and it is certainly true in a text I just recently published in *Enchoria* 13(1985): 41-49. Particularly with family property, where you can't split up a house, with each child from a proper marriage getting a piece of it. It is something that can't really be broken up practically.

Discussions at the End of Day Two

Cruz-Uribe: First, I would like to respond to something Prof. Allam said earlier today about the office of the God's Wife of Amun. In my own understanding of the office, it was a religious office which was revived or seems to have been utilized for purely political reasons during the Third Intermediate Period. There isn't any evidence that the God's Wife of Amun was celibate because none of the documents that refer to them ever tell us that the God's Wife could not marry, or should not marry. We just don't have any evidence that they did. Kitchen, in his book on the Third Intermediate Period did mention that there may be a son of a God's Wife of Amun, in which case perhaps the God's Wife of Amun did marry. The problem is that the office needs to be studied more, because there are two offices which we should have a look at, the office of God's Wife, and the office of Divine Adoratrice of Amun, and sometimes these two are confused by Kitchen himself when he is talking about their role. So more study needs to be done. There is no other evidence that the God's Wife ever was and had to be celibate, it's never said in the Adoption stele, plus it always was the daughter of the king, and she was placed for political reasons, to break up the power or to replace the High Priest of Amun office.

B. Lesko: Let me interject for the benefit of the Assyriologists. The Third Intermediate Period Divine Adoratrice occupied a position very similar to Sargon's daughter Enheduanna: both were made priestesses for political reasons. Another thing, people have thought that because the Egyptian priestess was adopting her successor in the office implies celibacy. I think that is where that idea started.

Cruz-Uribe: It is evident that the present holder was adopting her successor, but since we have up to three or four generations being adopted at once, or in succession due to changes in the political structure, it sort of destroys the idea that the adoptions were due to celibacy. One last thing, I wanted to respond to Prof. Menu's talk this morning, the general tone of her talk. Professor, you indicated that in the Nubian and Saite periods in Egypt there seems to be an increase all of a sudden of women showing up in legal texts. Could this have anything to do with the fact that the Nubian Meroitic society was much more matrilinealy based, and that this was sort of percolating into the Egyptian society or was it just the revision or the apparent revision of the forms of contracts.

Menu: Yes I think that the multiplication of contracts implies the multiplication of the presence of women in contracts and this is also a phenomenon that appeared in the reign of Psammetichus I with necessary modifications of the rights of women.

Allam: I should like to inquire about an item which she has discussed in her paper. She said she was speaking about women dealing freely without any control of their relatives, but in one sentence I would say she went too far in being cautious and stated that women could run their affairs freely perhaps only under the control of their relatives. I know the material coming from the third and the second Millennium I would say quite well, and I am not unaware of the material coming from the Demotic period and from the first Millennium and I would say I have never come across one single text where the woman is deeding, or is contracting with another under the control of anyone, whether father or brother. So I would think Prof. Menu was going too far in her caution when she stated this. Could you quote one single text where it is really clear that the woman was acting under the control of someone else?

Menu: There is a very great difference between the texts of the Twenty-first and Twenty-third Dynasties.

Allam: Well, another observation: the term adoption has repeatedly been mentioned and, I myself have also been occupied with this institution as far as ancient Egypt is concerned. I would like to compare this institution with a similar institution in Mesopotamia. And I am aware of a book written by David on this subject, but it is now rather old. I would like to know from our colleagues, experts in the material, whether Babylonian women were capable of adopting women, and whether adopted women could inherit the property of their adopted mother.

Grosz: Well, I have some very definite views on adoption, especially adoption of women by women which do not really conform with the views of Martin David, because he used the definition of adoption, such as we understand it today, that is a person without children who adopts someone to become an heir, an heir who takes over the adoptive parents' status, he sort of steps into his shoes. To my knowledge in Nuzi I can guarantee it never occurred. Adoption is not conceived of in this way. I think the problem with David's definition of adoption was partly that it was derived from our legal and conceptual framework and partly because he based his argumentation on a collection of legal formulae, probably used in scribal schools to train scribes who were writing these documents. A part of this series concerns adoption, and some strange cases of adoption, such as adopting children found in the street, or then they go on to describe children found in a ditch, and found in a well, and found in a hole in the earth, and so on and so forth. I don't really believe that this form of adoption ever existed in Mesopotamia.

Westbrook: Oh yes it did.

Grosz: You have documents where people are adopted, but they are never given the status of full heirs.

Westbrook: Why not?

Roth: In the Old Babylonian Period and especially in the Neo-Babylonian period adoption is common. Adults adopting children when they have no children of their own, explicitly say in the adoption document "I have no other heir. I wish to adopt this child. I will raise him. He will become my heir." Adults adopt other adults, certainly in a similar fashion. The provisions are that the adopted child or adult is to provide for and support the adoptive parent in his or her old age and he will certainly inherit property.

Allam: Well we have in the evidence coming from Egypt many, many documents where it is stated this man is a son of this other man or this man is a father of this man. And I would never dare say this isn't adoption.

Westbrook: To answer your question of whether there is adoption of women by women. Yes there are. The naditu documents specifically say a naditu (this is the priestess) adopts a young girl, she is called *redit warkalisa*, the "follower of her inheritance," and the inheritance documents set out what she is going to get, or that she is going to get everything after the death of the *nadītun*. So there can be no doubt that it was adoption.

Grosz: Well, I don't doubt that you can adopt her into property, but what about into the family? For instance in Roman times a person who is adopted receives a new family name, cannot marry his adopted sister or brother, or whatever, This doesn't happen in Mesopotamia.

Roth: Yes, it does. I can think of at least one case off the top of my head of a child who is adopted and is later known as A son of B, and so he is truly adopted.

Figure 35

Seated woman with spindel. Stone relief from Susa, 8th-7th century B.C. Courtesy National Museums of France, Louvre # SB 2834

Western Asia in the First Millennium

The first millennium B.C. will be known to many of you as the millennium of empire: Assyrians, Babylonians, Persians, Greco-Macedonians, Romans, Parthians. The Assyrian empire was revived, in fits and starts, during the first part of the first millennium. By the seventh century, Assur ruled from southwestern Iran to the fringes of Kurdistan, Syria-Palestine, and even Egypt. The records of this great empire are predominantly administrative, diplomatic, and commemorative in character, though some private documents exist.

After the destruction of Assyria by the Medes and their allies, towards the end of the seventh century, the kings of Babylon were able to step in as heirs to much of the Assyrian domains. Babylon was to become the greatest city of its time; this is the city that was the wonder of the Greeks, the image too of luxury and usury through the dark glass of Biblical tradition.

Babylon's power was taken from her by Cyrus the Persian who, by his own account, marched into the city peacefully and deposed the last Babylonian ruler, Nabonidus, a man whose religious convictions and political program have left him a fascinating enigma. Under Cyrus and his immediate successors, Babylon was to prosper as she never had before, now as the commercial center and wealthiest province of an empire stretching from Thrace to Afghanistan. Enterprising Babylonians were not slow to recognize the commercial and political opportunities of the new world order.

One significant social development of this period was the extraordinary growth of chattel slavery, hitherto not a factor of great economic importance in Mesopotamian society. Even at this time slaves were more successfully used in domestic service than in production. The latter was in the hands of free and unfree peasantry who were at the mercy of absentee landlords and an increasingly rapacious imperial bureaucracy and nobility. In fact, slaves acquired considerable social and economic importance as managers, agents, and even property owners.

Another important change was the "internationalization" and prosperity of Babylonia. Under the Achaemenids, as under the Babylonian dynasts, Babylonia was a major center of commerce. Her agriculture was sustained by large-scale irrigation works. Although various ill-starred attempts to break away from Persian rule caused damage and oppression, in the main Babylonia benefited from the new conditions of Persian domination.

A wealth of documentation exists from Babylonia under the Neo-Babylonian dynasty and the early Achaemenids. Under the Seleucids, the records become narrower in scope and tend to deal with the concerns of a few large temples and their staffs. Aramaic and Greek, written on perishable media, replace the durable Akkadian tablets, and our sources dwindle dramatically with the outgoing millennium.

Benjamin R. Foster

Non-Royal Women in the Late Babylonian Period: A Survey

Amélie Kuhrt

Introduction

Before attempting to discuss the position of 'ordinary women' in the Late Babylonian Period it is imperative to define that period briefly, and consider the main sources. All of these aspects are crucial to the enterprise: patterns of social behavior can and do change, subtly or radically, in the course of time and sometimes directly as a result of particular political events, as, for example, the rapid shift from relative freedom to the severe restriction of women in Syriac Christianity;[1] or the marked difference in attitudes to the centrality of the mother-child relationship in healthy child development traceable in Britain during the Second World War as opposed to the post-war period.[2] Similarly, documentary material can by its very sparseness highlight how limited a place was assigned to women in public life,[3] how this role was essentially subservient to male (=family) interests[4] and hence the implication that where women *do* figure in official transactions, their cases are atypical or limited to specific status-groups and the larger interests of such groups.

The historical background

[1]S.A. Harvey, "Women in Early Syrian Christianity," in A. Cameron and A. Kuhrt (eds), *Images of Women in Antiquity*, (London, 1983), 288-298.

[2]J. Mitchell, *Psychoanalysis and Feminism* (London, 1974), 228ff. Cf. for an overall critical re-examination of this complex issue D. Riley, *War in the Nursery*, Theories of the Child and Mother (London, 1983).

[3]E.g. S.C. Humphreys, "*Oikos* and *polis*," *The Family, Women and Death*, Comparative studies, (London, 1983): 1-21, (2).

[4]Cf. H. Sancisi-Weerdenburg, "Exit Atossa: images of women in Greek historiography on Persia," in Cameron and Kuhrt (eds) *Images* (above note 1), 20-33.

'Late Babylonian' is in itself no more than a linguistic classification defining the increasingly Aramaic influenced Akkadian language[5] preserved in the large number of cuneiform texts emanating from Babylonia (=roughly, area stretching from modern Baghdad to the Persian Gulf) in the period from approximately 626 B.C. (although the immediately preceding decades could be included) until c. 75 AD: in other words, a very long time-span. I have generally confined myself for this paper to the period of Neo-Babylonian and Persian rule (626-330 B.C.), and as the greater bulk of documents preserved date to before 400 B.C., the range of time is more or less limited to just over two hundred years.

The period begins at a time of long drawn-out armed struggles (626-616 B.C.) against Assyrian imperial rule accompanied by internal dissensions (different cities supported different sides) which resulted in the ravaging of the country-side. These were particularly disastrous for the cultivation of date-palms, as these only produce fruit after six years growth, require artificial pollination in addition to careful tending[6] and are one of the staples on which the Babylonian population depended for basic food.[7] In their major dietary value, the long-term investment and regular management they require, and their vulnerability in wars, they play a comparable role to the olive-tree as amply documented for Greece.[8] Certainly by 616 B.C.,[9] the main area of the war had moved outside the boundaries of Babylonia (as defined above) although the fragility of the political situation (the Assyrian empire was still in place) meant that royal and official intervention aimed at restimulating the economy was limited. In 605 B.C. the Egyptian allies of the Assyrians were

---

[5]See W. von Soden, *Grundiss der akkadischen Grammatik* (Analecta Orientalia 33/47, Rome, 1969),§2h.

[6]Fully studied by D. Cocquerillat, *Les palmeraies et cultures de l'Eanna d'Uruk (559-520)* (Ausgrabungen der Deutschen Forschungsgemeinschaft in Uruk-Warka 8, Berlin, 1968); briefly, M. Silver, *Economic Structures of the Ancient Near East* (London, 1985), 109-110.

[7]For its possibly crucial role in urban development in south Iraq see R.McC. Adams, "Factors influencing the rise of civilization in the alluvium: illustrated by Mesopotamia" in C.H. Kraeling and R. McC. Adams (eds), *City Invincible*: A symposium on urbanization and cultural development in the ancient Near East, (Chicago, 1960), 24-34; for its important nutritive role in Mesopotamian diet cf. Rosemary Ellison, "Diet in Mesopotamia," *Iraq* 43 (1981): 35-45 (36).

[8]L. Foxhall, "Greece, Ancient and Modern--subsistence and survival," *History Today* 36 (July 1986): 35-43. For the cutting down of datepalms as a deliberate strategy used by invading armies in Babylonia cf. D.D. Luckenbill, *Ancient Records of Assyria and Babylonia* 2 (Chicago, 1927), 32.

[9]A.K. Grayson, *Assyrian and Babylonian Chronicles* (Texts from Cuneiform Sources 5; Locust Valley, N.Y. 1975), no. 3.

decisively defeated and effectively driven out of the Levant--a major achievement which had important consequences.

First, it resulted in the Babylonian ruler (Nebuchadnezzar II) controlling a vast territory--in fact an empire that easily bears comparison with the Assyrian one it had defeated. The continuous organizing and securing of this empire meant that military activity was a constant which resulted in attracting mercenary soldiers,[10] as well as the deportations of peoples from consistently rebellious centers, such as Jerusalem, and their settlement in family-groups and ethnic communities in Babylonia,[11] on plots of land requiring reclamation work. Such deported groups, their numbers swelled by prisoners-of-war, could and were also used for the construction and elaboration of buildings serving royal and military requirements (e.g. Nebuchadnezzar's 'Median wall,' city-walls, the palace in Babylon) as well as those of symbolic significance (temples, ziggurats, the *giparu* at Ur). Temples were also the beneficiaries in other respects of the kings' wars, inasmuch as they received increased offerings from them, as well as prisoners of war who became temple-slaves, flocks and precious items.[12] Despite some instability in the royal succession (Neriglissar's irregular accession [559 B.C.] and even more that of Nabonidus [556 B.C.] are cases in point), political challenges to the régime (such as that against Nebuchadnezzar II, or against Nabonidus soon after his accession[13]), and occasional military set-backs, such as Nebuchadnezzar's abortive attempt to invade Egypt,[14] the peace established and fairly successfully maintained over such a large area resulted in the resumption of long-distance trade[15] and the concomitant industrial and

---

[10]Including Greeks cf. J.M. Edmonds, *Lyra Graeca* (Loeb ed.), 1 (London, 1928), Alkaios no. 133. For possible Greeks in a text from the Neo-Babylonian dynasty, see E.F. Weidner, "Jojachin, König von Juda, in babylonischen Keilschrifttexten" *Mélanges syriens offerts à Monsieur René Dussaud par ses amis et ses élèves* (Paris, 1939), 923ff.

[11]Cf. M.D. Coogan, "Life in the Diaspora: Jews at Nippur in the Fifth Century B.C. *Biblical Archaeologist* 37/1 (March 1974): 6-12 (repr. as chapter 14 in E.F. Campbell and D.N. Freedman (eds) *The Biblical Archaeologist Reader*, 4 (Sheffield, 1983), 249-256.

[12]S. Langdon, *Die Neubabylonischen Königsinschriften* (Vorderasiatische Bibliothek 4; Leipzig, 1912), Nabonid Nr. 8.

[13]Evidence of treason against Nebuchadnezzar II: E.F. Weidner, "Hochverrat gegen Nebukadnezar II," *Archiv für Orientforschung* 17 (1954/6): 1-9; for opposition to Nabonidus' accession: C.J. Gadd, "The Harran Inscriptions of Nabonidus," *Anatolian Studies* 8 (1958): 35-92, cf. W. Röllig, "Erwägungen zu neuen Stelen König Nabonids," *Zeitschrift für Assyriologie und verwandte Gebiete* 56 (1964): 218-260.

[14]See E. Edel, "Amasis und Nebukadnezar II," *Göttinger Miszellen* 29(1978), 13-20.

[15]A.L. Oppenheim, "Essay on Overland Trade in the First Millennium B.C.," *Journal of Cuneiform Studies* 21(1967): 236-254.

entrepreneurial activities. The long-term picture of the economy is an increasingly prosperous one.[16]

In 539 B.C. the new expansionist régime in Iran founded by the Achaemenid Cyrus in 550 B.C. with his defeat of the Medes,[17] confronted the Babylonian army at Opis. The bloody battle, followed by a massacre of the local population and looting, ended in defeat for the Babylonians and Cyrus' triumphal entry into Babylon marked not only the conquest of Babylonia itself but also that of the vast regions it had controlled. Despite the care taken by the new Persian rulers not to offend local interests but instead to manipulate existing ideological structures for their own purposes,[18] the new and differently constituted imperial structure of which Babylonia was now a part inevitably led to changes in social organization which can be detected from around the middle of the reign of Darius I onwards.[19] This was largely related to the gradual development by the Persians of the mechanisms needed by a mature state, such as their system of provinces, regular demands for tax payable in silver and state-service on royal building schemes in Persia, and its tightening up of the system of land-parcels held in return for military obligations.[20] Although Babylonian temples probably received rather less in the way of lavish gifts than from the Neo-Babylonian kings,[21] they were certainly neither deliberately impoverished nor destroyed,[22] and continued to

16Cf. Cocquerillat, *Palmeraies* (above note 6); also M.A. Dandamaev, *Slavery in Babylonia* (trans.; DeKalb, Ill., 1984), 36-66.

17Grayson, *Chronicles* (above note 9), no. 7 col. ii, ll. 1-4.

18On this see A. Kuhrt, "The Cyrus Cylinder and Achaemenid Imperial Policy," *Journal for the Study of the Old Testament* 25(1983): 83-97; R.J. van der Spek, "Cyrus de Pers in assyrisch perspectief," *Tijdschrift voor Geschiedenis* 96 (1983), 1-27.

19Cf. Dandamaev, *Slavery* (above note 16), 43-44; 181-184; further M.W. Stolper, *Entrepreneurs and Empire*, The Murašû Archive, the Murašû Firm, and Persian Rule in Babylonia (Leiden, 1985), 7-9.

20For taxes payable in silver: Stolper, *Entrepreneurs* (above note 19), 27-28; for state-service on royal construction projects: R.T. Hallock, "The evidence of the Persepolis tablets, being one chapter of Volume Two of the Cambridge History of Iran," (Cambridge, 1971; reprinted as chapter 11 in *Cambridge History of Iran* 2, Cambridge, 1985); cf. M.A. Dandamaev, "Forced Labour in the palace economy in Achaemenid Iran," *Altorientalische Forschungen* 2 (1975): 71-78; for the reorganisation of the military fiefs: Stolper, *Entrepreneurs* (above note 19), 24-27 with notes.

21M.A. Dandamaev, "State and Temple in Babylonia in the fiirst millennium BC," in E. Lipínski (ed) *State and Temple Economy in the Ancient Near East*, Orientalia Lovaniensia Analecta 6 (Leuven, 1979), 2, 589-596.

22A. Kuhrt and S. Sherwin-White, "Xerxes' Destruction of Babylonian Temples," in H. Sancisi-Weerdenburg and A. Kuhrt (eds) *Achaemenid History II: The Greek Sources* (Leiden, 1987), 69-78.

function as the chief foci of civic activity. Again, despite the havoc and depredations of war--the initial conquest and its bloody consequence in 539 B.C.; the war between Cyrus the Younger and Artaxerxes II in 401 B.C. for which Babylonia provided the battleground; four revolts;[23] the temporary strain put on the economy by the dynastic struggles of 424-423 B.C.[24] and the massive Persian preparations made at Babylon to meet Alexander in 331 B.C.[25]--, the overall impression of Babylonia in the Achaemenid Period is one of prosperity and vitality.[26]

The Sources

Apart from a fragmentary collection of laws from this period,[27] the documentation available for gaining an insight into the society during this period consists of contemporary legal, economic and administrative texts and is potentially vast[28] but a number of problems such as incomplete publication and methods of acquisition which have resulted in the separation of archives limit their usefulness at present. A further inhibiting factor of the material should be stressed: there are no coherent state archives available for this period[29] so that the functioning and interests of the central governing organ--the superstructure within the restraints of which social behavior was

[23]Babylonia revolted twice in 521/0 B.C., cf. R.G. Kent, *Old Persian*, Grammar, Texts, Lexicon (2nd ed; New Haven, Conn., 1953), DB 16; §§18-20; §§49-50; and again in 484 B.C. and 482 B.C., cf. F.M.T. de Liagre Böhl, "Die babylonischen Prätendenten zur Zeit Xerxes," *Bibliotheca Orientalis* 19(1962): 110-114.

[24]See Stolper, *Entrepreneurs* (above note 19), 104-124.

[25]Described in some detail in Quintus Curtius Rufus, *The History of Alexander* 4/9, 1-6.

[26]Cf. G. van Driel, "Continuity or decay in the late Achaemenid period: evidence from southern Mesopotamia," in H. Sancisi-Weerdenburg (ed) *Achaemenid History I: Sources, Structures and Synthesis*, (Leiden, 1987), 159-181; A. Kuhrt, "Survey of written sources available for the history of Babylonia under the later Achaemenids," *ibid.*, 147-157.

[27]F. Peiser, "Die Zugehörigkeit der unter Nr.84, 2-11 im British Museum registrierten Tonthafelsammlung zu den Tonthafelsammlungen des Königlichen Museums zu Berlin," *Sitzungsbericht der Preussischen Akademie der Wissenschaften* (Berlin, 1889), 823-828. Cf. G.R. Driver and J.C. Miles, *The Babylonian Laws* (Oxford, 1955), vol. 2, 324-347; R. Borger, "Die neubabylonischen Gesetze," *Texte aus der Umwelt des Alten Testaments* Band 1/1: Rechtsbücher (Gütersloh, 1982), 92-95.

[28]Dandamaev, *Slavery* (above note 16), 6-29; A.L. Oppenheim, "The Babylonian evidence of Achaemenian rule in Mesopotamia," *Cambridge History of Iran*, 2 (Cambridge, 1985), 529-587; Amélie Kuhrt, "Babylonia from Cyrus to the death of Xerxes," *Cambridge Ancient History*, 4 (Cambridge, 1988), 114 and cf. list, 816-821.

[29]J. Oelsner, "Erwägungen zum Gesellschaftsaufbau Babyloniens von der neubabylonischen bis zur achämenidischen Zeit (7.-4. Jh.v.u.Z.)," *Altorientalische Forschungen* 4(1976), 131-149.

formulated and to which it had to accommodate itself--remains extremely poorly understood. An example of how the absence of this kind of material may limit understanding of the topic under review here may serve to indicate the seriousness of this situation:--

For the Late Assyrian Period rich state archives are available some of which reflect an important state concern, i.e., prophecy. Such prophecies were directly relevant to the king in particular, as well as the royal family, and reports of prophetic utterances were sent from all sorts of places within the empire to the court. Some have been preserved in letters, others in *Sammeltafeln* on which successful predictions were preserved. The name and home of each prophet was noted[30] and it is clear that a significant proportion of these prophets stood, more often than not, outside an organized cultic context and were female.[31] It has been argued[32] that this type of revealed prophecy was limited to Assyria and did not exist in Babylonia, a view with some consequences in trying to assess, for example, the ambiguity of attitudes to women in Babylonia: i.e., this type of activity in which women were perceived at one and the same time outside organized religion yet powerful as transmitters of divine will is entirely absent from the Babylonian cultural sphere. But, is one in a position to make such a far-reaching judgement? It should be noted that ABL 437, written in the 670's B.C. from Babylonia and concerning the enactment in Babylon of a major ritual with crucial political resonances, repeatedly refers to the role played on that occasion by a prophetess (*ragimtu*) who, one has every reason to assume, was a local woman.[33] It could thus well be that an entire area of influential female activity remains inaccessible simply as a result of a lacuna in the sources.

The nearest to a government archive extant from this period and of a very different nature from the varied Nineveh archives, are the Elamite texts from Persepolis (509-458 B.C.) recording primarily disbursements made to

---

[30] They could and did claim recompense for uttering prophecies that came to pass, see S. Parpola, "The Murder of Sennacherib," in B. Alster (ed), *Death in Mesopotamia*, XXVIe Rencontre Assyriologique International (Mesopotamia 8; Copenhagen, 1980), 171-181.

[31] Cf. M. Weippert, "Assyrische Prophetien der Zeit Asarhaddons und Assurbanipals," in F.M. Fales (ed), *Assyrian Royal Inscriptions: New Horizons in literary, ideological, and historical analysis* (Oriens Antiqui Collectio 17; Rome, 1981), 71-115.

[32] By H. Tadmor, "Assyria and the West: the ninth century and its aftermath," in H. Goedicke and J.J.M. Roberts (eds), *Unity and Diversity*, Essays in the history, literature and religion of the ancient Near East (Johns Hopkins Near Eastern Studies; Baltimore, 1973), 36-48 (43).

[33] Cf. B. Landsberger, "Brief eines Bischofs von Esagila an König Asarhaddon," *Mededelingen der Koninklijke Nederlandse Akademie van Wetenschappen, afd. letterkunde* (Nieuwe reeks 28/VI; Amsterdam, 1965): 46-49.

groups working as craftsmen and laborers on the royal building projects there, as well as to shepherds, vintners, brewers, scribes, etc.[34] As Babylonians took part in this work and certainly some labor-groups consisted of families, they can shed some light on the experience of some Babylonian women, although more study is needed.

Apart from this, archives are available dating to the sixth to early fifth century B.C. from the large sanctuaries in Sippar and Uruk,[35] with rather more scattered material from other temples. But their primary concern is the administration of temple-property (especially land) and connected matters. As women generally played no role in the upper echelons of temple-bureaucracy, their appearance in this context is naturally incidental--they tend to appear most frequently in the role of temple-slaves (see below) and occasionally as workers charged with producing items needed for temple-service.[36] Only once (to my knowledge) does a female cultic officiant figure in a text[37] and in that instance the document is solely concerned with resolving the position of a temple-slave who had been placed as a pawn at her disposal, after her death. One therefore only knows her title: *sagittu*--but as this happens to be the only attestation of it, its very meaning, never mind the function of her office, remains totally obscure.[38]

The other main sources consist of texts emanating from family concerns. There are two major archives of 'business firms': first, that of the Egibi family (690-480 B.C., although it was in existence already earlier), important merchants, international traders and bankers,[39] and secondly, the famous Murashû firm (middle to end of the fifth century B.C.) which acted as property managers, agricultural creditors and also marketed agricultural

---

[34]Texts: G.G. Cameron, *The Persepolis Treasury Tablets* (Oriental Institute Publications 65; Chicago: 1948); R.T. Hallock, *The Persepolis Fortification Tablets* (Oriental Institute Publications 92; Chicago: 1969). Discussion: Hallock, *Evidence* (above note 20); Dandamaev, *Slavery* (above note 16), 568-584.

[35]For survey cf. Oelsner, "Erwägungen," (above note 29).

[36]E.g. weavers, cf. F. Joannès, *Textes économiques de la Babylonie récente* (Études Assyriologiques, Cahier 6; Paris, 1982), no. 5:5.

[37]Published V. Scheil, "La libération judiciaire d'un fils donné en gage sous Neriglissor en 558 av. J.-C.," *Revue d'Assyriologie* 12(1915), 1-13; further discussion: R.P. Dougherty, *The Shirkûtu of Babylonian Deities* (Yale Oriental Series Researches 5/II; New Haven, Conn., 1923), 29-31; Dandamaev, Slavery (above n. 16), 541-5.

[38]*AHw* s.v. *sagittu*; cf. Dandamaev, *Slavery* (above note 16), 541: note 107: 'Some sort of priestess.'

[39]S. Weingort, *Das Haus Egibi in neubabylonischen Rechturkunden* (diss. Berlin, 1939); A. Ungnad, "Das Haus Egibi," *Archiv für Orientforschung* 14(1941-4): 67-64.

produce.[40] Given the commercial concerns of these firms it is not surprising that documents in which women figure relate invariably to property interests, reflecting *either* something of the position of very wealthy women in their role as consolidators of family property *or* the life of female slaves who constituted some of the property being exchanged. The texts not forming part of these archives reflect closely comparable transactions: the problem in these cases when one is trying to pin-point their significance is the difficulty inherent in reconstructing the original archives--a painstaking process in which progress has and is being made,[41] but inevitably a slow and frustrating one.

Beyond this, there is scholarly and literary material: proverbs, admonitions, incantations, medical texts, epics, myths which might provide a deeper insight into female images, sexual behavior, definitions of the female body, attitudes to prostitution, normative female roles, standard expectations of women's behavior in marriage, female aspirations--in sum, the conceptual framework and moral texture of the society. The problem with this body of material, however, is that it stands within a stream of tradition in some cases reaching back over two thousand years, in others certainly over one thousand. Now, I certainly do *not* subscribe to the view that texts of this type were simply used as scribal training-fodder and thus entirely divorced from contemporary behavior[42]--the selecting of texts being copied and hence preserved was a deliberate act which must echo a kind of dialogue with material composed at earlier periods. A good example of its continued value and relevance is the sophisticated reshaping and reinterpreting of some of it by Berossus in the early third century B.C.[43] and this should serve as a caveat to those who simply use these texts to fill gaps in earlier versions and ignore the historical context of later copies. On the other hand, apart from the example of Berossus, the bare existence of these texts makes it exceedingly difficult to divine how *precisely* they may have functioned in this period. Just as for most of us the Bible is a text with which our culture has maintained a dialogue over two thousand years so that while providing parameters for debate it is also an ever fluid entity from which different generations, social and ethnic groups have derived entirely different messages--so these Mesopotamian traditions

---

[40]G. Cardascia, *Les archives des Murašû, une famille d'hommes d'affaires à l'époque perse (455-403 av. J.-C.)* (Paris, 1951); Stolper, *Entrepreneurs* (above note 19).

[41]E.g. M. San Nicolò and A. Ungnad, *Neubabylonische Rechts- und Verwaltungsurkunden* (Leipzig, 1929-35); Joannès, *Textes* (above note 36); van Driel, "Continuity," (above note 26).

[42]A view proposed by A.L. Oppenheim, *Ancient Mesopotamia: Portrait of a dead civilization* (Chicago, 1964), 20-21.

[43]Cf. A. Kuhrt, "Berossus' *Babyloniaka* and Seleucid rule in Babylonia," in A. Kuhrt and S. Sherwin-White (eds), *Hellenism in the East: the interaction of Greek and non-Greek civilizations from Syria to Central Asia after Alexander* (London & Berkeley, 1987), 32-56.

were for the cultural participants undoubtedly both a static given and a pliable mass that could be moulded. But what is almost entirely lacking in the Assyriological realm, unfortunately, is a corpus of anecdotes and stories drawn from everyday life whereby this wealth of material could be appreciated within a historically specific social context. Some progress has been made in this direction by a considered use of Old Testament stories,[44] but more often the material is used to provide impressive compendia that are veritable treasuries of valuable information on women,[45] but which gloss over the problems of historical and cultural developments.

The one relevant narrative source on Babylonia in this period is, of course, Herodotus (writing after the middle of the fifth century) who had visited Babylonia and gives some information on prostitution (I, 199), former and present marriage practices in villages (I, 196), the sacred marriage ritual (I, 180), and sexual intercourse between husband and wife (I, 197). But using his information is fraught with difficulties: how good were his informants? To what extent did he misinterpret what he saw? How much did he shape his material to provide stories that fitted in with Greek literary models?[46] It is, therefore, essential to tread very carefully with the Herodotean reports and bear in mind the presence of distorting factors in them.

With the scene set and the provisos indicated above in mind I should now like to examine briefly some of the documents in order to provide a rough sketch of the contents of the material.

Neo Babylonian Laws

---

[44]Particularly by E. Cassin; see her "Pouvoirs de la femme et structures familiales," *Revue d'Assyriologie* 63 (1969): 121-148; also id., "Virginité et stratégie du sexe," *La première fois, ou le roman de la virginté perdue à travers les siècles et les continents* (Paris, 1981), 241-258 (repr. as ch. 13 in Elena Cassin, *Le sembable et le différent: symbolisme du pouvoir dans le proche-orient ancien* (Paris, 1987), 338-357).

[45]Such as J. Bottéro, "La femme en Mésopotamie," in P. Grimal (ed), *Histoire mondiale de la femme: préhistoire et antiquité* (Paris, 1965), 155-223; also M. Stol, *Zwangerschap en Geboorte bij de Babyloniërs en in di Bijbel* (Leiden, 1983).

[46]For Herodotus' informants: W. Baumgartner, "Herodots babylonische und assyrische Nachrichten," *Archív Orientální* 18/1 (1950), 69-106. Assumed misunderstanding by Herodotus: J. Bottéro, "L''amour libre' et ses desavantages," *Mésopotamie: l'écriture, la raison et les dieux* (Paris, 1987), 229; Dandamaev, *Slavery* (above note 16), 132. Greek literary motifs in Herodotus: H. Sancisi-Weerdenburg, "Exit Atossa" (above note 4), 29-30.

The fragmentary nature of these[47] and their lack of a clear date makes it difficult to discern their precise *Sitz im Leben* as well as impeding clear understanding of specific clauses. One, for example, was interpreted by Driver and Miles[48] as relating to a part played by women in the cult of dead kin; however, a new translation of the laws by Borger[49] suggests that it concerns the punishment of women performing magical rites in a public place or on private property. As it is not the performance of the rite, but the damage done to private property which seems to be the only concern of the law, little can be gleaned of the role of women in such rituals from this, while Borger's substantial rerendering of the clause indicates the difficulties inherent in merely reading the text correctly.

Apart from this, the laws in part concern rules relating to questions such as the sale of female slaves (§6, see below) and to matrimony among citizens enjoying full legal rights. Where these latter can be compared to preserved marriage-agreements of the Late Babylonian period they largely harmonize with them. General principles relating to daughters of propertied families are thus delineated (§§8-15) and deal primarily with dowry regulations (of which more below). I shall examine here only two that are not reflected in other documents. Thus according to §8 once the bridegroom's father has agreed to settle a sum for marriage on his son, the bride's father has fixed a dowry (*nudunnu*) for his daughter and the transaction has been 'committed to paper (=clay)', the groom's father may not backtrack on the agreement by trying to reduce his contribution. Yet if, conversely (§9), the property of the bride's father has diminished after the dowry had been agreed, he is entitled to deviate from the sum by giving her one commensurate with his reduced circumstances while the groom and father-in-law are not allowed to renege on the original arrangement. Underlying such regulations is clearly the rule that a daughter's inheritance usually *was* her dowry,[50] while sons would continue to share automatically in their father's property at his death. The tendency naturally was to make as advantageous a marriage as possible in order to augment the conjugal fund and hence homogamy was encouraged by families and recognized by the law. Nevertheless misfortunes beyond the control of the bride-giving family could mean that an agreed 'match' might be contested by the wife-takers as no longer suitable in which case the betrothed girl and her family received legal support in holding them to the agreement.

---

[47]For references see note 27 above.

[48]Driver and Miles, *Babylonian Laws* (above note 27), 326-327.

[49]Borger, "Die neubabylonischen Gesetze," (above note 27), 93-94 (§7).

[50]The system dubbed 'diverging devolution' by J. Goody, *Production and Reproduction: a comparative study of the domestic domain* (Cambridge Studies in Social Anthropology 17; Cambridge, 1976), 10-11.

What further emerges clearly from this whole complex of laws is that precisely because women were the "receivers of 'male' property (by dowry)"[51] their marriages were closely controlled and every attempt made to maintain status. Thus, even if family fortunes declined, the legal compulsion to honor an agreement made in more prosperous days meant that the remainder of the family could have at least some access to privilege and status via the well-married daughter as opposed to dropping totally out of sight among the ranks of the poor.[52]

Marriage practices and strategies

Marriage practices and strategies within the propertied section of Late Babylonian society are perhaps best illustrated further by picking out some of the not very numerous documents relating to agreements and dowries.[53] Although the overwhelming tendency in this period was for monogamy (which a society with diverging devolution will tend to prefer as a means of guarding against impoverishment[54]), and the preserved Late Babylonian laws do not consider secondary wives, it is clear from one marriage document (VS 6,3=NRVU 1) that adding a wife (wives) *was* a strategy used on occasion by some, presumably extremely wealthy, men in preference to the more widespread adoption-practice to extend their alliance network and create male heirs. Thus in this instance (dating to 624 B.C.) the man specifies that his present wife has produced no sons, for which reason he requests the hand of the nubile girl (*batultu*[55]) from her father to be his wife (the regular term *aššatu* is used of the girl as well as the existing wife). The one proviso made is that if his first wife should after all bear a son he will be entitled to two-thirds of the father's property while male offspring of the younger, second wife will only be able to claim a one-third share of the patrimony. This accords precisely with the provision made in one of the laws (§15) in the case of the remarriage of a widower: the sons of the first union obtain two-thirds, the sons of the second one-third of the property. But this differential in access to property applied only to the father's estate: a widow who had borne children

---

[51]Goody, *Production* (above note 50), 13.

[52]Ibid.

[53]For detailed discussion of this, see M. Roth, this volume.

[54]Persuasively argued by Goody, *Production* (above note 50), 32-34.

[55]For *batultu* as an age-group term only, cf. B. Landsberger, "Jungfräulichkeit: ein Beitrag zum Thema 'Beilager und Eheschliessung'," in J.A. Ankum et al. (eds), *Symbolae Iuridicae et Historicae Martino David dedicatae*, Tomus Alter--Iura Orientis Antiqui (Leiden, 1968), 41-105. For arguments that the term probably designated a 'virgin', cf. M. Roth, "Age at Marriage and the Household: a study of Neo-Babylonian and Neo-Assyrian forms," *Comparative Studies in Society and History* 29 (1987), 742-745.

was able to enjoy the usufruct of her dowry, keep any gifts bestowed on her by her husband and if she remarried and produced more children, the offspring of the first and second union had equal claims on her property (§13). Further, the same law stipulated that she might marry "whom she pleased," i.e., without the permission of her male kin.

But at this point one can discern a definite divergence between this legal right and actual practice--dictated, undoubtedly, by the strong family pressure to keep property as far as possible together by strategic marriages--in a series of texts treated in part by San Nicolò and restudied recently by Joannès.[56]

In this instance one can trace a series of marriages between two families in the second half of the sixth century B.C. In 551/50 B.C. Nadinu, son of Luṣi-ana-nur-Marduk of the Ili-bani family in Borsippa married Nubtâ, the daughter of Nabû-šum-iškun (his cousin), who died shortly afterwards. As a result of this her dowry, consisting of a date-palm orchard, uncultivated land and slave girls, was returned to her father.[57] Clearly in order not to lose these valuable assets, Nadinu immediately (in 550) married his dead wife's sister, Kabtâ, and thus secured his access to the original dowry (land and slaves), as well as some household items. The offspring of this marriage were two daughters who on his death (some time after 542/41 B.C.) became heirs to his landed property together with their father's brother, Širiktu. Technically at this point Kabtâ could have demanded an income from her dowry and gone off to marry someone else thus risking another family obtaining a claim to it. What in fact happened is that she herself married her dead husband's brother, Širiktu, (producing two sons) so that the dowered property remained securely within the family. Further, Širiktu and Nadinu had a sister, Hubbuṣitu, who was married to Nabû-ereš, son of Zer-Babili. On his death, her dowry was secured for her husband's family by her remarriage to her dead husband's brother, Mušezib-Bel; moreover, on Hubbuṣitu's death, her second husband (Mušezib-Bel) married her niece, Amti-Sutiti, one of the daughters of Nadinu and Kabtâ, thus augmenting and keeping intact property that had come from the same original patrimonial fund. This particular example is simply one of several such instances of endogamy that are traceable and indeed to be expected among propertied groups in Babylonia, and highlights the role of

56M. San Nicolò, "Due atti matrimoniali neobabilonesi," *Aegyptus* 27(1947), 118-143; F. Joannès, "Un cas de remariage d'époque néo-babylonienne," in J.-M. Durand (ed), *La Femme dans le Proche-Orient Antique*, XXXIIIe Rencontre Assyriologique International (Paris, 1987), 91-96.

57This is in accordance with *Neo-Babylonian Laws* §11.

women as channels for the acquisition and reproduction of wealth, as well as the difference between actual practice and legal right.[58]

In a society where men control the marriage of their women so strictly because of their function in securing property, creating alliance and maintaining (or providing access to) status, the opportunities for spontaneous romance and 'love-marriages' are extremely limited. Yet there do appear to have been attempts to try to force the hands of parents, though only two are attested. The serious nature of these cases can be judged by the steps that were taken to prevent the situation developing any further. Cyr. 307 is the record of a court-case held in the presence of a mother of a girl, Ṭabat-Iššar, who had been 'going out' with a boy called Kulu without the consent or knowledge of his father. The girl is warned that if she does not stop meeting Kulu or if she marries him without the consent of his father she will be turned into a slave (cf. similarly Cyr. 312). The strategy that may be reflected in the behavior of this couple may well be analogous to the planned elopements in Andalusia, as analyzed by Pitt-Rivers,[59] which were certainly used to force parental consent to 'unsuitable' matches. One wonders, indeed, whether there were not some instances where these attempts were successful--naturally they would not appear in the written record.

But what, of course, this case illustrates succinctly is that, while the prevailing wisdom might be that the only natural state for women was the married one (as expressed in the proverb: 'a house without an owner (is like) a woman without a husband'[60]) what *kind* of woman a husband married was certainly not left up to his, let alone her, personal whim. Rather it was

---

[58]Several other aspects of marriage are either scantily or not yet fully elucidated. The details of the marriage ceremony beautifully delineated for the Old Babylonian period by S. Greengus, "Old Babylonian marriage ceremonies and rites," *Journal of Cuneiform Studies* 20 (1966): 55-72, are not recoverable from the Late Babylonian material, although one of the sayings of Ahiqar may reflect a general similarity (cf. Greengus ibid., 72 and n.114); it is possible that a proverb preserved in a Late Assyrian text, W.G. Lambert, Babylonian Wisdom Literature (Oxford, 1960), 238, implies that a value was placed on wives who were intelligent or sophisticated, but precise interpretation of the proverb is difficult and it can be read differently; references to punishment by death for adultery of the wife occur but are not easy to comprehend fully, cf. M. Roth, "'She will die by the iron dagger': adultery and Neo-Babylonian marriage," *JESHO* 31 (1988): 186-206; divorce is yet another important aspect which still requires a full study--for some remarks see Roth, *ibid.*

[59]Julian Pitt-Rivers, "The moral foundations of the family," *The Fate of Shechem, or the Politics of Sex*, Essays in the Anthropology of the Mediterranean (Cambridge Studies in Social Anthropology; Cambridge, 1977), 92.

[60]Lambert, *Wisdom* (above note 58), 232.

carefully overseen and managed by the families involved who were prepared to demote a daughter to slave-status if she persisted in pursuing an unsuitable match.

Women and Property

A woman's life in wealthy families must have been an exceedingly restricted one, yet women's importance as heirs and dowry-bearers meant that they played a crucial role as property-owners, although the active exploiter of female property appears frequently to be the husband.[61] This raises the question to what extent not only dowry but all female property was simply a family resource which to all intents and purposes functioned primarily in the interests of husbands. Oppenheim[62] has suggested that the status of women in this period was lower than in the Old Babylonian period because women do not appear as witnesses in legal documents. Whether the equation legal role = status is correct or not, it indicates the possibility that while men may have had to act on behalf of their wives in conducting public business or because of prevailing legal custom, the latter nevertheless retained fairly full control of their possessions. And one should note that despite the prominence of the role of husbands in handling women's property transactions, her presence in court during such proceedings is always noted and was clearly, therefore, indispensable.

Further, the fairly strong legal position of women of substance at this period is supported by the fact that they could be held responsible for debts incurred by a male relative (Cyr. 147); stand bail to obtain the release of relatives from prison (PBS 2/I: 17); make contracts; occasionally owned seals[63]; could bring a court-case against someone (Nbn. 13); and vindicate a claim to slave-status on oath.[64] This is not to deny that there were clearly limitations on them in disposing of their own property which certainly existed (cf. C1 and 2, above), but, at present, I am not quite clear what precisely to make of this when it is juxtaposed with their fairly wide legal competence in other fields.

An important role played by women was in the transmission of the lots (*isqu*) associated with a great variety of temple functions.[65] While women

---

61Cf., e.g. VS 6,90 and 91; cf. NRVU 14.

62A.L. Oppenheim, *Letters from Mesopotamia* (Chicago, 1967), 45.

63Dandamaev, *Slavery* (above note 16), 48.

64Dougherty, *Shirkûtu* (above note 37), 36-37.

65The best and clearest discussion of this can be found in L.T. Doty, *Cuneiform Archives from Hellenistic Uruk* (diss. Yale University, 1977), 119ff.

themselves very rarely appear as the holders of cultic office that carry incomes (land or rations) with them, they could nevertheless own shares in them by receiving them as a pledge (VS 5,83=NRVU 62), by inheritance or gift (cf. VS 5,21=NRVU 12). VS 5,21 is a particularly interesting text in that it describes the somewhat unusual circumstances as a result of which a woman becomes heir to one of these shares in cultic office. The man who owned it had fallen ill and those to whom he would normally have looked for care and support, i.e., his brother and son, had abandoned him. He therefore asked his daughter to take him in and provide him with a home, food and clothing. In addition he would continue to have the usufruct of his temple-office income, but undertook neither to sell it, give it away, pledge it or diminish it in any way so that on his death his daughter would inherit it intact. Shares in temple-offices and income derived from them constituted a valuable resource as well as being presumably an indicator of some status within the community; certainly, in Seleucid Uruk (third century B.C.), it has been possible to trace the substantial, calculated investments made by local families in them.[66] The fact that women, despite not being entitled to perform the relevant functions, could provide access to these sought-after sources of revenue and rank, thus further enhanced their desirability as marriage-partners, and emphasizes their importance as maintainers of a family's social standing.

A number of texts indicate that slaves, particularly slave-girls, frequently constituted part of the dowry of a wealthy woman. Their practical usefulness (apart from pure market and profit-value) is illustrated by cases in which propertied women were left without husband or children to look after them. A small number of texts indicate that in this situation they sometimes manumitted their slaves on condition that the latter look after their owner until her death (Cyr. 339). A slightly more frequent expedient (though scantily attested) seems to have been for a woman to adopt a slave as her heir,[67] which also resulted in her/his manumission. Yet another way in which possession of slaves could be exploited to provide comfort for a solitary woman is the complex transaction of VS 6, 184 (=NRVU 27). In this case Hanna, who owns seven slaves, gives them to Gigitu (who had been married to a slave) and Gigitu's son, Bel-ibni. Hanna herself has adopted Bel-ibni thus almost certainly manumitting him. As long as Hanna lives the seven slaves will continue to serve her in any way necessary, but at her death will become the outright property of her adoptive son and his mother. This text illustrates neatly the interdependence of slave and owner, as well as the diverging fortunes of women. Hanna must have been a wealthy person to own as many

[66] Doty, *Cuneiform Archives*, 189-302.

[67] Cf. Nbn. 626+334; Dandamaev, *Slavery* (above note 16), 439-440 and n.470.

as seven slaves,[68] but seems to have been without close kin to look after her or inherit. Gigitu was almost certainly a free poor woman who had lost status by marrying a slave. She was, however, lucky enough to have a son whom she could provide as an heir to the childless Hanna. This was doubly advantageous as it allowed her son to regain eventually the social standing she had forfeited as well as opening the doors to greater worldly fortune than she had known, as she and Bel-ibni would be joint-owners of seven slaves on Hanna's death. Hanna in her turn gained a son and heir while not losing the services of her slaves during her life-time. The elderly, wealthy woman without children must have been as sought-after (and perhaps exploited?) by the socially and materially less fortunate at that time as she has been at other periods and places.[69]

Women as Slaves

Precisely because almost all the material at our disposal is concerned with regulating property and business transactions and thus reflects exclusively the wealthy section of Babylonian society, something of the fate of women at the very opposite pole of the social scale, i.e., slave-women, can be discerned. Almost half[70] of the population at this period has been estimated to consist of slaves, and their possession constituted a major indicator of wealth. Different categories of slaves can be defined: first, royal slaves--of whom virtually nothing is known given the absence of palace archives (see above, section B), although it is clear that female royal slaves did exist as they are mentioned in guarantee-clauses of slave-sales (e.g. VS 5,35 = NRVU 67). Another group were the temple-slaves dedicated to the deities of particular shrines who are rather better attested particularly in the extensive Eanna archives from Uruk.[71] Both palace slaves and temple slaves could not be sold as is clear from the sale-deeds of ordinary slaves, and hence constituted a constantly reproduced body of labour and profit for these large institutions. The third category were household slaves who could be given as gifts, inherited, sold, form part of a dowry, etc. A way of distinguishing these groups existed by virtue of the markings they bore: temple slaves were usually tattooed (or branded) with an appropriate divine symbol (such as the star of

68For estimates of numbers of slaves per household, see Dandamaev, *Slavery* (above note 16), 215-218.

69The lone, elderly woman exploited by young men on the make is a stock figure in much popular fiction and entertainment, e.g. Agatha Christie, *Mrs. McGinty's Dead*; Barbara Pym, *The Sweet Dove Died*; and the romantic film starring Katherine Hepburn and Sir Laurence Olivier, *Love among the Ruins*.

70Although no more than half, cf. Dandamaev, *Slavery* (above note 16), 218.

71The only study so far of this institution is Dougherty, *Shirkûtu* (above n.37).

Ishtar, the stylus of Nabu) as were the temple-herds, while privately-owned slaves frequently bore the names of former owners and the present one on their wrists.[72]

There were, of course, important differences in the expectations and experiences of slave-women depending on whether they were privately or institutionally owned: slave-girls in households frequently bore children to their owners (note the fact that household-slaves are usually identified by the name of their mother only) and had, one assumes, little chance of either fending off their master's advances nor any legal claims on their owner as a result of bearing him children--in a sense he was increasing his disposable stock and could sell them at any time;[73] indeed, there is one instance[74] where a slave-woman was sold immediately after giving birth. Because of their reproductive and sexual function, moreover, those who were beautiful were highly prized (CT 22, 201; 202), and lost their value as they aged, cf. Nbn. 388 where an old slave-woman is sold for fourteen shekels when an average rate for female slaves was about fifty shekels.[75] Further, they could be sold to a foreigner who might remove them from the place with which they were familiar or be acquired by a master less considerate than their former one. Yet they did have the hope of manumission (see above, C3).

By contrast, female temple slaves were less vulnerable to sexual advances as of right since their owners were institutions, and as they were inalienable temple-property their age, physical attributes, state of health etc. could not affect their market-value and hence insidiously influence (in that respect, at least) the regard which they were accorded. A significant difference between temple and private slaves is that temple-slaves were almost always identified by their patronymic suggesting the existence of a regular family-structure among this group. Clearly the absence of an individual owner and the impossibility of sale made for greater stability and continuity in their existence. An interesting example of this is provided by YOS 7,66 which deals with the case of a slave-woman, Nubtâ. Her owner had marked her with a star, thus dedicating her to Ishtar and indicating his wish that at his death she should belong to the Eanna temple at Uruk. Instead what had happened was that the owner's brother took her over as part of his inheritance, and fathered three sons on her. Nubtâ herself brought her plight to court and the decision arrived at was that she remain with her present owner and work for him until

[72]For the marking of slaves cf. generally Dandamaev, *Slavery* (above note 16), 229-234.

[73]Cf. Dandamaev, *Slavery* (above note 16), 186.

[74]A.B. Moldenke, *Cuneiform Texts in the Metropolitan Museum of Art*, Part 1 (New York, 1983), 11.

[75]For prices of slaves, see Dandamaev, *Slavery* (above note 16), 186-206.

his death. However, the court placed severe restrictions on the owner's rights over her: he was not 'to desire' her (one is tempted to see this as forbidding him to have sexual intercourse with her, but the meaning is unfortunately uncertain); he was forbidden to sell her; and could not marry her off to another slave. In addition the court upheld the temple's claim on Nubtâ once her present owner died. Although it has been argued that temple-slavery was probably more brutal (as well as everlasting) than private slavery,[76] in this particular instance one can grasp fairly clearly some of the advantages and securities it could and did offer.

Beyond these major and significant differences many other aspects of the life of female private and temple slaves were largely similar, inasmuch as one can reconstruct it, as they appear far less frequently than their male counterparts. This is very probably connected to the type of work that slave-women usually carried out, which one suspects was largely domestic and/or less demanding agricultural work.[77] Such work is much less likely to be reflected in the types of documents available, indeed it seems probable that the texts at times conceal the kind of productive work women almost certainly performed such as textile production.[78] Further, in a predominantly male-oriented society it is men who obtain professional training rather than women. So while one can see slave-owners investing in their male slaves by having them apprenticed as barbers, shoemakers, bakers, and smiths,[79] there is only one instance where a female slave was set up in business in this way, probably as a tavern-keeper (Camb. 330;331). Similarly, although slave-women do appear as owners of land (Dar. 470) and acting as agents for their owners,[80] attestations of them in these roles is quantitatively tiny compared to male slaves. Associated with their lesser status is the fact that while they do (like free women) have a legal persona they never have seals in contrast to some of the prominent, wealthy male slaves of this period;[81] indeed there seem to have been no similarly well-endowed slave-women. A frequently attested way in which female (as well as male) slaves were used was either to secure loans or work them off in the creditor's house (*antichresis*). But the most striking method by which female slaves were exploited (both by private owners and

---

[76]A view expressed by I. Mendelsohn, *Slavery in the Ancient Near East* (New York, 1949), 104 and Dandamaev, *Slavery (above note 16), 555,*

[77]Such as the gleaning carried out by Ruth in the Old Testament Story, cf. Esther Boserup, *Women's Role in Economic Development* (London, 1970), 50; Goody, *Production* (above note 50), 32-34.

[78]See NRVU 376; cf. Dandamaev, *Slavery* (above note 16), 294-295.

[79]For these and further examples see Dandamaev, *Slavery* (above note 16), 295-296; 336.

[80]Dandamaev, *Slavery* (above note 16), 313;319.

[81]For seals owned by slaves cf. Dandamaev, *Slavery* (above note 16), 401-402.

temples) was to hire them out to brothels (Nbk. 409) or individuals (Nbn. 679) as prostitutes, the fee paid augmenting the income of their master or that of the god/goddess to whose house they belonged (UCP 9/1 1 53).

Poor Women

An associated question that needs consideration at this point concerns the sources of slaves and methods of acquisition, apart from physical reproduction. Certainly military campaigns and the resulting prisoners-of-war were one, and probably an economically important one given the emphasis on military prowess as a royal virtue by both Babylonians and Persians. Certainly temples received some of their slaves as gifts from the king's military exploits,[82] and there is one clear example of an Egyptian woman with a three-month old daughter who had been the war-booty of a Babylonian soldier being sold to a member of the Egibi family as slaves (Camb. 334). Similar methods of acquisition must have been originally employed to account for the presence of other foreign slave-women in Babylonia such as Gandharans and Bactrians.[83] Apart from this, precise knowledge of slave acquisition is sparse, although the suspicion exists that in the cases where daughters from free families were used as a security for a debt (e.g. TCL 12,42), the possibility (at least) of them ending up as slaves because of a failure to repay it did exist--and the fact that a free man could not pledge his wife in the same way[84] may imply that the social position of a free married woman was protected in a way that the offspring of free families were not.

Despite this, it seems that debt-slavery did not play a major role in this period and there is only one instance of a self-sale because of destitution, and that occurs very early in the period under discussion.[85] It happened during a crisis, namely the long siege of Babylon by Assurbanipal (650-48 B.C.), when a woman sold herself in order to obtain food. The seriousness and unusual character of her enforced action is stressed by an additional clause in the text which specified that once the siege was lifted any member of her family had the right to redeem her. One can, therefore, certainly not assume that this was a regular practice.

---

[82]Nabonidus presented 2850 prisoners-of-war to temples, cf. Langdon, *Königsinschriften* (above note 12), Nbn. 8, col. IX: 31-32.

[83]See Dandamaev, *Slavery* (above note 16), 107-110.

[84]Cf. Dandamaev, *Slavery* (above note 16), 168-169.

[85]Mid-seventh century B.C., cf. E.F. Weidner, "Keilschrifttexte nach Kopien T.G. Pinches. Aus den Nachlass veröffentlicht und bearbeitet. 1. Babylonische Privaturkunden aus dem 7. Jahrhundert v. Chr.," *Archiv für Orientforschung* 16 (1952/3): 35-46: no. 2.

Similarly, in the case of the children (eight out of nine of them small girls) sold by their parents during the drawn-out siege of Nippur in the 620's B.C.,[86] all the documents emphasize that the children were sold only to keep them alive. Again the circumstances were extreme and the selling of children a last resort to ensure their survival. Interestingly, the sellers in seven out of the nine documents are the mothers which, Oppenheim argued, suggested that the women had been left to fend for themselves as a result of either the death of their husbands or their absence on military duty. In these cases slavery, particularly perhaps for girls who had less opportunities for independent productive work, provided a strategy for their survival. Temples, whose slave-personnel could be acquired through private dedications,[87] also functioned to some extent to help the offspring of women who had fallen on hard times. YOS 6,154 records the dedication by a widow of her two sons to the Eanna temple because there was a famine in the land. She marked them with a star, the boys were declared to be temple-slaves for life and taken from her to be fed.

Naturally, how such women might survive after losing their children, is not recorded and indeed very little is known of the lives of poorer, free women. The occasional glimpse reveals that married women could be imprisoned and then hired out to work (TMH 2/3, 203). Free women could be used to work off debts[88] or simply hired out to work (NRVU 156)--sometimes by their mothers (NRVU 158)--, while in one instance a daughter is hired out as a wet-nurse for one year (BE 8, 47). Undoubtedly, poorer families frequently exposed infants they could not support in the streets, and the fate of a majority of those who survived and were picked up was slavery. But it is unclear that this was invariably the case. VS 6,116 (=NRVU 712) records the declaration made by a woman called Ṣira who had found a girl, Šepitta, abandoned in the street, brought her up and now that she had married wished to record the fact that Šepitta belonged to her and her husband 'having placed her feet on clay.' While it is not impossible that this is a formal recording of the ownership of Šepitta as a slave,[89] the curious terminology is far more reminiscent of the adoption-procedure to be followed in cases of foundlings, hence without kin, recorded in the Old Babylonian series *ana ittišu* (II-III:38-44). In which case this document would reflect something much more akin to the course taken by Pharaoh's daughter on finding the abandoned Moses and bringing him up (Exodus 2). One could then reconstruct the affair thus: Ṣira,

86A.L. Oppenheim, "'Siege documents' from Nippur," *Iraq* 17 (1955): 69-89.

87Cf. above section C4, the case of Nubtâ.

88As already mentioned above; cf. also Joannès, *Textes économiques* (above note 36), 69.

89The interpretation offered by M. San Nicolò, "Über Adoption und die Gerichtsbarkeit der mâr-bânî im neubabylonischen Recht," *Zeitschrift der Savigny-Stiftung* 50 (1930), 450.

a young girl from a well-off family, had come across a baby-girl abandoned in the street whom she was allowed by her family to take in and bring up. At this point Šepitta's actual status must have been indeterminate and ambivalent. On Ṣira's marriage she needed to resolve this situation as she both wished to keep Šepitta with her and include her in the new family of which she was now a member. Her husband was willing for this to happen and the couple legitimized her by 'placing her feet on clay', i.e., a form of adoption interestingly not unlike one practised by the Nuer.[90] If this interpretation is correct, it would be one of the very rare documented acts of charity extended by a woman of high rank to one of the lowest.

Women as prostitutes

I mentioned above the widespread use of slave-women as prostitutes (C4). What is far less clear and, indeed, extremely hard to grasp with any clarity is the role played by free women as prostitutes and attitudes to them. On the one hand the existence of a whole range of prostitutes is attested in such text groups as incantations and admonitions[91] where they are regarded as potentially dangerous and certainly unsuitable as wives. On the other hand there is a text which may record the expectation that a prostitute (*harimtu*) will make a socially distinguished marriage (*An.Or.* 8, 14). Further testimony of a kind is provided by Herodotus I 196 who maintained that after the Persian conquest all girls of the lower classes were prostituted by their families--presumably to acquire dowries for marriage as it is contrasted with an earlier marriage-practice among the same social group. And, of course, in any consideration of this question his notorious statement at I 199 that every Babylonian woman must once in her life have sexual intercourse with a strange man must also be included.

How can these seemingly contradictory pieces of evidence be resolved? It seems probable that quite frequently poorer girls turned to prostitution to support their families and themselves--a practice which might or might not be associated with cultic activities (cf. the use of household and temple slave-women, above). The real problem is raised by An.Or. 8, 14 which concerns the adoption by a man of his sister's baby (a boy), where the

---

[90]E.E. Evans-Pritchard, *The Nuer*, A description of the modes of livelihood and political institutions of a Nilotic people (Oxford, 1940), 222. Cf. further the penetrating remarks on this practice by Elena Cassin, "Symboles de cession immobilière dans l'ancien droit mésopotamien," *Le semblable* (above note 44), 280-337 (esp. 298, n.4); (first published *L'Année sociologique* 3ème série (1952), (Paris, 1955), 107-161.

[91]Incantations: G.R. Meier, *Die Beschwörungssammlung Maqlû* (Archiv für Orientforschung Beiheft 2; Berlin, 1937), col. III: 40ff. Admonitions: Lambert, *Wisdom* (above note 58), 102; 103.

sister is described as 'practicing prostitution'. The term for her profession (*hari'utu*) relates to the common term for prostitute (*harimtu*) used, for example, in Gilgamesh VII, iii: 10ff., where Enkidu pronounces the prostitute's destiny in no uncertain terms as one debarred from any family-life, subject to physical abuse from drunkards, living alone in the recesses of the city-walls, poorly clothed, barefoot and a prey to all insults.[92] Yet nothing of these dire circumstances is revealed by the text mentioned although clear comprehension is uncertain. A possible reading is that Baltâ's (= baby's mother) brother, Innin-šum-ibni, asked to adopt her seventeen-day-old son (Ilu-dannu-ahhe-ibni), whom he will inscribe as next-in-line to his own son. The boy is to continue living with his mother while she works as a prostitute--which suggests that Baltâ was making enough to feed, clothe and house him adequately. But when she marries a free citizen (*mar banê*), Innin-šum-ibni undertakes to pay her a regular sum of money as well as provide food and clothing for him--presumably because she will then lose her income but her child will not be her husband's responsibility.[93] The text ends with the adopter's promise that he will not give the boy away to his brother or other sister, and that the adoptee will serve the king and the 'Lady of Uruk' (=Ishtar) together with Innin-šum-ibni's own son. Because of this final statement it is generally assumed that Baltâ was in fact working not as a 'common prostitute' but as a hierodule and that her son's future would also be devoted to temple service.[94] Certainly, the available material is not sufficient to determine what precise shades of meaning the term *harimtu* may have acquired at this period. But the interpretation is based to a large extent on assumption rather than hard fact. I would prefer to see the text as a reminder of the enormous number of aspects of Late Babylonian society, particularly in respect to women that are

---

92Cf. also Bottéro, "L''amour libre'," (above note 46), 235.

93This rendering of the text is a possible reading (cf. M. San Nicolò and H. Petschow, *Babylonische Rechtsurkunden aus dem 6 Jahrhundert v. Chr.* (Abhandlungen der Bayerische Akademie der Wissenschaften, Phil.-hist. Klasse, Neue Folge, Heft 51; Munich, 1960), no. 4). Martha Roth has suggested to me another interpretation: the term 'go to the house of a *mar banî* (taken to mean 'marry') could simply mean precisely that, i.e., she may at some stage as an unprotected woman place herself in the care of a well-placed citizen. [It is also possible to read the action to be taken differently (due to the use of unspecific pronouns): The brother adopts and *he* will raise the child and support his sister as long as she works as a prostitute. When she 'goes to the house of a *mar banî*,' the *mar banî* will repay the brother for the expenses incurred in supporting the woman and child.] For marriage agreements entered into by women who had been sexually active and the apparent absence of any moral judgement, cf. Roth, "Age at Marriage," (above note 55), 743-4.

94As done by M San Nicolò, "Parerga Babyloniaca 15-16," *Archiv Orientální* 7 (1935): 16-28 (18, n.2) and Dandamaev, *Slavery* (above note 16), 132-3.

not understood rather than push the problem aside by 'sanctifying' this particular prostitute.

Concluding remarks

As a conclusion to this and, indeed, to all that one may glean of the position of women in the Late Babylonian Period, I would like to stress this final, negative point. It is an inescapable fact that our understanding of Late Babylonian society is very incomplete. Thus when, as is usually done, scholars explain Herodotus' problematic statement that Babylonian women prostituted themselves (I 199, and preceeding section) by saying that he was confused by the sacred prostitutes at the Ishtar temple[95] then the problem of explanation is avoided rather than directly confronted. If one is going to admit Herodotus' evidence at all, then what he is describing is something that applied, according to him, to *all* Babylonian women, rich and poor, and which happened *once* only. It thus sounds far more like a *rite de passage*, than a description of temple-prostitutes, although of what type remains opaque at present.[96] But alternative approaches to the prevailing one should at least be considered.

Other important aspects of how female behavior was regarded, circumscribed, or regulated are tantalizingly hinted at in some texts, e.g. *Camb.* 273 in which the widow of a priest is forbidden to remarry before her sons have 'grown up'. This is not in keeping with the usual practice nor the preserved laws. Is this then a special case related to the safe-guarding of property? Were the wives of certain temple-functionaries more restricted than other married women? Or did she[97] not have any property and was thus being allowed to remain in her home? Or consider the problematical statement in YOS 7, 167 in which a man is examined by the temple-authorities as to his fitness to carry out the office of temple-brewer. To establish this, witnesses were asked whether his mother was 'pure' (*elletu*), "so that he is fit to be

---

[95]So Bottéro, "L''amour libre'," (above note 46), 229; Dandamaev, *Slavery* (above note 16), 132.

[96]Various possibilities suggest themselves to me from unsystematic reading (there are doubtless more): 1) A rite that serves to define girls as ready for marriage (cf. A. van Gennep, *The Rites of Passage* (trans.; London, 1960), 70; 2) A rite intended to bridge the gap between apparent physical readiness for marriage (menstruation) and repressed female fertility (for the physical aspect cf. Susan Brownmiller, *Femininity* (New York & London, 1984), 28 quoting A. Montagu, *Sex, Men and Society* (New York, 1969; 3) a practice connected with a collective offering of sanctuary, cf. Pitt-Rivers, "Women and sanctuary in the Mediterranean." *The Fate of Shechem* (above note 59), 123; finally, 4) ritualised sexual hospitality, cf. Pitt-Rivers, "The Fate of Shechem," *ibid.*, 158-160.

[97]Suggestion of Martha Roth (personal communication).

consecrated." It has been argued[98] that this question was intended to establish that his mother had not been a slave. But the primary meaning of the term is 'clean' and hence has derived meanings of 'pure' and 'sacred,' which could indicate particular store set in such circumstances, by a woman's 'purity' in a sexual and/or spiritual sense which entirely escapes us.

While one may glimpse something of the ambivalence of attitude to prostitutes--Enkidu after his initial curse of the whore repents and forecasts a somewhat more attractive fate for her (Gilgamesh VII, iv: 1-10)--the circumstances under which women inspired fear remain very shadowy. The only indicator occurs in the incantation series *maqlû* where all types of witches,[99] sacred prostitutes as well as extremely devout female cultic officiants[100] are listed together as liable to attack men by supernatural, magical means. What is the significance of this grouping in such a context? I would suggest on the basis of the limited evidence available that, first, all these women were 'abnormal' in that they stood outside the routine of home and family, or even, in the case of prostitutes directly threatened it (cf. Enkidu, *loc. cit.* '[on thy account] shall be forsaken the mother (though) a mother of seven'). Secondly, the factor of significance that links these categories of women is that they all escaped regular masculine authority which, in the male-dominated society of Babylonia represented an inversion of the correct social order. In such a society, as pointed out by Pitt-Rivers,[101] women, not under the direct control of men, were automatically dangerous and bound to inspire fear.

Finally, I would like to delineate two specific problems that deserve further consideration. One concerns the question of how one might get closer to defining any shifts in the position of women during the period of Persian rule. Herodotus maintained that poor women were worse off at this time

---

[98]By M. San Nicolò, "Parerga Babyloniaca 12: Einiges über Tempelfründe (isqu) and hemerai letiourgikai in Eanna," *Archiv Orientální* 6 (1934): 196.

[99]Meier, *Maqlû* (above note 91), 29 col. III; 40ff. For the types of witches mentioned cf. S. Rollin, "Women and Witchcraft in Ancient Assyria," in Cameron and Kuhrt, *Images* (above note 1), 34-45.

[100]Who were certainly at times of very high social status such as the *naditu*, cf. R. Harris' many articles devoted to this topic and her contribution to this volume; for a brief introduction cf. U. Jeyes, "The *Naditu* Women of Sippar," in Cameron and Kuhrt, *Images* (above note 1), 260-272. The *naditu* are not attested after the Old Babylonian period, although it is possible that an attempt to revive the institution was made by Nabonidus, cf. E. Sollberger, "The Cruciform Monument," *Jaarbericht Ex Oriente Lux* 20 (1967-8): 50-70.

[101]Pitt-Rivers, "Moral foundations," (above note 59), 81ff.

because the country had become poorer, but recent work on Babylonia[102] has shown this not to be the case. Yet the substitution of a Persian satrap for a Babylonian king and court and the extensive ownership of land in Babylonia by members of the Persian nobility must have had substantial repercussions in the socio-economic sphere of Babylonian life that affected and modified the role of the wealthy Babylonian families. The other is: How, specifically, did the cult of Ishtar function in this period? A significant change in her cult at Uruk took place at the end of the fifth century B.C., possibly related to the development of the royally sponsored Persian cult of Anahita.[103] This shift is not even remotely understood; yet as a deity closely associated with female sexuality, Ishtar both reflected and helped to support the status quo of the social hierarchy, fixing women firmly to their place within it.[104] A clearer picture of her worship is a major *desideratum* if one is to gain a closer insight into the position of 'ordinary women' in Late Babylonian society.

---

[102]van Driel, "Continuity," (above note 26).

[103]J. Oelsner, "Kontinuität und Wandel in Gesellschaft und Kultur Babyloniens in hellenistischer Zeit," *Klio* 60/1 (1978): 101-115 (p. 103); A. Kuhrt, "Written Sources," (above note 26), 151.

[104]In this respect the cult of Ishtar, I suggest, functions analogously to that of Mary, cf. M. Warner, *Alone of all her sex: the myth and cult of the Virgin Mary* (London, 1976; pb. 1985), 104 ('Maria Regina').

Responses to Prof. Kuhrt's Paper

Delaney: This is the first paper that we have heard at the conference that seems to have any awareness of the whole concept and issue of gender, a word that has not even been mentioned here in the past couple of days. Instead there seems to be a bias that both Sherrie Orton and Harriet Whitehead talked about in their book called *Sexual Meanings: Construction of Gender and Sexuality*, we've seen a bias in the assumptions of the approaches to woman's role and position in society, as well as in the issue of male dominance; a bias that assumes that we know what men and women are, in other words that they are basically predominantly natural objects rather than cultural constructions. At least in your paper you were talking about the things that we don't know about, about how people think about women, what would be necessary for gender definition. At least you were aware of that. The other papers, in general, it seems to me, assume that there can be a natural history of women somehow separate and independent from the cultures in which they are imbedded, this hinders theorizing on the whole issue of gender, and I think these issues need to be talked about generally later on today; but I did want to say that I really appreciate your awareness of this issue.

Kuhrt: Yes, I was struck when trying to gather the material for this paper by the kind of assumptions that are made, particularly in the case of some of the prostitutes. For example, the assumption that there is a sort of natural kind of easy way of knowing what women are about, and it grew upon me more and more that I do not really understand it. I couldn't completely grasp what the situations were, and also what the attitudes, positions, functions of women were in the different groups, in the various different realms, not just one woman, one ordinary woman. Every time I would put "ordinary woman" in this paper I would put it in inverted commas because I felt that that was another way of flattening out the perspective.

Zagarell: You may be aware of similar institutions in some of the neighboring regions. Just as a possible model, at least an area that one could look into, would be in fact in south India, the whole Devadasi structure, which are formally called temple prostitutes, or literally "slaves of the gods," that's what the word means. They are formally connected with the temple, they're not dedicated to the temple; they go through high-status marriages to the temple and the temple god. Nevertheless they are allowed to have sex with the patrons, in fact they are encouraged to have sex with the patrons of the temple. Nevertheless they have the legal status of celibate, that is they are considered unmarried, celibate, having sexuality, considered high-status: a high status individual and in fact also at the same time a prostitute in the temple. Because of their high status the patrons often provide money.

Bird: My frame of reference is a different culture, but I want to say that the question about prostitution, sacred prostitution, is an important question that has been confused by the looseness of the terms and transfers of meaning from one term to another, namely those of prostitute and hierodule.

There are also distinctions that need to be kept in mind, there are clear distinctions in the terminology. I think that this issue is sufficient for a conference in itself, and I would love to see a discussion of this, but I think that bringing in the question of the Devadasi may be somewhat confusing to the issue because the way these women, the Devadasi, are described, they may be the bride of the god, but all this is described basically as entertainment. That's the kind of identification of the woman's role in the cult, which I think is not associated with cultic offices in Mesopotamia. I'm not sure, but at least the model there is that the terms for prostitute are used of the women in the cult. So greater care needs to be taken.

Kuhrt: Yes, I think I have to do a lot more work to look at other kinds of ethnographic possibilities, but it does seem to me that there are in fact enormous different numbers of women working in very different ways as prostitutes in Babylonia at this time, and of course, separate from that is the situation mentioned in Herodotus, as I think Jean Jacques Glassner emphasized also, but that is not in any way related to prostitution or cultic prostitution; it clearly reflects a quite different sort of activity that is unique and falls into an entirely different area.

B. Lesko: I would like to follow up on that. It struck me that if indeed it is true that what Herodotus described was some type of *rite de passage* this would, would it not, indicate a tremendous change of thinking from Old Babylonian or Middle Assyrian society where such a high value was placed on a daughter's virginity, and the family received accordingly a higher reward for marrying her off to somebody. Would this mean that in Neo-Babylonian society girls did not have to be virgins when they were married?

Kuhrt: That is an interesting question. In fact Oppenheim maintained that virginity only became important in the Neo-Babylonian period. You have this particular term, *batultu*, that appears and that was then counter-argued by Landsberger, who said that this is simply an age definition of somebody who is of marriageable age, so that throws that all open again. On the other hand I think I would agree with what Martha is suggesting now in her work, that these girls were very, very, young when they were married and that they were almost certainly virgins. I think they were pretty certainly, don't you?

Roth: There are two terms in the marriage agreements and occasionally also in dowry donations that refer to these brides, *batultu* and *nu'artu*. They were however young. The brides who had previous marriages or previously bore children are never called *batultu* or *nu'artu*. I therefore suspect that these terms indicate that they were still virgins.

Kuhrt: Yes, and I think in fact what I have to look much more into are other possible kinds of *rite de passage* in other societies to perhaps help provide some possibilities for interpreting it, but someone has told me, although I haven't yet checked it out, that there are some kinds of rituals where you have problems particularly concerning those who are married at a very young age. They do then mature, of course gradually, and there is a gap in their apparent physical maturity and their ability to conceive. If they don't appear to be conceiving, you can sometimes have particular sorts of rituals, or rites of passage, to try to resolve this seemingly contradictory situation. So, in fact, it just wouldn't necessarily reflect that these women would not be virgins at marriage. It could actually happen after they were married at the time that they might be expected to be producing children, or becoming pregnant. Have you come across anything like that?

Roth: I have no evidence of girls married before menarchy.

Kuhrt: But they are somewhat young, and they actually have a depressed fertility, some women do, even though they are menstruating they can't actually conceive.

Roth: Well, I don't know. Do we have a doctor here? I do not think that there is regular ovulation with the onset of menarchy immediately, is that right?

Shute: It is certainly true with most women that there is diminished fertility from the period of the onset of menstruation until about the age of 15. Of course, there may be variations, but in general that is so.

Roth: I hadn't thought of that. It is very interesting.

Kuhrt: Yes, Yes.

Van de Mieroop: Did owners breed slaves?

Kuhrt: No, but I do think that the fact that a female slave could become pregnant and that her offspring would be his property, and that this would in fact actually increase the sort of stock at the master's disposal was an important element in the manner in which they were looked at. But I can't detect any evidence of people deliberately setting out to breed slaves as such. However, it is an important element, physical reproduction, this reproduction created an increase of slave-stock for temple institutions as well.

Roth: Do you know of any cases in which it seems to be that the slave's father was mentioned? I know slaves married among themselves; obviously then increasing the slave pool. I don't recall any instance on which I can put my finger that the father of a slave was the master. Do you?

Kuhrt: Well, there is the instance of Nubta, a woman who was a private slave. Her master wanted to dedicate her to the Ishtar Temple as a temple slave but at his death she went over with his property to his brother. And the brother fathered three sons by her, and she then went to the court and said "you know I was meant to go to the temple, what are you going to do about it?" And then they forbade him to try and marry her off to another slave.

Marriage and Matrimonial Prestations in First Millennium B.C. Babylonia

Martha T. Roth

Sources

The Neo- and Late Babylonian period (roughly the seventh through second centuries B.C.) is exceptionally well documented. Tens of thousands of cuneiform tablets from these centuries have been excavated, and about 15,000 legal and economic tablets have been published--mostly in autograph hand copies still accessible only to the specialist. From published and unpublished tablets, I have found documents directly concerned with matrimonial affairs--such as marriage agreements, dowry promises and receipts, and lawsuits over dowries--and documents in which matrimonial property figures only secondarily--such as inheritance divisions and directives, sales, loans, or pledges involving matrimonial property, and real estate descriptions in which borders are identified as adjacent to some woman's dowry land. As a result, I have been able to find at least some evidence of the matrimonial property or matrimonial affairs of about two hundred women.[1] In addition to this evidence of "real" women's marriage prestations, the "Neo-Babylonian Laws" include several provisions relating to matrimonial property, indicating hypothetical conflicts and their resolutions[2]--although their value for social history (and more generally the relationship between formal rules and social practice in Mesopotamia) remains elusive.

[1]This paper presents some summaries and conclusions as of November, 1987, from my ongoing research on Neo- and Late Babylonian marriage and matrimonial property. References to the cuneiform sources may be found in my articles "Age at Marriage and the Household: A Study of Neo-Babylonian and Neo-Assyrian Forms," *Comparative Studies in Society and History*, XXIX (1987): 715-47, and "She Will Die by the Iron Dagger: Adultery and Neo-Babylonian Marriage," *Journal of the Economic and Social History of the Orient*, XXX (1988): 186-206. Manuscripts providing editions of all the marriage agreements and a study of the matrimonial properties are in preparation.

[2]For the Neo-Babylonian Laws (LNB) see R. Borger, *Rechtsbücher*, Texte aus der Umwelt des Alten Testaments I/1 (Gütersloh, 1982), pp. 92ff., with collations and previous bibliography.

In comparison to other periods of cuneiform documentation, the Neo-Babylonian period provides us with an abundance of matrimonial information. However, given the enormous Neo-Babylonian corpus, and the more than four centuries covered, the fact remains that we have evidence for only two hundred women. At least 50,000 persons are named in the published documents. No more than two percent of the named individuals are women, and a conservative estimate would allow that at least three-quarters of these named women were slaves. I also have had access to another three thousand plus unpublished tablets, and can confirm that this gross under-representation of the female half of the population is a constant in the documentation--and not a product of selective publication by preceding generations of scholars. Women are not only marginalized in our standard history books; they are marginalized in our primary sources. The few women about whom our sources do speak are known to us when their lives intersect with the economic worlds of their fathers, brothers, husbands, and sons. This means that the evidence of the matrimonial history of the two hundred women about whom we know anything is preselected by the concerns of the males involved.

Terminology

I have been using some terms and labels that should be defined before continuing. And I want to use this digression to point to the dangers of indiscriminately drawing conclusions and comparisons from labels alone.

I use "dowry" to translate Neo-Babylonian *nudunnû*, property brought to the marriage provided by the bride's family (it is this prestation with which I will be most concerned today); "bridewealth" translates *biblu*, property given by the groom or his family to the bride's family. Property given by the husband to the wife in anticipation of her maintenance needs as a widow, *širiktu*, is translated "widow's settlement." And finally, property given to the husband at the time of his marriage by his own father is labeled *nungurtu* in our sources, and translated--in time-honored assyriologese--"*nungurtu*-settlement."

Those of you familiar with matrimonial prestations in other periods of Mesopotamian history, and in other societies, will immediately recognize the terminological labyrinth we are negotiating. In Mesopotamian legal and family studies, *nudunnû* (my Neo-Babylonian "dowry") is the label for the widow's settlement in the Old Babylonian Laws of Hammurabi and in the Middle Assyrian Laws, and the label for "dowry" in functional Old Babylonian and Neo-Assyrian legal documents. *Biblu* marks the Old Babylonian, Middle Assyrian, as well as the Neo-Babylonian "bridewealth." *Širiktu* is the widow's settlement in both Old Babylonian and Neo-Babylonian sources, but the "dowry" in the Laws of Hammurabi. Another term, *terḫatu*, is used throughout the cuneiform record, except in the Neo-Babylonian period, for "bridewealth," while *mulūgu* marks "dowry" in Amarna and Nuzi.[3]

If I have failed to confuse you with the Akkadian terms, allow me to try with English and Latin. Most (but not all) anthropological and legal literature uses "dowry" and "bridewealth" as already defined, "dowry" for property from the bride's family brought to the marriage (*maritaguim* of English law, *dos* of canonists and Roman legal historians[4]), and "bridewealth" for property given by the groom's family to the bride's family. But social anthropology may further distinguish dowry as "direct" when the bride receives it from her own family, and "indirect" when it derives from the groom's family.[5] Some anthropological literature also uses "groomwealth" for property from the bride's family to the groom's family, and another term, "dower," for the property from the groom's family for the marriage[6] (comparable perhaps to my Neo-Babylonian *nungurtu*)--while canonists use "dower" to translate the *donatio propter nuptias*, as the groom's gift to the bride,[7] and in Anglo-Saxon law, "dower" is used for that portion of the husband's estate to which the wife is entitled to life interest for her maintenance.[8]

There is a reason I have subjected you to this tortuous exercise. When we find "dowry" in both India and Neo-Babylonian Mesopotamia, for example, or *nudunnû* in the Old and Neo-Babylonian periods, we must not assume that the same social and legal phenomena are in operation.

---

[3]Additional marriage prestations or sub-categories of the prestations include *zubullû*, a sub-category or alternate term for "bridewealth" in OB and MA; and *mulūgu* and *quppu*, both sub-categories of the Neo-Babylonian *nudunnû* "dowry," restricted respectively to slaves and cash.

[4]See R. Saller, "Roman Dowry and the Devolution of Property in the Principate," *Classical Quarterly*, XXXIV (1984): 195-205.

[5]See J. Goody, "Marriage Prestations, Inheritance and Descent in Pre-Industrial Societies," *Journal of Comparative Family Studies*, I (1970): 37-54; slightly different emphasis is found in Goody's "Bridewealth and Dowry in Africa and Asia," in J. Goody and S.J. Tambiah, *Bridewealth and Dowry* Cambridge Papers in Social Anthropology 7 (Cambridge, 1973), pp. 1-58 (see the table on p. 1). For "direct" and "indirect" dowry, see J. Goody, *The Development of the Family and Marriage in Europe* (Cambridge, 1983), particularly pp. 240-61.

[6]M.E. Spiro, "Marriage Payments: A Paradigm from the Burmese Perspective," *Journal of Anthropological Research*, XXXI (1975): 80-115.

[7]See M. Sheehan, "The Influence of Canon Law on the Property Rights of Married Women in England," *Medieval Studies*, XXV (1963): 109-24.

[8]See Pollock and Maitland, *The History of English Law*, 2 vols., 2nd ed., (Cambridge: 1968), II, pp. 420-428.

Specifically, given the concerns of this conference, we must not infer the comparability of marriage patterns and of the realities of the social, legal, and economic status of women from the appearance of similarly labeled prestations--either in the native terminology or in their second-hand translations.

Neo-Babylonian Dowry

We can turn now to an examination of the marriage prestations in the Neo-Babylonian period. I will describe briefly the mechanisms of transfer, the use and devolution of these properties--especially of the *nudunnû* "dowry." I will draw attention to the effects of these transactions upon the lives of the women involved, and simultaneously to women's limited roles in the processes.

I know of dowries (*nudunnû*) provided by the families of one hundred and sixty-one Neo-Babylonian women. In the overwhelming majority of cases, the dowry is provided by the bride's father or--if he is no longer living--by her mother or brother. There is little difference--in the size or value of the dowry, in the legal mechanics of the transfer, in the rights and obligations outlined in the marriage agreements--between those cases in which the bride's father is the dowry donor and those in which it is her brother or mother. This implies that there was a full transfer of authority over the woman, after the death of her father, to the new head-of-household. She was not, in other words, made legally independent by her father's death.

However, there are a few cases--four to be precise--in which a woman either contracted her own marriage or gave her own dowry to her new husband. And, after the death of the bride's father, she is almost as likely to be represented by her widowed mother as by her brother. This suggests that a woman's legal dependency was conditioned at least as much by her age and the presence of an adult male or female family member--father, mother, or brother--as by her sex. If she had no living parent or brother and/or was old enough (though how old in chronological terms cannot be determined), she might contract her own marriage; and after her husband died, she could in turn contract her daughter's marriage. (Note that the father's authority was never transferred outside of the nuclear family, to a father's brother, for example.)

This situation in which the bride was dependent on the legal authority of a parent or brother in her marriage agreement and dowry donation is paralleled by the groom's lesser but still clear legal dependency, for men too were legally dependent upon their fathers to arrange their matrimonial affairs. Men married at a later age than did women--my research shows that they were at least a decade older at first marriage--and there were fewer men than women marrying with living fathers. But when a man's father was living, it was almost always the father who arranged his son's marriage and who accepted his daughter-in-law's dowry. There are even cases in which marriages were annulled due to failure to obtain the groom's father's permission.[9] (In the absence of a living father, there is one case of a mother arranging her son's marriage.[10]) Curiously, there has been little study of legal dependency in Mesopotamia; I cannot tell you whether men were always legally and economically dependent as long as they had living fathers, or in which public and private arenas this dependency obtained. It is clear, however, that in first-millennium Babylonia, most men and women remained legally dependent upon a living parent to arrange their marriages.

I have been talking about the Neo-Babylonian "dowry" (*nudunnû*) as property given by the bride's family--usually her father--when she marries. Almost universally, the dowry is seen as a transfer of wealth *to* the bride, and is considered an expression of her inheritance rights; usually, the dowry represents the final economic obligation of the paternal estate to a daughter. The dowry in the Neo-Babylonian period, however, is never given "to" the bride when she marries, but "to" (*ana*) the groom or his father, and "with" (*itti*) the bride. The only exceptions are inheritance directives in which a man, in anticipation of his death, gives a dowry "to" his unmarried daughter, or to his son "for" the unmarried daughter. Yet these are not really exceptions at all. The ultimate intended recipient of the dowry will be the future groom; the daughter or her brother holds the designated properties only until such time as a marriage can be arranged and the dowry transferred to her husband.

The fact that it is the husband, and not the wife, who is the recipient of the *nudunnû* raises the very basic question of whether we are justified in understanding the *nudunnû* as a "dowry" at all. Would it be more appropriate to see in the *nudunnû* the rare prestation "groomwealth"?[11] Certainly, if we look only at the formal donors and recipients of the *nudunnû*--the bride's family and the groom or groom's father--and no further, the *nudunnû* looks like "groomwealth." But closer examination of the operation and composition of the prestation makes it clear that the *nudunnû* is not groomwealth intended for the groom's kin, but dowry for the conjugal couple, whose economic and social head was the husband, and ultimately for their offspring.

---

[9]See *Comparative Studies in Society and History*, XXIX (1987): 725 note 22.

[10]*TBER* 78 AO 26775.

[11]See J. Goody, *Journal of Comparative Family Studies*, I (1970): 44; and J.L. Comaroff, "Introduction," in *The Meaning of Marriage Payments*, ed. J.L. Comaroff (London and New York, 1980), p. 4 with note 1.

The material composition of the *nudunnû* includes two categories of property. First, cash (silver or gold), slaves, and real estate--wealth that is of immediate and practical use for the husband's outside economic activities;[12] and second, jewelry, textiles, household furniture, and household utensils--wealth whose utility is restricted to the household's inside activities. Each dowry will consist of a different selection of items of differing value. But it is clear from the range of possible dowry items that the intention of the transaction was at least in part to help establish the new household.

There is some indication that the dowry was fully transferred to the husband only after the wife's childbearing capabilities were established. First, although dowries were promised to the husband at the final stage of marriage negotiation, some documents refer to promises of dowry property that have not yet been fulfilled, and to partial outstanding balances due on the dowry. Such delayed delivery schedules could be explained as due to occasional economic necessity, but they are common enough to demonstrate a tendency to wait for the marriage to produce offspring. Additional explicit evidence for this tendency comes from five marriage agreements, with dowries, that include a clause referring to children born prior to the agreement: "(The children) (sometimes named) who were born before her dowry agreement was sealed are the children of (the husband)."[13] Yet other marriage agreements also allude to this postponement of the dowry delivery. In one such marriage agreement, the husband--presumably childless--contracted to marry the sister of his deceased wife. In the itemization of the dowry for this second wife, we learn about the earlier dowry promise of her sister--a dowry which had never been delivered to the husband.[14]

Once the dowry did change hands, it was not absorbed into the general estate of the bride's husband (or her father-in-law if he was still living), but remained a discrete part of that estate. We find husbands using dowry silver to extend loans, to purchase slaves, or to settle their own debts; they lease dowry real estate to third parties, or include it in property exchanges. But, when our sources allow us to follow the history of the dowry property, the husband's right to use the dowry is successfully challenged by his wife or her family. If the husband does wish to use some component without restriction, he could resort to what I call a "conversion" of the property, substituting some other commodity of comparable value. This new

---

[12]In addition to these common components, one dowry includes a share in a prebend (*VAS* 6 95 with *VAS* 5 54/143), and one includes livestock (Evetts *Ner.* 25 [=Strassmaier *Liverpool* 115]).

[13]*OECT* 10 313, BM 66005, *OECT* 9 73, *CT* 49 165, *JCS* 1 350 No. 3.

[14]*TuM* 2-3 1.

commodity then becomes part of the formal dowry, and the husband is free to utilize the old dowry elements.

The reason for this legal maneuvering becomes clear at the moment the marriage ends. There is little indication in our sources as to the fate of the dowry in case of divorce. In fact, there are no records of divorce extant; no lawsuits, no settlements, no letters--nothing that provides us with an actual case of divorce. What we do have is a "divorce clause" in marriage agreements, outlining the obligations of the husband should he seek to end the marriage. In such a case, the husband is to pay his wife a (prohibitively) substantial divorce settlement of one, five, or six minas of silver. She is then free to leave the conjugal home. I suspect from the circumstances outlined in the divorce clauses that the only possible (or at least admissible) grounds for the husband ending the marriage was the failure to produce offspring. (In fact, in the only certain case of bigamy, the husband states his reason for the second marriage: "I have no child; I desire a child. Please give me your daughter in marriage."[15]) And if I am correct in inferring that the dowry generally was transferred only after the birth of a child, then it is not surprising that the disposition of the dowry does not enter into the divorce resolutions.[16]

It is when the marriage ends by the death of one spouse that the integrality of the dowry becomes most important. If the wife is widowed, she needs her dowry to support herself and perhaps her young children. If she predeceases her husband, her children will inherit the dowry. It is for this final disposition that the dowry has been maintained (relatively) intact during the life of the marriage.

There is ample documentation of widows claiming their dowries from the estates of their dead husbands. They sue or defend their rights against their husbands' brothers and fathers, and even against their own sons. While married, they might have been able to exercise only minimal control over the dowries held by their husbands; but now as widows they come into full control of their dowries. They use the capital to engage in business, lend out their dowry silver, lease their fields or houses, use the dowry as collateral for loans. Now widowed and possibly still young, a woman is socially, legally, and economically independent of her father, brother, and husband. The dowry

---

[15]*VAS* 6 3.

[16]The single exception is *TBER* 93f., a document from Susa, in which the principals and several of the witnesses have Egyptian names, suggesting a non-Babylonian background. *TBER* 93f. provides for the return of the dowry to the wife in addition to the payment of a five-mina divorce settlement.

also, of course, could enhance her prospects for a second marriage, delaying or preventing this "independence."

If it is the wife who dies before her husband, he will continue to hold her dowry until his estate too is divided and inherited by their heirs. If she had sons by a previous marriage, however, the dowry is divided upon her death between the offspring of the two marriages, and her second widowed husband will retain control over only that share which eventually will be inherited by his own sons.

Right of inheritance in first millennium Babylonia was almost always restricted to males, and this ultimately also includes the right to inherit dowries. As in many other societies, the dowry itself serves as a woman's effective share of her patrimony, and it is sons and not daughters who usually inherit from their fathers. A woman's dowry, however, can go upon occasion to her daughter, granddaughter, or even niece as part of the latter's own dowry. This is particularly the case with the "inside" dowry goods and with single dowry slaves (to both of which I will return later). But such a dowry-to-dowry donation only delays by another generation the final disposition of the properties. Eventually, the dowry, which originated in a bride's father's estate, will be inherited by males--by her sons, grandsons, or great-grandsons. At that point, and not before, the specific properties that comprised the dowry and that remained discrete for decades will re-enter the general economy as undifferentiated wealth.

Other Prestations

Prestations other than the dowry are rarely mentioned in our sources, and I therefore suspect that they were far less common. Bridewealth (*biblu*) given by the husband to the wife's kin is attested for only three marriages,[17] in two of which there are also dowries. A prestation from the husband's father to the husband (*nungurtu*), allowing the husband to establish an independent household before he receives his inheritance, is known for only two marriages.[18] And widows' settlements (*širiktu*) from their husbands are a frequent phenomenon. I suspect that most widows receive a share of their husbands' estates primarily when they have no dowries to retrieve from that estate. Such settlements are sometimes designated by the husband during his

---

[17]*Nbk.* 101, *TBER* 78 AO 26775, *TBER* 93f.

[18]BM 54158 and *VAS* 6 61. The situation in which both the groom's and bride's fathers provide prestations to their offspring and the new marriage is also foreseen, however, in LNB §§8 and 9; it is possible, therefore, that the practice of making an outright gift to a son upon his marriage, independent of his future inheritance, was more widespread than our documentation reveals.

lifetime, and he might charge his sons not to evict or dispossess their mother. In other cases, when a husband fails to make explicit provision for his wife, she might have to resort to judicial intervention to secure her maintenance needs.

Summary of the Prestations

The wealth that is the dowry or the widow's settlement is almost the only wealth accessible to most women in the first millennium, and her access to even this wealth is restricted. Before marriage, she is economically as well as legally dependent upon her father, mother, or brother. On those infrequent occasions when an unmarried orphaned woman's dowry was assigned directly to her, she probably could do no more than hold it for her future husband. No pre-marriage dowry award included a house (although several did include fields), and where and how such an unmarried woman lived remains unknown. During her marriage, a woman's husband or father-in-law controlled the dowry wealth. We do not know if her domestic activities contributed to the family's income (for example, by spinning or weaving?--note that no dowry includes items identifiable, for example, as looms), or if they did, whether she secured for herself some disposable income. Only after she was widowed did a woman enjoy a significant measure of legal and economic independence. She now had control--although still not unlimited control--over the dowry awarded by her father and perhaps over properties for her support awarded by her husband. These two categories of property would form the basis of her maintenance, and-if of sufficient value to allow some discretionary income--they could allow her to enter the larger (male) economic arena.

Questions

I now want to shift my focus away from male-derived and male-controlled matrimonial property. As I emphasized at the beginning of this paper, our cuneiform evidence is dominated by male economic concerns. But there are scattered and indirect suggestions of the concerns and actions of women, raising questions with which I want to conclude this paper.

The first question concerns the "inside" dowry items--goods primarily of use to the internal affairs of the household, and of little use to the husband's outside economic activities. These "inside" components--the woman's jewelry, the beddings, linens, cushions, textiles, the beds, tables, and chairs, the pots and pans--can represent considerable amounts of wealth and a substantial investment by the bride's family. They are instrumental in the formation of the new, independent, conjugal household. They formed the basis of the household's production and preparation of clothing and food, and the bearing and rearing of children. But we do not know where these goods come from, who wove the textiles, who manufactured the furniture, who crafted the utensils. (Often we do not even know how to translate the Akkadian words for these items. The terms identify exclusively(?) "inside" or female-associated goods, and about one-fifth of the terms are unattested except in dowry lists. They therefore enter our dictionaries as "mng. unkn.," "mng. uncert.," or "a vessel.") And the archaeologists' ubiquitous clay pots are almost never mentioned in dowry lists;[19] were they not part of the household goods a bride brought to her new home? Or were they so common and of so little economic value that no accounting of them was necessary?

The second question involves that part of the cash component of the dowry that is labelled *quppu*[20] and kept distinct from other monies in the dowry itemizations. For example, "Eight minas of silver together with one mina of silver of the *quppu*."[21] What is the function of this *quppu* and how do *quppu* monies differ from unlabeled dowry cash?

The transactions associated with the *quppu* apparently are no different than the transactions associated with other dowry cash. Although in practice the *quppu* monies appear indistinguishable from other monies or properties of the larger *nudunnû*, in theory at least the wife may have a greater degree of control over the *quppu*, and her husband more restricted access to it. The *quppu* might represent an attempt by the bride's family to provide her with some cash that her husband cannot appropriate (her own "nest egg" or "pin money").

The third and final question I want to raise concerns the place of dowry donations by female kin *in addition to* the dowry awards made by a bride's father. These female-to-female property transfers consist mostly of slaves: mothers award a single slave to their daughters; a paternal grandmother assigns two female slaves; one paternal aunt awards one slave, and another paternal aunt awards three slaves and a field; a wife's maternal grandmother assigns three slaves, silver, and perhaps household goods.

The frequency with which slaves are involved in these awards suggests more a personal than an economic motive. As S.D. Goitein remarked in his study of the 9th-11th century A.D. Cairo Geniza material, "The well-to-

---

19The only dowry list with clay pots is found in L 1634, which includes "twelve empty, used, storage jars."

20In non-dowry contexts, the *quppu* is a box or chest, often used for holding temple silver offerings.

21*Dar.* 530+:1ff.

do girl brought in with her, as usual, one maidservant, a confidante from her mother's home, who would help her overcome the difficulties awaiting her in a strange household dominated by her mother- and sisters-in-law."[22] The Neo-Babylonian bride, in contrast, only infrequently entered an existing household. Nonetheless, these donations by female relatives of slaves--perhaps a young companion or the bride's old nursemaid--could very well have been motivated by similar personal concerns.

The few such female awards of which we are aware are noted in the documents only secondarily, as postscripts to the more valuable awards that concern the contracting (male) parties. If we proceed from the assumption that a witnessed tablet will be used only to record the transfer of items of significant economic value either to the party who comes into possession of the dowry (the husband or husband's father) or to the party who gives the dowry (the bride's father or brother), then the paucity of documentation for such female-to-female dowry transfers is not surprising. If a bride's female relative wanted to give her household items such as pots and pans, it is possible that the donation would not be documented. It is likely, therefore, that such supplemental donations were common, although--because they were of minimal concern to the male economic world--they remain largely invisible to us.

Conclusion

There is evidence from first-millennium cuneiform sources about matrimonial prestations, marriage patterns, and other social and legal phenomena involving women; but the evidence does not always illuminate questions of concern either to feminist historians or to historians of women. Our legal and administrative documents, no less than the literary and scientific, were written by, for, and mostly about the concerns of the adult, male, free, and usually elite population. The pictures we try to reconstruct from these sources will always be incomplete. We must scrutinize enormous quantities of raw data (with their problems of reading and assessment) with but small return. But, finally, it is up to those of us trained in the specialized esoterica of our traditional disciplines to ask the questions.

---

[22]S.D. Goitein, *A Mediterranean Society: The Jewish Communities of the Arab World as Portrayed in the Documents of the Cairo Geniza*, 4 vols., (Berkeley, 1983), IV, p. 311.

Responses to Prof. Roth's Paper

Robins: At the end, you make the point that we are dealing with the elite--these are presumably families of high status, --and the main aim of this institution that we are calling marriage seems to do with property. On the other end of the scale, Dr. Kuhrt was talking about slaves, women themselves as property and the situation is very different. Do we have any idea what marriage meant for the people in between?

Roth: Yes. I did say that our picture by and large is one of male elite population, but I hope I didn't say that it is exclusively that. Yes, I have, for example, marriage agreements between manumitted slaves and free-born women, at one end of the spectrum, and at the other end the marriage of the king's daughter to a high temple official. Unfortunately it's broken at the dowry, because that would be very nice. But I also have dowries that consist of nothing, maybe one pot.

Robins: Do they take the same form?

Roth: Yes, they do. By and large this is an urban population. It is a population that is for other reasons as well accustomed to recording certain types of transactions and not relying exclusively on the oral transaction, and it is more a propertied population than a very poor one. But my impression is that it is a fairly representative population.

Westbrook: Can we have a go at trying to clear up some of this terribly confusing dowry terminology? As far as I know the term *širiktu* in the Old Babylonian period appears only in the laws. Am I right?

Roth: Yes. The phenomenon is attested, however....

Westbrook: The phenomenon. Yes, good. Let us begin with the Old Babylonian period. There we have these two terms, *nudunnû* and *širiktu*. Now the *nudunnû* in the Old Babylonian period and in the laws of Hammurabi is the totality of the property of the wife, or what is assigned to the wife. It includes what we call dowry, the daughter's share of her father's estate, and also any other gifts that come in from any side. That all makes up the *nudunnû*. So that she can have *nudunnû* that her husband gave her, as the laws of Hammurabi put it, as a part of the *nudunnû*. Now one understands within this all-embracing term for the very narrow dowry so-called that which comes from her father's house and is the functional equivalent of her share of the inheritance. It's important, usually because it is subsumed into one mass during the course of the marriage. Both at the end of the marriage, depending on the mode of distribution, on who is the survivor, the devolution of the separate parts of the marital property may differ and therefore it is at that point that we ought to distinguish them. Now this system of terminology, continues into the Middle Assyrian period where it is called *širiktu* and *nudunnû* and I think that the same system probably survived into the first millennium. Unfortunately the terminology didn't and what we called the *širiktu* disappears, its meaning is lost and therefore it is confused with the Neo-Babylonian laws and called things that are some things given by the husband, it doesn't represent reality anymore. Instead we have in the first millennium a different word from that which we were dealing with in the second millennium, the word *mulūgu* which is the equivalent of the *širiktu*, it's that narrow part, which is *mulūgu* and this turns up at El-Amarna and at Nuzi. You see it is also found at Ugarit and in the late Talmudic sources. Is it found in Neo-Babylonian?

Roth: In Neo-Babylonian *mulūgu* defines a class of dowry slave.

Westbrook: There were *mulūgu* slaves?

Roth: I believe it was an inherited status.

Westbrook: I hope this makes the terminology a little bit more clear.

Roth: Well, in fact the terminological labyrinth is meant to confuse many. I have some different ideas about what happens in Hammurabi. My point, however, in subjecting you to that exercise was that the labels themselves are insufficient and labels must be seen just as labels, we have to find out what is going on behind them, who is doing what and what the prestation is about. The labels are not enough in themselves.

Kuhrt: I think an appropriate point is the point of Bienveniste who said to understand the names of institutions is not the same as understanding the institutions, and that I believe is the point that Martha is making, and it's a very fundamental and a very important one.

Westbrook: If they saw fit, if the native terminology sees fit to distinguish between various institutions then that should be our starting point, we can't possibly ignore this distinction.

Stone: Responding to two different points that you made: first of all you talked about the terms of independence, especially men's, in terms of whether they have to wait until their father's death to become independent, which is what most inheritance documents tend to suggest. The other aspect which you dealt with was the age of marriage when you suggested that men are considerably older than their wives, that they still tend to be in their twenties. And then at the end you suggested that there are a few brides who would be moving into existing households, Now my understanding, at least the way that I have been interpreting the bits and pieces we have for this period and earlier periods, is that we have tended to assume that in fact joint households, even after the death of the father, very often continue. Thus in many cases I think rather than seeing the bride as coming in (especially when they are often very young girls) and in fact running a household, she is rather coming in to one that is much more established. In fact, if you have a look at what her status is at marriage, she has to adapt herself mostly to an already existing situation.

Roth: Yes, I think that is right, a very good point. What I meant was that since the groom's father was probably no longer living in most cases when the groom takes a bride the household....

Stone: So are you suggesting that in fact the grooms don't very often get married until then?

Roth: I would say can't. The patterns seem to be that most grooms have no living fathers, whether they waited until their fathers died, or societal expectation was that a man did not get married until he was about twenty-seven or twenty-eight-- at which point most men no longer had living fathers. I'm not going to choose one or the other. But you are right, of course if the groom's mother is a decade or more younger than his father she may still very well be living, and we have brothers and other sisters-in law and his own sisters, so that the young bride will be moving into a very large house with a lot of other women and social dynamics.

Stone: I think this late age of marriage might explain the large incidence of prostitution.

Stuard: Prof. Roth, there has been a contest for about the last twenty to twenty-five years between those of the historians and anthropologists looking at the subject of dowry and I would like to see what a historian looking at it within its historical context finds. The anthropologists like Jack Goody would find a great deal of difficulty with your identification of bride wealth in a system with dowry, because he sees them as characteristic of two different locales, and you see them together. But those anthropologists do raise a question that I would like to pose to you and that is, for instance, that Goody would see dowry as essentially a means of the transmission of wealth generationally. There are aspects of that in your presentation. He would see bridewealth as a means for the maintenance of status of the woman in her marriage. Now your bridewealth doesn't seem to be doing that, but dowry does seem to be doing that at times and would you tell us a bit more about those two aspects of your question.

Roth: I think dowry is a strategy by which a man tends to transmit his wealth, but not to his daughters, he transmits his wealth to his grandson via his daughter. Now bridewealth, you say Goody says that bridewealth is a maintenance of her status? Yes? Alright, I suppose that if bridewealth is given by the groom's family to the bride's family, it may maintain the equal status of the families....

Herlihy: I may be wrong on this but I think you should distinguish between brideprice and bridewealth. Brideprice goes to the bride's family, bridewealth goes to her.

Stuard: It maintains her status within her marriage. So those have often been seen as two different very different purposes for marriage prestations and they seem to appear together in this particular treatment. I think that is interesting.

Foster: I would say that your particular question is an example of the kind of questions that Assyriologists have not been able to answer, they always bring us up short.

Roth: About the bridewealth, we have so little, I have three documents that have this prestation from the groom's family to the bride's family and in at least one it is counter-dowry. The groom's family contributes one and one half minas of silver and the bride returns one and one half minas of silver.

Delaney: You said something about children born before the marriage agreement was sealed belonging to the father. Now is this an exception, because it seems that later on after it is sealed they also belong to the father. Do they always belong to the father, and if they belong to the father after it is sealed then why do they belong to the father before it is sealed? It doesn't really make too much sense.

Roth: This is something that I am speculating on at the moment and whatever I say now is purely preliminary. Within the body of the marriage contract five marriage contracts have a clause that refers to a document that has not yet been sealed and makes reference to children, existing, named children in one case, given by age, and these children have been born to the woman.

Delaney: This is just what I was trying to say, that in general, then, you could also imply that before it is sealed normally the children belonged to their mother. In other words these things are exceptions.

Roth: My most recent understanding of this clause was that the dowry is the document that has not yet been sealed and transferred, and they did not transfer the dowry until she had proven her child-bearing capability, so they are now saying there are children and they are living and we now seal this document and the children are legitimate, whatever that means, and at any rate will inherit from the father.

Figure 36

Terracotta figurine depicting a female frame-drum musician. Its exact provenance is unknown; but it belongs to a type found widely in Cyprus and occassionally in Palestine in Iron II contexts. Courtesy The Semitic Museum, Harvard University, #5755. Photo by Sharon Wright.

Introduction to Ancient Israel

In the final sessions of formal papers in this Conference, we turn our attention to ancient Israel, that aspect of the Ancient Near East which has been accessible to the world through its written traditions for the longest period of any of the parts of the Ancient Near East included in this Conference. Indeed, there has been virtually an unceasing opportunity to focus on the literary remains of ancient Israel since its demise. In an unbroken chronology the written traditions of Bible were preserved and studied in the religious communities of Formative Judaism and Early Christianity which received those traditions and treasured them as scriptural. Other evidence, external to the Bible, written on leather, stone, or clay has been recovered primarily in modern times and amplifies our understanding of ancient Israel. While the monuments of all other ancient Near Eastern peoples stood in mute testimony to the lives of their creators, waiting for those who would unlock the written traditions of Egypt, Sumeria, Assyria and Babylonia in modern times, students and scholars of ancient Israel have been able to pursue their interests without linguistic barriers since the end of ancient Israel in the latter years of the first millennium B.C.E.

This continuing access has not been without its problems, however, since the access was gained almost exclusively through a single source, the Hebrew Bible. Not unlike the remainder of the Ancient Near East, it was not until the development of modern archaeology in the nineteenth century that we have been able to enlarge our vision of life in ancient Israel beyond the vignettes of the Bible and gain a better understanding of the boundaries of the Bible as a source for understanding the social history of ancient Israel and the role of women in Israelite culture. Archaeology, formal and informal, has presented us with an impressive array of textual discoveries signalled by such names as Qumran, Amarna, Ugarit, Ebla. Such activity has also provided a basis for further linguistic attention to the traditions of surrounding groups such as Moabites, Elamites, Ammonites and the like. We may observe further that modern access to ancient Israel through archaeological and linguistic studies has reduced the tendency to study ancient Israel through the succeeding religious traditions which inherited and transformed that tradition.

Multiple sources of access and lessened dependency on the views within Formative Judaism and Early Christianity may modify the misogynous views associated with the Christian missionary, Paul, reared a Jew or the assumption that the Jewish view of women is that embedded in the prayer, "Blessed art Thou, O Lord God, who has not made me a woman." Such traditions as these have provided the glasses through which ancient Israelite woman has been viewed and concomitantly reduced the tendency to look at Israel more especially as a part of the Ancient Near East.

The intention to look at ancient Israel through its contemporaneous setting in the Ancient Near East rather than through the major religious traditions which look to Israel for their foundations provides an initial contrast with the other Ancient Near Eastern groups identified for attention in this Conference. It is important, however, to note several distinctions:

1. The relative brevity of ancient Israel, or at least of the period in which its traditions took their final written forms. If, e.g., we view ancient Israel with respect to Ancient Near Eastern concerns of the second millennium, we must note that views of Israel relating to that second millennium are encased in traditions from later periods and, in any event, reflect a people in formation who are portrayed as experiencing significant influence from the peoples of the Tigris-Euphrates river valley and from Egypt. Indeed it is important to be as precise as possible since using the term "ancient Israel" in any sense which conveys a society with social, economic, and political forms is largely possible only in the first millennium B.C.E. Traditions such as those in the Book of Genesis may be useful for later reflections of gender roles, but the admixture of mythological and legendary materials provides a barrier to be surmounted.

Even if one thousand years looms large in the eyes of the beholder, there is a further observation pertinent to the analysis of ancient Israel. Most of that millennium was spent under a series of occupiers of Israel or as parts of various Egyptian, Assyrian, Babylonian, Persian, or Hellenistic empires or kingdoms.

Only at the beginning of the period of ancient Israel under the control of the Davidic dynasty and at the end of ancient Israel under the Hasmoneans would Israel know the development of institutions free politically of external influence. Even in this instance we may exaggerate the freedom of cultural expression and cultural change which is a by-product of political independence. Insofar, however, as political independency has any bearing on the nature of female roles in Israel, the opportunity for that expression would be limited to two periods of approximately a century each rather than a millennium of Israelite life.

2. A related factor is one of size. ancient Israel, or Palestine, comprised an area that would in contemporary terms include portions of the modern nations of Israel, Jordan, Lebanon and Syria. In antiquity the coastal strip of land provided a bridge between the dominant centers of Egypt and Mesopotamia. ancient Israel occupied an area not much different in size than the state of Vermont, though on occasion dreaming of world empire. Throughout the Biblical tradition it becomes clear that Israel's views of its greatest political achievement measured in the extent of land controlled are bound up with the accomplishments under the rule of David. It was the kingdom of David which provided the model for retrospective views of what Israel might be as a world power. Save for the religious heritage of Israel which would provide a basis for the subsequent development of Formative Judaism and Early Christianity, this small nation-state might well have become of no greater interest to modern investigators than other small national states in and near the Syro-Palestinian area.

Once we are no longer threatened by questions of Israel's accommodation to its environment, there is no necessity to publish books with titles that suggest that the Hebrew Bible stands "against its environment." Originality becomes a better model of investigation than uniqueness. Issues of cultural diffusion, of explanations of similarity and difference become primary and require the use of anthropologically-oriented methods of research.

However, the acceptance of ancient Israel as a small vassal state for most of its history does not solve the problem of defining the role(s) of women in ancient Israel, nor satisfy us with the answer that the role(s) of women in ancient Israel are no more than the reflection of the major states controlling Israel's economy.

3. Further, we can comment that this small vassal state, regularly trying to preserve its existence by debating alternative political alliances, sits strategically placed between the two major power areas of the Ancient Near East, Mesopotamia to the northeast and Egypt to the southwest. Power shifted between these areas and Israel's concern for continued existence was regularly involved in maintaining acceptable relations with whichever area was in control in a given period.

4. Among the factors influencing gender roles in ancient Israel is the rise of urbanization during the last millennium before the Common Era, though the scale of that urbanization needs to be carefully watched. Again,

this is an agrarian economy as a whole with little industrial expression and with all that such an assertion may mean for the nature and extent of roles for women.

5. Lastly I would note as a general aspect for the study of gender roles in ancient Israel what will be developed at greater length by the presenters of this section, namely, the nature of the sources by which the focus of this Conference is researched.

Much of the work to date in the discussion of women in ancient Israel has been done through analysis of the Hebrew Bible, a complex literary document bearing the heavy imprint of the religious communities which created, received, edited, and preserved it. Indeed, the current generation of scholarship on ancient Israel is very aware of assertions about the patriarchal and androcentric character of the Hebrew Bible.

The continuing use of the Hebrew Bible for the study of women in ancient Israel requires attention to the analytical approaches by which it is studied. Secondly, this literary source is accompanied by a paucity of epigraphic evidence from Israel (and the absence of such data as wall painting of the type available to certain other Ancient Near Eastern historians). The premises of the presenters today is to urge that we must try to supplement literary data with artifactual evidence and gain a more comprehensive understanding of the roles of women in ancient Israel.

Ernest S. Frerichs

Women and the Domestic Economy of Early Israel

Carol Meyers

Introduction

The investigation of women's history no longer needs justification. Nearly two decades of research have made the recovery of the female past a field of its own, or a sub-discipline within the various fields of historical research.[1] The energies and resourcefulness of the current generation of scholars are meeting the difficulties of a remote subject matter and of a relative paucity of sources.

When it comes to investigating women in the biblical past, a particular problem emerges that is not present, or at least is not felt so strongly in other areas of historical inquiry. Modern western culture has been shaped by biblical[2] images and ideas. Yet these images and ideas typically do not exert their influence in their original context or with their Iron Age meanings, but rather as they have been transmitted and interpreted by post-biblical Christian and Jewish traditions. This is particularly true with biblical materials that relate to women. Many of the traditional interpretations of biblical texts dealing with gender implicitly or explicitly involve ideas of female inferiority or submissiveness as they emerged in late biblical or post-biblical settings. A case in point is the Eden story. Our familiarity with that narrative and our sense of what it means are colored more by the New Testament (especially I Timothy 2: 11-15) and by Milton's *Paradise Lost* than by an analysis of the

---

[1] For a perceptive discussion for the emergence of feminist scholarship and its impact on several of the major disciplines, including history, in the academy, see E. C. DuBois, G. P. Kelly, E. L. Kennedy, C. Korsmyer, and L. S. Robinson, *Feminist Scholarship: Kindling in the Groves of Academe* (Urbana, 1985).

[2] In this paper, references to the "Bible" are references to Hebrew Scripture, which is called the Old Testament by Christians.

original Hebrew text.[3] Similar readings or misreadings of biblical texts on the ideological level, and to the detriment of women, are present in all sorts of contemporary secular as well as religious contexts. Consequently, recovering the position of women in the Israelite world means not only searching for clues in the texts of ancient Israel and in the material remains of the Israelite world, but also breaking through the incredibly strong web of post-biblical interpretations.

The focus in this paper is not on women in the Bible or on biblical women but rather on women in ancient Israel. As the methodological discussion will make clear, these two groups are not necessarily the same. Even though there is a general assumption that the Bible is an accurate reflection of at least some aspects of Israelite society, and although this assumption may be valid at many levels, when it comes to gender it must be carefully examined. Theologians and feminists alike need to be cautious in drawing conclusions about Israelite women from biblical texts[4] not only because an overlay of interpretation may occlude the texts but also because the texts themselves may not have a one-to-one correspondence with reality.

Methodological Considerations and Analytical Perspectives

1. Perhaps the most difficult problem confronting the researcher's attempt to discover the role and status of women in Israelite society is the procurement of data. To be sure, the Bible is an unparalleled source of information about ancient Israel. Without it, even with all that archaeology and other Near Eastern materials have provided, we would be quite in the dark about Israelite life and history. Yet the Bible as an informant about gender relations is a biased source of information; and those biases must be recognized.

Just what are its biases? First and foremost, from the perspective of feminist inquiry, is the fact that the Bible was written almost entirely by males.

---

[3]Some of the consequent misunderstandings of Genesis 2-3 are listed in my paper "Recovering Eve: Biblical Woman without Post-biblical Dogma," *Women and a New Academy: Gender and Cultural Contexts*, ed. J. F. O'Barr (Madison, Wisconsin: 1989). See also P. Trible, *God and the Rhetoric of Sexuality* (Philadelphia: 1978), 72-74, and J. Higgins, "The Myth of Eve the Temptress," *JAAR* 44 (1976): 439-47.

[4]One of the most blatant examples of a prominent feminist theologian erroneously presuming that biblical texts portray Israelite reality is R. R. Ruether's pronouncement about the "enslavement of persons [women and slaves] within the Hebrew family." See Ruether's "Feminist Interpretation: A Method of Correlation," *Feminist Interpretation of the Bible*, ed. Letty M. Russel (Philadelphia, 1985), 119.

The Pentateuch, complicated and ancient as its components may be, is in its final redaction a product of priestly activity (and only men were priests). Most of the historical books stem from the royal court in Jerusalem and its bureaucrats, that is, from a king and his male courtiers. Occasionally women's voices can be heard. Some early poems are attributed to women; and one biblical book, the Song of Songs, may be a woman's composition. But the bulk of biblical writings must be attributed to male authorship. The social distance of females from the shapers of sacred tradition has its effect in the androcentric orientation of biblical writings. This androcentric aspect of the Bible has several implications for attempts to understand women's lives: 1) Relatively little attention or mention is given in the Bible to women's lives or concerns, except insofar as they are part of "all Israel," which is the overriding focus of the biblical authors. 2) The perspective on issues which do impinge on women's lives is a male one and cannot be expected to represent situations as they might be seen from a female perspective.

Second, the Hebrew Bible by its very nature is largely concerned with public and/or national life. For most (but not all; see below) of Israelite history, public life was almost exclusively male life. Leadership positions, with several notable exceptions, were held by men. Israel's very existence, in the much fought-over territory of Iron Age (1200-587 BCE) Palestine, was contingent upon military and political manipulation. The army was a male institution, as were the political and government bodies. With the public sector being almost exclusively male, the chief public document (the Bible) was inevitably the result of male literary and chronistic activity.

Third, the Bible is in large measure a product of urban life, and mostly the life of one atypical city, Jerusalem, the seat of the political and religious institutional life of Israel for the greater part of its existence. Because of this, the Bible does not properly deal with rural and/or non-Jerusalem life. But Jerusalem was an exceptional city in the ancient Levant.[5] Thus the biblical orientation to Jerusalem is at the expense of a perspective on rural life and even on life in other cities. Even though there were a number of other urban centers in Israel, they were not cities like Jerusalem and certainly not like cities in our post-industrial world. Ancient Palestinian cities were tied to the agricultural hinterland.[6] Israel was an agrarian society; and the urban

---

[5]Most of the sacred Priestly and Deuteronomic traditions were shaped in Jerusalem after the eighth century, when urban expansion made the capital of Judah at least ten times larger than other contemporary Palestinian cities; cf., Y. Shiloh, "Archaeology and the History of Jerusalem," graduate seminar at Duke University, 1986.

[6]F. S. Frick, *The City in Ancient Israel* (S.B.L. Dissertation Series, 36; Missoula, Montana, 1977), 6-8, 91-97.

segment of such societies was never larger than ten percent and was more likely to have been below five percent.[7] The large majority of the population were peasant farmers living in small, relatively isolated villages.

A fourth point, not itself a bias but nonetheless a problem deriving from the nature of the biblical materials, is a chronological one. The Bible spans almost a thousand years in its compositional history and even longer in the history of its subject matter. Hebraic society underwent radical changes during that span. Hence biblical materials concerning gender cannot necessarily be lumped together for an overview of biblical women let alone of Israelite women; the chronological place of individual texts must be taken into account, and this is sometimes impossible.

For all these reasons, and others that our next few points will touch on, the Bible is a biased informant and must be used very cautiously as a source for women's history.

2. Our next methodological consideration concerns the relationship between formal gender arrangements and social reality. Ethnographic research has revealed that there is normally a disjunction between societal ideas or ideology (as expressed in laws, for example, or in normative narratives) and social behavior. Sir Edmund Leach's warning to anthropologists is relevant to investigators of Israelite antiquity: "The observer must distinguish between what people do and what people say they do; that is between normal custom as individually interpreted on the one hand and normative rule on the other...[The researcher] must distinguish behavior from ideology."[8] Insofar as we are interested in behavior, ideology bearing sources must be treated circumspectly. For ancient Israel as for any society, ideology cannot be simply equated with daily reality, which can diverge from the normative expression contained in the sacred texts.

Related to the above point is the difficulty in evaluating the existence of the signs of patriarchal structures, such as the patrilineal transferral of property across generations and the patrilineal organization of social units, in terms of the effective power of such structures in the dynamics of gender relationships in daily life. The apparent hierarchical control of men over women may have been functionally far less powerful than might be expected. Again, anthropologists have pointed out that formal rights may favor males but that daily informal interaction may exhibit a "balance of gender power" or

---

[7]G. E. Lenski, *Power and Privilege: A Theory of Social Stratification*, 2nd ed. (Chapel Hill, 1984), 199-200.

[8]E. Leach, *Social Anthropology* (Glasgow, 1982), 130.

even some signs or areas of female dominance.[9] This is particularly true in certain social and economic circumstances, such as those obtaining in early Israel (see below). While agrarian societies exhibit clear gender distinctions that have great functional value and that are often "elaborated in cultural ideologies,"[10] such distinctions do not necessarily signify actual differentials of power.

3. Our contemporary assumptions that male prerogatives and privileges are innately more valued than those of females[11] should not be automatically superimposed upon an ancient society. Such assumptions have been shaped by the course of events in the industrialized West and may not be appropriate for the assessment of a pre-modern, oriental culture. For this reason, the very use of the term "patriarchal," which has implicit connotations of hierarchical arrangements that devalue females, cannot be easily applied to Israelite society. The term itself is controversial. Not only are there a variety of definitions attached to it, but also the origins and functions of patriarchal systems are much debated.[12] Some researchers would prefer not to use it.[13] For ancient Israel, especially for the pre-state period to which we shall soon turn our attention, the idea of patriarchy and its assumptions of male

---

[9]The research of several anthropologists has demonstrated this. See S. C. Rogers, "Female Forms of Power and the Myth of Male Dominance: A Model of Female/Male Interaction in Peasant Society," *American Ethnologist* 2 (1975): 727-56; C. Cronin, "Illusion and Reality in Sicily," *Sexual Stratification: A Cross-Cultural View*, ed. A. Schlegel (New York, 1977), 67-93; and E. Friedl, "The Position of Women: Appearance and Reality," *Anthropological Quarterly* 40 (1967): 47-108.

[10]S. LeVine and R. J. LeVine, "Age, Gender, and the Demographic Transition: The Life Course in Agrarian Societies," *Gender and the Life Course*, ed. A. S. Rossi (New York, 1985), 30. LeVine and LeVine review characteristic features of agrarian societies, with respect to age and gender, that are helpful in reconstructing early Israelite village society.

[11]For a classical statement of this assumption see M. Z. Rosaldo's pioneering essay, "Women, Culture, and Society: A Theoretical Overview," *Women Culture and Society*, ed. M. Z. Rosaldo and L. Lamphere (Stanford, 1974), 18-21. Rosaldo's claims have been subjected to considerable discussion, and she defends them more recently in "The Use and Abuse of Anthropology: Reflections on Feminism and Cross-cultural Understanding," *SIGNS* 5 (1980): 393-96. See also M. Gould, "Review Essay: The New Sociology," *SIGNS* 5 (1980): 464.

[12]See e.g., S. Rowbotham, "The Trouble with Patriarchy," The New Statesman (21/28 December, 1979): 970-71. See my chapter on "The Problem of Patriarchy" in *Discovering Eve: Ancient Israelite Women in Context* (New York, 1988) for a discussion of patriarchy, its use in feminist research, and its relationship to patrilineality and to power structures.

[13]P. Bird, "Images of Women in the Old Testament," *Religion and Sexism*, ed. R. R. Ruether (New York, 1974), 77, n.1, explains her judicious avoidance of the term in her discussion of biblical passages dealing with women.

superiority should be avoided. Contemporary western measures of status, role, value, etc. cannot be simply transposed to a radically different setting.[14]

4. Related to the above point about assumptions of gender value in contemporary versus ancient societies is the very problem of the legitimacy of evaluating the role of an individual person living in an ancient agrarian society. As for most agrarian or peasant societies, the Hebraic concept of the individual was not developed in ways in which it is in the modern world.[15] Although it is normal for us to think of persons as autonomous human beings and to differentiate ourselves as individuals from social relationships and family ties, it would have been rare for the ancient Israelite to have done so in quite the same way. People experienced themselves relationally rather than through individuation and separation. Thus, while males and females had sharply defined roles, such roles were seen as integrally related, as parts of a whole piece that contributed to the survival and welfare of the group. This communal orientation means that one cannot really consider the exploitation of individuals in the same way that we do in the modern world. Individual existence is subsumed into a corporate structure in a way essential for group survival. Thus the possibility of dehumanizing or abusive behavior toward categories of individuals that were integral to the basic units of social organization may have been virtually nonexistent.

The probable lack of a separate concept of individual identity does not mean that highly differentiated roles for individuals did not exist. On the contrary, defined roles--positions in society filled by individuals in response to recurring needs--were of critical importance.[16] But the very fact that specific roles along age and gender lines were of crucial importance meant that the social group depended on the individuals fulfilling those roles and that those individuals operated to meet group needs, not individual needs.

5. Finally, as the above considerations have indicated, biblical texts alone are not sufficient nor reliable for the reconstruction of gender roles in early Israel. The potential for reaching the Israelite woman lies in the use of extra-biblical materials provided by archaeology as well as in the examination of biblical texts; and it also involves the application of social scientific analytical perspectives. The task of investigating the lives of Israelite women must begin with the Iron I Period, ancient Israel's formative period. Patterns

---

[14]As demonstrated by the research of M. K. Whyte, *The Status of Women in Preindustrial Societies* (Princeton, 1978).

[15]LeVine and LeVine, 31; cf. J. Pedersen, *Israel: Its Life and Culture* (2 vols.; London, 1926), 1, 259, 263.

[16]G. E. Lenski and J. Lenski, *Human Societies*, 5th ed. (New York, 1987), 75.

of gender relationships, as of many aspects of Israelite life, were established in the early centuries of Israelite existence. Despite the often radical shifts in political and social organization that subsequently occurred, residuals of the pattern established early in Israelite history would have been sustained well into the Iron II Period, the era of monarchic rule.

Thus our focus is on the reconstruction of the social fabric of Israelite life in the pre-monarchic age. Archaeological work in the past two decades, as influenced by the goals and methods of the "new archaeology,"[17] has made significant strides in investigating the small, isolated, highland villages that all too often had been ignored by earlier generations of archaeologists, who were interested in political history and monumental remains. The work on those villages of the hill country that most investigators are willing to call "Israelite" enables us to establish, first, what the environmental conditions were for emergent Israel, and then what the economic, social, and political responses were to those conditions. This kind of analysis draws heavily upon social scientific methodologies for understanding the structure of the society represented by the inhabitants of these villages.

As helpful as archaeology is in establishing the setting in which Israelite women lived, it has frustratingly little to tell us about their lives. Like the Bible, archaeology cannot easily or directly be used to reconstruct the place of women. While archaeology is extremely helpful in its attention to the physical context of the ancients, direct correlation between artifacts or structures and gender is rarely possible. Archaeological remains, however we wish it were otherwise, are rarely "gender noisy." Yet the information now available about early Israelite villages lends itself to the application of further social scientific models. Using analogies from the study of societies with similar economic and domestic patterns, we can begin to visualize what roles women played in Israelite life in a way that would not be possible were we to use only the biblical text or only the artifactual remains.

Women in Early Israelite Society

1. Establishing the place of women in Israelite society depends, first, on examining the nature of early Israel's environment and technology as they

[17]A useful description of the new archaeology as developed by W.W. Taylor, L.R. Binford, and others, can be found in D. H. Thomas, *Archaeology* (New York, 1979): 44-60. The influence of the new archaeology on "biblical" archaeology is discussed by W. G. Dever, "The Impact of the 'New Archaeology' on Syro-Palestinian Archaeology," *BASOR* 242 (1981): 15-29.

would have impinged upon gender roles. Much recent research material[18] deals directly with Israel's environment and with the technological and social adaptation of early Israel to that environment. The conclusions of this historical, material-cultural research as it relates to gender roles can be briefly summarized, especially as it reveals aspects of the labor requirements in the highland villages of the early Iron Age.

First, early Israel was a pioneer society. The numerous highland sites assumed to be Israelite were situated in underdeveloped areas of the central hill country, areas that were rocky, forested, and under-watered. The demands of such an environment involved substantial commitments of labor, largely by men, for clearing the overgrowth, digging cisterns to create a year-round water supply, and constructing terraces to help retain water and to provide flat land for horticultural development and also for field crops where the intermontane valleys were few and small. All of these activities required large outputs of labor.[19] The construction of terraces, for example, while a great boon to the Israelite settlers and perhaps the *sina qua non* of dry farming in the highlands, required not only substantial initial efforts but also an ongoing, relatively large investment of labor, particularly during the rainy season and often at times when the agricultural calendar imposed other heavy labor demands.[20] That is, the agrarian economy of the highland villages involved labor-intensive periods.

Second, Israel came into existence at a time in which the population of the eastern Mediterranean world in general was in decline, in which famine, disease and warfare in the preceding Late Bronze Age had reduced the already short life expectancy of the ancients.[21] Excavation of tombs and paleopathological analysis indicate lowered life-spans for both males and females, with female life expectancies being up to ten years less than those of males.

---

[18]E.g. F. S. Frick, *The Formation of the State in Ancient Israel* (The Social World of Biblical Antiquity Series, 4; Sheffield, England, 1985), and D. C. Hopkins, *The Highlands of Canaan* (The Social World of Biblical Antiquity Series, 3; Sheffield, England, 1985). Cf. N. K. Gottwald, *The Tribes of Yahweh* (New York, 1979), 650-66.

[19]In horticultural societies, and presumably also agrarian ones, those pioneer tasks are close to constituting a male monopoly, so E. Friedl, *Women and Men: An Anthropologist's View*, (New York, 1975), 53-54.

[20]Hopkins, 173-86, 213-35.

[21]See the data presented in my article "The Roots of Restriction: Women in Early Israel," *BA* 41 (1978): 95-99.

These factors--the demographic decline of that era, along with the existence of a labor-intensive economy and the extra labor needs of the pioneer period--would have had several important implications for women's lives. First, the labor requirements of Israelite families, as of all farm families, meant an emphasis on large families. The domestic use of child labor was critical for the maintenance of food supply, which is the overriding priority of agrarian peoples.[22] The maternal imperative was thus especially strong for early Israel. Biblical passages emphasizing female fertility and the overcoming of barrenness must be understood in this context: they give ideological sanction to the adaptive strategy of increasing birthrate. As in many agrarian societies, beliefs and practices promoting fertility are "fundamental to the adaptive strategies by which agrarian parents" obtain their immediate survival and also secure their long-term security.[23] Second, high labor demands meant the active participation of women in agrarian work. The intensification of woman's productive as well as reproductive tasks is typical of agrarian societies with an agricultural calendar involving labor intensive periods. Especially when there exist pioneer tasks that typically fall to males and when there are sporadic military encounters drawing males away from the family lands, females participate in more of the "everyday" agricultural jobs than might otherwise be the case.[24]

These two female roles--the productive and the reproductive--should not be seen as competing or incompatible, as they are in the modern western world. Bearing and caring for children are subsumed into the daily routine in agrarian settings, and the labors of childbirth do not radically disrupt female subsistence labors.[25] Having children was normally not viewed as a discrete role that precluded or interfered with other social and economic roles.

2. This general picture of the highland setting and its labor and reproductive imperatives for women can be supplemented by delineating the specific social setting--the actual structures--in which the villagers lived. In

---

[22]LeVine and LeVine, 31.

[23]*Ibid.*, 30. Note that the familiar biblical charge, "Be fruitful and multiply," uses plural verbs in the Hebrew. God's command to increase population is addressed to society as a whole and thus indicates that the female maternal role is embedded in community goals, the securing of highland territories, as well as in family labor needs.

[24]The social scientific and biblical evidence for this situation existing in early Israel is presented in my article "Procreation, Production, and Protection: Male-Female Balance in Early Israel," *JAAR* 51 (1983): 569-93.

[25]L. Tilly, "The Social Sciences and the Study of Women: A Review Article," *Comparative Studies in Society and History* 20 (1978): 167.

looking at living arrangements, both the physical and social configurations of daily life are significant.

The archaeological recovery of highland village sites has revealed a number of salient features. First, the relative absence of imported wares or other indications of a market economy suggests that the villages were relatively self-sufficient. Second, the fact that the living units are mostly the same size points to a relatively egalitarian social structure. Third, the existence of individual installations, within each household area, for commodity processing and storage, and the concomitant absence of public works as would indicate centralizing governmental structures, shows the household units to be relatively autonomous. These general features of highland villages and their component units have been supplemented by further sociological analysis, most notably by Stager's work on the "Archaeology of the Family."[26] His study of the village plans and of the configuration of structures has produced an understanding of the dwelling units themselves and also a sense of how they relate to levels of social organization.

The highland villages in the early Iron Age consisted not of nuclear family dwellings but rather of dwelling clusters or residential compounds, with two or three small dwellings structurally linked and sharing facilities for food production, processing and storage. Such units, which can be related, though imperfectly, to the biblical term *beth 'av*, were occupied by compound family groupings. Social scientific study of the history of the family[27]--in this case better designated "family household" to accommodate the way in which the household involved related persons and also the residential quarters, out-buildings, tools and equipment, livestock, and even fields and orchards[28]--indicates that such groupings were atypical. Compound families, whether extended vertically or horizontally, are difficult to manage and often involve complex and tense interpersonal relations.[29] They apparently emerge in response to particularly difficult problems of subsistence, when the pooling of labor and of resources increases chances of survival.

---

[26]L. A. Stager, "The Archaeology of the Family in Ancient Israel," *BASOR* 260 (1985): 1-36.

[27]E.g. by R. McC. Netting, R. R. Wilk, and E. J. Arnould (eds.), *Household: Comparative and Historical Studies of the Domestic Group* (Berkeley, 1984); see especially the editors' "Introduction," xiii-xxxviii. Cf. S. J. Yanagisako, "Family and Household: The Analysis of Domestic Groups," *Annual Review of Anthropology* 8 (1979): 161-205.

[28]This inclusive aspect of the ancient Near Eastern household has been pointed out by, among others, I. J. Gelb, "Approaches to the Study of Ancient Society," *JAOS* 87 (1967): 5.

[29]B. Pasternak, C.R. Ember, and M. Ember, "On the Conditions Favoring Extended Family Households," *Journal of Anthropological Research* 32 (1976): 109-23.

Therefore, in a setting in which women have a large economic role, by supplying labor through their children and on their own, we see households that are larger and more complex than the norm. This datum must then be set against the fact that in tribal Israel, with its relative lack of social, political and economic hierarchies, the locus of power was at the bottom of the social structure,[30] viz., with the family household. (Thereafter, with the rise of the monarchy and centralized structures, the base of power shifted to the top.)

3. The role of women within such autonomous and complex household groups can be theoretically reconstructed. The economic role of the female was, as we have already suggested, crucial. Women were undoubtedly involved in all aspects of economic life: in producing, transforming, and allocating resources. Much of what they did required considerable technological skill. While we cannot be sure exactly which tasks they performed, we can be fairly certain that the differentiation of tasks by gender (and age) meant female expertise in and control of a range of indispensable activities. The economic roles of women included not only tasks performed but also, with respect to senior females in a multiple family compound, the management of the activities of others: other females to be sure, and probably also younger males. Fulfillment of distinct economic roles by both females and males in agrarian societies creates efficiency in carrying out tasks essential for food production and thus for survival. It also functions socially, stimulating cooperation and interdependence and thereby strengthening group life.[31]

Female participation in societal roles, of course, was not limited to the crucial economic tasks.[32] Parenting--the socialization and education of the young--was inextricably linked to maternity and was interwoven with the technological specialties of the females. Transmission of many aspects of culture was thus part of the female's role; children of both genders absorbed modes of behavior, cultural forms, and social values from the direct or indirect instructions of the mother. One particular aspect of this culture transmission function, which another paper in this collection describes,[33] is the place of women in the formal and informal religious or ritual activities that took place

---

[30]A.D.H. Mayes, *Judges*, Old Testament Guides (Sheffield, England, 1985), 46-51.

[31]Lenski and Lenski, 44-45.

[32]My chapter on "Household Function and Female Roles," in *Discovering Eve* explains in considerable detail the reconstruction of economic and of other female roles in pre-monarchic Israel.

[33]P. Bird, "Women's Religion in Ancient Israel," in this volume; cf. Bird's paper on "The Place of Women in the Israelite Cultus," *Ancient Israelite Religion*, ed. P. D. Miller, Jr., P. D. Hanson, and J. D. McBride (Philadelphia, 1987), 397-420.

within the household and in local village settings. Clearly women played active, diverse, and vital roles in the complex households of early Israel.

Although the existence of complex families is believed, in many traditional social scientific arguments, to be related to hierarchical structures in which males dominate, this predicted relationship is *not* borne out for pre-state societies. On the contrary, the power accruing to women by virtue of their technical contributions to family subsistence is augmented when there are more family members involved.[34] Thus, in their managerial roles, senior females gained authority--the recognized right to control--by virtue of having more people with whom to interact. As expressed for ancient Israel by the fifth command of the Decalogue and by the seemingly harsh case laws related to that commandment,[35] filial obedience to mother as well as father was imperative for maintaining order and accomplishing subsistence activities, and was no doubt sanctioned in customary and then in Pentateuchal law.

We can thus re-vision the place of women in pre-monarchic village households and suggest that the vital productive and reproductive roles of women, along with their essential social and socializing roles, created a situation of gender complementarity that is consonant with the date supplied by cross-cultural studies.[36]

4. The implications of this reconstruction of female roles in early Israel, in which a situation of near parity of female and male contributions existed and in which females exerted control over significant tasks and over numbers of persons, become clear when the context we have delineated is set against the analytical opposition of domestic and public realms found in much of the social scientific discussion of female roles and status.[37] Thus far we have refrained from using the term "domestic" in reference to the arena of female activity in early Israel because, in the pre-monarchic period, there was a marked lack of formal supra-household structures or professions that would be labeled "public." Thus, to use the term "domestic" for household would be to suggest an alternate "public" realm, which hardly existed at all during the tribal period. With the family household being the dominant level of social organization, the role of the female therein constituted a general, one might

---

[34]Whyte, 135.

[35]Exod 20:12 and Deut 5:16; Exod 21:15; Lev 20:9; Deut 21:18-21; Deut 27:16.

[36]See the works cited above in n.9.

[37]For a critique of this dichotomizing distance between public and private realms, see DuBois et al, 113-25; S. C. Rogers, "Woman's Place: A Critical Review of Anthropological Theory," *Comparative Studies in Society and History* 20 (1978): 147-53; and Rosaldo, "Uses and Abuses," 396-401.

even say a "public," role. As long as the society was based on a household production system, and as long as there was a relative absence of the public hierarchies that usually favor males, females would have had great social impact, beyond the household. Female control of certain aspects of household life was not a trivial matter in a context in which the family household was the primary economic and social unit and in which determinative social forms lay at the bottom rather than at the top.

5. This discussion can come full circle now by suggesting that there are, in fact, biblical texts that reflect the social situation we have described and that have survived the growing androcentrism of Israelite society as it moved into its long centuries of monarchic existence. I have treated some of these texts elsewhere at considerable length; some have been discussed by others; and still others remain to be examined. All such texts deserve more extensive analysis than can be provided here. But nonetheless several examples can be mentioned briefly.

First, consider the exceptional nature of the Book of Judges. With respect to women it deals specifically with the pre-state period, and it is marked by an unusual number of stories involving females. Perhaps women are not so marginalized in these narratives as they are elsewhere in Hebrew scripture because the pre-state social milieu of the Judges stories is one in which women were central figures.[38]

Second, consider the Song of Songs, with its largely non-public setting and its concomitant favoring of female figures and modes over male ones, despite the basic mutuality of the relationship of the woman and the man in the poems. Note also that the figurative language of Canticles contains power imagery--military forms and fierce animals--exclusively in relationship to the female.[39]

Third, consider the function of the Eden story in Genesis 2-3 as a wisdom tale, to enhance the acceptance by both females and males of the often harsh realities of highland life and to provide ideological sanction for large families and for intense physical toil in subsistence activities.[40]

---

[38]Another possibility is that women are prominent in Judges because the book as a whole deals with marginalization; see M. P. O'Connor, "The Women in the Book of Judges," *Hebrew Annual Review* 10 (1986): 277-93.

[39]Analyzed in my "Gender Imagery in the Song of Songs," *Hebrew Annual Review* 10 (1986): 209-23.

[40]See my "Gender Roles and Genesis 3:16 Revisited," *The Word of the Lord Shall Go Forth*, ed. C. Meyers and M.P. O'Connor (Philadelphia, 1983), 337-54.

Fourth, consider, as C. Camp had done,[41] the images of female wisdom against the backdrop of female creativity, female instruction in household contexts, and possibly superior female skills in interpersonal relationships (females being less able to resort to force and therefore more adept at finding alternative, indirect ways to resolve conflict).

Fifth, consider that many of the legal materials that seem to most favor males over females are related to property transmission and may be a response to informal female controls interfering with the expected male domination in a patrilineal system.[42] Furthermore, it is not appropriate to generalize authoritative or dominant behavior from one category of interaction to all categories or even to assume that the concept of dominance always existed and meant the same as it does in our urban, industrial world.[43]

Looking at such passages, and others too, suggests that despite the increasing hierarchization of Israelite society along gender lines (and other lines as well) during the monarchy, some materials from a time of socially significant female power have survived in the canonical literature.

[41]*Wisdom and the Feminine in the Book of Proverbs* (Bible and Literature Series, 11; Sheffield, England, 1985), and "The Wise Women of 2 Samuel: A Role Model for Women in Early Israel," *CBQ* 43 (1981): 14-29.

[42]Meyers, *Discovering Eve*, 38-40, 155, 183-87..

[43]R. R. Reiter, "Introduction," *Towards an Anthropology of Women*, ed. R. R. Reiter (New York, 1975), 15.

Responses to Prof. Meyers' Paper

Stone: I just want to say how really nice it was to have someone who started her paper with a discussion of the sources. Most of us dealing with written sources only provide a fraction of the picture of what was really going on, no matter how detailed the texts are. I think that before we can even begin to suggest whether the written materials or archaeological material or whatever are really telling us about the position of women or anyone in these societies we've got to decide what sample we're using, and I really appreciate that.

Delaney: I was also really glad to hear your discussion of domestic versus public, I think that is a very important area to address, and I would say that there were a lot of interesting things in your paper, but one thing I don't understand (even from my work in contemporary agrarian society in Turkey) is that women can do a great deal of the economic work and support the basic economic roles in a society and yet that really doesn't make a bit of difference about gender definition. Now I think there is a difference between gender law and gender definition and I think that's really the crux of the matter. No matter how much work they do, women still are not valued in a way that is equal.

Meyers: I think that you are absolutely right about that and that in some senses the more that women do in society, even if they do too much, it tends to have a reverse effect. That by virtue of their control of too many activities they can be seen as threatening and therefore become limited, or are seen as limited in other ways. The thing that I suspect may set this part of the population apart a bit is the fact that, unlike, for example, contemporary agrarian societies, which nonetheless are still part of a larger structure which includes a central government and hierarchies and political roles being held by numerous non-royal males, I think there was a limited time here in antiquity in which such positions for common born men were virtually nonexistent. So that in ancient times, symbols that reflect value, and that tend to be male symbols, would not have existed to the same extent that you find in agrarian societies today which are part of a larger polity. That may help explain why I seem to come to a different conclusion about what it may have meant to be a woman in this kind of ancient nonurban setting you are so correct in referring to.

Bird: I think that I'm still not persuaded that women had a significantly higher status, and I think that the evidence that you cite from Judges and the Song of Solomon might be interpreted within a system which in general women have to support. What I wanted to ask about was the evidence for a shift toward a more egalitarian ideology, that is this perplexing countering to the one which you sketched as evidenced in the juxtaposition of the two forms of the slave law in the Covenant Code in Deuteronomy in which Deuteronomy treats the possibility of a woman enslaving herself, suggesting higher status of a woman, a shift there, and this general Deuteronomic effort to make exclusive the inclusion of women in the congregation in the community. So it seems to me the picture that you sketch of a stronger role for women in the community being eroded by increasing an extensively patriarchal structure is in fact the case, and that some account must be made for what appears to be counter productive.

Meyers: Let me just preface this by saying that I find a great deal of difficulty in any period knowing exactly how to look at the laws in relationship to the reality of society. And so whatever I may say is really kind of guesswork, but the Deuteronomic laws are part of a reform movement that is in part fueled by prophecy, by prophetic motivations and which consciously to some extent tries to recapture earlier periods. I wonder whether it may be the kind of humanistic tradition that seems to pervade Deuteronomic legislation, it may be recapturing some of that.

Nugent: I wondered about the text in Proverbs, I think it is thirty-one, which describes the ideal woman, and the good wife. What struck me as I listened to papers over the last couple of days, is the complete difference in that text--it prescribes that women do things like weaving, but also that she work out in the field, planting and so forth. I was just wondering whether that is a large ideological difference: that a woman's place in all of our materials seems to be fairly exclusively, at least in the ideal, posited within the household. Is that a product of what you describe of the agrarian non-urban society rather than some other?

Meyers: Well, let me first explain spatial concept, and I don't mean in the usual way " indoors", because the *beit* of a household could be taken to include the land and agricultural fields, and so domestic or household activity is not just scrubbing floors and cooking meals. This is a portrait of an urban woman, a marginal woman. This is notoriously difficult to deal with; at least it is difficult for me to deal with because I would need to put it in a political, social, chronological setting and I've never seen any kind of consensus about where it (The Book of Proverbs) should be. Some people would put it at the very beginning of Israelite history, and some people would put it post-exilic or even later. So, while it is very interesting in showing the range of activities of a woman we don't know when this job description might apply, or how to take it: as a reflection or an opposition of some sort of reality?

Women's Religion in Ancient Israel

Phyllis Bird

This essay is concerned with women's religious practice and experience, a narrow topic in the social history of women in ancient Israel, but of particular importance because the only surviving literature from that society represents it as a religiously defined community. I approach the question of women's religion as part of a larger effort to reconceive and reconstruct the religion of ancient Israel as a comprehensive system of belief and practice, inclusive of female as well as male activity, private as well as public devotion, and heterodox as well as orthodox expression.[1]

For most of this century scholarship on the place of women in Israelite religion has been intent to deny any substantial distinction between men's and women's religious practice or privilege, insisting on women's essential equality with men in all but priestly roles.[2] Standard histories of religion suggest by their generalizations that women were the silent partners of men in their religious practices except where special obligations or restrictions required explicit note or where peculiar practices (usually interpreted as syncretistic or foreign) or outstanding figures (e.g., Miriam and Deborah) demanded attention.

This qualified inclusive and egalitarian reading may be seen as a reaction to the views of Old Testament scholars at the turn of the century who interpreted Israelite Yahwism as the expression of an essentially male cult in which women had little if any place. Some argued that they had little interest

[1]For a fuller statement of the project and its presuppositions see P. Bird, "The Place of Women in the Israelite Cultus," *Ancient Israelite Religion: Essays in Honor of Frank M. Cross*, ed. P. D. Hanson, P. D. Miller, and S. D. McBride (Philadelphia, 1987), 397-419.

[2]Ibid., 397-98. The earliest and most positive treatment was that of I. Peritz in 1898: "Women in the Ancient Hebrew Cult," *Journal of Biblical Literature* 17 (1898): 111-48. Other studies include M. Löhr, *Die Stellung des Weibes zur Jahwe-Religion und -Kult* (Leipzig, 1908); G. Beer, *Die soziale und religiöse Stellung der Frau im israelitischen Altertum* (Tübingen, 1919); and more recently C.J. Vos, *Women in Old Testament Worship* (Delft, 1968).

either, suggesting that women's religious needs were better served by non-Yahwistic ("foreign") cults, especially those with female deities.[3] Recently this argument has been revived by U. Winter, who has attempted to show the continuing significance of a goddess in Israelite women's religion and the inadequacy of a male deity for women.[4]

I share Winter's conviction that we must distinguish male and female religious practice and belief in ancient Israel, but my argument has a different theoretical base and draws on different sources. It is grounded in observations concerning patterns of male and female activity in pre-industrial and non-Western societies and generalizations concerning gender roles and status in cross-cultural perspective as formulated in the new anthropological literature on gender.[5] It follows from the recognition of gender differentiation as a universal phenomenon in the structuring of social roles, responsibilities and values, extending far beyond the fundamental division of labor from which it is commonly derived. This basic principle of gender differentiation has been ignored or denied in most modern scholarship on Israelite religion, with a

---

[3]Cf. J. Wellhausen, *Israelitische und jüdische Geschichte* (3d ed.; Berlin, 1897): 89-90; I. Benzinger, *Hebräische Archäologie* (Freiburg i.B. and Leipzig, 1894): 140; W. Nowack, *Lehrbuch der hebräischen Archäologie* (Freiburg i.B. and Leipzig, 1894): 154, 348; B. Stade, *Biblische Theologie des Alten Testaments* (Tübingen, 1905), 1.40; and E. König, *Geschichte der alttestamentlichen Religion* (Gütersloh, 1912): 216 n.1.

[4]*Frau und Göttin. Exegetische und ikonographische Studien zum weiblichen Gottesbild im alten Israel und in dessen Umwelt* (Freiburg und Göttingen, 1983).

[5]This fast growing literature can only be sampled here. Since the field of gender studies is developing so rapidly and gaining increasing sophistication, works only a few years old, including some cited below, may already be dated. A recent useful guide to the literature is M. I. Duley and M. I. Edwards, *The Cross-Cultural Study of Women* (New York, 1986). Works on gender theory that have informed my thinking include M. Z. Rosaldo and L. Lamphere, eds., *Women, Culture, and Society* (Stanford, 1974); M.Z. Rosaldo, "The Use and Abuse of Anthropology: Reflections on Feminism and Cross-Cultural Understanding," *Signs* 5 (1980): 389-417; J. Shapiro, "Anthropology and the Study of Gender," *A Feminist Perspective in the Academy: The Difference It Makes* (ed. E. Langland and W. Gove; Chicago, 1981), 110-29; S. B. Ortner and H. Whitehead, eds., *Sexual Meanings: The Cultural Construction of Gender and Sexuality* (Cambridge, 1981); M. K. Martin and B. Voorhies, *Female of the Species* (New York and London, 1975); D. Hammond and A. Jablow, *Women in Cultures of the World* (Menlo Park, 1976); and M. K. Whyte, *The Status of Women in Preindustrial Societies* (Princeton, 1978). Helpful ethnographic studies include the following: N. A. Falk and R. M. Gross, eds., *Unspoken Worlds: Women's Religious Lives in Non-Western Cultures* (San Francisco, 1980); E. Fernea, *Guests of the Sheik: An Ethnography of an Iraqi Village* (Garden City, NY, 1969); and E. Bourguignon et al., *A World of Women: Anthropological Studies of Women in the Societies of the World* (New York, 1980). See further Bird, "Place of Women," 413-14 ns. 14-18.

resulting depiction of the religion as a male dominated system in which women's roles were simply a pale copy of men's. That construction, I believe, seriously misrepresents Israelite religion and women's roles in it.

Methodology

Any attempt to reconstruct ancient Israelite religion or society must begin with the problem of sources and methodology. Although I have laid out my arguments elsewhere,[6] I must repeat the main points, since they determine my starting point and my use of the biblical sources. Briefly summarized they are as follows:

1. Our sources for ancient Israel are limited almost exclusively to writings preserved in the Hebrew Bible, a collection whose form and function as canonical literature points to origins and/or transmission in male circles representing the dominant religious "schools" (priestly, prophetic and sapiential) in the southern kingdom of Judah during the Monarchy and Restoration. The limited and skewed perspective of these sources has particular consequence for the effort to describe women's religious practice and experience.[7]

a. We have, I believe, no epigraphic sources that come directly from women (in contrast to the letters, hymns, contracts, etc., from Mesopotamian women). The portrait of women given to us by the Bible and the words of women it transmits are all framed, selected and/or redacted by men for the purposes of a male-centered and male-dominated cult.[8]

---

[6]"Place of Women," 399-400.

[7]A further significant feature of this literature as a source for the historian is its continous use as a sacred and authoritative text by communities of faith for whom it is not simply a source of memory but a guide to present belief and practice. Thus, unlike the sources for other ancient Near Eastern cultures, the Bible has a long and complex history of interpretation invested with deep personal and communal meanings. This history of interpretation has not been confined, however, to the religious communities in which it has been cultivated. The profound influence of the Bible on the common intellectual tradition of the West, including legal and literary traditions, has affected the way in which the question of women in "patriarchal" society has been understood in secular as well as religious thought.

[8]It is increasingly common today to hear suggestions of female authorship for particular biblical books or portions of scripture (see, e.g., E. F. Campbell, Jr., *Ruth*, The Anchor Bible, 7 [Garden City, 1975], 22-23, who suggests "wise-women" as the story-tellers who cultivated the genre of tale found in Ruth and other short stories; others have suggested the Psalms, Proverbs and the Song of Solomon as composed by women). I do not reject the possibility out of hand; the Hebrew Bible itself clearly attributes some literary works to women (e.g., the "Song of Miriam," Exod 15:21 [a

b. We have very little account of women's religious practices, either as distinct from or identical to men's practices. Moreover, because of the nature of our sources, we have little or no means of determining the meaning for women of either shared or distinctive practices.

c. Because of the androcentric language of the texts as well as the androcentric organization of social and religious life, we are unable to determine the extent to which actions or prescriptions presented as referring to "all Israel," or lacking explicit gender qualification, were actually intended to include women. We cannot assume without further evidence that such designations as "the people" (*hāᶜām*), "the congregation (*haqqāhāl* or *hāᶜēdâ*), or "Israel" include, or exclude, women.[9]

2. Extra-biblical sources for the period and territory of ancient Israel, either in its homeland or in diaspora, are fragmentary, largely non-epigraphic, and either androcentric or mute (female figurines, cultic installations and paraphernalia) with respect to women's practice and point of view. It is unlikely that this situation will be altered significantly by new discoveries.

3. The dearth of our sources for reconstructing the religious (or social) life of women in ancient Israel and the bias that characterizes them means that we cannot create an adequate or meaningful picture on the basis of the fragments of evidence imbedded in the biblical text or gleaned from extrabiblical Israelite/Jewish sources. We need a model that will enable us to construct a portrait of the society in its total social, economic, political and religious organization, by means of which we can locate and interpret the bits of information we possess and identify types and/or loci of missing data.

---

couplet thought by many to be an incipit to the hymn (vv. 1-17) attributed to Moses in v. 1]; the "Song of Deborah," Judg 5:1-31; the "Song of Hannah," 1 Sam 2:1-10; and the instructions of Lemuel's mother in Prov 31:1-9). But these few works have all been transmitted to us in the compositions of scribal guilds, which I would view as male associations. Hence I believe that we have no *direct* or *unmediated* access to the words or lives of women in the Hebrew scriptures. It may well be that some genres of literature, especially oral genres (such as the victory song, lament, some forms of story-telling, or parables), were especially associated with women, but the move from oral to written forms involves a social as well as a literary shift. Therefore it is not sufficient as an argument for female authorship of biblical writings to show that women wrote or that they could and did compose songs or stories. Rather one must explain the presence of women in those religious circles that shaped and transmitted Israel's canonical writings.

[9]Examples of restrictive (male) use of the term *ᶜam* ("people") may be seen in the following passages: "Jeremiah said to all the people and all the women," Jer 44:24; And he (Moses) said to the people, 'Be ready by the third day; do not go near a woman,'" Exod 19:15. Cf. Bird, "Place of Women," 402.

a. The model we employ must be able to recognize changes over time and variation related to region and class. Careful attention must therefore be given to the dating of sources and to their nature and function. Socio-literary analysis must precede historical reconstruction.[10]

b. The blank spaces in the construct are as important, or more important, for the total picture than the known data. Any structure built according to a plan that fails to recognize them will collapse. The blanks must be held open by labeling or other place-holding devices or imaginatively filled through the use of analogies from better-known societies.

c. The results of any reconstruction (of men's as well as women's practice and experience) must be viewed as tentative and subject to revision.

4. Anthropology, especially in its subfields of gender theory and ethnography, provides an indispensable tool for the construction of interpretive models and the identification of women's places within them. Cross-cultural studies identify significant patterns and variables in the roles and status of women in different types of societies, while ethnographic studies supply concrete examples of women's activity needed to flesh out schematic constructs. Thus anthropology aids the historian by stimulating, and disciplining, the imagination required for reconstruction.

5. Reconstruction must depend heavily on analogy to supply the missing data on women's religious practice in ancient Israel. The closest and best analogies are to be sought in other ancient Near Eastern societies, especially those that share most fully the type and complexity of economic and social organization and the broad cultural and religious horizons of ancient Israel. Nevertheless, the available sources from the ancient Near East suffer from many of the same defects as those from Israel, in that they are written, fragmentary, stem largely from men and relate primarily to public institutions and activity. In addition, few deal directly with the religious life of women--even when they pertain to women identified by cultic associations.

---

[10]This is the most serious problem for any reconstruction, because there is at present no consensus among biblical scholars about the dating, or even relative chronology, of many key texts. Although it is generally agreed that the history to which the texts refer covers a span of some one thousand years (ca. 1200-200 B.C.), with even earlier periods reflected in some of the traditions, it cannot be assumed that all of the traditions in a given book, such as Genesis or Judges, stem from the period described or even from the same period. Rather each text (and sometimes each verse) must be tested by literary-historical analysis before it can be used as evidence for the social thought or practice of a particular period in the life of ancient Israel.

6. The gap in the ancient sources with respect to women's activities and experience may be filled, at least partially, by modern studies of women in non-Western cultures, especially those based on field studies carried out by women. Through such investigations we gain access to women's lives and experiences that are out of the range of most written documents, or distorted by secondhand male transmission. Persons and activities that may be judged unimportant by indigenous historians and reporters, or too obvious to mention, emerge into view in these studies to be assessed. In them we are able to encounter for the first time the differing perceptions of women concerning community events or actions hitherto known only through male eyes.[11]

Steps Toward a Reconstruction

Essential to any reconstruction of the religious life of women in ancient Israel is an analysis of the larger economic, social and political contours of the society. For purposes of this essay, a summary statement must suffice.[12]

During most of the Old Testament period Israel may be characterized as village agrarian society engaged in diversified subsistence cultivation supplemented by livestock husbandry, but drawn increasingly into a market economy dominated by urban political centers and influenced by external military and trade relations. From an original segmentary organization of patrilineages, variously linked in larger "tribal" associations, it developed through a transitional chiefdomship (Saul's "kingship") into a monarchic state, represented during most of the period by two separate and often hostile states (Israel and Judah). The final period is marked by colonial dependency in dispersed centers of religious and cultural life, though Jerusalem retained priority, with an externally authorized native hierocracy replacing monarchic

[11]In addition to the ethnographic literature cited above (n. 5), I have found particularly illuminating and thought provoking the study by S. S. Sered, *Women as Ritual Experts: The Religious Lives of Sephardi Jewish Women in Israel* (unpublished Ph.D. dissertation, ca. 1986).

[12]Fuller analysis may be found in recent, sociologically informed descriptions of ancient Israel, although most concentrate on the earliest ("formative") period, before the development of a monarchic state, and give little attention to sexual differentiation in describing social tasks and roles. See especially N. K. Gottwald, *The Tribes of Yahweh* (Maryknoll, NY, 1979); idem, "Early Israel and the Canaanite Socioeconomic System," *Palestine in Transition: The Emergence of Ancient Israel*, ed. D. N. Freedman and D. F. Graf, SWBAS 2 (1983): 25-37; D. C. Hopkins, *The Highlands of Canaan: Agricultural Life in the Early Iron Age*, SWBAS 3 (1985); and F. S. Frick, *The Formation of the State in Ancient Israel*, SWBAS, 4 (1985). For an analysis of women's roles in early Israel see C. Meyers, "Procreation, Production, and Protection: Male-Female Balance in Early Israel," *JAAR* 51 (1983): 569-93.

rule. Although most sociological and theological studies of Israel stress the premonarchic period as determinative for its distinctive ethos, the preserved texts derive almost exclusively from the period beginning with the monarchy (ca. 1000-587 B.C.), a period characterized by increased urbanization, stratification and centralization of political and religious institutions, which impinged in numerous significant ways on village and family organization and activities.[13]

As a premodern agrarian society, ancient Israel belongs typologically to a class of societies exhibiting a relatively sharp sexual division of labor and differentiation of roles marked by significant asymmetry of power and prestige.[14] Although this asymmetry (typically described as "patriarchal"[15]) is variously explained and exhibits considerable variation in degree and expression, even within a given society, the pattern requires note, particularly in its implications for women's religious roles and activities.[16]

It has been commonly linked to a distinction between public and domestic spheres in which women are identified with the tasks of nurture and home maintenance, whatever their activities outside the home (which are often economically significant), and men are identified primarily by activities outside or beyond the home, including agricultural production, craft specialization, commerce, and government.[17] To the public realm of male

---

13Despite the dangers of bringing together data from widely differing periods and situations, I have chosen to treat the whole biblical period, rather than a segment thereof, because the total available data on women's religion are so few and because synchronic study does not permit observance of patterns that appear over time.

14Martin and Voorhies, *Female of the Species*, 276-332; Whyte, *Status of Women*, 153-82.

15I have avoided the term "patriarchy," although it is an appropriate descriptive term, because in popular usage it has acquired an overload of negative connotations and is not sufficiently discriminating to be of much help as an analytical tool.

16For an attempt to generalize about women's religious roles in cross-cultural perspective see Hammond and Jablow, *Women in Cultures of the World*, 120-26.

17While this dichotomous distinction often strains or obscures actual relationships within the society, it corresponds rather closely to traditional Israelite views. A paradigm for Israel's understanding of the sexual division of labor as a distinction between procreation and production may be seen in the Genesis 3 account of the punishment of the first couple for their disobedience of the divine command. For the man, the consequences of sin are experienced as pain in his labor of tilling the soil (3:17); for the woman, as pain in her labor of childbirth (3:16). The two statements are parallel and balanced and use the same terminology to describe both the man's and the woman's pain. (I read *ᶜiṣṣĕbônēk wĕhērōnēk* in 3:16 as hendiadys, with most commentators, and cannot accept C. Meyers' view that the verse speaks of multiplying the woman's work and pregnancies or Meyers' elimination of the sense of painful labor from the parallel clause, *bĕᶜeṣeb*

activity and male control belong most, if not all, of the extra-familial or trans-familial activities and institutions, including political, legal and religious institutions. As a consequence of this distinction of realms, women are to some degree always outsiders (treated as marginal or as intruders) in the institutions and activities of the public sphere, even when they may have regular and essential duties there. (Are areas of activities of the public realm where women have regular recourse, such as the market place, redefined as extensions of women's realm? Is there any neutral ground?)

At the same time that women are restricted in the public sphere they also lack full authority in the domestic sphere, where final authority in the family is given to the husband or father. Furthermore, since the overarching and integrating institutions of the society (in particular, legal and religious institutions), which give expression to the society's values and norms and attempt to regulate behavior, belong to the public sphere and are designed and governed by men, the values they articulate and seek to impose are essentially male values, although formulated as "general" rules and norms.[18] Women have little or no role in the determining decisions. Thus asymmetry between the spheres of male and female activity has the character of encapsulation and penetration of the domestic sphere by the public sphere.

One consequence of this asymmetry of power, in which men or male-dominated institutions play a determinative role in shaping the culture and defining values and norms, is that women commonly accept the male-articulated values as their own, or at least as legitimate, even when this involves negative appraisal of their own practices and/or inability to achieve

---

tĕlĕdî bānîm ["Gender Roles and Genesis 3:16 Revisited" (*The Word of the Lord Shall Go Forth. Essays in Honor of David Noel Freedman*, ed. C. L. Meyers and M. O'Connor [Winona Lake, 1983], 337-54), 344-46]. Cf. Bird, "Sexual Differentiation and Divine Image in the Genesis Creation Texts," *Image of God and Gender Models*, ed. K. E. Børresen (Oslo, Atlantic Heights, NJ, forthcoming). While the public/domestic distinction continues to be useful, it needs to be qualified by more complex models for understanding male and female realms of activity and contribution to the society, such as the three-fold division employed by Meyers in "Procreation, Production, and Protection" (especially 574-76). Cf. J. K. Brown, "A Note on the Division of Labor by Sex," *American Anthropologist* 72 (1970): 1074-78; M.Z. Rosaldo, "Women, Culture, and Society: A Theoretical Overview" (Rosaldo and Lamphere, *Woman, Culture and Society*, 17-42) esp. 18, 26-27; and P. R. Sanday, "Female Status in the Public Domain" (ibid., 189-206).

18This is exhibited in numerous ways in the Hebrew Bible, including the formulation of laws and exhortations in second person masculine forms (singular-collective or plural), with third person references to women (e.g., "You shall not covet your neighbor's wife," Exod 20:17). See Bird, "Place of Women," 402-403.

the norms.[19] Male values are understood as general, or "universal," values, while female values and views are seen as limited, aberrant or special. (The same pattern is observable in the language, where only female forms are gender-marked.)

Failure to recognize the asymmetry of power and authority in patriarchal societies such as ancient Israel leads to misreading of the data by interpreting complementarity of roles, especially when accompanied by expressions of honor, as evidence of equality. On the other hand, overemphasis on the structures and symbols of overt power may blind the interpreter to the informal exercise of power by women (in influencing decisions, obtaining favors, etc.) and to authority exercised through wisdom and affection (e.g., in teaching and the formation of values in the home). The complex and mutual relationships between men and women are often ignored or misconstrued in simplistic judgments about the distribution of power in patriarchal societies.

Women in Israelite Religious Practice

A survey of the variety of religious activities attested either directly or indirectly in the Hebrew scriptures yields a picture of predominantly male participation and almost exclusively male leadership in documented (descriptive and prescriptive) cases of public and kinship-based communal worship.[20] Such a pattern is to be expected from the nature of the sources and from cross-cultural studies. But as a picture of religious life based on evidence deriving from the spheres of male activity and control it cannot be taken as descriptive of the whole and is itself in need of interpretation. While it is possible to suggest some modifications of this picture, we are not now in a position to construct an alternative portrait.[21] What is needed at this stage, I believe, is questions, not answers. Thus what follows is primarily a series of questions with supporting examples and comments. I begin with a broad set of questions arranged according to class or activity and/or documentation and then continue with selective commentary and more questions.

19See E. Friedl, "Islam and Tribal Women in a Village in Iran," Falk and Gross, *Unspoken Worlds*, 159-73: 163.

20The analysis in this section is based on a preliminary outline of Israelite religion in which I attempted to identify all types of religious practice in ancient Israel, both attested and inferred. For purposes of this essay I have had to eliminate the outline and limit my observations to several broad categories of activity.

21For a broad, preliminary attempt to sketch women's roles in Israelite religion see Bird, "Place of Women," 401-11.

Documented communal activities (pilgrim feasts, national convocations, communal fasts, victory celebrations, clan feasts, etc.): What, if any, role did women play in the public ceremonies? What role, if any, did they play in private or home-based activities accompanying or paralleling the public rituals? Does prescribed male activity require female preparation or support? Is the latter considered religious activity? What is the meaning for women of the communal observances in which they participate? From which they are excluded? Is "communal" activity by nature (or social definition) male or male-dominated activity?

Women in documented religious roles: What are these roles? Are they cultic, associated with a sanctuary and requiring specialized knowledge or expertise? What kind of specialized knowledge? Are they in contexts of exclusively or predominantly female activity? What are the implications of specialized cultic activity for women's other responsibilities (to husband, children, father?).[22] Are the roles or activities regarded as orthodox or heterodox?

Inferred roles: Where should we look for female religious activity behind or beyond documented practices? What were women's individual religious practices? In what ways did they differ from male practices? Were there female communal practices? What was their nature (e.g., peculiar to women's life circumstances or counterparts of men's practice)?

Communal Activities

It is clear from the narrative of 1 Samuel 1-2, as well as the later Deuteronomic legislation for the Passover, that women were not excluded from the appointed pilgrim feasts, even when obligation was laid only on males.[23] Furthermore, Hannah's request to stay at home with the infant until he is weaned suggests an expectation that a wife would normally accompany her husband on the pilgrimage, thus making it a family affair (since the children would accompany their mother). But Hannah's appeal to counter-obligation (nursing the child) is also accepted as a legitimate excuse. Since she makes the request of her husband, it would appear that whatever obligation she had to the cult was mediated by him. Is her obligation to be understood as solely to him?

---

[22]One of the features of asymmetry in Israelite society may be seen in recurring evidence of conflict for women, but not for men, between social and religious obligation (ibid., 402).

[23]Exod 23:17; 34:23; Deut 16:16. Ibid.

We must ask further what the women did at the sanctuary on the occasion of a pilgrim feast. From 1 Sam 1:4 we learn that they shared the communion meal following the sacrifice (in this case, performed by Elkanah). But who prepared the meal? Did women accompany men on the pilgrimage primarily to prepare the meal after the sacrificial slaughter, or did they have their own, possibly distinct reasons for participating? Should pilgrim feasts be thought of primarily as family affairs in which women and men play essentially the same sexually differentiated roles they do in the home?

The question about the role of women in preparing the communion meal may be applied to other types of religious celebrations involving special meals, whether in connection with appointed feasts, family celebrations, or observances by special groups. Since women normally prepare the food, at least in the household, the requirement of a special meal for a religious celebration would appear to place a special responsibility, and burden, upon them. How was this service interpreted--by the women, and by the "society" or the cult? Was it understood as a religious duty or simply an added burden of labor?[24] Does the action performed in the home carry a different value from that performed at the sanctuary?

In the earliest practice, reflected in the accounts of sacrifice at the old sanctuary at Shiloh, the person who presented the offering appears also to have performed the sacrifice (1 Sam 1:4) and cooked the meat (2:13-15). While the former action is clearly a male prerogative,[25] the latter might well be performed by a woman. With increasing clericalization and the specialization and stratification of clergy functions in the Jerusalem temple cult, sacrifice became a priestly (or royal) prerogative, and in Ezekiel's vision of a restored temple, priests cook and bake the offerings of the inner court while "ministers [masculine plural participle] of the house" (*mĕšārĕtê habbayit*) boil the "sacrifice of the people" (*zebaḥ hā*ᶜ*ām*) at the hearths located in the outer court (Ezek 46: 21-24). Since the pattern of male usurpation of female activities when they move outside the home is well documented in both the secular and sacred realm, it is difficult to say who prepared the sacrificial meal at any time and what connection, if any, might have been made between the action at the sanctuary and the activity in the home.

---

[24]See especially Sered, *Women as Ritual Experts*, 52-59, 64-65, 71.

[25]N. Jay, "Sacrifice as Remedy for Having Been Born of Woman," *Immaculate and Powerful: The Female in Sacred Image and Social Reality*, ed. C. W. Atkinson, C. H. Buchanan, and M. R. Miles, (Boston, 1985), 283-309, 284. While Jay's thesis fails to persuade, her study contains many useful observations about sacrifice and patrilineal societies.

A further question may be asked about the sacred meal, viz., who ate it--or, what role did women have in the activities associated with its consumption? While the women are clearly included in the shared meal of the sacrifice at Shiloh (1 Sam 1:4-5, 9) and are explicitly named in the Deuteronomic directions for the pilgrim feasts of Weeks and Booths (Deut 16:9-15, 16; though omitted in the case of Passover [vvs. 1-8], which is described as a home celebration in Exodus 12, including the entire household), their inclusion cannot be assumed for all types of religious meals. Biblical evidence as well as comparative studies suggest that religious meals were often all-male affairs, with women present only as servants or entertainers (e.g., the meal at the high place in the land of Zuph, 1 Sam 9:12-13, 22-24; cf. the last supper of Jesus), a pattern also exhibited in secular banquets (Esther 1: 3, 9). Who participated in the *marzēaḥ*?[26]

If women may be expected among the men enjoined to observe the major pilgrim feasts, then we must also look for, or speculate about, their presence in other communal religious actions, such as general fasts, which have a pronounced inclusive nature (parodied in Jonah 3:7-8, though not with attention to gender), and victory celebrations. In the latter case, we have evidence of a special leadership role played by women (Exod 15:20-21).[27] A comparable women's specialization in a communal religious observance may be seen in ceremonies of mourning for the dead (Jer 9:17 [H 9:16]). But if women may be understood to be included in some communal activities known only from men's participation, we must take care not to assume in our reconstruction that the women's roles will be the same as the men's. Where we have specific information, gender-differentiated role specialization seems to be the rule.

This gender-related role specialization raises a question of interpretation. Many commentators would deny that either Miriam's action or that of the keening women was a *religious* action.[28] The same problem of

---

[26]According to M. Pope, the *marzēaḥ* was a religious institution organized for the purpose of celebrating funeral feasts of bacchanalian character, which were held in special houses called a *marzēaḥ*-house or "drinking/wine house" (Jer 16:5; cf. Amos 6:4-7 and Song of Sol 2:4-5). *Song of Songs*, The Anchor Bible, 7C (Garden City, 1977), 214-222.

[27]R. J. Burns, *Has the Lord Indeed Spoken Only Through Moses? A Study of the Biblical Portrait of Miriam*, SBL Dissertation Series, 84 (Atlanta, 1987). Burns argues that the activity described in Gen 15:20-21 should be understood as a liturgical event at a shrine, not a spontaneous celebration. Miriam's role is, accordingly, that of a cultic leader (p.40).

[28]E.g., Miriam's action is commonly seen in the context of secular victory celebrations in which women greeted the victorious warriors with dance and song (1 Sam 18:6; Judg 11:34). And mourning, which takes place in a home or at the gravesite, rather than at a sanctuary, may likewise

interpretation is encountered here as in the case of women's roles in the preparation of sacred meals. Ultimately it is a question of what makes a given act religious and who determines the criteria. The answer at one level is obvious: the "society" defines what is religious, and more particularly, the priests or other religious specialists. But if men and women in that society have distinct or separate roles in activities patterned in such a way that men have the central or public roles, then male activity will reinforce social perception of their roles as essential and determinative, and shape both male and female understanding. Comparative studies show women reacting to such imbalance of religious authority in a variety of ways: they may accept the definitions of male authorities as normative and view themselves as deficient or deprived (having a lower level of religious understanding and/or ability to perform required religious acts) or as simply "not religious" (associating religion with male activities);[29] they may develop women's religious activities parallel to those of men, including female leadership;[30] or they may invest their traditional secular roles with religious meaning, creating rituals of their own by the way they perform essential functions.[31]

An example of the differential religious meaning and value assigned to male and female roles may be seen in the case of activities relating to death. While some aspects of mourning may have been confined largely or exclusively to family members, requiring no special expertise, others called for ritual specialists.[32] We hear of laments composed by men (David for Saul and Jonathan [2 Sam 1:19-27], and for Abner [2 Sam 3:33-34]; Jeremiah for Josiah [2 Chron 35:25]), but also of a class of female specialists, "keening women" (*mĕqônĕnôt*, Jer 9:17 [H 9:16]), whose skill is passed from mothers to daughters (Jer 9:17 [H 9:19]).[33] While this class does not include all women,

be judged a "secular" ritual. These examples demonstrate the need to clarify the way in which the terms "cultic," "ritual" and "religious" are understood and used. They are not coterminus, and the distinctions can be instructive.

29Friedl, "Islam and Tribal Women," 168-69.

30Fernea, *Guests of the Sheik*, 107-115; and A. H. Betteridge, "The Controversial Vows of the Urban Muslim Women in Iran," Falk and Gross, *Unspoken Worlds*, 141-55.

31Sered, *Women as Ritual Experts*, 55-59 (sorting rice for passover) 75-77 (throwing candles at tombs of saints) and passim. Cf. R. A. Fernea and E. W. Fernea, "Variation in Religious Observance among Islamic Women," in *Scholars, Saints and Sufis: Muslim Religious Institutions in the Middle East since 1500*, ed. N. R. Keddi, (Berkeley, 1972), 385-401.

32Or was this only in cases where the deceased was a prominent person, demanding public or communal mourning?

33The distinction between male and female roles cannot be between male composers and female performers, since 2 Chron 35:25 mentions both male and female "singers" (*šārîm* and *šārôt*) and Jeremiah's composing (*yĕqônēn*) is described by the same term used as a participle to describe the

it appears to be a women's specialty and may be understood as a professionalized form of the wailing performed by women generally. The keening women perform an essential, public role in rituals for the dead, but is it a religious action? Keening women are not a part of the sanctuary personnel and have no other ritual duties.[34] They are simply the skilled among their sisters in performing and leading expressions of grief. In a burial service described in a modern Islamic setting, women's wailing was an essential part of the ceremony, but was understood to be preliminary to the religious service, which consisted of prayers and readings from the Quran. When the "religious" action began, the women were required to leave.[35]

Home-centered Activities

I must abbreviate my comments on home-centered religious activities, which are for the most part hidden. Those that involve sacrifice, stress lineage, or emphasize family solidarity would appear to focus on male participation and assume male leadership. Thus "all-family" celebrations would appear to exhibit the same patterns of participation and leadership as "all Israel" celebrations. The patriarchal family at worship replicates the patterns of the patriarchal society at worship, or vice versa.[36] But this male-

---

keening women in Jer 9:17 (H 18). Is the male leadership related to the status of the deceased and the locus of the mourning?

34The singers mentioned in 2 Chron 35:25 appear to represent a more general class of performers, who included dirges in their repertoire. There was in addition to the common mourning ceremony a specialized cultic form of murning performed by women in the cult of Tammuz (Ezek 8:14)--though in this case the simple verb for weeping (*BKH*, though in the rare Piel stem: *mĕbakkôt*) is used, not the special term related to the dirge, thus suggesting that the women devotees were enacting the role of the grieving mother, not the professional role of the keener.

35Friedl, "Islam and Tribal Women," 163.

36A recent interpretation of the biblical *teraphim* (commonly translated "household gods") as ancestor figurines (K. van der Toorn, "Ancestor Figurines in Ancient Israel and Their Near Eastern Environment. A Reinterpretation of Biblical *Terāfîm*," paper delivered at the 1987 Annual Meeting of the Society of Biblical Literature [Boston, Dec 5-8]; *Abstracts* [ed. K. H. Richards and J. B. Wiggins] 320: S133) renews attention to the domestic cult in Israel. Since *teraphim* are twice reported in the Hebrew Bible in the possession of women (Rachel, Gen 31:19, 34-35 [identified as belonging to her father]; and Michal, 1 Sam 19:13, 16) and similar figurines are associated, in admittedly unusual circumstances, with women in Mesopotamia who have inherited family land and attendant responsibility for the family gods/ancestral cult, the question of women's role in any ancestral cult persisting in Israel needs to be reexamined. Although earlier studies argued for the exclusion of women from the Yahwistic cult on the basis of its supposed origins as an ancestor cult (Stade, *Biblische Theologie* 1.40), Sered's study of the religious practices of elderly Kurdish Israeli women found that the women saw themselves as "the link between the generations...responsible

headed social unit with its associated living and work space is also the primary locus of women's life and work and, we may hypothesize on the basis of cross-cultural studies, of women's religious life. It is, however, by its very nature a sphere of activity from which we can expect little or no direct documentation. Thus any attempt to identify likely or conceivable actions in this category must be based largely on comparative studies and hints suggested by fragments of traditions (e.g., Exod 4:24-26: a reference to female participation/leadership in a circumcision rite?]). This is the area most in need of illumination from cross-cultural studies. The home as women's space needs to be envisioned not simply as the place of individual acts of piety but as a possible locus of female communal religious activity, which may or may not be parallel to men's public practices.

Individual Religious Activities/"Private" Practices

In treating communal activities, both public and family centered, I have already given attention to inferred, but undocumented, roles of women. A further type of women's religious activity may be inferred from the story of Hannah's vow. As the account in 1 Sam 1:9-18 shows, the occasion of a pilgrim feast might also provide opportunity for private or individual religious actions not directly related to the sacrifice, in this case a prayer of distress and a petition accompanied by a vow. Since pilgrimages to shrines and the making of vows are described in comparative ethnographic literature as among the most characteristic religious acts of women,[37] we may view Hannah's action as typical and as an example of the use of a male-oriented communal feast as a vehicle to serve a personal, and typically female, need.

Evidence for women as cultic specialists is meagre, but not insignificant. I have not attempted to treat it in this essay, however, because responsible interpretation requires detailed analysis of the complex textual, linguistic and cultural problems that attend the texts. The polemical nature of the sources in which most of the evidence is found makes reconstruction

---

for soliciting the help of ancestors whenever their descendants are faced with problems such as illness, infertility, war, or economic troubles." The rituals by which they "remember" their ancestors "range from lighting candles on the Festival of the New Moon to visiting cemeteries and holy tombs" (*Women As Ritual Experts*, 29). In view of these evidences of continuing religious activity associated with ancestors and of continuing involvement of women, I would suggest that we may need to reconceive the domestic cult to include a transgenerational aspect ("ancestor worship") and a place for women in their role as mothers, guardians and supplicants.

37See e.g., *ibid.*, 165; Betteridge, "Controversial Vows," 144; F. Mernissi, "Women, Saints and Sanctuaries," *Signs* 3, no. 1 (1977): 101-112; and J. M. Freeman, "The Ladies of Lord Krishna: Rituals of Middle-Aged Women in Eastern India," Falk and Gross, *Unspoken Worlds*, 110-126.

exceedingly difficult, while the persistence of the evidence in the hostile sources demands the effort. Miriam leading the celebration of Yahweh's victory at the sea (Exod 15:20-21; cf. Num 12:2-8 and Mic 6:4); women "ministering" at the tent of meeting (Exod 38:8; 1 Sam 2:22); qĕdēšôt (lit. "consecrated ones," commonly translated "sacred prostitutes") at local, and possibly, central sanctuaries (Hos 4:14; Deut 23:18; cf. Gen 38:21-22; cf. the masculine plural [often construed as inclusive] used in 2 Kngs 23:7); weaving vestments for Asherah in the Jerusalem temple (2 Kngs 23:7); these at least describe women in cultic roles, and they may be only the tip of the iceberg. Recognition of male leadership and control of the cult does not in itself require the denial of cultic roles to women. But the patterns of sexual differentiation exhibited elsewhere in the society should lead to the expectation of sexually differentiated cultic roles.[38]

[38]See further Bird, "Place of Women," 405-408.

Responses to Prof. Bird's Paper

Westbrook: Just one question about keening women, a question about whether this is at all religious in something preceding the religious ceremonies. But what about the weeping women of Tammuz in the temple?

Bird: Yes, well that is clearly a religious rite. As part of the Tammuz celebration, its a religious practice that is based on a more common, widely distributed, general practice of women in the society. So it doesn't answer the question of what the meaning of normal mourning practices are. The reason that I raise this issue is precisely because of this example from the Iranian village and my own experience when I was digging in Jordan. When one of our workmen died, I sat with the women on the side of the hill away from where the religious ceremonies were taking place with the men around the burial. It's this question about definition that is raised by those two incidences. In the case of the village in Iran it was clear that the definition of the actions in that society made only the males' actions religious.

Westbrook: Yes, but to get back to the question, do you see the women who are in the temple weeping over Tammuz, as just women weeping over Tammuz or were they professional keening women?

Bird: Oh, I see. You're suggesting that the professional group of keening women are related to the cult of Tammuz.

Westbrook: It seems to me that there must be a connection because they are weeping over a dead god.

Bird: Yes, but the problem here is that I treat that as a special case, and I think that these are all sorts of particular cultic observances at particular times but the practice of women's mourning for the dead is a more general practice. Furthermore it is clear from the way that the material was introduced that the cult of Tammuz is depicted as an illegitimate cult while there are frequent references to keening women as a recognized part of Israelite practice. And so for example we have references in the Prophets to keening women.

Westbrook: I'm not sure that Ezekiel liked the idea of women in the Temple, but obviously it was established.

Bird: Again, the place of the keening women is not in the temple.

Westbrook: But they're there. It says so.

Kuhrt: It's not the same situation, is it, what you're discussing and what she's discussing. You're talking about a specific ritual related to a god, whereas she's discussing a specific rite relating to real dead people who have died where they would perform a natural kind of religious function. What struck me as interesting in relation to the keening women is that it seems to be very widespread, we've seen in many societies that same kind of differentiation which Dr. Robins, I think, was pointing out, particularly in the Egyptian material. You have the keening women there as a kind of professional group very much in the background while the males are performing the actual funerary rites, so it seems to carry a great importance.

Bird: Yes. The one is a general practice and the other represents a special ritualization and a special ritual situation that draws upon this general action of women.

Westbrook: Well, could you argue then that if the Tammuz rite and weeping was sufficiently religious to be included in these rites of the god, then perhaps one should redraw one's definition of religious ritual. What the women are doing, was just in a separate part. Why should we regard it as secular rather than as religious? It seems to me to be missing the point.

Bird: That's a good argument. You might take that to that Iranian village.

Fischer: Speaking of women preparing the body before burial, this is recorded by Zola as happening in small communities in France. Clearly this is an everyday sort of respect for the dead, it doesn't, I think, have religious connections, at all. It is a kind of household thing for them to do. As far as Egyptian mourners are concerned, this is very, very religious, because as I said in my talk they impersonate actually the goddesses Isis and Nephthys. Actually there is a model boat from the Middle Kingdom in which the people are identified by so-and-so is Isis and so-and-so is Nephthys. It is very specific.

Harris: I just want to say that I agree with Dr. Fischer, I'm not sure that putting mourning and burial and keening into the same category of religious is really quite correct. As a matter of fact in early Jewish tradition in earlier times anybody could bury anybody. Marriage is not a sacrament either. So I'm not sure that it really belongs to the category of religious. I'm not sure what category you would put it in, if not religious, maybe a temporary ritual. But I don't know if that dichotomy is correct, religious over against non-religious. Women are part of the burial process and they play a role in that, but it has nothing to do with religion as I see it.

Bird: My main reason for raising this question is to suggest that we need greater sensitivity to the assumptions that have been made about what practices constitute religious practices and how to draw the lines when we go about describing the religion of a certain culture and in particular when we don't have access to women's understanding of them. I found very constructive this dissertation of Sered's on the practices of the Kurdish women that describe in great detail the importance they invested in preparation for the Passover and the preparation of the food, not because they were following particular Rabbinic or particular culticly prescribed patterns, but rather they created on their own by the way in which they cooked the passover they made it into a blessing. And so she describes in one place a woman's sorting the rice and sorting all the kernels of rice very carefully and then having concluded that went back and did the same thing over again seven times and Sered asked "why are you doing this, once is enough." And the response was that this makes it a blessing.

Harris: Let me point out that there is separation between men and women in all sorts of activities which have nothing to do with the religious domain at all, and by the way they may be following Islamic tradition here among the Kurds.

Bird: Well, that is precisely my point, where and how does one define the religious domain?

Nathanson: In addition, it seems to me that in Rabbinical literature, meaning in both the Talmuds,(one of which is probably dated to the close of the fourth and the beginning of the fifth century and the other, the

Babylonian Talmud, which probably dates to the middle of the sixth century), in terms of what Prof. Bird has said, there indeed show up women mourners, women mourners are hired. It is also interesting to observe in terms of Professor Meyers' comment concerning the problems of sources the need, for example, to exercise caution in the use of the Hebrew Bible as a source for talking about women's Israelite religion. A very similar set of problems exists, for our main literary source is the canon of Rabbinic literature which reflects the attitudes of Rabbis over a span of several centuries.

Recent trends in social history of Jewish women in Roman and Byzantine Palestine have really attempted to do the kinds of things that Bird and Meyers are doing. For example, you read Rabbinic literature and you're barely aware that Rome existed. But of course Palestine is under Roman rule and what the rabbis are doing, they're doing basically with Roman permission. Recent excavations and surveys are making clear that you have a highly urbanized, highly Romanized situation. Very few towns and villages have other than these populations. There are no longer the isolated highland villages that Prof. Meyers described. In the nooks and crannies of Upper Galilee or of the Golan, in towns which are regarded off the beaten track, you nonetheless find mixed populations in the very heartland of what is generally thought of as a Jewish population.

So it is a very basic question of how the rabbis described the role of women. They're interested in the property and transfer of property at certain critical moments like marriage or divorce or widowhood, they're interested in life-cycle issues like puberty or marriage. Yet on the other hand you have this growing body of evidence that indicates that actually most Jewish women in Palestine during the Roman and Byzantine periods are living in centers of mixed populations. We still do not know exactly what are the implications that her neighbor is Christian or pagan at one time or another, or a Samaritan woman. What does it mean that there are always Roman forces going on among the rabbis and Rabbinic literature? Again if you look at, for example, the few caches of papyri that you have from Jewish women, the growing body of inscriptional evidence seems to suggest that at least some Jewish women did control property and dispose of property, and initiate divorces. The situation is somewhat different than what one might expect from the Rabbinic literature. I suspect that their lives were much like the lives of their pagan and Christian sisters.

Concluding Discussions

B. Lesko: Dr. Allam and Dr. Menu: Sarah Pomeroy has written that there is evidence for the corvée labor involving women, a state obligation of labor, in the Ptolemaic Period in Egypt, and certainly there is an example in the Brooklyn Papyrus from the early Middle Kingdom. Now have either of you ever found evidence for the corvée labor of women in the New Kingdom?

Allam: Well, your question is quite correct, I'm not quite sure whether you could find something about text material in the book by Černý about the workmen of Deir el-Medina. There, if I'm not mistaken, there is mention of a *ḥmw*, servants, or if slaves, men slaves, women slaves, but we don't know exactly what work they were doing.

B. Lesko: I have checked Černý. The only labor that he connected with slave-women was the grinding of the grain. They went from house to house in that community and ground the grain for the housewives, because that was an arduous task, as Bill Ward pointed out the other day. Why would Ptolemaic Egypt have involved women in the corvee? It seems to me strange that something like this would die out for a while and then come back, and yet Pomeroy states in her book on women in Hellenistic Egypt, that they were involved in corvee labor during that period. Surely for an institution to exist during the Middle Kingdom and the Ptolemaic period and not during the New Kingdom is odd unless there is some other very good reason operating. That is also what I would like to discover, what changes within the society affect women's roles.

Allam: I would like to formulate some hypotheses with regard to the paper given by Prof. Roth. I am very interested in the subject of marriage and I have occupied myself on several occasions with this subject as far as ancient Egypt is concerned. I think you mentioned that the transfer of the dowry to the man occurred sometime later after there were children born. This struck me because we have also an analogous situation in Egypt. From the demotic manuscripts we know that the marriage contract as such was written sometimes in a situation many, many years after the celebration of the marriage itself and I would like to ask the same question of Prof. Roth, whether we could separate neatly, with regard to the institution of marriage in ancient Mesopotamia, between the celebration of marriage on the one hand and on the other hand the written contract. We believe that in Egypt's Late Period the mass of property which the bride brought into the household was divided into several items. We could compare it with the dowry which you were speaking about. So the bride comes with her mass of property and she surrenders this property to her husband. Also, the husband has the right to use this property, has the right of usufruct. He could also sell this property with the condition that he would be able to give its value back to the wife. Of course, as long as the marriage goes on, there is no dispute, but the dispute arises when the marriage comes to an end in divorce. The woman brings not only her dowry to the marriage, but her bridewealth that is not surrendered with the property, she has that in her proprietorship. Her husband has the right to use, only to use, this property, and I would say this is quite clear in ancient Egypt, and I have the feeling that Prof. Roth, from her material comes to the same conclusion, but I feel that she is too cautious to use the terms. I would like to ask her for what reason did she refrain from using these terms which are well known? If a marriage ends by divorce, what happens with these properties? The dowry the groom gives back to the wife, her property, but the man has been working maybe twenty to thirty years on his acquisitions during this time he has acquired much of his property and it would have been also with the help of his wife, so as far as Egypt is concerned, the wife has the right to at least one third, sometimes two thirds, sometimes even all the acquisitions of the marriage. I couldn't see in the texts which you have spoken of, something similar, and it might be that something is missing here. What we term in Egyptological literature "acquisitions," the acquisitions which the couple acquired during the marriage, what happens to these things?

Roth: First of all, you asked about the dowry in the case of divorce. I did say something in my talk this morning about that. In fact we know nothing about any real divorces, we have no real cases of divorce. There are, however divorce clauses in 13 of the 23 extant Neo-Babylonian marriage agreements. In all these cases it is the husband who wishes to end the relationship, I assume from the circumstances the marriage has so far failed to produce offspring. He must pay the wife a substantial amount of money, and then she goes free. There is no mention of the dowry in a divorce. I think it is because if she hasn't been able to produce children there is no dowry to return. Now there is one marriage agreement that does consider the dowry in a divorce. This is a document that is found at Susa and the principals in this document bear Egyptian names; it probably dates to Artaxerxes, around 435 B.C., mid fifth century. And in this document there is bilateral divorce, the woman can also divorce the man, and it says in this one case that, if he divorces her, he returns to her her dowry. If she divorces him she forfeits her dowry. Well, the property that they acquired during the course of marriage would have been acquired exclusively from the husband's goods unless there were children and he acquired her dowry. Now I am speculating, I must admit that I am not 100% convinced that the dowry is only transmitted after she bore children, so I may change my mind on this. Don't hold me to this for too long, but if in fact she has already borne children and they have received her dowry they are not going to get a divorce. What does happen, however, is that she does sometimes end up as a widow, and wants to claim goods which were purchased with partial dowry funds. And there are also lawsuits in which a woman goes to court and she says that her husband used 4 1/2 minas of her dowry as 1/3 payment of a house, he put up another 1/3 and an outside partner put in some money and now the husband has died and they need to sell the house and sort it all out and there is an adopted child and there is a slave, and there is a daughter who needed a new dowry and there were no funds in the estate to deal with all these claims, and the court had to sell off the entire estate to deal with these claims, and give her back her original funds. The real question is concerning the mortal elements of the dowry. We have slaves in our dowries. There is one dowry that has livestock. What happens when you give a slave in your daughters dowry and later the slave dies, or the slave bears children and then the time comes when you have to return the dowry, when the woman dies? What do you do with the mortal elements of the dowry?

Allam: But you have pointed out in your paper that the right of the man to the dowry has been successfully challenged.

Roth: You asked me to use certain legal terms that you use in your Egyptological sources. As I understand some of that is related to actual translations of Egyptian terms, technical terms; but we don't have that in Neo-Babylonian sources. The dowry is given to the husband; by that I understand that he has control over it. He never gets anything like a title to it, and the dowry is properly the wife's throughout the life of the marriage. If the husband does something with the dowry, if he buys a slave with his wife's dowry, it is identified as her dowry property. So I hesitate to use legal terms which I think are not applicable to what happens.

Herlihy: The system you describe is very Roman in many ways, but one inconsistency, I think, is the fact that you did say that this dowry is going to meet the expenses of creating a household. If that is true how could it be delayed? It includes pots and pans, the things that you need to create a household. Why would they delay it? Not that social systems have to be consistent....

Roth: No, that is very true. There is one very clear example I have of a dowry promise where the entire possessions of the bride, silver, some plates and household goods, all listed in detailed amounts, and it says the husband is taking right now the silver and when he marries, when he cohabits, with this woman he gets the rest. In fact we have two more documents when he seems to get things in at least two more stages, the real estate is transferred and another piece even later. I am not sure whether this was simply because her family was reluctant to trust the man, to give him everything at once. Did they feel that they could give things like pots and pans at the beginning so that they could set up an independent household, or would it be a household in which the brides mother-in-law and sisters-in-law may also be living, and you shouldn't need pots and pans. I don't know. These are really questions I have to explore more.

Herlihy: I have a general comment, but its not on this subject which would take us far from marriage. I wanted to make a general comment about social systems that we have heard a great deal about, patrilineal systems, patriarchal systems, and I think one must be open to the possibility of the existence of superimposed social systems each governing a different aspect of social life, existing simultaneously, but not all of equal visibility. New patrilineal systems usually enjoy great visibility because they frequently control property and property devolution , but therefore they break through into a written record far more easily than other social systems, but they are not necessarily the most important. I want to give an example out of medieval Europe: in terms of the devolution of property, Medieval Europe does develop patrilineal systems particularly from about the 11th and 12th centuries. But the patrilineal system still does not govern mate selection, for example. You still cannot be independent. Matrilineal relationships are of fundamental importance in determining whom you can marry. Quite clearly the ties of patrilinearity regarding property devolution do not touch the older bilateral kinship system. Now that is only in terms of law. Also in terms of what we might call communities of support, there is a famous relationship in medieval Europe known as the avunculate, which is the special tie between a man and his sister's child. Now this was a matrilineal relationship, and even under the patrilineal system of property devolution this avunculate remained very, very strong. And there is also a factor of prestige, that if you want to claim nobility, your mother's family counted too, so you have to show your quarters of noble descent, including descent from the mother. Thus even under the apparent patrilineal system you have several definitions of kin that are there simultaneously.

Also I want to say a word about patriarchy. I'm sorry to say that I have great trouble with that term, patriarchy, for the reason that one has to ask what is a system attempting to do. Now is patriarchy attempting to preserve male dominance? Now clearly it is not, in terms, preserving the dominance of a male slave, or a male prisoner, or a male impoverished person. What it seems to be doing is trying to preserve the prominence of a *lineage*. So in other words what you want to do is to preserve your line and also the status, primarily of the males within it. Now the difficulty with that system is that under societies of very high death rates frequently that line of descent will depend upon women. This comes up again and again and that if you create a system of law that is too obstructive concerning the rights of women to hold and manage property you are in a sense going to defeat the purpose of the system, which is to preserve your line. The importance, and the prestige and the wealth of the line will depend upon female linkages, so that means you have to be very very careful in the way you create laws affecting women. So one has to be careful of treating patriarchy as an absolute system. In other words you have to be aware of some of the mechanisms and how it is really operating and even if you can see that it was definitely to promote male strains you have to ask what males, and how could it best be done.

Roth: What happens in our cuneiform material from Mesopotamia is that individuals are identified as so-and-so the son of his father, and in certain periods the descendant of your grandfather, or other male ancestor. Very, very seldom do we find individuals identified in terms of their mothers and then only in very special cases like in lawsuits where a woman says "my son so-and-so, the son of mister whatever."

Zagarell: I have one or two points that I would like to make, sort of general statements, and perhaps raise a question. In general the papers are very rich and I think accomplish something in emphasizing questions in each and every area and this leads to important progress. Nevertheless I would like to say that in general what we have are descriptions of conditions in the ancient Near East. The point I would like to stress is that a *description* is conceptually quite different from explanation. Even a sequence of descriptions can never substitute for explanation and therefore there has to be now an attempt to go through the process of explanation and ask the questions which people are asking outside of ancient Near Eastern studies when they are discussing these kinds of questions. Why, for example, for extended periods of time do we have what appears to be women having a right to immovables? They had rights to inherit, they even had rights to distribute their property, yet over a few thousand years at the end of that time what we have is essentially women still retaining those rights but the control over it is still concentrated in the hands of males.

This seems odd because historical experience teaches that through time everything changes. This has to be explained, why things don't change and why things do change. We need explanations for both, because theoretically there are a number of concepts, the concept of social reproduction of institutions, for instance, that have to be reinstituted every generation. That explains why things remain the same and then in reproducing the whole thing how change occurs. That is a major area of discussion. This has to be explained, not only described.

The second point I found to be an area that we have yet to look at, is the question of the effects of the institution where women are involved. What we are doing here, in separating out the institutions, and I don't mean that all the papers did this, is separating out the women from the whole society. That can be done consciously in terms of analysis, but women have to be put back into society because they exist as part and parcel of the system. You can only understand men when you can understand the position of women.

So if I can give one example, the question of weaving. The question of weaving, of course is not of women staying at home or working in other institutions, but the product of their act enters into the society in one form or another, even if it never goes into trade. But sometimes it does go into trade and therefore it is appropriated by the state, in some cases by the state system itself. That means that there is a whole section of society that is dependent on that element of production. In some sections it doesn't go into exchange, and in not going into exchange what it does is limit the development of a commodity within that society. So it seems to me, at least, that if you can analyze the role of women in society you have to look at how they fit into the society, how they integrate into society, not simply a list of attributes, although that might be a necessary first step.

Kuhrt: May I just make a very brief comment? My impression was that Dr. Grosz's paper made precisely the same point as you, that women are not in opposition to the patrilineal system but play a role precisely in order to ensure its continuity. I don't know whether I'm misrepresenting her view but I think she actually emphasized that particular point.

Fischer: When I gave my talk I emphasized that in the Old Kingdom that although the father was far more mentioned in situations apart from the funerary establishment, that in the tomb frequently the wife was emphasized and there were certain situations in which the mother held property during the marriage before her husband's death, she could give it to her sons. And so obviously marriage did not truly restrict women's roles.

B. Lesko: I am struck with the very basic but important role that ordinary women and men could play in producing wealth. In Egypt cloth and clothing was used in barter. Thus a housewife at home at her loom had, in effect, a significant role to play in affecting her family's financial status.

Shute: I would like, if I may, to raise a point relating to interpretation. It's a general one which relates particularly to Egyptian material, possibly to New Kingdom Egyptian material, and that is whether in the representational material one can be sure to recognize different levels of interpretation of which the Egyptians themselves might have been aware. Now take a simple example which seems trivial, which perhaps isn't quite so trivial. It relates to the point which was made that women pull flax, men cut grain, and Dr. Fischer made the point that flax and the weaving of flax into material was originally associated with women. He said that he did not think that the cutting of grain required more strength than the pulling of flax. I'm not sure that's true, actually because I have myself cut grain with a sickle and I think it's extremely hard work, and flax, I haven't actually pulled it myself but I know the plant, it's not as robust as it looks in Egyptian representations.

But what I wanted to say is that possibly there is another level of interpretation that should be considered. That is to say, there could have been a taboo on showing women wielding knives. Is there some reason that possibly women used knives in their kitchens to dice vegetables or to peel fruit, or whatever; they're not shown doing so? The only examples of women holding knives appear to be in the Book of the Dead where the deceased occasionally, but not always, cuts the grain. So would there have been a taboo on women being represented holding knives. It might be related to the fear of women, which of course all men have, now as then, and which was referred to by Dr. Robins in her talk.

Robins: The first point about the possible different levels of interpretation of the representations I think is very important because we are using the representations as source material and possibly we can't really trust the source material to tell us something about real life. I think it is a problem. It must mean something. It is there, but we have to know what to do with it, and I'm quite sure that there are different levels, the Egyptians were very subtle people, and I think they were very visual people and managed to get into their art a lot of different meanings. I think that it is quite clear over time a new interpretation might have been developed and was added to the old ways.

A very different example, I think is the fishing and fowling scenes. I talked about them having an erotic meaning in the Eighteenth Dynasty with the woman dressed up in clothing quite unsuited to going out into the wet marshes to have a day watching her husband spear fish, but this develops out of a scene which originally had no such interpretation. It was a straightforward scene of the tomb owners fishing and fowling. I suspect that in the New Kingdom we have the two levels side by side and it would be read in both ways, as representing both ideas, so I think we really have to recognize that in order to interpret the material you can't just ignore it. I made it quite clear in my paper, I hope, that this material is produced by men for men and we have to reckon with these different levels of interpretation. As for the question of women in tomb paintings not apparently holding knives or sickles it could again be that it was considered inappropriate for a woman to do this in the environment of a tomb designed for a man. I think you would agree with that.

Fischer: Well, I'm not so sure about this because again I'm thinking of Old Kingdom scenes. There in one case you have a woman overseeing flax production even though she has a title connected with weaving. Also in the matter of butchering, of course men were involved in that, and then I think that leads to their cooking the meat, and unfortunately all the cooking scenes in the Old Kingdom show men cooking meat. So then you have to ask yourself "did women cook?" I think they did because for one thing we have a woman whose name means cook. I don't think you would give a woman such a name if women never cooked. And then of course you do have that scene which I showed, a very dramatic one in which women are wielding knives with a vengeance and killing the invading army.

Robins: I think the last point is unusual.

Fischer: Very.

Robins: As a last resort men allow women to defend their lives, their homes and their children when all else is lost. I'm not denying that in real life they used knives, I can't believe that women who worked in the village of Deir-el-Medina sat for nine days without lifting a knife because their husbands were off at the tombs. No, what I'm suggesting is that for some reason in the Eighteenth Dynasty tombs, anyway, there seems to be some avoidance of showing women wielding these sharp objects.

Fischer: There is one other exception, that is that women have razors, they shave, I suppose, their bodies, and....

Robins: But that would not be shown on tomb walls.

Fischer: No, it would not be shown on tomb walls. In any case women did use razors.

Robins: But this is the difference between reality and the male image that we are getting on these tomb walls.

Kuhrt: I'd like to ask Profs. Delaney and Zagarell, it seems to me that you have brought up the same point several times over in the course of this conference, and it's a very important point, and for some reason we all seem to continuously ignore it, and I think the main reason is that we are all slightly startled and have perhaps not thought about the question too much, but there is a particular problem, an area in which we need specific help from anthropologists who are experienced in these matters as to what kinds of questions we should be asking our material in order to pay more attention to this question of social reproduction, in which women play a crucial role, as Dr. Zagarell pointed out. It seems to me that our material from Mesopotamia, Egypt and Israel is terribly difficult, and we are struggling with the whole nature of the family but I think that what this conference is about is that you should perhaps try to point us in the direction of what we should be looking at and what questions we should be addressing. For example, the whole creation of the concept of what is gendermen's role, what is women's role, what do boys do, what do girls do, what is a boy and how do we actually define him, and who does the defining, how long do boys and girls stay together, at what point are boys separated off and take off to start doing things which lead to becoming men? Those are all questions that occur to me, what is the sort of specific difference of the life experience of a boy in a particular society as opposed to a girl? Dr. Roth has been suggesting very persuasively, that boys marry much later in Neo-Babylonian society than girls. There was a very marked difference then between boys and girls, and that is but one example I have been able to think of.

Delaney: I think that one of the main things is not to think of men and women as somehow only natural objects. You cannot have separate histories of men or of women totally removed from any cultural context, and that also implies that cultures are looked on as wholes, and therefore not as patrilineal systems, but cultural systems in which there are different kinds of world views that form the ways people think about each other.

Zagarell: The underlying question is how are males and females created, under what conditions and how changing the conditions changes in fact who they are.

Fischer: It struck me that we are talking about material that isn't parallel. You couldn't take all these papers and then make comparisons because in the first place our evidence is obviously so different, in some of the first papers we have a great deal of epigraphic evidence, which is lacking in Mesopotamia. On their side they have much more textual evidence than Egyptologists could produce, and we were reading quite disparate things, in some talks we could tell quite a lot about occupations of women, in other cases practically nothing. So to put together a synthesis of these papers would be extremely difficult.

Now this is extremely obvious, of course. Perhaps someone would care to comment on it some more. Occasionally you can see parallels and contrasts, but it is very kaleidoscopic.

Roth: I think you're right, but I think that we don't want to make a single synthesis. We all have different types of evidence, we approach our evidence with different biases, but basically everyone here today is a philologist, and the fact that we can benefit from seeing the kinds of questions you ask of your material and we can be thinking of our own material to see whether similar questions might in fact apply, which we have never thought of before. I wouldn't want to come up with any single conclusion from this conference. In fact, its diversity has made it most interesting to me.

Robins: In looking for a model it would be terribly incestuous just to look for models from each other. What we have to do is to take a different point of view and look far outside of our range in areas in time, and take those models. We are never going to find exact parallels but look and see whether they can suggest questions that we can put to our materials and interpretations of our material perhaps would grow out of this, from learning from a very wide area.

B. Lesko: I agree. I was thinking just before this conference began that I wished I had invited a a scholar familiar with pre-colonial African tribal societies because, after all, Egypt is an African culture, and I have recently read a description of African queens in pre-colonial Africa who married other women in order to gain greater social status and wealth with reciprocal relationships. Perhaps this is what Bill Ward has with the burials around King Mentuhotep's temple. Perhaps that is the real intention of the queen's harem of the Empire Period. This is a suggestion from Africa's own cultural heritage. We have to remain open to anthropology, ethnology, and all other disciplines to guide us in interpreting and analyzing our material.

Nugent: As a comparative outsider, listening to the material over the last three days, this methodological, theoretical question is exactly what stood out most for me and it seems to me that we are dealing very much with the life-force of a discipline or various disciplines and it does seem to be inadequate. The first must be philology, but it is important to move on from that stage, and I was thinking also of feminist studies. I think that many different kinds of feminist critics now would accept that the first stage of feminist criticism was the so-called images of women, but that then one moves beyond images of women, to perhaps a more complex notion of the *construction* of images of women, and this is to some extent responding to your comment, Prof. Robins, about the art reflecting life. It certainly does, but in its own way. I would want to claim that reflection is very strongly mediated through cultural and ideological concepts and I was struck very much by the kinds of treatments of enumeration, as you said description, that was very much what was at stake here, and maybe that is an inevitable first step.

Hegedus: If we could compare ostraca, papyri, graffiti, and grave finds of the commoners with artistic representations then maybe we would get a more varied picture. Because the presentations are ideologically influenced by the elite class they represent only a certain ideology and not the real life. We cannot believe that women were only harvesting flax or banqueting or enjoying the smell of lotus, for instance. It is ridiculous.

L. Lesko: We have significant differences in the ideal representations of these Egyptian tombs and the conflicts we find in their literature, in letters, letters to the dead, letters to the living, for that matter, that record women plotting the execution of people that they were angry with. They record concern for spirits, the theft of property, all of these things were recorded, indicating that the Egyptians were no more secure than people nowadays, that they did not live the idyllic existence that we see portrayed in their tomb art.

Robins: I'm certainly not suggesting that women did nothing, the majority of women are engaged in that incredible task of running a household. Before the age of conveniences the food came in as grain, your payment was made in grain, and to get anything to eat you had to sit there and grind your grain, you had to bake it, you had to brew the beer, and that's just a small part of it. You would keep weaving, presumably a woman was responsible for clothing her household, her family. I'm not implying that women sat there idle. I think they had their hands full, but I think that what we see very often in the tomb scenes are things that women did at home, on the domestic side, moved up into the public sphere and taken over by men. Then we see the men cooking, we see the male launderers doing the washing. But I think that the women, the invisible women that we don't see, actually spent their time this way. It was a full time occupation, let alone going to the market, or producing what might go to exchange for other goods that they didn't make themselves.

Kuhrt: I think the question, though, is *who* decides that it is the woman that has to grind the grain. Who decides that it is the woman who has to feed the household and wash the clothes?

B. Lesko: Why is it that the men are shown doing these things portrayed in a tomb? Is this really life?

Robins: Because you're not interested in an individual household, you're interested in the tomb owner's estate. The men employed, what they are doing, has come out of the household and it's in a larger sphere.

Kuhrt: Absolutely. I quite agree with you, but I think that the debate and question that Georgia and Carol and Allan have been suggesting, is that we should be going even further back, and asking when did all this begin.

Zagarell: For example, Dr. Bird talked about the encapsulation of the gender-related role. And just to give you an example, everyone knows that not too long ago people used to say that women don't work. What they meant was women don't go out and have a job outside the house. What they did was denigrate the labor that was carried out within the house. It says that certain work doesn't exist.

Robins: I have the same thing in the tomb paintings.

Zagarell: Exactly.

Nugent: A question close to that, is who decides what will be represented in what kind of scene and so forth. My own experience is with amphoras' representations of the Greek stage which seem to bear no relationship to Greek reality in the fifth century. So men first want ideal images of women, but very, very quickly would tend to realize that that was by no means sufficient, or even any kind of picture of reality reversed, and that's what seems to me a possibility for some of the material that has been brought up.

Zagarell: The papers as a group represent both the strengths and the weaknesses of ancient oriental studies. They reflect the erudition and dedication of ancient Near Eastern scholars to the solution of regional and area problems. It is also clear how much ancient Near Eastern scholarship has suffered because of its largely self-imposed isolation from scholarly work in other related fields. In most of the papers presented there were no or few references to sources outside the ancient Orient. The papers simply don't represent a discourse with the external scholarly world.

For example, these papers referred quite clearly to several questions that are the subject of much debate in feminist studies. Material presented by Christine Gailey (see among other articles Gailey 1985 and Gailey and Patterson 1987) and Karen Sacks (1979) and others, directly pertain to the position of women, their changing status, in emerging state societies and yet there is no reference to their work. Similarly, Conkey and Spector have discussed the unconscious biases of scholars when dealing with questions of gender (Conkey and Spector 1984), but again there is no reference to this body of literature. Of course, this lack of reference to broader, non-Orientalist discussions is not simply characteristic of this conference but permeates much of ancient Near Eastern scholarship. I am afraid unless we alter our modes of analysis, unless we begin to discuss these kinds of problems, unless we take into account the broader scholarly discussions taking place outside our immediate disciplines, we may, indeed, continue to make progress, but with few radical conceptual breakthroughs. However, the intimate knowledge of the data-base represented by ancient Near Eastern materials, may, when combined with broader theoretical concerns, provide the basis for a radical leap in understanding for gender studies as a whole.

B. Lesko: I'd like to conclude this by reiterating the observation made before that the specialists in the ancient Near East face two major problems: first, the spotty survival of the ancient documents--which hides at least as much as it suggests or states--and also the general lack of awareness on our part of the diversity which human institutions and attitudes can take is a hindrance. This last can be overcome by studying social anthropologists' reports, such as those of Martin King Whyte who studied ninety-three preindustrial societies. For instance, from him we learn that there is no pattern of universal male dominance, or, put another way, no general status of women, and that, rather, quite a lot of variation shows up from culture to culture regarding the position of women relative to men. Knowing this, we should be free to examine our ancient records with an open mind but also be ready to measure the information they present against a standard based on the new schools of thought about gender.

We must rely on the most accurate and up-to-date translations the philologists can provide of the ancient written documents, while hoping that the next turn of the archaeologist's spade may reveal still more evidence which will increase the corpus of women's earliest records.

Bibliography

Ancient Egypt

A bibliography for the study of women and society in ancient Egypt:

Books

Allam, Shafik *Some Pages from Everyday Life in Ancient Egypt*, Giza: 1986.

Baer, Klaus *Rank and Title in the Old Kingdom*, Chicago: 1960.

Bakir, Abd el-Mohsen *Slavery in Pharaonic Egypt*, (Supplement aux *ASAE*, 18) Cairo: 1952.

Bénédite, G. *Tombeau de la Reine Thiti*, Cairo: 1892.

Bierbrier, Morris *The Late New Kingdom in Egypt*, Warminster: 1975.
The Tomb-Builders of the Pharaohs, London: 1982.

Brunner-Traut, Emma *Der Tanz im Alten Ägypten*, (*ÄF*, 6) Glückstadt, 1958.

Buttles, J. *The Queens of Egypt*, London: 1908.

Černý, Jaroslav *Catalogue des ostraca hiératique non-littéraires de Deir el Médineh*, 6 vols. Cairo: 1937-70.
A Community of Workmen at Thebes in the Ramesside Period, Cairo: 1973.

Desroches-Noblecourt, Christiane *La femme au temps des Pharaons*, Paris: 1986.
and Kuentz, C. *Le petit temple d'Abou Simbel*, Cairo: 1968.

Dunham, D. and Simpson, W.K. *The Mastaba of Queen Mersyankh III G 7530-7540*, Boston: 1974.

Edel, Elmar *Das Akazienhaus und seine Rolle in den Begräbnisriten des alten Ägyptens*, (*MÄS* 24), Berlin, 1970.

Fischer, Henry George *Egyptian Titles of the Middle Kingdom*, (3 parts) New York: 1985.
Varia (*Egyptian Studies* I), New York: 1976.

Gaballa, G.A. *The Memphite Tomb Chapel of Mose*, Warminster: 1977.

Galvin,M. *The Priestesses of Hathor in the Old Kingdom and the 1st Intermediate Period*, (Brandeis Dissertation), Ann Arbor: 1981.

Gardiner, A.H. and K. Sethe *Egyptian Letters to the Dead*, London: 1928.

Gitton, M. *L'Épouse du dieu Ahmes Néfertary*, Paris: 1975.
Les Divines Épouses de la 18e dynastie, Paris: 1984.

Graefe, E. *Untersuchungen zur Verwaltung und Geschichte der Institution der Gottesgemahlin des Amun vom Beginn des Neuen Reiches bis zur Spätzeit* (*Äg. Abh.* 37: 1-2), Wiesbaden: 1981.

Hari, R. *Horemheb et la reine Moutnedjemet ou la fin d'une dynastie*, Geneva: 1964.

Hayes, Wm. C. *A Papyrus of the Late Middle Kingdom in the Brooklyn Museum*, Brooklyn: 1955.

James, T.G.H. *The Ḥeḳanakhte Papers and other Early Middle Kingdom Documents*, New York: 1962.

Janssen, Jac. J. *Commodity Prices from the Ramessid Period*, Leiden: 1975.

Jéquier, J. *La pyramide d'Oudjebten*, Cairo: 1928.
Les pyramides des reines Neit et Apouit, Cairo: 1933.

Keimer, Louis *Remarques sur le tatouage dans l'Égypte ancienne* (*MIE* 53), Cairo: 1948.

Kitchen, K.A. *The Third Intermediate Period in Egypt*, Warminster: 1973.

Klebs, Luise *Die Reliefs des Alten Reiches*, (*AHAW* 3), Heidelberg,1915.
Die Reliefs und Malereien des Mittleren Reiches, (*AHAW* 6), Heidelberg: 1922.
Die Reliefs und Malereien des Neuen Reiches, (*AHAW* 9), Heidelberg: 1934.

Kuchman [-Sabbahy], L. *The Development of the Titulary and Iconography of the Ancient Egyptian Queen from Dynasty One to Early Dynasty Eighteen*, (unpubl. Diss.), Toronto: 1982.

Lesko, Barbara S. *The Remarkable Women of Ancient Egypt*, Berkeley: 1978, 2nd rev. ed., Providence: 1987.

Lüddeckens, Erich *Ägyptische Eheverträge*, Wiesbaden: 1960.

Manniche, Lise *Sexual Life in Ancient Egypt*, London: 1987.

Menu, Bernadette *Recherches sur l'histoire Juridique, Economique et Sociale de l'ancienne Egypte*, Versailles: 1982.
Le Regime Juridique des Terres et du Personnel attache a la terre dans le Papyrus Wilbour, Lille: 1970.

Mertz, B. *Certain Titles of the Egyptian Queens and their Bearing on the Hereditary Right to the Throne*, (unpublished dissertation), University of Chicago: 1952.

Millard, A. *The Position of Women in Society and in the family in Ancient Egypt, with special reference to the Middle Kingdom*, (Unpublished dissertation, University College London), London.

Pelizaeus Museum (Hildesheim) *Nofret-Die Schöne: Die Frau im alten Ägypten. "Wahrheit" und Wirklichkeit*, Mainz: 1985.

Perepelkin, J. *The Secret of the Gold Coffin, Moscow*: 1978.

Pestman, P. W. *Marriage and Matrimonial Property in Ancient Egypt*,(Papyrologica Lugduno-Batava, no. 9), Leiden: 1961.

Pinch, Geraldine *New Kingdom Votive Offerings to Hathor*, Warminster: 1989.

Pomeroy, Sarah B. *Women in Hellenistic Egypt*, New York: 1984.

Ratié, A. *La reine Hatchepsout*, Leiden: 1979.

Redford, Donald B. *History and Chronology of the Eighteenth Dynasty*, Toronto: 1967.

Reiser, Elfriede *Die Königliche Harim im Alten Ägypten und seine verwaltung*, Vienna: 1972.

Reisner, G. and Smith, W.S. *A History of the Giza Necropolis II: The Tomb of Hetepheres*, Cambridge, MA: 1955.

Ruffle, J. and Kitchen, K.A. *Glimpses of Ancient Egypt*, Warminster: 1979.

Sampson, Julia *Nefertiti and Cleopatra*, London: 1985.

Sander-Hansen, C.E. *Das Gottesweib des Amun, Copenhagen: 1940.*

Schulze, Peter H. *Frauen im Alten Ägypten*, Bergisch Gladbach: 1987.

Simpson, Wm. K. and Dows Dunham *The Mastaba of Queen Meresankh III*, Boston: 1974.

Tefnin, R. *La statuaire d'Hatshepsout:pourtrait royal et politique sous la 18e dynastie*, Bruxelles: 1979.

Thausing, G. and Goedicke, H. *Nofretari-Eine Documentation der Wandgemälde ihres Grabes*, Graz: 1971.

Trigger, Bruce et al. *Ancient Egypt: A Social History*, Cambridge: 1983.

Troy, Lana *Patterns in Queenship in Ancient Egyptian Myth and History*, Uppsala: 1986.

Valbelle, Dominique *Les ouvriers de la tombe Deir el Medineh à l'époque Ramesside*, (*BdE* XCVI), Cairo: 1985.

Ward, Wm. A. *Essays on Feminine Titles*, Beirut: 1986.
Index of Egyptian Administrative and Religious Titles, Beirut: 1982.

Werbrouck, Marcelle *Les Pleureuses dans l'Égypte ancienne*, Brussels: 1938.

Wenig, Steffen *The Woman in Egyptian Art*, New York: 1969.

Wente, Edward F. *Late Ramesside Letters*, (*SAOC*, 33) Chicago: 1967.

Winlock, H.E. *Bas-reliefs from the Temple of Ramses I at Abydos*, New York: 1921.
The Tomb of Queen Meryet-Amun at Thebes, New York: 1932.
The Treasure of the Three Egyptian Princesses, New York: 1948.

Winter, U. *Frau und Göttin: Exegetische und ikonographische Studien zum weiblichen Gottesbild im Alten Israel und in dessen Umwelt*, (*Orbis biblicus et orientalis*, 53), Freiburg-Göttingen: 1983.

Articles

Aldred, C. "Hairstyles and History," *BMMA* 15(1957) 199.
"Queen Mutnodjme-a correction," *JEA* 56(1970) 195-196.

Allam,S. "Zur Stellung der Frau im Alten Ägypten in der Zeit des Neuen Reiches," *BiOr* 26 (1969) 155-159 and *Das Altertum* 16(1970) 67-81.

"De l'adoption en Égypte pharaonique," *Oriens Antiquus* 11(1972) 277-295.

"Zur Adoption im pharaonischen Ägypten," *Das Altertum* 19(1973) 3-17.

"An Allusion to an Egyptian Wedding Ceremony?" *GM* 13 (1974) 9-11.

"Ehe," *LÄ*, I, coll. 1162-1181.

"Familie," *LÄ*, II, coll. 101-113.

"Geschwisterehe," *LÄ*, II, coll. 568-570.

"Les obligations et la famille dans la société égyptienne ancienne," *Oriens Antiquus* 16(1977) 89-97.

"Quelques aspects du marriage dans l'Égypte ancienne," *JEA* 67(1981) 116-135.

"La Vente dans l'Egypte ancienne (Particulièrement à l'époque du Nouvel Empire," *Revue historique de droit français et étranger*, 60 (1982) 377-93.

"Eheschliessung und Scheidung in Altägypten," *Das Altertum* 29(1983) 117-123.

"Familie und Besitzverhältnisse in der altägyptischen Arbeitersiedlung von Deir-el-Medineh," *R.I.D.A.* 30 (1983) 17-39.

"Un contrat de Mariage (Pap. Démotique Caire J. 68567)," *RdE* 35 (1984) 3-21.

"Trois lettres d'affaires (P. Caire CG 58056, 58058, 58060)," *BdE* 97/I (1985) 19-30.

"Sinuhe's Foreign Wife (Reconsidered)," *Discussions in Egyptology* 4(1986) 15-16.

"Zur Stellung der Frau im Altägypten," *Discussions in Egyptology* 5 (1986) pp. 7-15.

"Women as Owners of Rights (during the Egyptian Late Period)," *JEA* (in press).

Allen, T.G. "A unique statue of Senmut," *AJSLL* 44 (1928) 49-55.

Altenmüller, H. "Die Stellung der Königsmutter Chentkaues beim übergang von der 4. zur 5. Dynastie," *CdE* 45 (1970) 223-235.

"Tausret und Sethnacht," *JEA* 68 (1982) 107-115.

"Das Grab der Königin Tausret im Tal der König," *SAK* 10 (1983) 15-20.

d'Auria, S. "The Princess Baketamun," *JEA* 69 (1983) 161-169.

Bakry, H. "The Discovery of a Statue of Queen Twosre (1207-1194? B.C.) at Medīnet Naṣr, Cairo," *Revista degli Studi Orientali* 46 (1971) 17-26.

Berlandini-Grenier, J. "Senenmout, Stoliste royal sur une statue-cube avec Neferouré," *BIFAO* 76 (1976) 111-132.

Bierbrier, M.L. "Terms of Relationship at Deir el-Medina," *JEA* 66 (1980) 100-107.

Blackman, A.M. "On the Position of women in the ancient Egyptian Hierarchy," *JEA* 7 (1921) 8-30.

Blankenberg-van Delden, C. "Additional Remarks on Queen Ahhotep, Consort of Senakhtenre Tao I?" *GM* 49 (1981) 17-18.

"Ahmes Merytamun and Ahhotep I, Consort of Senakhtenre Tao I?" *GM* 47 (1981) 15-19.

"A genealogical reconstruction of the kings and queens of the late 17th and early 18th dynasties," *GM* 54 (1982) 31-45.

"Ahmes Satamon," *GM* 68 (1983) 37-39.

Bleeker, C.J. "The Position of the Queen in Ancient Egypt," in *The Sacral Kingship* (Studies in the History of Religion vol. 4), Leiden: 1959.

Borghouts, J.F., "Monthu and Matrimonial Squabbles," *RdE* 33(1981) 11-22.

Brunner-Traut, E. "Das Muttermilchkrüglein: Ammen mit Stillumhang und Mondamultett." *Die Welt des Orients* 5(1970) 145-164.

Bryan, B.M. "Evidence of Female Literacy from Theban Tombs of the New Kingdom," *BES* 6(1984) 17-32.

"The Career and Family of Minmose, High Priest of Onuris," *CdE* 61 (1986) 5-30.

"Non-Royal Women's Titles in the 18th Egyptian Dynasty," *ARCE Newsletter*, 1984 13-16.

Caminos, R. "The Nitocris Adoption Stela," *JEA* 50 (1964) 71-101.

Capart, J. "La reine Thenti-Hapi," *CdE* 16 (1941) 39-49.

"Nefertari, Isisnefert et Khaemouast," *CdE* 17 (1942) 72-82.

Carter, H. "A Tomb prepared for Queen Hatshepsut," *JEA* 4 (1917) 107-118.

Černý, J. "Consanguineous Marriage in Pharaonic Egypt," *JEA* 40 (1954) 23-29.

"A Note on the Ancient Egyptian Family," *Studi in onore di A. Calderini e R. Paribeni* II (1957) 51-55.

"Papyrus Salt 124," *JEA* 15 (1920) 243-58.

"The Will of Naunakhte and the related documents," *JEA* 31 (1945) 29-53.

and T.E. Peet "A Marriage Settlement of the Twentieth Dynasty," *JEA* 13 (1927), 30-39.

Cruz-Uribe, E. "On the Wife of Merneptah," *GM* 24 (1977) 23-31.

Daressy, G. "Inscriptions de la Chapelle d'Ameniritis à Medinet-Habou," *RT* 23 (1901) 4-18.

"Une princesse inconnue d'époque Saite," *ASAE* 8 (1907) 280-281.

"La reine Aahmès-Henuttamehu," *ASAE* 9 (1908) 95-96.

"La stèle de la fille de Chéops," *RT* 30 (1908) 1-10.

"Les parents de la reine Teta-Chera," *ASAE* 9 (1908) 137-138.
"La tombe de la mère de Chefren," *ASAE* 10 (1910) 41-49.

von Deines, H. "*Mwt rmṯ* Mutter der Menschen," *MIO* 4 (1956) 27-39.

Desroches-Noblecourt, C. "'Concubines du Mort' et Mère de Famille au Moyen Empire à propos d'une supplique pour une naissance," *BIFAO* 53 (1953) 7-47.
"Touy, mère de Ramses II, la reine Tanadjmy et les reliques le l'experience armamienne," *L'Égyptologie* II, 227-243.

Engelbach, R. "Recent Acquisitions in the Cairo Museum III. Sphinx of a Queen," *ASAE* 31 (1931) 128-129.
"Notes on the Coffin and 'Mummy' of Princess Sit-Amûn," *ASAE* 39 (1939) 405-407.

Eyre, C.J. "Crime and Adultery in Ancient Egypt," *JEA* 70 (1984), 92-105.

Fischer, H.G. "A Daughter of the Overlords of Upper Egypt in the First Intermediate Period," *JAOS* 76(1956) 99-110.
"The Butcher *Pḥ-r-nfr*, IV. Additional note: A female overseer of the *ỉm3.t*," *Orientalia* 29(1960) 187-190.
"The Nubian Mercenaries of Gebelein during the First Intermediate Period," *Kush* 9(1961) 44-56.
"Three Old Kingdom Palimpsests in the Louvre," *ZÄS* 86(1961) 21-31.
"The Cult and Nome of the Goddess Bat," *JARCE* 1(1962) 7-23.
"Redundant Determinatives in the Old Kingdom," *MMJ* 8(1973) 7-25.
"*Nbty* in Old Kingdom Titles and Names," *JEA* 64(1974) 94-99.
"A feminine example of *wḏ ḥm.k* 'thy majesty commands' in the Fourth Dynasty," *JEA* 61(1975) 246-247.
"Some Early Monuments from Busiris, in the Egyptian Delta: The Fitzwilliam Museum False Door," *MMJ* 11(1976) 14-22.
"Boats manned with women (Westcar V, 1ff.)," in *Fragen an die altägyptische Literatur: Studien zum Gedenken an Eberhard Otto*, Wiesbaden, 1977, 161-165.
"Deux stéles villageoises du Moyen Empire," *CdE* 55(1980) 13-15.
"The request of a wife to her husband: an unusual expression of asserveration," *ZÄS* 105(1978) 44-47; addenda in *ZÄS* 107(1980) 86-87.
"Deux stéles curieuses de la Premiére Période Intermédiaire," *Supplément au BIFAO* 81(1981) 235-239.
"Notes on two tomb chapels at Giza," *JEA* 67(1981) 167-168.
"Priesterin," in *Lexikon der Ägyptologie*, 1100-1105.

Galvin, M. "The Hereditary Status of the Titles of the Cult of Hathor," *JEA* 70 (1984) 42-49.

Gardiner, A.H. "Adoption Extraordinary," *JEA* 26 (1941) 23-29.

Gauthier, H. "La titulature des reines des dynasties Memphites," *ASAE* 24 (1924) 198-209.

Gauthier-Laurent, M. "Les scénes de coiffure féminine dans l'Ancienne Égypte." *Mélanges Maspero* I (*MIFAO* 66), Cairo: 1938 673-696.

Gitton, M. "Le rôle des femmes dans le clergé d'Amon àla 18e dynastie," *BSFE* 75(1976) 31ff.
"Le résiliation d'une fonction religieuse: Nouvelle interpretation de la Stéle de Donation d'Ahmes Néfertary," *BIFAO* 76 (1976) 65-89.
and Leclant, J. "Gottesgemahlin," *LÄ* 2, col. 792-812.

Goedicke, H. "Was Magic used in the Harem Conspiracy against Ramesses III?" *JEA* 49 (1973) 71-92.
"An approximate Date for the Harem Investigation under Pepy I," *JAOS* 74 (1954), 88-89.
"Die Laufbahn des *Mṯn*," *MDAIK* 21 (1966), 1-71.

Grapow, H. "Die Inschrift der Königin Katimala am Tempel von Semne," *ZÄS* 76 (1940) 24-41.

Habachi, L. "La reine Touy, femme de Sethi I et ses proches parents inconnue," *RdE* 21 (1969) 27-47.
"The Tomb of the princess Nebt of the VIII dynasty discovered at Qift," *SAK* 10 (1983) 205-213.

Harari, I. "La Fondation Cultuelle: Notes sur l'organisation cultuelle dans l'Ancien Empire égyptien," *ASAE* 54 (1957), 317-344.
"La capacité juridique de la femme au Nouvel Empire," *RIDA* 30 (1983), 41-54.

Harris, J.R. "Nefemeferuaten," *GM* 4 (1973) 15-17.
"Nefertiti Rediviva," *Acta Orientalia* 35 (1973) 5ff.
"Kiya," *CdE* 49 (1974) 25-31.
"Contributions to the History of the Eighteenth Dynasty," *SAK* 2 (1975) 95-101.

Hohenwart-Gerlachstein, A. "The Legal Position of Women in Ancient Egypt," *Wiener Völkerkundliche Mitteilungen* 3, Jahrgang Nr. 1 (1955) 90 ff.

Hollis, Susan T. "Women of Ancient Egypt and the Sky Goddess Nut," *Journal of American Folklore* 100 (1987) 496-503.

Jacquet-Gordon, H. "A statuette of Ma'et and the Identity of the Divine Adoratress Karomama," *ZÄS* 94 (1967) 86-93.

Janssen, J.J. "Absence from work by the Necropolis Workmen of Thebes," *SAK* 8 (1980) 127-152.
"An Allusion to an Egyptian Wedding Ceremony?" *GM* 10 (1974) 25-28.

"La Reine Nefertari et la succession le Ramsés II par Merenptah," *CdE* 38 (1963) 30-36.
"The Rules of Legal Procedure in the Community of Necropolis Workmen at Deir el-Medina," *BiOr* 31 (1975) 291-96.
with P.W. Pestman: "Burial and Inheritance in the Community of the Necropolis Workmen at Thebes," *JESHO* 11 (1968) 137-170.

Kaplan, H.R. "The Problem of the Dynastic Position of Meryet-Nit," *JNES* 38 (1979) 23-27.

Kaplony, P. "Denkmäler der Prinzessin Neferure und der Königin Ti-mienese in der Sammlung A. Ghertsos," *RdE* 22 (1970) 99-109.

Kees, H. "Das Gottesweib Ahmes-Nofertere als Amonpriester," *Orientalia* 23 (1954) 57-63.

Keimer, L. "Remarques sur les 'cuillers á fard' du type dit á la nageuse." *ASAE* 52(1952) 59-72.

Kemp, B. "The Harim-Palace at Medinet el-Ghurab," *ZÄS* 105 (1978) 122-133.
"Wall Paintings form the Workmen's Village at el-'Amarna," *JEA* 65 (1979) 47-53.

Kuchman [-Sabbahy], L. "The Titles of Queenship," parts I & II *JSSEA* 7 & 9 (1977 & 1979) 9-10; 21-25.
"The Titulary of Queens Nbt and Ḫnwt," *GM* 52 (1981) 37-42.

Kuhlmann, K. "Ptolemais-Queen of Nectanebo I. Notes on the Inscription of an Unknown Princess of the XXXth Dynasty," *MDAIK* 37 (1981) 267-279.

Leach, E. "The Mother's Brother in Ancient Egypt," *Royal Anthropological Institute News*, 19-21.

Leclant, J. "Tefnout et les divine adoratrices thébaines," *MDAIK* 15 (1957) 166-171.

Lesko, B. S. "True Art in Ancient Egypt," *Egyptological Studies...Parker*, 85-97.
"Women of Egypt and the Ancient Near East," in *Becoming Visible: Women in European History*, R. Bridenthal, C. Koonz, S.M. Stuard, eds., Boston: 1987, 41-77.

Lesko, L.H. "A Little More Evidence for the end of the Nineteenth Dynasty," *JARCE* 5 (1966), 29-32.
"Three Late Egyptian Stories Reconsidered," *Egyptological Studies...Parker*, 98-103.

Malék, J. "Princess Inti, the Companion of Horus," *JSSEA* 10 (1980) 229-241.

Menu, B. "Quelque remarques à propos de l'étude comparée de la stèle juridique de Karnak et de la "stèles" d'Ahmès-Néfertari," *RdE* 23 (1971) 155-163.
"La gestion du 'patrimoine' foncier d'Hekanakhte," *RdE* 22, (1970) 111-129.

"La "stèle" d'Ahmès-Néfertari dans son contexte historique et juridique," *BIFAO* 77 (1977) 89-100.

Newberry, P.E. "Queen Nitocris of the Sixth Dynasty," *JEA* 29 (1943) 51-54.

Nims, C. "The Date of the Dishounouring of Hatshepsut," *ZÄS* 93 (1966) 97-100.
"Some Notes on the Family of Mereruka," *JAOS* 58 (1938) 638-647.

Nord, D. "The Term *ḫnr* 'harem' or 'musical performers' in *Fs. Dunham* Boston: 1981, 137.

Nur El-Din, M.A. "Some Remarks on the Title *mwt-nsw*," *Orientalia Lovaniensia* 11 (1980) 91-98.

Ogdon, J.R. "An Exceptional Family of Priests of the Early Fifth Dynasty at Giza," *GM* 90 (1986) 61-65.

Peet, T.E. "Two Letters from Akhetaten," *Annals of Archaeology and Anthropology* 17 (1930) 82-97.

Perdu, O. "Khenemet-Nefer-Hedjet: Une princesse et deux reines du Moyen Empire," *RdE* 29 (1977) 68-85.

Pestman, P.W. "The Law of Succession in Ancient Egypt," in *Essays on Oriental Laws of Succession*, (Studia et Documenta ad iura orientis antiqui pertinentia, 9), Leiden: 1969, 58-77.
and J.J. Janssen "Burial and Inheritance in the Community of the Necropolis Workmen at Thebes," *JESHO* 11 (1968), 137-70.

Pfluger, K. "The Private Funerary Stelae of the Middle Kingdom and their importance for the study of Ancient Egyptian History," *JAOS* 67 (1947) 127ff.

Pinch, G. "Childbirth and Female Figurines at Deir el-Medina and el-Amarna," *Orientalia* 52 (1983) 405-414.

Pirenne, J. "La statut de la Femme dans l'ancienne Egypte," *Recueils de la Société Jean Bodin* 11 (1959) 63-77.

Radwan, A. "Ramses II. und seine Mutter vor Osiris," *SAK* 6 (1978) 157-161.

Reisner, G. "Nefertkauw, the eldest daughter of Sneferu," *ZÄS* 64 (1929) 97-99.
"The tomb of Meresankh, a great-grand-daughter of Queen Hetep-heres and Sneferuw," *Boston Museum of Fine Arts Bull.* 25 (1927) 64-79.

Riefstahl, E. "Doll, Queen or Goddess," *Brooklyn Museum Journal* (1943-1944) 7-23.

Robins, G. "The God's Wife of Amon in the 18th dynasty in Egypt," in A. Cameron and A. Kuhrt, *Images of Women in Antiquity* Detroit: 1983, 65-78.
"The Relationships specified by Egyptian kinship terms of the Middle and New Kingdoms," *CdE* 54 (1979) 197-217.
"Meritamun, daughter of Ahmose, and Meritamun, daughter of Thutmose III," *GM* 56 (1982) 79-87.
"A Critical examination of the theory the right to the throne of ancient Egypt passed through the female line in the 18th dynasty," *GM* 62 (1983) 67-77.

Samson, J. "Royal names in Amarna History," *CdE* 51 (1976), 30-38.
"Nefertiti's Regality," *JEA* 63 (1977) 83-97.
"Akhenaten's Successor," *GM* 32 (1979) 53-58.
"Akhenaten's coregent Ankhheprure-Nefemeferuaten," *GM* 51-54 (1981-82).

Schubart, W. "Die Frau im griechisch-römischen Ägypten," *Internationale Monatsschrift für Wissenschaft, Kunst und Technik* 10(1916) col. 1503-1538.

Silverman, D. "Priestess of Hathor, *ᶜnḫ-Ḥwt-Ḥr*," ZAS 110 (1983) 80-89.

Simpson, W.K. "The Hyksos Princess Tany," *CdE* 34 (1959) 233-239.
"A Relief of a Divine Votaress in Boston," *CdE* 57 (1982) 231-235.

Smith, H.S. "Society and Settlement in ancient Egypt," in *Man, Settlement and Urbanism*, ed. P.J. Ucko et al London 1972, 705-719.

Spalinger, A. "Remarks on the family of Queen *Hᶜ.s nb*w and the problem of kingship in Dynasty XIII," *RdE* 32 (1980) 93-116.

Spiegelberg, W. "Note on the Feminine Character of the New Empire," *JEA* 15(1929) 199.

Tanner, R. "Untersuchungen zur Rechtsstellung der Frau im pharaonischen Ägypten," *Klio* 46(1965) 45-81.
"Untersuchungen zur ehe- und erbrechtlichen Stellung der Frau im pharaonischen Ägypten," *Klio* 49(1967) 5-37.

Théodoridès, A. "Le Droit matrimonial dans l'Égypte pharaonique," *RIDA* 3e serie, 23 (1976) 15-55.
review of T.G.H. James, *The Ḥeḳanakhte Papers and Other Early Middle Kingdom Documents*, *CdE* 41 (1966) 295-302.
"Du Prestige de la procédure oraculaire parmi le personnel de la nécropole thébaine sous le Nouvel Empire " in *Acta Orientalia Belgica* 31 (1963) 185-200.

"Frau" in *Lexikon der Ägyptologie*, ed. by W. Helck and E. Otto, bd. II, Weisbaden: 1977, 280-295.

Troy, L. "Good and Bad Women," *GM* 80 (1984) 77-81.
"Ahhotep--A Source Evaluation," *GM* 35 (1979) 81-91.

Vandier, J. "Iousâas et (Hathor)-Nébet-Hétepét," *RdE* 16 (1964) 55-146.
"Iousâas et (Hathor)-Nébet-Hétepét (suite)," *RdE* 17 (1965) 89-176.
"Iousâas et (Hathor)-Nébet-Hétepét (suite)," *RdE* 18 (1966) 67-142.

Vercoutter, J. "La Femme en Égypte Ancienne" in *Histoire Mondiale de la Femme* ed. P. Grimal, Paris: 1965, 63-49.

Vittmann, G. "Zwei Königinnen der Spätzeit namen Chedebnitjerbone," *CdE* 49 (1974) 43-51.

van de Walle, B. "La princesse Isis, fille et épouse d'Aménophis III," *CdE* 43 (1968)36-54.

Ward, W. "The Case of Mrs. Tchat and her sons at Beni Hasan," *GM* 71 (1984) 51-59.
"The supposed *s.t nt ḳnb.t* "Female Member of a Judicial Council" of Pap. Boulaq 18," *GM* 100 (1987) 81-83.

Winlock, H.E. "On Queen Tetisheri, Grandmother of Ahmose I," *Ancient Egypt* (1921) 14-16.

Syro-Mesopotamia

A representative bibliography of recent works on women and society.

Books

Asher-Greve, Julia M. *Frauen in Altsumerischer Zeit* (Bibliotheca Mesopotamica 18) Malibu: 1985.

Batto, Bernard F. *Studies on Women at Mari*, Baltimore: 1974.

Cameron, Avril, and Amélie Kuhrt *Images of Women in Antiquity*, London: 1983.

Cassin, Elena *La semblable et le different: symbolisme du pouvoir dans le proché-orient ancien*, Paris: 1987.

Driver, G.R. and John C. Miles *The Babylonian Laws*, 2 vols. Oxford: 1952 & 1955.
The Assyrian Laws, Oxford: 1935.

Durand, Jean-Marie *Les Femmes dans le Proché Orient Antique*, XXXIIIe Rencontre Assyriologique International, Paris: 1987.

Falkenstein, A. *The Sumerian Temple City*, Introduction and translation by Marie de J. Ellis, Malibu: 1974.

Hallo, William W. and J.J.A. van Dijk *The Exaltation of Inanna*, New Haven: 1968.
and Wm. Kelly Simpson *The Ancient Near East: a history*, New York: 1971.

Harris, Rivkah *Ancient Sippar: A Demographic Study of an Old-Babylonian City*,Istanbul: 1975.

Joannès, F. *Textes économiques de la Babylonie récente* (*Études Assyriologiques*, Cahier 6), Paris: 1982.

Kramer, Samuel Noah *Sumerian Mythology*, revised edition New York: 1961.
The Sumerians, their history, culture and character, Chicago: 1963.
The Sacred Marriage Rite, Bloomington: 1969.

Lipiński, E. (ed.) *State and Temple Economy in the Ancient Near East*, *Orientalia Lovaniensia Analecta* 6, 2 vols., Leuven: 1979.

Macdonald, Elizabeth Mary *The Position of Women as Reflected in the Semitic Code of Law*, Toronto: 1931.

Maidman, M.P. *A Socio-Economic Analysis of a Nuzi Family Archive*, Dissertation University of Pennsylvania (1976).

Oppenheim, A. Leo *Mesopotamia: Portrait of a Dead Civilization*, Chicago: 1964.

Owen, D. & M. Morrison *Studies on the Civilization and Culture of Nuzi and the Hurrians*,Winona Lake: 1981.

Pritchard, James B. ed. *Ancient Near Eastern Texts relating to the Old Testament*, 3rd. ed. Princeton: 1969.

Redman, Charles *The Rise of Civilization*, San Francisco: 1978.

Romer, W. H. *Frauenbriefe über Religion, Politik, und Privatleben in Mari*, (Archiv royale de Mari, 10) Paris: 1967.

Roth, M. *Babylonian Marriage Agreements, 7th-3rd Centuries B.C.* (forthcoming).

Saggs, H.W.F. *Everyday Life in Babylonia and Assyria*, London: 1965.
The Greatness that was Babylon, London: 1962.

Schmandt-Besserat, Denise ed. *The Legacy of Sumer*, (Bibliotheca Mesopotamica, 4) Malibu: 1979.

Saporetti, Claudio *The Status of Women in the Middle Assyrian Period*, (Monographs on the ancient Near East, 2) Malibu: 1979.

Seibert, Ilse *Women in the Ancient Near East*, New York: 1974.

Articles

Adams, R. "Mesopotamian Social Evolution. Old Outlooks, New Goals," in T. Earle, ed. *On the Evolution of Complex Societies. Essays in Honer of Harry Hoijer*, 1982, 79-129.

Albende, P. "Western Asiatic Women in the Iron Age: Their Image Revealed," *BA* 46(1983) 82-88.

Alster, B. "Gestinna as Singer and the Chorus of Uruk and Zahalan," *JCS* 37 (1958) 219-228.

Artzi, P. and A. Malamat "The Correspondence of Sibtu, Queen of Mari," *Orientalia* 40, (1971), 75-89.

Azarpay, G. "Nana, the Sumerian-Akkadian goddess of Transoxiana," *JAOS* 96 (1976) 536-542.

Barstow, A. "The Uses of Archaeology for Women's History: James Mellart's work on the Neolithic Goddess at Catal Huyuck," *Feminist Studies* 4, no. 3 (1978), 7-18.

Batto, Bernard F. "Land Tenure and women at Mari," *JESHO* 26 (1983) 209-239.

Bigga, M.G. "Matrimoni dinastici nel Viceno Oriente antico," *RSO* (1977) 1-5.

Bottero, Jean "La femme dans l'Asie Occidentale ancienne: Mesopotamie et Israel," in *Histoire Mondiale de la femme*, ed. P. Grimal Paris: (1957), 155-266.
"La femme en Mésopotamie" in *Histoire mondiale de la femme: prehistoire et antiquité*, Paris: 1965.
"La Femme, l'Amour et la Guerre en Mesopotamie Ancienne," in *Poikilia: Etudes offertes à Jean-Pierre Vernant*, Paris: 1987, 65ff.
"L'amour librè et ses desavantages," *Mesopotamie: l'écriture, la raíson et les dieux*, Paris: 1987.

Buccellati, G. "The Descent of Inanna as a ritual journey to Kutha?" *Syro-Mesopotamian Studies* 4 /3 1982 3-7.

Cassin, E. "Pouvoir de la femme et structures familiales," *RA* 63 (1969) 121-148.

Civil, M. "Enlil and Ninlil: The Marriage of Sud," *JAOS* 103 (1983) 43-66.

Cooper, J. S. "New Cuneiform Parallels to the Song of Songs," *JBL* 90, 157-162.
"Heilige Hochzeit," *Reallexikon der Assyriologie* 4, 259-269.

Dandamaev, M.A. "State and Temple in Babylonia in the first Millennium B.C.," in E. Lipiński (ed.), *State and Temple Economy in the Ancient Near East*, Leuven: 1979, vol. 2, 589-596.

Dunaud, J.-M. "Les dames du palais de Mari à l'époque du royaume de Haute Mesopotamie," *M.A.R.I.* 3(1984).
"Ehe" in *Reallexikon der Assyriologie*, 2, 281-299.

Eichler, B.L. "Another look at Nuzi sisterhood Contracts," *Studies in Memory of J.J. Finkelstein*, edited by M. de Jong Ellis, (Hamden, CT, 1977),45-59.

Ellis, M. dJ. "An Old Babylonian Adoption Contract from Tell Harmal," *JCS* (1975) 130-151.

Fensham, F. "Legal and Wisdom Literature," *JNES* 21 (1962) 129-139.

Finkelstein, J.J. "Sex offenses in Babylonian Laws," *JAOS* 86 (1966), 355-372.

Fisher, E.J. "Cultic Prostitution in the ancient Near East?" *Biblical Theology Bulletin* 6 (1976), 225-236.

Foster, Benjamin "A New Look at the Sumerian Temple State," *JESHO* 24 (1966) 225-241.
"Frau" in *Reallexikon der Assyriologie*, 3, 100-104.

Freedman, D. "A New Approach to the Nuzi Sistership Contract," *JANES* 2(1969-70).

Garelli, P. "Femmes d'affaires en Assyrie," *ArOr* 47 (1979), 42-48.

Gelb, I.J. "From Freedom to Slavery," *RAI* 18 (1970) 81-92.

Glassner, J.J. "La famille Mesopotamienne," *Histoire de la Familie* ed. A. Colin, Paris: 1985.

Gordon, C.H. "Fifteen Nuzi Tablets Relating to Women," *Le Museon* 48 (1935) 113-132.
"The Status of Women Reflected in the Nuzi Tablets," *ZA* N.F. (43) 1936, 146-169.

Grayson, A.K. and J. Van Seters "The Childless Wife in Assyria and the Stories of Genesis," *Orientalia* 44 (1975) 485-486.

Greengus, S. "Old Babylonian Marriage Ceremonies and Rites," *JCS* 20 (1966) 55-72.
"Sisterhood Adoption at Nuzi and the 'Wife-Sister' in Genesis," *HUCA* 46 (1975) 5-31.
"The Textbook Case of Adultery in Ancient Mesopotamia," *HUCA* 40-4 (1969-1970) 33-44.

Grosz, K. "Dowry and Brideprice in Nuzi," in Owen and Morrison *op. cit.*
"Bridewealth and dowry in Nuzi," in *Images of Women in Antiquity* ed. A. Cameron and A. Kuhrt London: 1983, 193-206.
"On some aspects of the Adoptions of women in Nuzi," in Owen and Morrison *op. cit.*
"Daughters Adopted as sons at Nuzi and Emar," in *Compte Rendu de la XXXIVeme Rencontre Assyriologique*, 1986, Paris.

Hallo, Wm. W. " Women of Sumer," in Schmandt-Besserat, *op. cit.*, 18ff.

Harris, R. "The Naditu Women," in *Studies-...Oppenheim.*
"Women in the ancient Near East," in *Interpreters Dictionary of the Bible, Supplementary Volume* K. Crim ed. Nashville: 1976, 960-63.
" On Kinship and Inheritance in Old Babylonian Sippar," *Iraq* 38 (1976) 129-132.

Heimpel, W. "The Nanshe Hymn," *JCS* 33 (1981), 65-139.
"A Catalogue of Near Eastern Venus Deities," *Syro-Mesopotamian Studies* 4/3 (1982) 9-22.
"Hierodolen" in *Reallexikon der Assyrologie*, IV.

Ichisar, M. "Un contrat de Mariage et la question du Levirat a l'Époque Cappadocien," *RA* 76 (1982).

Jacobsen, T. "Primitive Democracy in Ancient Mesopotamia," *JNES* 2 (1943) 159-172.

Jeyes, U. "The Naditu Women of Sippar," in Cameron and Kuhrt, *Images of Women in Antiquity*, 260-72.

Joannes, F. "Contrats de Marriage d'Époque Recente," *RA* 78 (1984) 71-81.

Koschaker, P. "Fratriarchat, Hausgemeinschaft und Mutterrecht in Keilschriftrechten," *ZA* 41(1933) 1-89.

Kramer, S.N. "Poets and Psalmists, Goddesses and Theologians," in Schmandt-Besserat *op. cit.* 12-18.

"The Weeping Goddess: Sumerian prototype of the *Mater Dolorosa*," *The Biblical Archaeologist* 46 (1983) 69-80.

Lacheman, E.R. "Real Estate Adoption by Women in the Tablets from URU Nuzi," *Studies Presented to Cyrus H. Gordon, AOAT* 22 (1973) 99-100.

Lambert, W.G. "Morals in ancient Mesopotamia," *JEOL* 15 (1957-58) 84-96.

Lewy, H. "Nitocris-Nagià," *JNES* 11(1952), 264-286.

Mackawa, K. "Female Weavers and their children in Lagash-Presargonic and Ur III," *Acta Sumerologica* (1980) 81-125.

Michalowski, P. "The Bride of Siamun," *JAOS* 95 (1975) 716-19.
"Royal Women of the Ur III period, Part II Isime-Ninlila," *JCS* 31 (1970) 171-176.
"On the Fowler and his wife," *RA* 75 (1981), 170.

Moorey, P.R.S. "What do we know about the people buried in the royal Cemetery?" *Expedition* 20, no. 1 (1977), 24-40.

Morrison, M. "The Family of Šilwa-Tešub," *JCS* 31 (1979) 3-29.
"The Southwest Archives at Nuzi," *SCCNH* II 167-201.

Owen, D. "Widow's Rights in Ur III Sumer," *ZA* 70 (1981) 170-184.

Paradise, J. "A Daughter and her father's property at Nuzi," *JCS* 32 (1980), 189-207.
"Daughters as Sons at Nuzi," *SCCNH* II 203-213.

Parr, R.A. "Ninkilia: Wife of Ajakala, Governor of Umma," *JCS* 25 (1974) 90-111.

Postgate, J. "On some Assyrian Ladies," *Iraq* 41 (1979) .

Renger, J. "Untersuchungen zum Priestertum in der altbabylonische Zeit," *ZA* 24 (1967) 110-188.

Roellig, W. "Politische Heiraten im Alten Orient," *Saeculum* 25 (1974) 11-23.

Rohrlich, R. "State Formation in Sumer and the Subjugation of Women," *Feminist Studies* 6 (1980) 76-102.

Rollin, S. "Women and Witchcraft in Ancient Assyria," in Cameron and Kuhrt *Images of Women in Antiquity*, 34-46.

Roth, M. "Age at Marriage and the Household: A Study of Neo-Babylonian and Neo-Assyrian Forms," *Comparative Studies in Society and History* 29(1987) 715-747.
"'She will die by the Iron Dagger' Adultery and Neo-Babylonian Marriage," *JESHO* 31 (1988) 186-206.

San Nicolò, M. "Due atti matrimoniali neobabilonesi," *Aegyptus* 27 (1947), 118-43.

Sasson J. "Notes on Some Royal ladies from Mari," *JCS* 25 (1973) 59-78.

Steinkeller, P. "More on the Ur III Royal Wives," *Acta Sumerologica* 3 (1981), 77-92.

"Two Sargonic Sale documents concerning women," *Orientalia* n.s. 51 (1982), 289-294.

Stone, E. "The Social role of the Naditu women in Old Babylonian Nippur," *JESHO* 25 (1982), 49-70.

Veenhof, K.R. "The Dissolution of an Old Babylonian Marriage according to C.T. 45,86," *RA* (1976) 153-164.

Weisberg, D.B. "Royal Women of the NeoBabylonian Period," in P. Garellied, *Le Palais et la Royauté* 447-454.

Zagarell, A. "Trade, Women, Class and Society in Ancient Western Asia," *Current Anthropology*, Dec. 1986, 415-430.

Ancient Israel

A select bibliography of books and articles concerning women, religion and society.

Books

Bal, M. *Lethal Love: Feminist Literary Readings of Biblical Love Stories*, Bloomington, in: 1987.

Boer, P.A.H. de *Fatherhood and Motherhood in Israelite and Judean Piety*, Leiden: 1974.

Brenner, A. *The Israelite Woman. Social Role and Literary Type in Biblical Narrative* (JSOT Supp. 21) Sheffield: 1985.

Burns, R.J. *Has the Lord Indeed Spoken Only Through Moses? A Study of the Biblical Portrait of Miriam*, (SBL Dissertation Series 84) Atlanta: 1987.

Callaway, M. *Sing, O Barren One: A Study in Comparative Midrash,* (SBL Dissertation Series 91) Atlanta: 1986.

Camp, C. *Wisdom and the Feminine in the Book of Proverbs,* Decatur, GA: 1985.

Campbell, E.F. *Ruth: A New Translation with Introduction and Commentary,* (Anchor Bible 7) Garden City, NY: 1975.

Collins, A. Y., ed. *Feminist Perspectives on Biblical Scholarship,* Chico, CA: 1985.

Cross, F.M. *Canaanite Myth and Hebrew Epic. Essays in the History of the Religion of Israel,* Cambridge, MA: 1973.

Falk, M. *Love Lyrics from the Bible,* Sheffield (England): 1982.

Fohrer, G. *History of Israelite Religion,* Nashville/New York: 1972.

Fox, Michael J. *The Song of Songs and the Ancient Egyptian Love Songs,* Madison: 1985.

Freedman, D.N. and Graff, D.F., eds., *Palestine in Transition,* Sheffield: 1983.

Frick, F. *The Formation of the State in Ancient Israel,* Sheffield: 1985.

Gerstenberger, E.S. and W. Schrage *Woman and Man,* (Biblical Encounter Series) Nashville: 1980.

Gottwald, Norman *The Hebrew Bible: A Socio-Literary Introduction,* Philadelphia: 1985.
The Tribes of Yahweh: A Sociology of the Religion of Liberated Israel 1250-1050 B.C. Maryknoll: 1979.

Gross, R.M., ed. *Beyond Androcentrism: New Essays on Women and Religion,* Missoula: 1977.

Hanson, P.D., et al eds. *Ancient Israelite Religion: Essays in Honor of Frank M. Cross,* Philadelphia: 1987.

Hopkins, D. *The Highlands of Canaan,* Sheffield: 1985.

Lang, B. *Wisdom and the Book of Proverbs: A Hebrew Goddess Redefined,* New York: 1986.

Lieberman, S. *The Eve Motif in Ancient Near Eastern and Classical Greek Sources,* Ann Arbor: 1975.

Maier, W. *'Ašerah: Extrabiblical Evidence,* Atlanta: 1986.

Mendenhall, G. *The Tenth Generation: Origins of the Biblical Tradition*, Baltimore: 1973.

Meyers, C. *Discovering Eve: Ancient Israelite Women in Context*, New York: 1988.

Muller, Herbert J. *Freedom in the Ancient World*, New York: 1961.

Ochshorn, Judith *The Female Experience and the Nature of the Divine*, Bloomington: 1981.

Otwell, J. *And Sarah Laughed: The Status of women in the Old Testament*, Philadelphia: 1977.

Patai, Raphael *Sex and Family in the Bible and in the Middle East*, New York: 1959.
The Hebrew Goddess, New York: 1967.

Poethig, E. *The Victory Song Tradition of the Women of Israel*, New York (dissertation): 1985.

Porter, J.R. *The Extended Family in the Old Testament*. London: 1967.

Pritchard, James B. *Ancient Near Eastern Texts relating to the Old Testament*, 3rd ed. Princeton: 1969.

Rogerson, J.W. *Anthropology and the Old Testament*, Oxford: 1978.

Ruether, R. ed., *Religion and Sexism: Images of women in the Jewish and Christian Traditions*, New York: 1974.

Russell, L. M. ed., *Feminist Interpretation of the Bible*, Philadelphia: 1985.

Sasson, Jack M. *Ruth: A New Translation with a Philological Commentary and a Formalist-Folklorist Interpretation*, Baltimore: 1979.

Stanton, E.C. *The Woman's Bible*, New York: 1885, 1898.

Terrien, S. *Til the Heart Sings*, Philadelphia: 1985.

Tolbert, M.A. ed., *The Bible and Feminist Hermeneutics*, (Semeia 28) Chico: 1983.

Tosato, A. *Il matrimonia israelitico*, Rome: 1982.

Trible, Phyllis *Biblical Narratives*, Philadelphia: 1984.
God and the Rhetoric of sexualtiy, Philadelphia: 1978.
Texts of Terror: Literary-Feminist Readings of Biblical Narratives, Philadelphia: 1984.

Vaux, Roland de *Ancient Israel: Its Life and Institutions*, New York: 1961.

Voss, Clarence J. *Women in Old Testament Worship*, Delft: 1968.

Wolff, Hans W. *Anthropology of the Old Testament*, Philadelphia: 1974.

Winter, U. *Frau und Gottin. Exegetische und ikonographische Studien zum Weiblichen Götterbild im alten Israel und in dessen Umwelt*, Freiburg/Göttingen: 1983.

Articles

Ackroyd, P.R. "Goddesses, Women and Jezebel," *Images of Women in Antiquity*, ed. A. Cameron and A. Kuhrt, Detroit: 1983, 245-259.

Adler, R. "A Mother in Israel, aspects of the mother role in Jewish myth," in Gross, *Beyond Androcentrism*, 237-255.

Ailen, C.G. "Who was Rebekah?" in Gross, *Beyond Androcentrism*, 183-216.

Anderson, F. "Israelite Kinship Terminology and Social Structure," *Biblical Translator* 20(1970), 29-34.

Andreasen, N.-E. "The Role of the Queen Mother in Israelite Society," *Catholic Biblical Quarterly* 45(1983), 179-194.

Andriolo, K.R. "A Structural Analysis of Genealogy and World View in the Old Testament," *American Anthropologist* 75(1973), 1657-1669.

Baab, O.J. "Marriage," *Interpreter's Dictionary of the Bible*, III ed. by Buttrick, Nashville: 1962, 278-287.

Bailey, J.A. "Initiation of the primal woman in Gilgamesh and Genesis 2-3," *JBL* 89 (1970).

Bass, D.C. "Women's Studies and Biblical Studies: An Historical Perspective," *JSOT* 22(1982), 6-12.

Bird, P. "The Harlot As Heroine in Biblical Texts: Narrative Art and Social Presupposition," *Semeia* (forthcoming).

"Images of Women in the Old Testament," in R.R. Reuther's *Religion and Sexism*, 41-88.

"Male and Female He Created Them: Genesis 1:27b in the Context of the Priestly Account of Creation," *HTR* 74 (1981), 129-159.

"The Place of Women in the Israelite Cultus," in *Ancient Israelite Religion: Essays in*

Honor of Frank Moore Cross, Patrick D. Miller, Jr., Paul P. Hansen, and S. Dean McBride, eds., Philadelphia, 1987: 397-419.
"Sexual Differentiation and Divine Image in the Genesis Creation Texts," in *Image of God and Gender Models*, ed. K. Borresen, Oslo/Atlantic Heights, NJ: (forthcoming).

Camp, C. "The Wise Women of 2 Samuel: A Role Model for Women in Early Israel," *Catholic Biblical Quarterly* 43(1981), 14-29.

Campbell, E.F. Jr. "Moses and the Foundation of Israel," *Interpretation* 29 (1975), 141-154.

Conkey, M.W. and Spector, J.D. "Archaeology and the Study of Gender," *Advances in Archaeological Method and Theory* 7(1984), 1-38.

Cowling, G. "Women in the Old Testament," *Ancient Society* 9 (1979), 96-115.

Delaney, C. "The Legacy of Abraham," in Gross, *Beyond Androcentrism*, 217-236.

Donaldson, M.E. "Kinship Theory in the Patriarchal Narratives , the case of the Barren Wife," *JAAR* 49 (1981), 77-87.

Dumbrell, W.J. "The Role of Women, a reconsideration of the Biblical Evidence," *Interchange* 4 (1977), 14-22.

Exum, C. "'Mother in Israel': A Familiar Story Reconsidered," in *Feminist Interpretation of the Bible*, ed. L. Russel, Philadelphia: 1985, 73-85.

Freedman, D.N. "Yahweh and His Asherah," *Biblical Archaeologist* 50(1987).

Gordis, R. "Love, Marriage and Business in the book of Ruth: A Chapter in Hebrew Customary Law," in *A Light unto my Path: Old Testament Studies in Honor of Jacob M. Myers*, ed. Bream et al, Philadelphia: 1974, 241-264.

Higgins,J. "The Myth of Eve the Temptress," *JAAR* 44 (1976), 639-648.

Hoftijzer, J. "David and the Tekoite Woman," *VT* 20 (1970), 419-44.

Horowitz, M.C. "The Image of God in Man--is woman included?" *HTR* 72 (1979), 175-206.

Kikawada, I. "Two Notes on Eve," *JBL* 91 (1972), 33-37.

Lyons, E.C. "A Note on Proverbs 31:10-31," in *The Listening Heart*, ed. K. Hoglund et al, Sheffield (England): 1987, 237-246.

Mendenhall, G. "Law and Covenant in Israel and the ancient Near East," *Biblical Archaeologist* 17 (1954), 26-46; 50-76.
"The Hebrew Conquest of Canaan," *BA* 25 (1962), 66-87.
"Social Organization in Early Israel," in *Magnalia Dei: The Mighty Acts of God*, ed. Cass et al. Garden City: 1976, 132-151.

Meyers, C. "Roots of Restriction: Women in Early Israel," *BA* 41 (1978), 91-103.
"Gender Imagery in the Song of Songs," *Hebrew Annual Review* 10 (1987): 209-223.
"Gender Roles and Genesis 3:16 Revisited," in *The Word of the Lord shall go Forth*, Philadelphia: 1983, 337-359.
"Procreation, Production and Protection: male-female balance in Early Israel," *JAAR* 51 (1983), 569-593.
"Adam and Eve," *World Book Encyclopedia* 1986 ed., I: 28.
"A Terracotta at the Harvard Semitic Museum and Disc-holding Female Figures Reconsidered," *Israel Exploration Journal* 37 (1987): 116-122.
"Recovering Eve: Biblical Gender without Post-biblical Dogma," in *Gender and Cultural Contexts: Feminist Reconstructions*, ed. J. O'Barr, Madison: (forthcoming).

Morgenstern, J. "Beena Marriage in Ancient Israel and its historical implications," *ZAW* 47 (1929), 91-110 and 48 (1931), 46-58.

Parker, S.B. "The Marriage Blessing in Isralite and Ugaritic Literature," *JBL* 95 (1976), 23-30.

Paterson, J. "Divorce and Desertion in the Old Testament," *JBL* 51 (1932), 161-170.

Phillips, A. "Some Aspects of Family Law in Pre-exilic Israel," *VT* 23 (1973), 349-361.

Prusak, B.P. "Woman, Seductive Siren and Source of sin," in Ruether, *Religion and Sexism* 89-116.

Ringgren, H. "The Marriage Motif in Israelite Religion," in *Ancient Israelite Religion: Essays in Honor of Frank Moore Cross*, Patrick D. Miller, Jr., Paul P. Hansen, and S. Dean McBride, eds., Philadelphia, 1987: 412-428.

Ruether, R.R. "Feminism and Patriarchal Religion: Principles of Ideological Critique of the Bible," *Religion and Sexism*, 54-56.

Sakenfeld, K.D. "Old Testament Perspectives, Methodological Issues," *JSOT* 22 (1982), 13-20.
"Feminist Perspectives on Bible and Theology: An Introduction to Selected Issues and Literature," *Interpretation* 42 (1988) 5-18.
"Feminist Uses of Biblical Materials," in *Feminist Interpretation of the Bible*, 55-64.

Sherlock, P. "Women and the Arguments from Creation," *Interchange* 20 (1976), 245-249.

Smith, Mark S. "God Male and Female in the Old Testament: Yahweh and His 'asherah,'" *Theological Studies* 48 (1987), 333-340.

Speiser, E.A. "The Wife-sister motif in Patriarchal Narratives," in *Biblical and Other Studies*, ed. A. Altman.

Stager, L. "The Archaeology of the Family in Ancient Israel," *BASOR* 260 (1985), 1-36.

Steinberg, N. "Gender Roles in the Rebekah Cycle," *USQR* 39 (1984), 175-188.

Taber, C.R. "Marriage" in *Interpreter's Dictionary of the Bible* III, ed. Buttrick, G.A. Nashville, 1976: 278-287.

Terrien, S. "Toward a Biblical Theology of Womanhood," *Religion in Life* 42 (1973) 322-333.

Trible, P. "Depatriarchalizing in Biblical Interpretation," *JAAR* 41 (1973) 30-48.
"Women in the Old Testament," *Interpreter's Dictionary of the Bible*, supp. volume, 963-966.

Van Seters, J. "The Problem of Childlessness in Near Eastern Law and the Patriarchy of Israel," *JBL* 87 (1968), 401-408.

Wilson, R.W. "The Family," in Harper's Bible Dictionary, San Francisco: 1985, 302-303.

Pertinent Publications in Anthropology and Gender Studies

Books

Auerbach, N. *Communities of Women: An Idea in Fiction*, Cambridge, MA: 1978.

Boserup, E. *Women's Role in Economic Development*, London: 1970.

Bottmore, T. *The Frankfort School*, New York: 1984.

Coward, R. *Patriarchal Precedents*, London: 1983.

Douglas, M. *Purity and Danger*, London: 1966.

Foucault, M. *The Order of Things*, New York: 1970.
The Archeology of Knowledge, New York: 1972.

Gilmore, D. ed., *Honor and Shame and the Unity of the Meditterranean*, Washington: 1987.

Goody, J. *Production and Reproduction: A comparative study of the domestic domain*, (Cambridge Studies in Social Anthropology, 17), Cambridge: 1976.

Lerner, G. *The Creation of Patriarchy*, Oxford: 1986.

MacCormack, C. and M. Strathern, eds. *Nature, Culture and Gender*, Cambridge: 1980.

Marcus, G. and M. Fischer *Anthropology as Cultural Critique*, Chicago: 1984.

Ortner, S. and H. Whitehead, *Sexual Meanings: Cultural Construction of Gender and Sexuality*, Cambridge: 1981.

Parkin, D. ed., *Semantic Anthropology*, New York: 1982.

Sacks, K. *Sisters and Wives: The Past and Future of Sexual Equality*, Westport, CT: 1979.

Schneider, D. *A Critique of the Study of Kinship*, Ann Arbor: 1984.

Vogel, L. *Marxism and the Oppression of Women. Toward a Unitary Theory*, New Brunswick, NJ: 1983.

Whyte, M.K. *The Status of Women in Preindustrial Societies*, Princeton: 1978.

Yanagiasako, S. and J. Collier, eds. *Gender and Kinship, Toward a Unified Analysis*, Stanford: 1987.

Articles

Conkey, M. and J. D. Spector, "Archeology and the Study of Gender," in M. Schiffer, ed. *Advances in Archeological Method and Theory*, vol. 7, New York: 1984, 1-38.

Delaney, C. "The Meaning of Paternity and the Virgin Birth Debate," *Man* 21 (N.S.) (1986) 494-513.

Gailey, C. "The State of the State in Anthropology," *Dialectical Anthropology* 9(1985) 65-90. and T. Patterson, "Power Relations and State Formation," in C. Gailey and T. Patterson, eds. *Power Relations and State Formation*, Washington: 1987, 1-27.

Smith-Rosenberg, C. "The Female World of Love and Ritual," *Signs* 1(1975), 1-29.

Wright, E.O.C., Costello, D. and Hachen, J. "The American Class Structure," *American Sociological Review* 47(1982), 709-726.

Zagarell, A. "Trade, Women, Class and Society in Ancient Western Asia," *Current Anthropology* 27(1986), 415-430.

Indexes

Index of Names

General Index

CPSIA information can be obtained at www.ICGtesting.com
Printed in the USA
BVOW011836061212

307344BV00008B/1441/P

9 781597 407700